Growing Up Male In America
Intimate conversations with young men

Dedication

I dedicate this book to the 30 interesting men who opened their lives to me during the interview sessions which I conducted between May 2000 and October 2001. I am indebted to each of them for being honest and forthcoming. These men, most of whom I did not know well before the interviews were conducted, admitted that they told me things which they had never uttered to another person before – a fact which supports my thesis for this book. I only regret that all 30 of these fascinating accounts could not fit in this book. Thanks to all of my anonymous interviewees!

Ronald G. Perrier

Copyright © 2002 by Ronald G. Perrier.

Published by:

AP | **Archie Publications**
P.O. Box 50154
Minneapolis, MN 55403

All rights reserved under International and Pan-American Copyright Conventions. Published by Archie Publications, P.O. Box 50154, Minneapolis, MN 55403. Telephone (612) 333-7922. E-mail address: archiepub@aol.com.

Ronald G. Perrier has taught at the secondary and college/university levels for 40 years. He holds M.A. and Ph.D. degrees from the University of Minnesota in Minneapolis and is Professor Emeritus of Film Studies at St. Cloud State University in St. Cloud, Minnesota. In his teaching career, Dr. Perrier has had nearly 50,000 students in his classes.

Designed by Joe Gohman of JG Design,
2450 Heimel Street, South St. Paul, MN 55075.
E-mail address: jgdesign@qwest.net.

Printed in the United States by Sentinel Printing, Inc., St. Cloud, Minnesota.

Cover Model: Mr. Tony McClay.

First printing: January 2002

ISBN 0-9704064-0-1

Preface

This book consists of 16 interviews with men between the ages of 21 and 31. The men are from numerous walks of life, educational backgrounds and work experience. In these candid conversations, the men discuss their fears, frustrations, successes, failures, and hopes and dreams in this post-women's liberation era. The men discuss their initiation into sexual experience and their success and failure in sexual relationships during adolescence and young adulthood. They reveal their relationships with parents, school friends, and male/female adult friends.

At the dawn of the new millennium, the young adult American male is often conflicted and without clear focus. He is thrust into a world without heroes and positive role models; his childhood is often the product of an upbringing with both parents in the work force and/or divorced; he receives contradictory messages about concepts of sexuality, maleness, sensitivity, male-bonding as well as relationships with women. Indeed, many men feel a poignant sense of alienation, estrangement and loneliness as they forge their way into the expectations of the adult world.

The men who were interviewed were not chosen in any scientific random selection; rather, men from a variety of experiences and backgrounds were sought out by me or were recommended to me by others. After each man was given an explanation of the scope of the interview questions, he was invited to participate. Each interview lasted between two and three hours and was recorded on audio tape. Each subject was interviewed with the guarantee of complete anonymity, thus assuring a high degree of openness and honesty in these conversations. Names of interviewees were never used, only code numbers.

In the true oral-history tradition, these conversations are the exact words of each subject rather than an editor's summary of what the interviewee said. Hence the dialogue format is utilized rather than a narrative one.

Since many of the points covered in the interviews center on sexuality, some readers may find the language rather graphic. But these are candid and honest utterances, and no effort was made by the interviewer to censor the language. Young people under the age of 12, however, might be cautioned not to read this book. Parental discretion is advised.

By professional training, I am neither a sociologist nor a psychologist. I am a professor of film studies, and in 40 years of teaching and encountering nearly 50,000 students in my classes, I am keenly aware of the personalities and behavior of young people. I think you will find my line of questioning to be non-threatening to the interviewee yet direct and incisive enough to elicit truthful answers.

Most people observe that men tend to be more private and enclosed than females. Suppressed emotions, unspoken fears and private fantasies seem to define maleness in large measure. Such interior aspects of a man's nature are rarely revealed or discussed, even in the confines of close male-male friendships. Because of this, the major outlets for pent-up male emotions are the battlefield or the athletic field. But pressures often do build up. Is it merely coincidental that school shootings are planned and executed by young men and not by young women? Is it not apparent that men far outnumber women as lawbreakers? Perhaps the interviews in this book will cast some light on the essence of the private nature of young men today.

I am indebted to a number of people for their contributions to this project:

Karen L. Mrja, for transcribing the interviews from the audio tapes and for typing all the subsequent revisions.

Sandy Perrier, Julie Barnes Weaver, Don MacPherson and Alan J. Fredrickson, for serving on an advisory committee. They provided me with an "eye outside" by reading transcripts and recommending to me which interviews they felt should be included in the book.

Don MacPherson, for proofreading the final manuscript.

The staff at Sentinel Printing, Inc., for their competent and professional advice and expertise.

I sincerely hope that readers of the 16 interviews in this book will gain insight into the world of young men. You will soon develop an empathy with these men, and you will wish that you could sit with each of them and have a long and detailed conversation. I had the privilege of getting to know them very well, and I am richer for that experience.

Ronald G. Perrier
January 2002

Growing Up Male In America

Interview 1	1
Interview 2	29
Interview 3	51
Interview 4	87
Interview 5	109
Interview 6	139
Interview 7	155
Interview 8	179
Interview 9	201
Interview 10	231
Interview 11	251
Interview 12	279
Interview 13	297
Interview 14	331
Interview 15	361
Interview 16	379

Interview 1

"I came home one day and thought something wasn't quite right."

This interview was conducted on June 19, 2001. He is 31 years old, 5' 6" tall, weighs 160 pounds and has brown hair. He likes to water ski and snow ski.

Ordinarily, I like to start these interviews with birth and early childhood, but I think instead, let's start with where you're at right now. So, what's your line of work?

I'm a plumber, and I also do heating work. I've been doing this kind of work with this one company for six years, and I was at another company for a couple of years before.

Okay. And this makes you about how old?

I'm 31.

Thirty-one. And people always tell you don't look 31, I'm sure. I'll bet people still card you at bars, don't they?

Yeah. All the time.

Because you have a young-looking face. What kind of training did you undergo to become a plumber?

I went to a trade school. It's a five-year apprenticeship program. Two nights a week, you go to school. The rest of the time, you work during the day and two nights a week. You learn through school. Welding, blueprints, isometric drawings. Water pipe and waste piping. Gas piping. So you can be a well-rounded plumber, so you can do service work or residential and commercial work.

Okay. So you start out with no training, virtually, and then it's on the job? And then school?

Exactly. Basically you become an apprentice, and you go through the program, and that's what it takes to train you to take your license exam.

And you do need to be licensed?

Growing Up Male In America

You have to be licensed in the state in which you work, and you have to be licensed in most of the cities, too.

Do you like what you're doing?

I don't mind what I do right now. I do service work, so it changes each day. If this is what I'm going to be doing for the next 10 years, probably not. I'll still be in the plumbing field, but I probably won't be doing service work.

So that would mean working up to administration?

Ownership. Or going into sales with a plumbing manufacturer or a wholesaler.

There must be a lot of disgusting things you have to do sometimes in your job. I mean, there are some pretty slimy things that happen in pipes.

I see a lot throughout my day. I see a lot of interesting people and get into a lot of interesting places.

[Laughs] Want to talk about that?

I've been kicked out of people's homes for quoting prices that they thought were too high. Our company charges for us to make a house call, and some customers refuse to pay us for that. I've had that happen to me twice. Let's see, what else have I experienced?

Has anyone tried to seduce you?

Yup. That's happened. Some girls trying to flirt with me. Also, I've had somebody steal my tools when I was on a job.

When you start unclogging drains and pipes, isn't that sometimes repulsive?

Oh, it gets pretty nasty at times. I've never really had too many bad experiences, except for one time. I was working on a sewage ejector pump, which is a pump that pumps sewer waste out from below grade to above grade and then back into the city main. I had to be tipped upside down. Another plumber was holding onto my legs, and I was dangling over a 100-gallon storage tank filled with sewage to undo the pump. I had to trust him not to drop me.

Do you swim? [Laughter]

I don't think you could swim in that.

Ugh! Plumbers have strange names for some of the tools and fittings that you work with. Some of those terms sound downright erotic or at least sexual.

Oh, yeah. I've got a good story for you. We had a lady who had just started working, answering the phones at our shop. I was out at a job site, and I needed some parts in my truck, so I called the shop and she picked up the phone to take my material order. I told her I needed a couple of ball cocks, a couple of two-inch nipples and some cockhole covers. Well, about a half hour to an hour went by, and I didn't get my materials. So I had to call back in. She thought I was playing a joke on her because she was a new girl up front. And it turns out

Interview 1

that that's the stuff I need for my job – ball cocks are water-filling devices for toilets, nipples are threaded pipes that screw in and out of iron fittings, and cockhole covers are chrome-covered plates that we put over the cuts and holes in walls.

And she thought you were ...

She thought I was talking dirty to her and trying to shock her.

That's interesting. Interesting, indeed. It's like somebody had a great sense of humor when they were naming these things.

I also have another interesting story about cleaning drains. One of our techs went over to a lady's house. Her drain for the laundry tub and the floor drain were plugged up. He did the work. She called back and wanted us to come over again because it was backed up but didn't want that same repair guy. Another tech went over, tried to clean the drain, got it to work, came back. She called up and didn't want that tech back over, either. Finally my boss sent me over there to go unclog the drain and take a look at what was going on, what the problem was. I went over there, got it fixed. I left. It backed up again. She called again and said she didn't want any of us over there but she was still having the problem and wanted my boss to come over. Well, here it turns out, when he went over there, he went to go take a look at the drain, and I went over with him. And she did not like the fact that I was there because I made her feel uncomfortable. It turns out, after my boss talked to her and we had got a camera put down the line, we found that what was happening was there was a break in her sewer line, and rats were coming up through her floor drain, taking her undergarments or underwear out of the laundry basket and dragging those things down the line. She insinuated that each of the three of us were stealing her underwear when we were over at her house.

Good grief!

That's why she didn't want to see us. She thought we were playing some joke. That's why she had my boss come over. So when the TV was hooked up and the camera went down the line, there were her undergarments.

Wow! That's incredible. And here rats were coming right up the drain and walking around her basement?

Rats were coming up through the floor drain because she had a busted floor drain cover. Rats in the sewers are quite common. They're not so bad, though. They're really not too bad in Minneapolis and St. Paul. Some bigger cities have major problems with them, though.

A friend of mine said that she was afraid to go to New York and sit on a toilet in a hotel for fear that a rat would come up through the pipes and bite her ass.

The place would have to be pretty bad for that to happen.

Yeah. I would think so. And the rats would have to hold their breath, I think, to

Growing Up Male In America

swim clear up to the eighteenth floor of a hotel!

Yeah. I worked at the home of a very famous football player about two years ago. He had a sewage ejector pump because his basement was below grade, and we went to clean out the pump, and he wanted to know why the pump was malfunctioning. We found a whole sewer ejector basket full of condoms that were getting jammed up into the pump and breaking the pump.

That would do it. You're not supposed to really flush those down the toilet, are you?

No.

Well. Your work sounds interesting. I'm not asking what your annual salary is, but I always hear that the hourly wage for a plumber is really quite good.

Yeah. Basically a journeyman licensed plumber should easily be able to make probably between $30,000 and $40,000 a year. Doing new construction, you could probably make $40,000 to $70,000. As to service plumbers and commercial plumbers, we don't have a split scale. But service plumbers can make anywhere between $50,000 to $100,000 or more, depending on how much they want to work. Service plumbers get a little bit better packages, bonuses, incentives. Not a lot of people like to do service work, especially if you work for a 24-hour service. It's a lot of on-call, so some companies will pay you just to be around for the weekend, whether you work or not. Some companies just pay you from the time you leave your house until the time you get back. Double time, time and a half, triple time. If you have your master's license, which I don't have at this time, most companies will pay you more for your master's license. It doesn't mean that you're a better plumber, but you have to have a master's license to own a business. So you can have people work underneath you.

Now, who makes that regulation?

The city does.

What's your preference? Do you like doing new construction?

I did new construction for a couple of years. If you get stuck on big buildings or apartments or townhomes, it's kind of repetitious. I wouldn't mind ... the hours are better. It's 6:00 to 2:30. No weekends, or during the summertime you can put long days in if you want and have three-day weekends. Or you put your time in during the summer and you have your winters off. I really have no preference at this time, but I would like to get more into commercial work. I've done a little bit of everything. I've done commercial service work, new construction, and now residential service work. Med-gas would be the only other thing that I would really be interested in at this time.

What's that?

It's running all your medical gas lines, your air lines, your nitrogen lines, in a hospital. It's basically everything that when you're hooked up to that bed, those

Interview 1

lines coming out of the wall, that's all plumber's work. There's glass waste piping in the walls, which is a specialty because of the acids that are used in hospitals and the blood and such things that break away normal plastic. Glass piping is a specialty in the plumbing trade.

Hey, I do have one more interesting story.

Go for it!

Okay. You were asking me if anybody's ever come on to me or if I've ever been seduced. Well, I went to this lady's house. Her kitchen faucet needed to be replaced, and I did the faucet. While I was working, I noticed she was talking on the phone or crying or something. And when she got done, I just asked her if she was okay. She kind of glared at me. I felt out of place, felt that it was a little bit too personal a question for me to be asking while I was working for somebody. So I was getting ready to leave. Well actually, before that, I was showing her how to work her faucet, and I took the spray hose, and when I went to turn it on it slipped out of my hand, and I ended up spraying her chest, so she really didn't like me at that point. I apologized, and I was getting ready to leave. I was walking out the door, and then she stopped me and said, "Are you nervous? Is something wrong? Because you were talking to me earlier." And I said, "Well, I thought that I asked too personal a question when you were talking on the phone." And she said, "Well, no not really. I'm not going to tell your employer or whatever. But thanks for asking." And I went on my way. When I got to my truck, I called my shop and told them that if this customer calls, I made a mistake, too personal, because a lot of times customers won't tell us in front of us. So sure enough, as soon as I stopped back at the shop, the phone rang. She said she wanted to speak to me. They asked if I had forgotten to fix any leaks or if I had left any tools there. No – but she wanted me to come back to her house. So they weren't too sure, and I didn't want to go back because I thought the lady was going to be upset with me. But I did go back to the house, walked in, and I was going to check the faucet. I had my pliers in my hand, and when I got out from underneath the sink, she took the pliers out of my hand, she told me I was scaring her, she gave me a big hug, asked me if I was single or seeing anybody, and then started kissing me. And one thing led to another. Ended up going into her bedroom on my lunch break.

Ah, your lunch break!

It was my lunch break.

Now, do you report that back to the office.

No! No. Besides you, I think there are only two of my close friends who know that story.

Well you know, I keep thinking of porn films and porn stories and fantasy. An attractive plumber comes in and he's on his back and he's screwing the gooseneck, and then somebody who lives there is standing over him thinking lecherous

Growing Up Male In America

thoughts.

I did go out with her a couple of times after that. I haven't talked to her in a while.

Now, she was 70 years old, you said?

[Laughter] Naw. She was 32 and very attractive.

All right. And there was no sign of a husband around there?

No, no. She was single.

See? You've got to stay in this business. You never know whom you're going to meet. Well, very interesting, indeed.

Well, let's go back to when you were just a little kid. You were born in California.

Yeah. Out there, my dad was in the military. It's right by a large air force base, which was one of the largest missile bases out there. I was born in 1970, so that was the time when we had the big military bases set up.

And are your parents still together?

Yup. My mom and dad are still together. I have one older sister, a year older than me. My mom's English. My dad met my mom in England when he was on assignment over there. My sister was born there. I was born in California, and we moved up to northern Minnesota for a while, but they closed that military base. Then we moved to England. Lived over in England for a few years, and then we moved back here. My dad was stationed out at Andrews Air Force Base, and then when my dad retired, and we came back to Minnesota so my sister and I could have a good place to finish high school and start college.

When you were in England, how old were you then?

I was between eight and 12.

So you went to school there.

Um-hum. I went to school on an American base. Not in the British school system.

All right. I guess that's what I would have thought. But it would have been nice if you had gone to a British school, wouldn't it? And then you could see how education differs from our system here.

Yeah. The education there, I think, differs a lot. Their school year's longer, and they also graduate when they're younger, too. They're a little bit more strict over there. My sister basically jumped a year ahead, not because we weren't in the British school system but just because of the American schools there and the teachers that they had there and the way everything worked. When we moved back here, my sister was a year ahead.

Are you still good friends with your sister?

Yes. My sister and I get along great.

Interview 1

So far you're rather unique compared to many of the men I've interviewed. Your parents are still together, and you get along with them and you get along with your sibling. Well, I guess this is the end of the interview. [Laughter]

I'm supposed to have dinner at her house tomorrow night. Mom, dad, my sister and my sister's husband.

Okay. So, you've been around. And to have experienced living in Europe at that early age, do you have any memories? Like, did you like it? Did you hate it? Was it just okay?

We never lived on base. My parents always made sure we lived off base, and we always did something on the weekends together. We were dragged up and down the whole country, wherever we moved to. When we lived in Maryland, we traveled up and down the whole East Coast. My parents kind of took advantage of wherever we lived. We learned and went and did things wherever we were.

Did you have advantages of going to the theatre and concerts and seeing some of the culture that was there?

Yeah. In England, as I said, we did a lot of different things. We went to all the different castles. I was into history back then. I learned a lot of different things with a group that we would travel with ... my friends ... on the weekends. But my parents always took us out to the theatre and shows, to dinner shows. I have quite a few memories. I've been back to England twice since to visit. My relatives are there.

When did you start thinking you wanted to be a plumber?

That didn't happen until a few years after I graduated from high school. After graduation, I started doing lawn and landscape work, outdoor work, with a company for a while. Then I started college, a community college, just for a two-year general degree. I had no focus on what I wanted to do. I did start going back to construction to pay to go through school, so I did a little bit of everything. Electrical, drywall. Not so much plumbing then. A little bit of tin work, stuff like that. It wasn't until a few years later, when I moved out to Colorado and was living in Vail, that I started working for another general contractor. Because I had taken two years of Spanish in college and a couple of years in high school, they made me a job-site foreman on all of their job sites.

Is there a heavy Mexican population in Colorado?

Lots. A lot of Mexican laborers out there. And so they made me a foreman, going around taking care of everything. On the weekends, I would help out the plumbers. I would go in on Friday or Saturday, stick around, because they worked four 10-hour days, and I would just go in because somebody had to be there from our company. And I would just start to help the plumbers out when I was there, and started talking to them about piping and some pipe fitters. So I

Growing Up Male In America

worked with them. My bosses back there, my superintendents, were all from Minnesota. They'd moved out there in the mid 1970s. They told me to go back to Minnesota, go through a trade school – whether electrical, plumbing, pipe fitting – come back, and they would double my wage. So I called mom and dad and told them I was coming back home, and I registered at a technical college. There was a little bit of a waiting list, so I took a different job for a while. After about a year of that, I ran into one of my friends whose dad was a contractor, and he found out that I was doing some plumbing out in Colorado before, and that's how I started. And then I got put into the apprenticeship program, and now I can work for anybody.

Whatever made you go to Colorado? To get out of town?

Yeah. I had an ex-girlfriend who had moved out there, and she was working out there for a little bit, and I went out to visit her one summer for a weekend. When I was out there, I picked up the local paper, and I just decided one day to go out to stay. She already moved ... she was in the process of moving back here, and I had moved out there. I just wanted to get away. No reason. I just thought I'd try something different. Actually, I was kind of making the decision as to what I wanted to go to college for. College or work. And I just couldn't see going to college without having a main focus.

But they told you at the community college that everybody pretty much goes through the general-ed classes, anyway, didn't they?

Right. But I wasn't too sure back then about that, so I didn't do it.

You say Vail, and I immediately think of skiing. Did you ski? Do you ski?

I love to ski. I love snow sports, and I love water sports. When I was out there, I worked during the day, so I couldn't be a ski bum. But whenever I had free time, I skied. I liked fly fishing. I did a lot of skiing and mountain biking. I like to mountain bike a lot. I used to have a lot of free time back then.

So that's where you developed your interest in what you're doing now, the plumbing. But then you came back here, went to school, and then hooked on with ...

A friend's dad's company. And then I moved on, from there to where I'm working now, and I've been with this company going on six years.

What's the turnover rate?

It's high in the service shop. It's very high. Since I've been there, there are probably at least 10 plumbers, if not more, within the past 10 years who've left. Some people come in and work in service shops to get out of the cold during the wintertime. Or you have some dishonest plumbers come in. Most service companies give you a truck and equipment, and when some of these guys get the truck and equipment, they go out to do side jobs or night jobs or scabbing, and they're using service trucks. In Minnesota, the union has to provide everything, except for a pair of work boots and a pair of pliers. They have to

Interview 1

supply everything else. So in new construction, a lot of people don't have service trucks that they take home, but plumbers do. These guys come in, they work for a service company, then they start doing cash jobs at night on their own using the company's service trucks. Until they get caught by the service company – when the boss calls them to come in at 7:00 in the evening and they're not there, and he goes to the house to get the truck and the truck's gone or the tools aren't there because they're out doing night jobs.

Is there a penalty for this, other than getting fired?

Yeah, there is. Well, in Minneapolis here, your contractor would fire you or give you a negative referral. Once you're in the plumbers' union, it takes a lot to get you out. If you had a problem with drugs, they'll put you through treatment. If people steal, they'll put you with a different contractor. I think last year, they just passed something – or they're trying to pass it – that if you have three negative referrals in a year, then they'll boot you out of the union. Or they'll take your license from you.

It sounds kind of like the teaching business, which I'm in. You really have to do something pretty gross to be fired. You may have run into a few teachers along the way whom you think should have been removed. [Laughs]

Yeah. A couple of them. For example, one of my college teachers didn't like men. It was a literature class. A very basic one. Very basic. A couple of us guys went to school together, and we'd sit in the back of the classroom and probably talk a little bit. But it seemed all the time that our papers would get marked down pretty low. Couldn't really figure that out, when another one of my friends who had her at a different hour did really well. Well, back in high school, I always remember that I did better than he did on the assignments. I couldn't really figure it out. So what I did was, I took my paper, gave it to him, he put his name on it, and he got a better grade. And it was my paper. It was actually the same paper that I'd turned in earlier. One was an A, and one was a C. And then I confronted her, and she went over a couple of things with me, and she just blew it off, said that it must have been overlooked or something. I dropped it at that, because I knew I would have to take her again the next semester. But I don't know if it was because a couple of us guys would always sit in the back together, or if she just didn't like guys.

That happens.

Other than that, teachers aren't bad.

Thanks! I needed that. Now, when you were in high school, were you involved in activities? Sports or clubs? Were you ever in a play?

Not in high school. Junior high. I used to be in band, and I started in middle school, junior high. I used to play a lot of concerts. I was in high-school band for a while. Did, like, Pep Fest, jazz band. I played the clarinet and sax. Mostly the clarinet. In high school, I kind of gave up playing the sax and just stuck

Growing Up Male In America

with the clarinet. I played baseball all the way up through high school. But towards my senior year of high school, I gave up band and I gave up baseball. No reason, I guess. I just wanted to do other things with my free time. I started getting a different group of friends, which I enjoyed doing other things with, like going fishing or riding a snowmobile.

When was your first experience with alcohol?

Junior year in high school.

Your dad was a military man. Was he a heavy drinker?

My dad doesn't drink.

At all? Never did?

He'll occasionally have a beer or occasionally have a mixed drink once in a great while. And the same with my mom. Maybe a glass of wine from time to time. My parents don't drink at all, hardly.

Now, was your dad a strong disciplinarian to you kids?

No. My dad was very relaxed. My dad was in the Air Force, and it takes a lot to make my dad upset. No. Very, very good. Actually, mom was the one who did most of the discipline.

Do you have a good relationship with your dad?

Yeah. Real good.

Did you then, when you were younger? You'd tell him most everything?

Um-hum. Yeah. All the way up through the year after high school. That was about the only time when things got a little tense. I guess I was pushing my parents at that time, and they were kind of pushing me. Mom was trying to figure out what I was going to do with my life, and I was saying I don't really know. I just want to hang out with my friends. So I went to college and started drinking, and that probably wasn't good. Not that I ever had any bad experiences with the law or anything because of it, but, you know, I'd come home on a Saturday night, and mom thought that I was drunk, and she always complained that I wasn't doing anything with my life.

How about drugs?

No. Never did any drugs.

Never tried marijuana?

Oh, well, yeah. I guess I forgot that.

Yeah. I smoked pot a couple of times. Probably in my senior year in high school, once or twice, if that, at a party. And maybe once afterwards, in my first year in college.

Do you remember the effect, if any, the first time?

Interview 1

No. I was drinking. No.

But you never got into heavier drugs at all? Have you ever thought why not? When people all around you must have been. I mean, they're doing lines of coke and they're taking all kinds of other things.

I saw that at a customer's house where I worked today. Sometimes people are smoking weed right in front of you, or you go upstairs and you see the coke right on their mirrors and stuff on their bathroom vanities. I just never was interested in that. I don't smoke and I don't do drugs. I just drink beer from time to time.

A lot?

Yeah. Sometimes.

I mean, when you go out ...

If I go out, I might have ... it depends. If I'm staying somewhere and not driving, with a group of friends, I'll probably drink a fair amount. Five or six beers or something like that. Nothing that would make me have to make an excuse not to show up to work the next day or that I'd be hung over. I gave that stuff up years ago, when I was, like, 21. That's another thing about being a service plumber. You've really got to watch that kind of stuff, because if you're going out and drinking all the time and you get home from work at 5:00, you sit back and have a couple of beers and you get a call to go to work, you have to say no. And so then that cuts into that thing we were talking about earlier, your salary. If you don't work much, you don't get paid much.

Plus, after a while, if the boss sees too many times ...

Then the boss kind of ... yeah. But it's not ... in service work, it's not cut and dry in our union bylaws, about how many hours we have to work or how many hours that we're expected to work. In service work, if I would turn down every weekend to work and every night call to work at this service company, they would not be able to get rid of me. I'm sure they would make things difficult for me, but they wouldn't be able to get rid of me.

Okay. Well, the idea of having a hangover every morning is not a pleasant prospect, either, even if you don't get called in.

It did happen one time, though. On a heating call. There were three of us. I think it was the night before Thanksgiving, so it must have been Wednesday night. A big night when a lot of people normally go out. The first tech went over and needed some parts. The second tech went over, brought some parts, and they were the wrong parts. The third tech – which was me – went over, brought the right parts, stuck around, gave a hand. Talked a little too much. Because on the comment card that we got back after we were there, we got, "Technicians: Wonderful job. Came out. Heat was on. The only company that would come out. But first tech smelled of booze. Drinking quite a bit. Second

Growing Up Male In America

tech was worse than first tech. Don't think he should have been over. Third tech [me] little too much ... very, very talkative." [Laughter] But when I saw that comment card, that's kind of when I realized that I'd better cool it with the drinking.

It's kind of a wake-up call, I guess. At least you, as a sensible guy, heard the call. Good!

I assume you got along well with your buddies and had some nice adventures together and everything in high school. When did you start noticing the young ladies?

Middle school. Before junior high.

Yeah. That's about the time puberty kicks in, I suppose.

I probably was about 13 or 14, and it was when I was living out in Maryland.

Are kids that age allowed to date? Or is it more like group activity things?

I don't know. My parents didn't let my sister date until I think she was at least 16. And with myself, I never really went out on any date-dates. I mean, I got together with my friends, maybe at a friend's birthday party or something like that, back then. But there was nothing ever serious. Nothing ever serious. Just kissing. That was about it, back then.

Do you remember the first time you had intercourse with a young lady?

Oh, yeah. Yeah. That wasn't until years later. It wasn't until I was 20, 21.

Really? First time?

I just never ...

You moved too much.

[Laughs] No, no. I was here. I did high school here and college for a few years. It's just that the girls I knew seemed either a little too easy, or the ones that I wanted didn't want anything to do with me. I was just waiting to meet the right one, I guess. I was never into just going out and going to parties and having sex. I guess I just wanted to know these women first, I guess.

The first time, was it successful?

Very successful.

Good! You know, most people, the first time you do almost anything, it's something of a flop.

Well, you know, I had experimented a bit before that. Foreplay and stuff with some other girls from time to time. But never the big one, actually having intercourse.

Okay. Do you remember – when puberty hit you – did you develop early or late or about the same as the other guys? Hair on the body and cock getting bigger and all

Interview 1

the rest of it.

I was probably past the middle to the later side.

Okay. And so you noticed in phy ed that there were guys with hair on their bodies already?

Oh, yeah. Exactly. I saw that I was later than they were.

Okay. Do you remember the first time you masturbated?

Probably back sometime in junior high, high school. Somewhere back there. Oh, it was different.

Now, there was a pretty big and important situation in your life, since we're talking about romance and all of that. You have been married. How old were you when you got married?

I was 25.

And had you known her for quite a while before?

Yeah. Quite a while. I've probably known her for … let's see, I met her in about 1989, and we got married in 1995.

Okay. This goes back to …

College. I met her in my first year of college. We went out a couple of times. Nothing happened sexually. Just went to a movie and a football game. She kind of went her way and I went my way. And when I came back from Colorado, I picked up the phone and gave her a call. She was going to another college then. So I gave her a call, and she wasn't seeing anybody. Over the period of years before, I'd give her a call from time to time. If she was seeing somebody. I'd just ask her how she was doing, and if she said she had a boyfriend, I just never asked her out. So when I heard she wasn't seeing anybody, I asked her if she wanted to go out on a date. So I took her out for dinner and a movie and went back home that night. And then we started dating for a year, then we were engaged for a year, and we were married for five years.

Any kids?

No kids. No.

Was that intentional?

Oh, no. We both wanted kids. At the beginning of the marriage, we both kind of agreed that we were going to maybe wait just a little bit, because I was working at my plumbing job, and I wasn't too sure exactly where that was going to be going. Also she was finishing up college, and she wasn't too sure what she exactly wanted to do. Plus, we just wanted to be together our first year or two. But we always did talk about having kids. Then my wife went through a few things, some different issues. She went through some depression issues. She went through treatment for alcohol. She also decided to go back to

Growing Up Male In America

school for something else.

Did she graduate from college?

No. Nope. She never did finish her degree. She only had a few credits left. Then she went into another program – a PTA, they're called. A physical therapist assistant. So she started that program a couple of years ago, and she was almost done with that, and one day she came home and just said, "You know, I really don't want to go to school. I've felt pressure to go to school by my family." Nobody from her side of the family has ever gone to school or completed anything. I said, "Okay," and the place where she had been working part time offered her a full-time job and she took it. Needless to say, a couple of months after working there, she met somebody and had an affair.

She had gone through treatment for alcoholism?

Yeah. First there was depression.

Was she ever hospitalized for depression?

Nope. No. But she went to some counseling and was on some medication. When we were getting married, her parents went through a real nasty divorce. They were on the verge of divorce for a few years before.

So she was raised in a rather unstable family.

Yeah. On her dad's side of the family, there are a lot of alcoholics. Her mom and two sisters were the only side of the family here, because they were from the Ukraine. She had two younger brothers, so everything was dumped on her. When they went through the divorce, everything was dumped on her, from my father-in-law, from my mother-in-law, from the brothers. If we spoke to the father-in-law, the mother-in-law would get mad. Just a lot of bad things.

Plus the pressure from them, for her, to go to school.

"Go to school. You're not going to amount to anything if you don't go to school."

But her heart wasn't in it.

Nope. Nope. She just thought that's what people were kind of pushing her to do, and then that's when I started doing my plumbing. So then I told her, "Well, why don't you take some time off?" So she took time off from school, and she tried to figure out what she wanted to go to school for. I told her, "Go back to school now, because that way you can have this done in case something happens to me or when we have kids here in the next year or two. But that way you don't have to be pregnant while you're going through school. So get it done now. And if you get pregnant along the way, that's okay." And so almost two years, now – that's when we decided we were going to have kids. In a year. Instead I found out the bad news.

Now, let's get back to the alcohol treatment. She felt she was drinking too much, or

Interview 1

did she have some run-ins?

It was a little bit of both. Both my wife and I, we really didn't drink much in our first year of marriage. But what I was finding out was when my wife wasn't going to school anymore and I was at work all day and when I'd come home, I could sometimes smell alcohol on her. Or her mood swings would be a little bit different, or we would go out and she would actually drink quite a bit, where the next day she'd be sleeping in or she might not feel like doing anything. And that's when I started to realize that she was drinking a little bit more than normal. She actually decided, made the decision herself, to seek treatment.

When she would drink too much, like at parties or when you were out with friends or something, did she get loud and obnoxious?

No, no. I couldn't even really tell sometimes. It was very hard to tell. She hid it very well. That's why it took a long time for me to figure it out. It took probably over a year to notice this problem, and it wasn't until when I would come home sometimes, or I'd get up in the middle of the night and go downstairs and she'd be having a drink and watching TV, that I got worried. It wasn't that she was abusive or loud or anything. But to me that behavior was a symptom of being depressed. Something was wrong there. She needed a drink maybe to sleep or think things through. I'm not like that when I drink. I guess when I have things on my mind, I don't drink, so I found that kind of strange. Then we talked about it, and we tried no drinking together first. That didn't seem to help too much, so then she wanted to go through an inpatient thing. Which was fine. So she checked herself in, and I stopped drinking with her and we went to some meetings together. And to this day, as far as I know, she's not drinking. Or at least that's what I'd like to believe. But I don't think she is.

All right. But you don't keep in touch with her now, after the divorce?

Oh, I talk to her now and then. Yeah. Through our first year after the divorce, it took a really long time. Although we didn't have any kids, there's just all this paperwork and property-settlement stuff that takes a while. Plus, all of our friends are friends to both of us, so it's kind of different. And I didn't see the divorce coming at all.

Now, let's talk about that.

Her alcohol treatment was all done.

So that was finished, and things were going along all right.

Yeah. Everything was going fine. Just over a year ago, it was in early spring or May. In May we went on vacation. We decided we were going to have kids one year down the road, when she got done with school. We were going to try to have a baby in the meanwhile, in between. Then in December, one day she came home and said she had started working at a part-time job. She worked in a government office downtown. Her aunt worked there, so she went in to help

Growing Up Male In America

her aunt part time. Well, they came up and said, "Good help is hard to find," and they offered her a full-time job. So she decided that she wasn't going to go to school anymore. So that was in December. In March I went to England to surprise my relatives. My uncle was having a triple bypass. I asked my wife to go with me, of course. She couldn't go because she had just started this job and couldn't get the time off. Well, I went to England for a week. I talked to her, and everything was great before I left. I sent her flowers. I mean, I had no idea. I came home one day and thought something wasn't quite right. Saw that her maiden name was written down on a sheet of paper, like a scrapbook thing. Wasn't too sure. I just happened to call one of my friends where she said she was, but she wasn't there. So I knew something was wrong. Then she told me that she had met a guy who worked in the same building she did.

At work?

At work, which is strange, because my ex never, ever dated anybody or even went out with anybody unless she'd met him through friends. She wasn't the kind of person who would just meet somebody in a bar and go home with him. You would always meet somebody, establish a relationship. Which kind of threw me off there.

And maybe that's what attracted you to her in the first place – that she wasn't a typical barfly. All right. You're in England with the relatives and the bypass operation. Only a week, did you say? So this had to have been happening before you left, right?

Yeah. Because she started work there in December, and she and I had a talk one day, and she told me she met him sometime in February. I mean, in January she and I had a great time. We went out of town for New Year's Eve to celebrate 2000. It was great, it was wonderful. We had a good time. And, you know, my wife hadn't worked for a few years because she'd been going through school, so with her first paycheck she bought me a really nice watch. Stuff like that. Which I'm wearing. But anyway, I thought things were going great with us.

And sex was good?

Oh, yeah. That's one thing I miss. No, we didn't have any problems there at all. My wife was very ... she was very caring. She was very caring with all of our friends and would do anything for anybody. Very creative, not materialistic. Strange! I had no clue why this affair she had ever happened.

How does she explain him?

She can't. I haven't talked to her about him much, though. I just don't have any reasons. I wish she could tell me I was an alcoholic or I was abusive to her or my career was more than hers or my friends were more than hers. I just have nothing to blame this on.

Interview 1

So I suppose she just chalks this up to meeting somebody and being very attracted. But it works two ways. He must have found her attractive, too.

Right. Yeah. It had to have been both ways. You know, I did have a conversation with him one time.

Oh, you know him?

Well, no. He called the house one time when I was leaving. I picked up the phone, and he asked me who I was. That was a couple of days right after I found out about him through her. And I told him, "I am her husband." And he said, "Not for long." So here's my wife, or my ex, who I think is a very good person – with the exception of what she was doing with this other guy, having this affair with somebody else.

That's a hell of a thing for him to say to you!

My mother-in-law – or ex-mother-in-law – to this day … it's been over a year … has not talked to her daughter. Shut her out 100 percent. Just because of the way she treated me.

Oh! But she talks to you.

Oh, yes. She talks to me like everything's just fine and I'm just great. Anyway, that made it rough for the first couple of months. My ex-wife's brothers, they're just now starting to talk to their sister and do things with her the past couple of months. But nothing like what we used to. Well, we would all go do things. My ex-father-in-law, now, he's been divorced for a few years, because he got divorced in 1995 – he's accepted her and her new boyfriend.

They're not married, your ex and her boyfriend?

They're not married, and the last I heard they're just living together. I've seen her. I've never been to her place … when she walked out on me, when she told me the bad news, that was the last time I had any physical contact with her. But I do see her. I've given her money from time to time or bought her some gifts here and there. I even helped her move into her new apartment, because she had no friends anymore. Because all of our friends … so I thought that maybe if I helped her and she had some space, maybe we could work on things. But she didn't want to talk about things. She didn't want to go to a counselor or talk. There was no reason. It was kind of like being lost. I don't know.

Well, who did the filing? Did you file for divorce, or was it mutual? How does it work now?

It was mutual. There's no separation in the state of Minnesota. You have to be divorced, and I waited until she made the decision, and then we went down and did it together. It took a long time. I don't talk to her anymore. I stopped talking to her about four or five months ago, stopped giving her a call to see if she's okay or to see how things are. But yet, about three weeks ago, she gave me a call out of the blue and asked me what I was doing. It was, like, 9:00 in

Growing Up Male In America

the morning on a Monday. I said, "I'm working." And she's working, too. But other than that, she didn't say anything.

When you made a conscious choice to stop calling her a few months ago, was that maybe to avoid the pain?

Yeah.

I mean, if she'd call and say she's having a great time ...

Yeah. And if she'd say she's happy ...

That's turning the knife.

Yeah. Exactly. And now I realize that her family is starting to accept this new guy. I don't know. It takes a really good person, maybe a few years down the road for me, to be able to block that out or get outside of it. But I'll never stop caring about her. But, yeah, I guess if I was to find out that she and this guy went to some of the resorts and other places that she and I used to go to and then she calls me and says, "We went to such-and-such a place, and we had a great time!" – that would really hurt me.

You have to, I suppose, cut it off at one point and move on.

And to complicate matters a little, she and I are godparents for some of my friends' kids. And then, once in a while, she calls me when some of her relatives need plumbing work. But other than that, it's pretty much done between us.

When was it final?

It will be a year next month, in July.

Now, is there payment? Do you have to make payment? Support?

No. No, no. We didn't have any kids, and she couldn't afford to buy me out on the house. But I offered her the house, told her to keep the house and the car, stuff like that. But that's all materialistic stuff. I mean, we'd bought a new car. I gave her that car. I gave her all the furniture. My wife made a lot of stuff. She's very creative. I just gave her everything. Everything. Figured that was just the easiest way to go. So, I had to make a new start.

You're a remarkable guy. There are a lot of people who would carry a whole lot of anger.

Yeah. Some of my friends talked to me about stuff like that. But you know, it's because I felt more hurt than angry, and that's why it took so long to break ties. You asked me if I talk to her. Well, you know, sometimes when I was out shopping by myself and saw something at a shop that we used to go to – if I'd see something in there and it reminded me of her or I knew she'd like something in there – I'd pick it up and I'd send it to her. I'd just send it to her at work. I don't know. It just made me feel good. But I didn't have any contact with her. But now I've stopped all that stuff. Been concentrating on myself lately. Just

Interview 1

doing things that I used to do. I was real worried about that – that when I got divorced, I'd start going back to how I was when I was single.

A lot of partying and that kind of thing?

Yeah, but that was also before I had a so-called career, I guess. When I didn't have a lot of responsibilities.

And also you were younger.

Yeah.

But even still, a lot of terrible things could have happened to you as a reaction to the divorce. You could have got lost in the bottle and all of a sudden turned into a problem drinker.

Well, it comes with being a plumber. [Laughter] Plumber's crack!

I suppose there's a course for that, right? How to wear your pants low enough so that when you bend over, you show a generous part of your ass crack.

Yeah, yeah. The Plumbing Heritage Class. [Laughter]

Well, now, since the divorce, have you been dating a little? Are you meeting some nice people?

Well, my one kitchen faucet customer.

Oh, that happened after?

Yeah. That happened after. Yeah. I never cheated on my wife. That happened afterwards. So I was … I don't think I would have ever done something like that before, so maybe I got a little lost there for a little time. I've been on a couple of dates.

She's the one who said, "Let me handle your tool." Is that what you said?

Yeah. So I put my pliers down because they were scaring her.

[Laughs] Oh, that's good stuff.

So, I went out with her a couple of times afterwards. And then I met a couple of girls here and there, but it's tough. It's tough now that I'm working a lot during the day and being more responsible. I actually never had the opportunities, when I was 21 and 22, going out and meeting girls at bars and things like that, because I had already found somebody when I was in college. From the time I was 19 or 20, all the way through. So now it's kind of like hopping back into the single life, but most of my friends are all married. So it's kind of hard to meet girls right now, but I've been on a few dates, but nothing special.

Well, whoever it is you meet, she will be a very fortunate woman, because you're a man of good conscience and good ethics, and you're sensible. That's good.

That's what my dad tells me.

It'll happen. You'll invite me to the wedding. I'll sit in the back and yell up to you,

Growing Up Male In America

"I told you you'd luck out!"

I just went to Florida this last weekend and met a girl there, so I might get some sun out of it. [Laughter]

Okay. The pain and loss of some things like divorce don't go away easily, but the pain gets a little less.

Yeah. I've talked to a counselor about it now and then. Just when I feel like it. But it's okay. Every day is different.

Yeah. Well, that kind of brings us up to the present. Let's see, we talked about early childhood. You had a regular childhood. You had parents who were married to each other, and you didn't go through the trauma of their divorce.

Well, moving along here. I always ask the men about the size of their penis, because I get some really interesting answers. Is yours less than average length, average or longer than average? I'm assuming you're circumcised.

Yeah. I'm circumcised. Well, I'd probably say average. But doesn't girth count? I get some compliments on girth, not so much as length. You never know if she's lying to you, though.

That's right. The second question usually is, "Well, what's average?" And if people watch a lot of porn films, they think that average is probably about 12 inches. And that's just not the case. They say the average length, erect, is about six inches.

Oh, I'm more than average, then, I would say.

Yeah, okay. So you never went through this thing in the locker room about being shy about your cock being too small or anything like that?

Oh, yeah. Actually, not so much about the size – not in the locker room – but I would have a problem with just going to the bathroom at urinals. Here I put these things in! [Laughter] At a sporting game or even just this last weekend, when I was down in Florida, going to the bathroom – I'm the one who usually will wait for the toilet stall instead of just standing there at the urinal. And it's not so much if someone looks at my cock – I've just never been able to pee in such situations. I just remember back in high school – no, it was after high school, somewhere in there – just one time, some of my friends one time, we were in the bathroom or something, and I just couldn't go. And they said, "Oh, it's stage fright! Stage fright!" My friend goes, "Just go in the toilet and shut the door and take your time." And he said, "Just go in there and stand there, and then you'll feel much better." And all my buddies were laughing. "He's got stage fright! Stage fright!" So now I just don't know ... whenever I use a public restroom, it always pops into my head that I'm going to have stage fright and won't be able to pee. But usually I just wait. But I have no problem. Like if I'm anywhere, if I'm working, if I'm outdoors and things like that, I'll just go to the bathroom anywhere. Out by the street sign. But it's in the public restroom, for some reason. And there can be nobody in there, and I still can't pee.

Interview 1

Oh! Oh! It's not because someone else is there.

No! Even when I go by myself, I'll still go into the toilet stall.

In terms of sex, do you have any trouble reaching orgasm?

No.

Well, good for you! Okay. So with you, we've got a slightly larger-than-average cock, and it has some fantastic girth, right?

That's just what my ex said. I don't know.

Okay. Good enough.

The following questions are quick-response ones. I'll ask you a question, and just answer it as quickly as you can. Just the first thing that comes into your mind. And sometimes nothing will come into your mind. Okay?

First: What is the most hurtful thing a friend or a relative has ever done to you? Let's leave out the divorce thing, because that probably would be at the top of the list. But what's the most hurtful thing a friend or a relative – somebody you trusted and loved or liked – did to you?

[Pause] A friend lied to me. After I helped one of my friends get into the plumbers' union and get a job at the same shop where I'm at. He lied to me about a couple of things. That kind of hurt. But nothing real terrible.

I agree with you. I think lying and stealing are about the same. Those things hurt. All right. Do you ever pose to attract women?

No. I'm usually the one that goes chasing after them.

[Laughs] Okay. Where do you see yourself when you're 50?

Hopefully retired. Pretty close to being retired. I don't know. Hopefully, by the time I'm 50, I would probably like to own my own company in the plumbing field. My own plumbing shop. Just comfortable, I guess. Just being comfortable by the time I'm 50.

And you're not really a materialistic sort of guy. I mean, it's not like you need this multi-level house.

No. No. Toys and things, stuff like that – that would be nice. But just being comfortable. Just that you don't have to worry about where your next paycheck is going to come from on Friday and whether it will cover all the bills. Just being comfortable, I guess.

As a plumber, do you ever feel not proud of that profession?

Oh, at times. It depends on what customers you work for. You can knock on a door and if right away they tell you, "The service door is in the back," well, right there you kind of want to make a little bit of a gulp. Maybe they do stereotype when you come walking in. And, of course, I always take my shoes

Growing Up Male In America

off. I do every time. And they're, right away, "Take your shoes off. Use the back door." I have a story, if we have time.

Sure!

I had a customer not long ago. I was working on some frozen pipes in a garage out back. A really nice house on one of the numerous lakes – a beautiful, beautiful house. And I was working on some frozen pipes and was up on a ladder, and the guy – he was probably about 55 to 60, somewhere in there – comes pulling in the driveway in a beautiful Mercedes convertible. His top was up and stuff, and he gets out of his car. Anyway, he comes walking in the garage. Now, the house is for sale, and this is why I'm there – because they're going to show the house. So I'd met with the wife earlier and started working in the garage. So he comes pulling in in this Mercedes, gets out of the car, and I said hello just to acknowledge that he was there, and he acknowledged me. So I said, "So where are you moving to? You moving further up the parkway, or are you moving out of Minneapolis?" And he said, "What the fuck does it matter to you? You're just a fucking plumber, and it's none of your fucking business." So at that point, I didn't know what to do, so I just kind of smiled and saw him go walk in the back door, and I took my pipe wrenches off the pipes, folded up my ladder, grabbed my stuff and started walking down to the parkway in front of my truck. As I was going down there, I was sitting in my truck and called the shop, saying, "I just got sworn at here. I'm going to see if he's going to leave here in a bit and then I'll go back in the house." Well, my foreman at the shop told me that they were going to send another plumber over, just in case, but they would pull me off the job site and have the other guy do the work. All of a sudden I go to look, and he's backed his car on the parkway and he's got his Mercedes parked there. His car is blocking traffic. Then he pulls up alongside my truck in the driveway, and he's yelling and honking his horn at me through my truck window, trying to tell me to roll it down. So I roll it down. And he starts swearing at me again. "I'm fucking sorry! I had a bad, fucking day! Can you please go fix my fucking pipes?" I'm, like, "Okay!" And then people are honking at him, so he starts saying the "f-word" back at them. So then I get back up there and I go into the garage again and I start working. Well, his wife comes outside, and that's when she told me that it's none of my business to know about their lives, that I'm too personal, that I asked too personal a question to be working there, and that I should maybe just concentrate on doing my work.

Did she say this kindly, or was this also direct?

It was very direct. It was very direct and a little bit arrogant. And then when she proceeded to walk away, she says, "You seem like you're a nice person. We're going through a divorce."

And everything was a little tense.

Right. So it turns out that at our company, it's happened three times that I've

Interview 1

put my foot in my mouth, and all three of those ladies are friends. It happened when I first started there with another customer, that we asked where the husband was. You know? "How's so-and-so? Is he at the manufacturing place?" And she replied, "No, he's off to younger and blonder." So right there was a personal thing at the house. And then one other time recently, at another customer's house, I actually saw him at a restaurant and I didn't see her. I thought maybe she was in the bathroom. I went to say "hi" and they weren't there, so I said, "Hey, how was the restaurant?" She said, "I wouldn't know. You'd have to ask his girlfriend. We're getting a divorce." And all these three ladies are all friends now. But there's another little plumbing story.

But you don't run into arrogant behavior often, do you?

You'd be amazed. A lot of the people who have money are some of the hardest people to work for, and impolite. But I get a lot of nice customers, too. But you know, I am in this service plumbing end of it, and service work is ... it's what it means: service.

But that still doesn't excuse that arrogance. I read something years ago about what it means to be civilized, and it means to make other people feel comfortable in your company. That arrogance you just described makes people feel very uncomfortable and hurt.

Well, to be honest with you, if people are polite – just being polite, you're going to get ... not that I do it, but you're probably going to get better service. Or they're going to go that little extra step that they probably wouldn't do. Instead of throwing your newspaper a couple of steps down, maybe the newspaper boy will put it up at your doorstep. And all you have to do is wave and acknowledge that they come there. [Laughs]

Isn't that the way you were raised, though?

Yeah. My parents were real respectful.

And you get it back if you are, too.

That was a good story. As you were describing the Mercedes in the parkway, I was kind of hoping – this is the cruel streak in me – that as his expensive car backed into the street, some garbage truck ran into him. I think that would be wonderful, and just dent the hell out of that pricey car And there's a nice metaphor in that image, isn't there? [Laughter]

Now, moving on. Where did you learn the most about sex? Another subpoint to this questions is: Did your mom and/or dad ever sit you down and tell you about sex?

Well, I learned a little bit from my friends. My parents caught me, probably when I was back in junior high, with some porno magazines. I had them stashed out in the little tree fort. My friends got the magazines from their parents or somebody, I can't remember. And Mom went out there one time to check on something, and she found these porno magazines. At 5:00, when Dad

Growing Up Male In America

came home, we had dinner. And right there on the dinner table were these porno magazines. And they sat me down, and my mom told me that this isn't how women are in real life. That's when we talked about the birds and the bees. And shortly right after that were some sex classes in school.

That's right. The schools are doing that, aren't they?

And that was in junior high, and then more classes on sexuality in high school.

And, of course, friends. I mean, guy talk.

And that wasn't until probably high school and moreso in college, really. My friends, we all kind of ... I don't know ... all probably had the same values, I guess. I don't know.

Did your friends – unless you knew them really well – did your friends back in high school ever talk about masturbating?

Well, some of my friends did. One of my friends is quite open about that stuff. He always talks about how large his cock is.

And what a lady killer he is?

Yeah. He's very open with all that kind of sex stuff.

All right. When you are with just guys, what is the main topic or subject of conversation?

Lately, with my single friends that I've been seeing quite a bit of – girls. Sex. Sex in general. Whoever they're dating or whatever.

Do you – I assume you do – do you have some close women friends?

I have some women friends, yeah.

Non-sexual. Just buddies.

Right.

What's the main subject of conversation with women?

Usually, lately ... a little bit of sex, but usually mostly it's trying to meet somebody who might be interested in marriage. Family values, I guess. A lot of my lady friends who are single now are coming up to their 30s, and they've just been talking about meeting guys.

Okay. How tall are you?

Five–six.

Does that ever bother you?

It used to.

Not any more?

Not any more. Actually, I probably didn't grow to five–six until my senior year of high school. I was usually five–four, five–five, somewhere in there. My par-

Interview 1

ents were worried there a little bit and went and had me checked out, but the doctors said everything was fine. And I kind of shot up a little later.

What is that, the pituitary gland?

I'm not too sure. But my dad's short, and his family is short. I can deal with it now. At times it's uncomfortable, but I've just learned to deal with it.

Sure. Like, what are you going to do about it, right? You can't change it.

No, you can't. You just wait in line at bars a little longer. [Laughs]

Okay. Finish this sentence: My biggest, greatest fear is …

[Pause] I guess being lonely.

Alone?

Alone. Forever. You've got to add forever on there. Alone temporarily is okay, but not always. I wouldn't want to be in my ex's shoes. That would be pretty frightening.

Well, you're hitting on loneliness or depression here. What can really put you into an emotional tailspin, into a depression?

When somebody lies to me or is dishonest to me. I'm divorced here, right now. Yeah, that was a big deal this past year. But when I put a lot of trust in the people that I know, and if they lie or do something dishonest to me – that, right there, means a lot to me and can depress me. Trust. Someone who shows no trust or is disrespectful – that would do it, too. That gets me mad, and I get in a bad mood and think about it and wonder why and how come it happened. Why would he or she say this or do this?

Disappointment.

Yeah.

Because you have higher expectations.

Yeah. For example, I helped this guy move into my house. I helped him out for a couple of months, and he totally took advantage of me. I told him he could live at my house for a while, and he was going to do some work on my house to show his gratitude. Some siding and stuff. And I paid him some money for the materials, and I still haven't seen my materials. And here I let him stay at my house, and he has my house torn apart outside. So lately, the past few days, something like that makes me a little down.

I can see why. Now, I assume you don't have any problem finding good, close friends. What adjectives do you think they use to describe you?

Probably, helpful. Caring. Loyal. Honest.

Sensitive?

Yeah, probably so, now. As the years go on. Not too many years ago, I wasn't a

Growing Up Male In America

very good listener. But I always cared. Always cared. Sensitive would be good.

All right. Some men are afraid to admit they're sensitive because ... that's one of the thrusts of my book. I mean, here we are, in the new millennium, and many men must wonder: Am I supposed to be macho-tough, thick-skinned? Or am I supposed to be a feeling man who's not afraid to cry, if the occasion arises?

I'm both, I guess. It depends on what the situation is. I care about my friends' kids, right now. I care about them, what's going on in their lives.

What is the importance of religion or spirituality in your life? And maybe you could talk how much of that you had in your growing up.

I believe in God. My parents left it open to my sister and me when we were growing up, because my dad was in the military and my mom is English, so she's well aware of the religious wars over in Ireland and parts of England. My mom is Church of England, which is Protestant, and my dad is Catholic. So as we were growing up, my parents encouraged religion. I was in Boy Scouts for many years, and when I would go on weekend camping trips, sometimes my dad would go with me if I chose to go to the Protestant services. I always believed in God. My sister found her own way and became a Methodist. I just never found one religion that I really liked until I was married, and then I went to classes to be Catholic because my ex was Catholic, and I had to promise that if we had kids, we'd raise them Catholic. But I was never confirmed Catholic. So when I do go to church I go on Sundays, and sometimes I will go on Sunday night, even. And if I do go, I usually go to a Catholic church. I usually go to the one by my house. But I'll go maybe a dozen times a year, if that.

So your religion is kind of a personal thing?

Yes. It's just my personal belief that there's a God out there, looking over me.

And you've pretty well established your own code of living, which is mutual respect and caring for other peoples' feelings?

Yes.

In your spare time, do you write? Do you read a lot? Do you ever write poetry? Do you ever try to express how you're feeling?

I used to read a little bit. Some history, some literature. I don't express myself in any ways in arts or make things or do creative or artistic things. I like going to galleries and festivals and things like that. I wish I could be creative like that. I'm kind of a nuts-and-bolts, two-by-four person. I could make a good square, but I can't make the stuff that goes in between it.

Do you ever pick up the clarinet?

The clarinet? Yeah. I haven't played it in a few years. Off and on, though. Around Christmastime. Currently, no. I gave it to my cousin to use in high school band.

Interview 1

Do you watch movies a lot?

> Not too often. Time right now is kind of important to me. To come home from work and then get some things done, some things that I'd like to do. I'll watch a movie occasionally. It's like football. I like football, but I won't plan my whole day around a certain game. If it's on when I'm home and it's there, I'll watch a game. If not, I won't watch it. But movies ... I like all sorts of movies, except for horror movies. I don't like scary movies. Just never have. Just can't sleep after seeing them. *It* by Stephen King ... that one. I saw that years ago, and it still bothers me if I see a clown. [Laughter] I like adventures, boy-meets-girl type movies. I just went and saw *Pearl Harbor*. It was okay.

Yeah. I saw that, too. A little romance laced in with history. Kind of like Titanic, *isn't it? Because everybody already knows the historical part, so you get romance injected into the history.*

I assume that some day you want to have a little flock of kids?

> If it happens, it happens. I don't know. I would have liked to have that happen by now, but we'll see. I guess I don't want to be so old with my kids that I can't spend time and enjoy certain things with them.

Well, I really thank you very much for being willing to sit in that chair and undergo this scrutiny. I really appreciate your comments in this conversation.

> You're welcome.

Postscript – December 2001

This man is recovering adequately from his painful divorce and is dating again. He continues to enjoy his work as a plumber.

Interview 2

"I can't believe we're from the same gene pool!"

This interview was conducted on June 21, 2001, when the subject was 29 years old. He is six feet tall, weighs 175 pounds and has blond hair.

I'm glad that you were willing to sit with me for this interview.

I hate to jump into sex right away – but I wonder if we could talk about your sexuality. If you were to put yourself on a continuum between heterosexual on one extreme and homosexual on the other extreme, where would you place yourself?

Well, on a scale of one to 10 – straight being a one and gay being a 10 – I'd probably put myself at six or a seven. Because I find both males and females attractive. I mean, for the last several years, I've been exclusively just with men, but my relationships with women have been good. But at this time in my life, women are not what I'm interested in. That's not part of me. And I don't know if I'll ever really go back to the woman thing again. You know, I always have had feelings towards men, even when I was with girls. But as we all know, when you're raised and stuff – not that my parents told me this – but the way society was, is that you're not supposed to think about being intimate with members of your own sex. And so that's why I went from women to men.

You were raised Lutheran?

Yeah. But we never talked about sex. We never were an overly affectionate family. We love each other, but we're not, like, hugging and stuff. I'd say we're very Swedish. It's a very Scandinavian thing. You know, like Italians, they talk with their hands and they're touchy and so on. Scandinavians historically aren't. That's how we are.

And when you were being raised, you never talked much about feelings, emotions.

Never.

Do you remember about how old you were when you started thinking about friend-

Growing Up Male In America

ships?

Oh, gosh. Four years old. Four or five. I remember way back when.

Okay. That's pretty young. In terms of the family, are your mom and dad still married?

No. My mom and dad separated and divorced when I was six. My mom died in 1987, when I was 16.

Well, how old was she when she died?

She was 47.

Ouch! So young! What of?

An aneurysm.

After your folks divorced, did you have visitation with your parents?

Yeah, I did. But it didn't go too well. I don't know the whole story behind it. I remember going over there and staying with my dad on overnights and weekends, but it wasn't that frequent. I think what happened is … my dad wasn't meant to have children. My dad is a good family man now, but when they had us they were young. And my dad wasn't ready. It's like all of a sudden they had an instant family, and they didn't want that. My mom was Catholic. My dad's Lutheran. And for my mom, abortion was completely out of the question. And so they had several kids together. And then they divorced.

When you say "several," how many siblings do you have?

I have four brothers and a sister.

Well, that is a big family, then.

Yeah. So I used to go over there occasionally to my dad's place before my mom remarried. My mom has been married three times. And my mom's husband – my mom married a year after my biological dad and she divorced, and her new husband was not a big fan of my dad's, so those trips to my dad's house came to a halt.

Did you ever have a visitation plan with your dad when he didn't show up and you had hoped he would?

Yeah.

Want to talk about that?

I vaguely remember it. But looking back at the pictures of myself as a little kid, I see now that a lot of stuff was going on. We're all smiling in those photographs. I was always a happy kid. My sister, on the other hand, took it in a different way. And then, you know, I have an older sibling above my sister, and I have four others under me. They were infants, so they didn't really notice it. But my sister and I would go over to my dad's place. My mom told me that one time she dropped us off and came back five hours later, and we were still

Interview 2

sitting on the steps outside his house in our Sunday clothes. Our dad wasn't there. I kind of remember that – but being a kid, you just kind of forget about it. But it taught me – in life, in later years – that I expect people to do what they say they're going to do, and if they don't, it disappoints me more than it probably should. I put a high regard on people who do show up and come through, and I put fairly strict expectations on people. And that's what's been frustrating for me, being in this "culture" – this gay culture. It's been very frustrating for me on that point, because it's hard to find that honesty.

People make promises: "Yes, I'll be there." "Yes, I'll call." "Yes, I'll ... whatever." And they don't live up to it. I wonder. Do you think that's a trend outside the gay culture?

I think it's probably moreso in the gay culture than it is in the straight culture. I mean, it's easier, I think, to be straight. Like everybody says, if I was straight, I wouldn't meet my wife in a bar. I mean, unfortunately, that's one of the few places that gay people meet each other. But men in general don't know how to be close to each other and cultivate relationships and friendships. And even my straight friends who are married or not married say it's hard to make friends and date as we get older. But they don't see the stuff that I've seen. I mean, sure there's some freaky women out there and stuff, but they have never seen the stuff that I have seen as a bartender.

Let's talk about that. You work at a bar. And how long have you been at that bar?

Almost two years.

And you're a bartender?

Yup.

Okay. What would you say are the positives and negatives about being a bartender?

Well, I like to socialize. I like that part of it. I like the bar itself, I like the people I work for and the money. I'm making a good living. It's my only source of income, and I do live well on it. On the downside, it's not a career. It's something that I can easily get stuck in. I need to get out of it eventually because I don't want to wake up one day and say, "Wow! I missed it." You know? And here I am, 50 years old. Which won't happen – but I don't want to be like that. I mean, it's a good living for most people, but I personally don't want to do it forever. The other thing is there's no job security there. You think you have it, but you don't. And I know people who say the same thing can happen at big companies, too. But it's nothing like a bar. I mean, you've got customers who can just have a hate for you and they can just sit there and tell the bosses, "He did this or did that." Also, people perceive me in a manner that – I don't understand why they do it – but some people just have it in for me and they turn around and call the owners. And that's where I feel like I'm on thin ice at this bar sometimes.

Growing Up Male In America

So some disgruntled customers can get on your case?

Yeah. I've had things said to me. I had a 70-year-old gay man who once called me a "fucking faggot" – like that. And I walked up to him and said, "You're calling me a faggot? What are you?" You know? I have seen a lot of crap that really makes me sad when people behave like that. It's tough enough to be gay, but yet, to be as mean as many are? It's like that's exactly what people think of the "gay community" – the pride, the "We Pride" Festival. What's there to be proud of? And that will go on later in this conversation. But things like that are the cons of bartending. People either think I'm arrogant or they think I'm the nicest bartender. The owners pulled me in once and talked to me when I came back from vacation, my first night back. They pulled me in the stockroom and talked to me. "People perceive you as arrogant and that you act like you own the bar." The bosses then said that several people were saying that I was overcharging them on drinks and pocketing the money. I looked at the bosses and said, "On my mother's grave, I would never steal from you. Never." And I said, "Was someone saying that? I don't know why they're saying that. Put a spotlight on me, turn those security cameras on me, whatever – but I don't steal. I never have. I don't need to steal."

I think the whole ageism factor is big. Young gay kids are ridiculing the old ones, and old ones are discounting the young and so on.

Well, okay. So you've been tending bar at the same place for about two years now. Were you a bartender somewhere else before that?

In Florida.

Okay. Now, what about Florida? How long were you down there?

Five years. I met a guy back in 1990, and I moved down there to be with him. And that lasted a short nine months, and then I moved from West Palm Beach down to Fort Lauderdale, and I graduated from college. I worked for Federal Express for a while in the national department in sales. I really liked it down there, but I came back home because I wanted to go back to the University of Minnesota for physical therapy.

You have a degree from Florida?

Yeah, in international business.

Okay. And have you started the physical-therapy program at the University of Minnesota?

Well, I did last September. I did it for two and a half months, and I didn't like it.

Okay. I see. You said you went down to Florida because of a relationship, but that lasted a little less than a year. And after that ended, did you have several relationships?

Interview 2

Well, I had two. First there was T—, and the other was B—. And B— was one person who I was with for two years. He was the longest relationship I've had. But it was easier for me to be myself down there than it is up here. Up here, I have a lot of history up here, and I don't like the gay scene. I don't like the attitude and the whole thing – you know, the ageism and all of this stuff. I mean, me at 29, I get it from people who are 21. I say to them, "You know what? I used to be 21. I used to have fresh-looking skin just like you. And I didn't walk around with an attitude. Because I'm telling you: your looks will fade, and you're going to be me someday." You know? I hate to be like that. I speak my mind, but they just don't like that. In Fort Lauderdale, the majority of my male friends are in their fifties. I find that the men who are older have been through all the crap and they're more grounded. Plus they all have yachts and big houses. They spoil me. [Laughs] Just kidding.

[Laughs] Sure! Well, here you are, on the very brink of turning 30. Do you think turning 30 is going to be difficult?

No.

No. It's just another year, huh?

I've been going out to bars since I was 16 years old. I remember being 18, and I met a guy who was 28. I said to myself, "I will not be going to the bar when I'm 28." I was so sure I wouldn't need to go to the bars when I was 28. But look at me now. It's happened. You know? The bars can be fun if you go out with your friends on occasion, but it's a false feeling, to me, of a community and of a good environment because it's really not. It's a bar. It's a meeting place for gay people, and it's a big club house that has liquor in it. You know? It's not really a very good environment, I don't think, for the most part.

I'll bet some people who have never done your kind of work think it's pretty glamorous to be a bartender. There you are, kind of on display, and everybody sees you and you get to see everybody. They forget the other big part: hard work, griefs, and some days you don't feel like being "on."

It's like being out in public and being under a microscope.

Yeah. And where everybody else is having a party – because they're there for that – you're working. But people don't always see that it's work for you, because you have to act like it isn't.

Do you ... at this point in your life, do you want a relationship?

Yeah, I would like one.

Have your ideas toward what you're looking for in a man changed from when you were 18 to 20, compared to now?

No.

What sort of things do you look for?

Growing Up Male In America

Honesty, first. Looks are important, of course, and a sense of humor. Masculine. Acting like a guy and not a queen or fem. I don't like effeminate guys to have a relationship with. Just a nice person about my age. And that's it.

Okay. When you were 18 or 20, did you like older people or people your own age?

My own age. I've always liked guys my own age. And thank god I'm like that now! I see younger ones and they think they're cute, but their personalities and mine don't mix. You know? And I'm glad I'm not like that. I feel sorry for people who are like that.

The "depth factor" is an important one. I mean, can you really talk with some of those people? Are you finding already that tastes differ in terms of music, for example?

Oh, yeah.

And values?

Yup. They're different. I went to another gay club on Thursday night, and it's mainly young guys who go there. I really hate to say that their behavior kind of irks me, because it's like I sound like my grandma. You know, "the younger generation." But I notice a difference in the attitude. They're not the nice guys that I think we were like when we were that age. I mean, we can be bitchy guys, too, but it was a nicer time. And we didn't sit there with such an attitude, and we didn't walk around with our shirts off. We weren't doing drugs. I mean, sure people were smoking pot back then, but there's all these designer drugs out there, and they're "on" them. I mean, they have glitter on their faces and they're walking around the bar like they're the cat's meow. And I wonder, what's wrong with just being yourself and being a nice person? Because this attitude is like, "Hey. I'm 21. I got it all going on." It repulses me. It does.

You realize, though, that nothing you can say will ever change them or that behavior. And all you can say or think is that, "Some day you'll be 30. Some day you'll be 50. Some day you'll be looking back," and they don't believe that either, so after a while you get tired of saying it.

Well, when I was 20, you know, in my twenties, I thought 25 was far away from me. And then, boom, there it was, you know. And it goes faster every year.

Yeah. I know. I'm 60.

Would you say your childhood was pretty much a normal sort of thing, aside from the things we've already talked about?

Yup.

Public or parochial grade school?

Public.

Here in Minneapolis? And can you think back to your one or two best friends in

Interview 2

first, second, third grade? What was it about them that made them friends? Were they male or female?

Males. R— was one, and D— was the other. D— was my neighbor. I lived in a suburb for a short time, too, and those were my kindergarten, first, second and third grades. R— I knew from school. D— went to my school but was also my neighbor. Right next door to us.

Now, what qualifications did they have as friends?

They were just nice kids. They were caring, and they were nice. They're like, I don't know … it's like your favorite pair of shoes you wear that are worn out. I don't know. They were just nice people. If someone's nice to me and it's genuine, they'll be my friend for life. But both of them moved away.

I suppose the element of trust comes in there. You didn't have to be on your guard with them?

Yeah. Well, it sounds corny to say it, but – at that age – in my thinking, I was a lot more advanced and had seen a lot more than most of these kids had seen. I saw my parents divorce. I remember meeting my mom's new husband for the first time. And I saw that. I mean, a lot of things at an early age, so I always felt older. I was always more drawn towards older people. But those few years – those are like my … what do they call it? … "golden years" in reversal. Because those were good times. It was fun, it was innocent. But then my mom and her new husband decided that we're moving. And that's when fourth grade came, and we moved. But those few years of grade school were just great. I mean, nothing existed outside my playground. You know?

How about school itself? Did you do all right?

Oh yeah.

Good student, and the teachers liked you?

No. I was a brat. [Laughter] I was the class clown. Got my mouth washed out because I called this girl Chrissy "pissy" once. The teacher grabbed me by the ear and put liquid soap in my mouth and washed my mouth out. But for the most part, yeah, I was an okay student.

But you were just a typical kid. What the hell.

Yeah. Exactly.

Yeah. Neighbors thought you were okay? They didn't mind having you come over and play with their kids?

Oh, no.

Which crowd were you in during those early school years?

I was in the popular crowd. I had a lot of friends, and that was one thing that was great about those early grades for me. But when I moved to a new school

Growing Up Male In America

district, the tables turned. It took me a long time to get my foot in.

Did you get involved in sports?

Baseball.

In terms of socioeconomic level, was your family income good?

My dad's side of the family is very wealthy, but here's what happened. When my mom and dad divorced, he said, "The kid's not with me. No support." Gone. And my mom farmed all us kids out, and she moved to an apartment in Minneapolis with only the stuff she could carry. He lives out in this beautiful lake mansion, and he cut us off. I mean, my mom didn't fight him on it. She said, "I'd rather have you kids and be broke than have you be with him. Because I'm not going to let you be with him." She had custody and he had visitation, but obviously he wasn't coming through. So he lost his visitation rights. But living with my mom at this transitional time was like driving a Mercedes Benz and then changing to public transportation. I remember having it all, and I also remember leaving and having only the clothes on my back. But I didn't sit there and go, "Gee, I miss this. I miss that." I knew it. You know, I looked at my mom and realized she was doing what's best.

Yeah. I see what you mean about being a little advanced. You had some experiences that most kids never have, and those things make you a little more mature.

Well, like when my mom brought her husband-to-be over to meet me for the first time. I was playing in this closet. You'd walk in one side and go into the other room through it. I used to like to go into little boxes and dog houses and make them my little house. So what happened is, she brought him over. And she said, "I want you come meet your new daddy." And I came out and I walked up to him, and I didn't like him the minute I saw him. And she said, "This is your new dad." And I took my foot and I kicked him in the shin and I said, "You're not my dad and you'll never be my dad." And I went right back in that closet. And that was how I felt. I knew I didn't like him and I never did like him. And he was part of our family for 10 years. So, yeah. I saw a lot. I never played with trucks or toys as a little kid. I wasn't interested in them.

Did you like to talk with people?

I talked too much. You should see my report cards. "Socialized too much." I always got that. Chatting. Chattering.

Disruptive in class?

Yes.

Okay. So, by the time you're hitting fifth, sixth grade, you'd been through your folks' divorce situation. You'd been through a separation that was kind of ugly, and you'd been through a pretty massive change in socioeconomic level, from one extreme to the other. But you maintained your equilibrium and you had good friendships.

Interview 2

Earlier, you mentioned drugs. As a bartender, you're kind of surrounded with that. What kind of drug involvement do you get involved with?

Well, I like to drink. Sometimes too much. I don't do other drugs, though. And I don't like seeing people do it, but it's their choice. I think it's ridiculous. I'm kind of naive, too, about the whole drug scene, I guess. Where I work, we don't get that kind of crowd like the bigger city bars do. But for me, I just don't care. It's bad enough that I drink. I like to drink. It makes me feel more comfortable going into a bar environment. I can't go in there and not drink. I just look around me and it's, like, "I need a drink. I want a drink." You know?

Okay. Tell me more about some of your most memorable teachers.

My kindergarten teacher, Mrs. W—. Also my fifth-grade teacher, who was 21 years old when she was my teacher. I didn't like her when I first met her, but then later she understood me. I had one teacher at the other school, and she was a feminist. You know, earth shoes and the octagon-shaped eyeglasses. She was married, and her name was Ms. V—. And I used to call her *Mrs. V—*, and she used to get so mad at me. So she and I had it out for each other. But those three ladies, yeah – they made positive and negative impacts on me.

In terms of religion, do you have your own personal faith or belief system or spirituality?

I don't know. I'd probably just say that I believe you live your life. I think you're down here for a reason. I'm sure there's something that created us here. I hate to talk like this, but I don't think there's someone upstairs in a robe looking down upon us. I believe you get the deck that you're dealt and that's it. Then you live your life and then you die and you come back. I believe in an afterlife. I think organized religion is what used to keep people in check, you know, supposedly sound and moral.

It also is the force that's been the reason for lots of wars and deaths in the history of humanity.

Okay. Moving along. Now you're about 13. Do you remember puberty happening to you?

In seventh grade, we had to shower in junior-high phy ed. That's when I saw guys who were really developed and guys who weren't. I don't remember when it happened with me. It was just all of a sudden, it was there. I remember that I developed at about the normal time. I wasn't late.

Do you remember your first sexual experience with another person?

What do you mean by sexual?

Perhaps to the point of ejaculation.

Well, I was too young to do that. And if we have to talk about that, we'd need to go way back.

Growing Up Male In America

Okay. Let's go way back.

We're talking kindergarten. A classmate of mine and his brother.

Okay. Tell me.

We were playing doctor. We took a blanket and put it over the ping pong table. We would climb under there and play doctor. You know? The youngest one was the patient. And I'll never forget my mom coming down, and I saw her leg, her feet. "Boys, what are you doing down there?" I said, "Doctors." And she goes, "What kind of doctors?" And I'm, like, "Special doctors." But what I did … I tried to take a clothespin and stick it in his butt. One of those wooden ones with those springs in it. I did get part of it in. Yeah. He was squirming, so I put my knee in the curvature of his back to hold him down, and his brother held this kid's arms down. I remember trying to cram it in there.

Well, the poor kid.

Yeah. And then my other friend and I used to play with each other once in a while, too. He and I used to. We went from first to second and third grades together. We had a choice of taking a language. We chose German. They'd close the curtains down in the classroom and they'd turn on TV, and there'd be a teacher teaching German. Well, this lady on TV would sit there and say, "Good morning, kinder." These two other boys and I would go back behind the table and sit there. It was a big table where you'd sit and read stuff. But we used to go back there and sit there and watch this German teacher, and we'd feel each other. We all had erections and stuff like that, but of course at that age nothing ever happened. But we used to do that, and we used to play with each other in the swimming pool. Just grabbing each other's cocks. Sometimes we'd turn over a two-man inflatable boat and flip it and swim under it, and we'd kiss and stuff like that. But I was a very sexual person at a very young age. I knew exactly what was going on.

How do you account for that? I don't suppose you ever talked about it. You just did it.

We just did it. And we didn't even talk about it the next day.

You were about how old, roughly?

About six, first grade. This happened until fourth grade. Then in fifth grade, it was the first time I remember I actually got off and had an ejaculation. I remember that.

Let's see. Fifth grade you're about 11, 12?

Yeah. I remember that because we were laying on top of each other naked. Then in sixth grade, three friends and I used to go above the garage in the rafters and watch one of them jack off. He had a big dick, and I remember he asked me to give him a blow job and I couldn't get my mouth around it. Then the other kid said to do it to him but I wouldn't because he was too small. Even

Interview 2

at that age, I wouldn't touch it because he was so small. But he was a beautiful guy, a gorgeous guy. We used to play like that. Then all of a sudden, seventh grade came and it never happened again. None of that stuff. It was like seventh grade was the exodus. It stopped.

Was it because there was a stigma or people might think you were queer?

We never really talked about it. We just did it.

And now, by this time, you're in full-fledged puberty. Did your interests, at the age of 14 and 15, go toward girls more than boys?

I'd look at the boys and notice they were cute, but I was sexual with girls. I mean, one guy and I used to have sex with this girl. We took her halter top once and said, "If you don't let us fuck you, you're not going to get it back." That was in seventh grade. We were messing around down on a river bank, and I pulled her halter top string off. We'd been with her before. She was a great lay. She was fun. We took her over on the sand on the bank, and we both did her. And that was, like, in seventh grade.

Seventh grade you're about 13, 14 or so. And she was experienced?

Yeah. She knew what she was doing. It felt great.

Any oral sex from her? Giving or receiving?

No. I like doing that to girls, but I liked having oral with guys. But nothing oral really happened at all with her.

Okay. Did you date much about this time?

I had girlfriends. I wasn't very sexual. I think it was more of a cover for me, in a way. I couldn't understand why I thought other guys were attractive, and I wondered why could girls say that, you know: "Oh, Betsy. She's so cute." And why can't boys say, "Yeah. John's a good-looking guy." I'm sure every other guy in my class thought that certain other guys were good-looking. I have a younger brother. I made a comment about his friend who was getting married and how I couldn't believe it because that guy was so damned ugly. My brother looked at me and said, "Only a faggot would say that." And I said, "Don't tell me you don't look at guys and think they're ugly or not." He goes, "No, I don't." I looked at him and said, "I can't believe we're from the same gene pool!"

But you never went through any great trauma with your noticing other guys?

No. I just felt different, and I went to great lengths not to go through it. Then I lived up north in a small town. There was nothing up there. But I'd see guys who were gay and I'd stay away from them. Like older guys who my mom had as friends. One Christmas we invited a friend of my mom's over. He was gay and our neighbor. I wouldn't go near him, because I thought he'd figure me out. So I avoided that.

Growing Up Male In America

And that was your secret. Never shared it with anybody, any friends at that time?

No. I look back now and I wish I could have talked to my mom about it.

In high school, did you know any close guys who were gay in whom you could confide about this?

No.

So you didn't have another person to share your secret with? You just went through this alone.

Yup. I know what it's like to go to a bar in the night and then get up in the morning and go to class the next day. Because I came back down here to the big city at age 16 and went to a fairly large school, and I was sneaking into gay bars then. That's when I lived with my great aunt.

Okay. Have you ever discussed your lifestyle with your siblings?

No.

Is there a reason? Or aren't you that close to them?

We're not that close.

Okay.

When my mom died, it kind of separated things out. My dad is like a friend to me. He's not like a father to me. We never had that "Hey, dad ..." sort of relationship. It's not that "father" quality. He's more like a good friend. Which is nice. I'm satisfied with it.

But you can't see yourself sitting down and talking about your lifestyle with your dad?

I don't want to talk with him about it, because I don't think it's any of his business. Besides, he doesn't ask. I mean, come on, figure it out. I'm almost 30. I'm not married. I don't talk about women in front of him.

Does he know that you work at a gay bar?

No.

Okay. Now, this is all hypothetical. What would you think if he walked into the bar some night?

I'll bet he might. I've had weirder things happen. I was talking to a customer the other day about this guy I used to mess around with when I was 18 and he was at the university. And this guy asked, "What's his name?" I told him and he said, "That's my nephew." And it was just, like, "Oh, wow." That was so funny.

Small world.

Yeah, it is. So it wouldn't surprise me if my dad came in some night. If someone wants to ask me if I'm gay and I think they need to know, I'll tell them.

Interview 2

But, you know, it's a sexual preference, and to me it never has been a lifestyle. I go to bars, I work and stuff like that, but I still don't live and breathe it. It's not me. I prefer the so-called "straight" environment more than I do a gay environment.

Along that line, who are your closest friends now: males or females?

Males. I don't really have any girl friends anymore. I'd say I have more close male friends now.

Do you find, as you get older, that your circle of friends enlarges? Or does it get smaller?

It fluctuates.

And you've learned to define the difference between acquaintance and friend.

Yes. I have five good friends who I consider best friends. They're the people I can count on. And because I bartend, I have a large circle of acquaintances. More than I care to, because then you're always going to have to be at your best. And sometimes I just don't want to bother.

I would think that would be the difficult part, but you have to because you're "on" all the time at work. And I think some people might assume that because you're nice to them in that working situation, you must be a close friend.

Yeah, that's right.

Do you anticipate a relationship in the future? Would this be a good thing?

I'd like it. I definitely would. But it just seems difficult to meet the right one. I mean, I'm not asking that much. Maybe I'm just too particular.

Well, there's nothing wrong with that. I mean, you're an attractive guy and you're intelligent, and I would imagine you're fighting them off. I'll bet they're lining up outside your door.

Well, they are and they're not. If you met my friends, you'd see that they're just nice people. That's what I look for in people. But there are so few men out there who are like that.

Yeah. It becomes a great detective story, doesn't it? Always investigating. What are their motivations?

Yes. And if you see someone and he's attractive, and you start talking to him, but then you discover that you just don't click. You meet guys and they're so "on" for you, but all of a sudden they just change and another side of their personality shows itself. You know?

Sex can be recreational and it can also be significant. Well, straight people say it's recreational or procreational. Are you able to be sexually active with somebody if you don't really care about him?

Yeah.

Growing Up Male In America

Just to get off?

Yeah. And I had never been like that before. But in the last two or three years, it's been nothing for me. In the past, if I was with someone, I liked them and then I would have sex with them, and then I'd like to be with them again. But I'm finding a lot of guys just want to do those one hits and go on to the next. I don't like to – but, you know, the way I look at it, why not? It doesn't screw up my mind like I thought it would. Some people tell me that I have too much sex, and it's going to make that right guy seem not anything special. I'm like, you're young for such a short time and you're going to be old for a hell of a long time, and if I'm single and there's someone out there and we know what this is all about, I'll do it.

Is sex the main reason for a relationship?

No, it's not the main reason.

Well, let's talk about relationships, if you don't mind sharing. The significant relationships you've had. Could you describe the one that lasted the longest?

Well, the longest one was two years when I was in Florida. I'm standing in this gay dance club, watching people dance, and all of a sudden I hear – this is so corny – he goes, "I like the way you shake your butt." I turn around and there he was. I thought he was from South America because he had brown hair and light blue eyes. He looked foreign, to a degree. Long story short, he turned out to be from Israel. He's Israeli. And he was 23 and very masculine. Nice guy. But he was very forward. He asked me how big I was and if I'm a top or a bottom, what I like to do in bed. And I'm, like, "Okay. The guy's a foreigner. Just let him have his talk." Anyway, we ended up going home that night together. We had a lot of fun. We clicked immediately.

We started seeing each other, and it was great. But then I realized there were certain cracks in his facade. And one of the cracks was an elderly man, and how they were really good friends. Right there I thought, "Sugar daddy." He admitted it to me later about this old guy because I dug and I dug. And the phone calls late at night. We were living together. At 3:00 in the morning it was this man, calling. And I realized that there's more to it than meets the eye. And that's what he admitted to me. They had met in Israel, and he admitted that he used to sleep with him for money. He said, "I used to be a male escort in Israel." It just took everything that I thought of this beautiful young man and twisted it upside down. I was floored by it.

How long into the relationship did all this information surface?

It was a year into our relationship.

Oh.

Yeah. Then I thought, "Oh, maybe I'm just being a conservative from Minnesota." I even went as far as to meet the old guy, and he was this craggy

Interview 2

58-year-old ... yuck. You know what I mean? There are young people in all ages and there are old people. He was 58 but he seemed like he was 88, and he was married with five kids. And he looked at me when my young friend walked to the bathroom and said, "You know what, you little son of a bitch? Don't you fuck with me. Because I swear to god I'll put you down." And I said, "Watch it, grandpa." You know? And I couldn't stand it. I had this mental picture of the two of them being sexual, and it really turned me off. It just really darkened things, and the relationship went downhill from there. Then I started going off with other people. I'd worked as a bartender, and I started going off with people I worked with. We'd go to the happy hour. We partied all night long. And yet this young man stayed with me for six months after all this stuff came out and basically waited for me to come around. Because I kept saying to him, "I just need some time to figure this out." But he stayed there. I'll pat him on the back for this one, without being sexual with me for that whole timeframe. Finally it got to a point where he wanted to go back to being a male escort, so I said, "Later." So now he's a male escort down there. But I thought he was the person I was going to spend the rest of my life with. I wanted to. He was perfect.

That image was there, but then reality revealed itself, huh?

Right. The image and the personality. I liked them both. But I have to admit it was fun. Now he's still a male prostitute down in Florida, lying about his age, saying he's 26 when he's not and telling people he's a college jock, when he's never played a sport in his life. It's hard for me to talk about it because I really did like him. I thought that was my last chance of a true relationship. Because I meet a lot of guys – you know – six months, nine months, one month, two weeks. You know what I mean? But this one, I really liked. I have five journals in my bedroom. There's a lot of him in those journals.

I'm happy to hear that you keep a journal.

Oh, yeah. I do a lot of writing. Anyway, I tried to be friends with this guy, even from here in Minnesota, but I couldn't. I just couldn't do it. It bothered me that he did that for a living, and I was hurt that he lied to me about it. I know we all have skeletons in our closets and stuff, but that was a little bit too much for me to take. I mean, he's sitting in a house with other male hookers and having men come in. He told me he did, like, 10 to 15 guys a day, and you know, I think that's just so weird. Because he told me, "It's only sex." And I said, "I don't care if it's only sex.... Go get a job somewhere. Have some respect for yourself." Not that I've been an angel with my sexual practices. But I'm not sitting in a room, doing things for money with men who I don't really even want to sleep with.

You mean he actually worked in a house of male prostitution?

A house. He used to sit in a room and guys would come in there, choose him and do him. And there were many wealthy regular customers who always

Growing Up Male In America

picked him when they came there. And I asked, "Are you an onion? Like every layer I'm pulling off, there's more crap to you." You know? He just said, "Oh, you stupid Americans."

Anyway, that bad experience with the hustler, is that what precipitated your leaving Florida?

Yes, sort of. but it was hard to meet genuine people there, and I really wanted to get home to Minnesota and get going with my schooling and just feel grounded, feel whole. Because I didn't feel whole down there. I was so freaked out by the trash down there that I came back.

Minnesota is not so bad, is it? Now, you take pride in being a good bartender. Do you have good friendships with some of your co-workers?

Well, I get along with one guy perfectly. He and I usually work the main bar together. We're a good team.

Would you call him a friend?

He's my best friend. Everybody says that we have a nice chemistry together.

Skipping back to when you were in high school, were you out for any activities? Did you do theatre? Chorus?

No. I wouldn't do theatre because it's too close to home. It might make people suspect I was gay.

Choir?

No.

Any sports?

Baseball.

Football?

No. I don't like football. I wanted to play tennis so bad. I wanted to be a cheerleader so bad. But those were things you stayed away from because they weren't the butch activities.

So the pressure was very strong, wasn't it?

Yeah. And I really wanted to be in theatre. The same thing.

Do you think there were any teachers when you were in high school who figured you out?

No.

Were there any teachers you figured out?

Yeah.

Did you ever have a teacher you trusted enough to feel that you could talk about your emerging gayness?

Interview 2

No. Because those who I suspected were gay were bitchy queens. One was the art teacher and one was the science teacher. They were obnoxious as hell.

Okay. Some gay men choose to be real queens and be out floating all over the place so that everybody knows they're gay. Such guys seem to think that to be gay means you have to be swishy and feminine. And that's what many straight people still think. That if you're a gay guy, you want to dress up and act like a woman.

Right.

Were you ever in the military?

No.

Did you ever think about it?

I thought about it, until I visited San Antonio and saw the kind of people who were in the military. I didn't want to be around it. It's a pretty rough crowd.

Have you ever been in love?

I've never been in love with anybody, I don't think. I don't think so. Well, maybe with the hustler guy in Florida. I don't know.

Maybe that's why that hurt so much. When you found out all the sordid details about his life.

Yeah. But other than him, no, I've never been in love. Women were just friends, girls that I had sex with. And that's why in my 20s, I put that involvement with women on the shelf for the most part, because I wanted to go out and be what I truly was – a gay man. I didn't want to be one of these guys who gets married and has kids, and then when he's 40 years old he is sneaking in the gay bars. You know? I did it the other way around.

You said something earlier about your career as a bartender, and that it's not the sort of thing you want to be doing when you're 50 years old. Where do you want to be?

Twenty years from now I'm going to be retired, so …

Oh. Good luck! [Laughter]

Yeah. Right. As to a career, I don't know. That's what I'm going through right now, figuring it out. I don't know what I want to do. There are several things, but it all involves going back to school, and I just don't know if I ever want to do that. You know? Part of me wants to go out and become a mason or something like that, and the other part wants to be a physician's assistant. The other part wants to go into computers.

Well, someday when you least expect it, the light bulb will flash on and your direction will be clearer.

Now for some random questions which need only quick responses. Over your whole life, what have you done that most embarrassed you?

Growing Up Male In America

Getting caught by the police on an Indian reservation with this guy I used to sleep around with in college in Arizona. I went to Arizona State for a short time. I was totally nude laying on the ground, with him on top of me. All of a sudden we heard the gravel, the car tires on the gravel, and there's this big spotlight shining at us. That was embarrassing!

What did they say?

They asked us to come out from under the tree, informed us that we were on Indian reservation land and asked us to leave. That was it. They were very nice about it. But it was still embarrassing, big time.

Oh. There weren't any arrests or anything?

No, yet we were both 18 and drunk.

Next question: You say you've encountered people for whom you had higher expectations and then they disappointed you, and then you sort of blamed yourself for being a poor judge of character.

Yup. My mom and dad always used to say, "Treat people how you want to be treated." I consider myself a nice person, and I do that. I'm not perfect and I am going to fail sometimes, but I expect my friends to understand when I do something, and I apologize and just let it go.

Right. You said earlier that the man you tend bar with is your best friend, even though he's really quite a bit younger, isn't he?

Yup. He's 22, soon to be 23. He's a young 22-year-old but he's a good kid, and I look out for him. And it bothers me in a way, because the tables are turning. I used to have someone say, "Don't do this. Don't do that." And here I am doing it with him.

Next question: Who are your heroes? Do you have any role models?

Martina Navratilova is. Greg Louganis. I understand why they didn't come out earlier. But in general, those two. They're not sexual pigs like George Michael, you know? I find a lot of gay people who are out there, they have to be so extreme it's repulsive to me. It's offensive. You know? So I don't find too many role models out there. You know what? I just like average, run-of-the-mill type people, but it's hard to find them.

Again, it's the bar crowd, again. Not that there are bad people there.

Look at the Pride Parade. You know? It's going to be a freak show. It's going to be skin and drag queens. Dykes on bikes and stuff like that. That's the saving grace about myself. Because I don't look like that. But as a gay man, I'm identified with that. But I wish people would see that there are people like myself who are out there. Unfortunately, not in droves. The only times I've gone out and you see people that you find attractive – and I learned to watch how fast their mouth moves or if they roll their eyes, or their hand movements, their

Interview 2

gestures, were too much. I won't waste my time if they do that, because often they come in all muscular and then they turn out to be swishy.

Well, look at the leather bars.

Oh, man! What is that all about? Big sissies dressed in leather.

Do you ever have a fear of failure performing when having sex?

No. Never.

Do you ever worry that the other person isn't enjoying sex? Do you worry that your partner isn't being satisfied?

No.

Do you feel okay about your body?

I wish my upper arms were bigger.

Do you go to the gym regularly?

Yeah. But still it's not going to happen with my upper arms.

Your weight's great for your height. You're six feet and 175. Do you consider yourself handsome?

Um ... I do. Yes and no. I don't know. I guess I'm good looking, for the most part. I mean, I guess I am. That's an odd question to be asked.

I know. It's a delicate question.

You do keep in touch with your dad, even though that divorce happened way back when you were six years old, right? Does he ever talk about the divorce or your mom?

Neither of them ever did. They never sat there and said, "He's a bad man" or "She's a bad wife." They're just not like that. My mom, my parents, if they didn't have anything good to say, they wouldn't say it. That's how they raised us to be. Unfortunately, I'm not like that. [Laughter] If I don't like something, I'm going to say it. You know? I've gotten better, though.

Well, you'll probably never have an ulcer from holding it in.

Exactly.

What's your frequency of masturbation?

Once every two weeks, at the most.

Is that because you are sexually involved with other people on a regular basis?

Yeah.

All right. Let's say you didn't have any involvement with another person.

I used to do it all the time when I was young, when I was in the teens and stuff. I had kind of an obsession with it. The older I get, the less I do it. But lately

Growing Up Male In America

I've just had such a bumper crop of experiences with guys, I don't need to.

Good for you!

I'm not too proud of that, but ... part of me says it's the whole numbers thing. Because I'm involved with all these different guys, and they know we're just having fun and that's it. But then if you meet someone who asks, "Well, how many guys have you been with?" My answer to that is, "None of your damn business." But I don't sleep with customers from the bar, though. That's one thing.

Why is that?

Just because I did it with this one guy when I first started, and it turned out to be a disaster.

Oh.

Well, I liked him a lot. And then he was coming in and he had his hand on this guy's knee at the bar, and that really hurt me. And I said to myself, "That's it. You got what you've got coming to you."

Of course, the question about AIDS has to come up when we're talking about gay sex. You certainly were aware of AIDS early on, weren't you?

I knew it was out there when I was 13, in 1983. When I first heard about it.

That certainly had to have affected your involvement in sexual activities.

Yeah. But when you first start out, you tend to believe that it's only the older ones that get the disease. That's where a lot of people messed up, because that's just not true.

What's your greatest fear? What scares you the most?

Growing older. Not being in a loving, committed relationship and going through my life by myself. And not having children.

Okay. If you find the right guy, you would adopt?

No.

No?

I want, you know, a biological child. I want to go to South America and find a woman who wants to move up to the United States in exchange for U.S. citizenship.

What depresses you the most? Do you ever go into periods of depression?

Not really.

Okay. But if you do get kind of blue or down, what do you do to get out of it?

I'll get in my car and drive up north. Or go to a movie or something like that.

Does it bother you to go to a movie alone or eat at a restaurant alone?

Interview 2

No.

Do you ever find yourself posing when you know somebody's looking?

I get a compliment when I know somebody's staring. That's what's so funny, because I bartend. Because people do look at you. I get very shy and embarrassed.

You do?

Oh, yeah. I'm actually somewhat of a shy person, in a way, and also I don't trust most men. I don't. For example, this one guy asked me for my telephone number on four different occasions. The fourth time I said, "You know what? I called you last time like you told me to, the next morning, to go for lunch. You didn't call me back, so don't ever come to me again and ask for my phone number." And you know what he said to me? "You're a bitch." I said, "You know what? I'm not a bitch. You're a loser." I said, "How old are you?" He goes, "Thirty." And I said, "You know what? You better get moving, because if you're going to behave like this you're going to be a really single, lonely man real soon for the rest of your life." I said, "You just stay away from me." You know? And my fellow bartender buddy was there, and he heard the whole thing and said, "I can't believe you said that." I said, "Hey, when I was 22, I would never have done that or said those things. But you know what? I'm almost 30, and I'm sick of it." And I'm not going to sit there and be Mr. Candy Ass about it and say, "Oh, that's okay." No, not me!

Well, we're almost at the end of this conversation. Is there anything you want to throw in that we haven't covered?

My 20s were a learning decade for me, to decide what I want and what I don't want. I learned a lot, and I take everything that happened to me and I see those things as lessons. It's not, like, "Oh, poor me." You know? It's all a lesson. I learned what I don't want. And I just hope that people who are younger will listen to older people or people like myself for guidance. When I was in my early 20s, I had someone who was my age tell me the same stuff, and I wish I would have listened to him. It's the nature of youth. But you know, there are people out there who do listen. I listened to my grandmothers talking about things. But when you're that young – like 21 – you think you've got the whole world ahead of you, and you do – but it still flies by. So I keep plugging along.

Well, I really appreciate your willingness to do this interview. It was nice of you to sit here and talk so openly with me.

I hope it was interesting, but I don't know. It's kind of interesting when you sit down – like we did here today – and talk about more intimate, personal things. I don't disclose this much about myself to many people, but now you know that side of me.

Thank you again, very, very much.

Growing Up Male In America

Postscript – December 2001

This man still works as a bartender, but he left the previous gay club and now tends bar at another gay club.

Interview 3

"He's probably my best friend. I know him really well and that bugs him."

This interview was conducted on May 23, 2001. This man is 21 years old, 6' 1" tall, weighs 235 pounds and has blond hair. He is an avid body builder and gets to the gym for weight training several times a week. A university student with a history major, he plans to teach on the secondary level.

Okay. Let's start. Let's start way back, as far back as you can remember as a kid. You were born where?

Michigan.

Michigan. And your dad was doing …?

A residency or an internship at a university hospital there.

Okay. And he's working where now?

At a clinic near the Twin Cities.

Okay. How old is your dad?

He is 48, I think.

And your mom, about the same?

I think she's 46.

Way back when you were just a kid – first of all, siblings. How many in the family?

I have an older brother who's 23, just about to turn 24. Because I am 21. And I have a younger sister who just turned 12.

Oh! A little space there, huh?

Yeah. A little space.

And she's spoiled?

Rotten. And at this juncture in the marital situation, she gets bribed, it seems to me. My dad kind of lavishes her to make up for time lost, so she won't be too forgiving towards my mother. But the inevitable split between my folks is com-

Growing Up Male In America

ing, I think.

And that's on the horizon?

Yeah. Very soon.

But they haven't started the divorce procedure?

No. They haven't started anything legally, yet. But being at home the last couple of days …

It's colder.

Yeah. A lot colder.

How does that make you feel?

Well, you know, both of them have been unhappy for a while. I remember in high school, I'd come home and dad wouldn't come home until 10:00 at night and leave at 7:00 in the morning. And for a guy who's not working at the plant two shifts to cover expenses – it doesn't seem like a doctor should have to work that long a shift because he stopped seeing patients at 5:00.

Sure. So where was he?

Well, it's not a question of where he was. I mean, we know he was at work because he just labors. Loves to labor. But you'd think that he would want to come home. And if he didn't want to come home, he could find stuff to do at the clinic for forever and ever. And he would come home with the look of a beaten man. When you've just given it everything and you just come home like that. He's had that look about him. And mom hasn't been happy for a while, either. So it has to change. It has to change. And, I mean, I don't think it's what either of them started out envisioning what married life would be like or how it would end.

I can't quite figure out what that must feel like. And I think for your younger sister, it's probably harder.

Yeah.

Because she's still a kid. At least you guys can …

Get a little perspective on it.

And go out. You've got your own life starting right now. With whom are you closer? Your dad or your mom?

It's … in different areas. I mean, emotionally, with my mom, of course. Intellectually, with my dad. There's just something there. I think it really started when I finished high school. When I went off to college. I realized I wasn't getting good enough grades to make dad proud, even when I was getting fairly good grades. Because this is what I wanted to do. I was starting my own life. I kind of realized what it was about. And if he could try to impress upon my sister that schooling is more about you than about anybody else, and taking what

Interview 3

you can get out of it. There was a lot of stress in high school about getting good grades and stuff. And so now I think me and my dad are on pretty good terms because I proved myself to him.

I see. That's good. And how about you and your older brother? How do you get along?

We're very close. Very close. He's probably my best friend. I know him really well, and that bugs him. He's a smart guy, too. By "too" I mean, I'm including him with my dad, when I say he's a smart guy, too.

How about you? Are you a smart guy? What's your grade point?

Three-point-two, right now. That's over a B average.

You're going to have a special high honors tassel on your graduation cap!

Unfortunately, because it's cheerleading season and in the winter, my GPA really suffers. In the spring, though, when cheerleading gets done and I've got a month and a half to just focus in on school work, it's better. I got a 3.86 last spring semester, and I got 3.8 this spring semester. So, I mean, spring semester is my time. But it's tough to juggle everything in the winter and the fall.

Yeah. I would imagine. What's the major?

History.

History.

And secondary education. I'm going to be a teacher.

All right! You're going to be a teacher.

Then I'm going to work on my master's and act all snooty. And maybe my PhD down the line. And then I will hardly be able to talk to half of the people I know. [Laughter]

Well, I totally understand that. [Laughter] You know, something you said a little bit earlier about cheerleading may need some clarification. Explain what you do at school. I don't mean academically, but in terms of cheerleading.

I'm a competition cheerleader, which basically entails tumbling and a little bit of motions, which is the only cheerleader thing that anybody who's not in the sport thinks it is. And mainly stunting, which is holding other people up in the air. Holding girls up in the air. By even one hand. Or stuff like that. That's what I do for nine months out of the year.

And for somebody with your excellent physique – when you say that you're a cheerleader – there must be an incredulous reaction from most people.

It's hysterical.

Because you are six–one, and you weigh 235 pounds. And you quite obviously work out, so you're in fantastic shape. Your muscles are bursting out in all directions.

Growing Up Male In America

And then you walk into a room and say, "I'm a cheerleader."

Um-hum. "What do you guys do?" When the occupation question flings around the room, I say, "I'm a competition cheerleader."

After I talked to you last week, when we scheduled this interview, I've asked friends, "What do you think of a male cheerleader?" And almost always they said, "They're the ones who tried to get on the team but couldn't." [Laughter] And, "Oh, they're some puny little guy." You know, like, "They had to go recruit him because he didn't fit in anywhere else." And it's certainly not the case, as you are living proof.

Do you think after you get into a teaching position, will you continue with cheerleading activity?

Oh, yeah. For sure.

Would you like to organize some kind of a group?

The office manager of the company I work for right now just had a conversation with me this weekend at staff training, and she said, "My goal for our company's growth is that by the time you finish college, you will have a job with us full time that pays better than you would get as a teacher." So that's their goal. And if I graduate and, you know, want to pursue teaching and that's what it's going to be, I'll do cheerleading workshops and clinics in the summer. Because I'll have my summers free for clinics and camps and competitions. I'm going to be at a cheerleading competition down in Georgia in the next couple of months. So, yeah. I'll keep it going. Until my body says "no." It is a lot of stress. The knees are pretty spent right now, and the shoulder's getting a little weak. I can't put it down. It's a lot of fun.

Well, that might surprise a lot of people, because they assume it's not a high-stress or greatly physical activity. Like being out playing the game.

People call me Pompom. Well, people that know me well. I'll come into work and have a cut on my face and be holding my wrist, and they'll say, "Drop your pompom out in the parking lot, there?" [Laughs] But, yeah, I've got bone chips in this eye and stitches in this eye, and my face gets smacked by elbows and arms. So much that my nose gets even wider than it is now, which is hard to believe. [Laughs] But it gets huge by the end of competition season. I fractured my third vertebra and my lumbar spine doing this. My knees ... you can probably see how crooked they are.

Uh-huh. When you move your knees, it sounds like gravel in there.

Yeah. Yeah.

Is that going to mean orthopedic surgery, eventually?

It's going to mean something. And I don't go to a real doctor. I just go over to the trainers physical education department, and they tell me not to lift weights so much. I do leg lifts, like a dead lift. And squats and the extensions and what-

Interview 3

not. They say on my right kneecap, there's no more cartilage on the back side of it, so it slides all funny. I don't know what that means.

Well. It surprises a lot of people that there are many rigorous things involved in what you do.

Oh, yeah. Well, I sweat through three pairs of clothes at practice.

That's a disgusting thought!

Yeah. Yeah. Yeah. [Laughter] Well, I'll just leave you with that one.

Okay.

The girls hate it, because I have to catch them and then I hold them and then they're going, "Let me go! Let me go! Let me go!"

Slimy!

Yeah.

Now, your dad's a doctor. Did that ever enter your mind – to be a doctor? Or did your older brother ever consider medicine as a profession?

Well, my older brother … I know that my dad being a doctor had a big influence on him. My brother got a degree from Madison in genetics, and so I know that the conversations they had in the early 1980s, when my dad was coming home and talking about genetics, got under my brother's skin. And he was trying to read microbiology college textbooks when he was in high school. I know that had a big effect. I kind of saw, though, that he didn't want that for his life. I mean, it wasn't, like, "I don't want that." But he didn't want those hours. Dad once described the environment at the clinic, and I remember it always seemed like you were in this big monolith downtown. And you were kind of being watched by Big Brother. It would feel to me like … if I was going to be a doctor, I'd have … I'd be living under a microscope, too. I'd have everybody breathing down my neck. And, I don't know … I wouldn't feel significant enough, and I know you'd get a chance to help people and stuff. But if they don't like my opinion, they'd go to somebody else for a second opinion.

I think you'll feel the pressure when you go into teaching, though, too. But it's different. You walk into that classroom and shut the door, and it's your domain. And, yeah, you'll be evaluated and people will question why you did what you did. But it's really pretty much your own thing there.

Um-hum. Well, when you're a doctor, you've got somebody's life right there in the palm of your hands.

But you can bury your mistakes! [Laughter]

Yeah.

What does your mother do?

She works at … well, back in the days … she was a secret shopper. She would

Growing Up Male In America

actually go around and have to order some food at a fast-food restaurant and then rate them on how they did. Stuff like that. She kept that going for a little while. But that's not really a real job. Now she works at a department store selling crystal. Waterford crystal and china plates and stuff like that. And she does the bridal registry thing. So she's always on the phone to me. "Guess who's getting married" and blah-blah-blah-blah-blah. And, you know. I guess I don't want to hear it and I want to be happy for all these kids, but it's kind of the double-edged sword. Like, you know, "What are you doing about that? When will *you* get married?" And I don't know. I don't ever think I've ever felt real pressure, but it's, kind of, like ... why would she tell me this stuff so much? Like about people I don't even know. Like, "Oh, do you remember Bill Blah-Blah-Blah? He was in your class. He's getting married." And I've never even heard of the guy before. Maybe once, might have seen him in the hall or something. "Oh, yeah. He's getting married. Blah-blah-blah."

It sounds like, "And will you marry?"

Yeah.

Is your older brother married?

No.

Is he close to getting married?

Yeah. Some days I think really close, and some days not so much. But he's talked about it with me. And I say, "Yeah," because I think she's a great girl, and they're really happy together. And he's dumb for her. Dumber than I've ever seen him for a girl before. I don't know if he's ready – but, yeah, I think he's probably going to get married to her.

Of the two of you – even though he's chronologically older – which of you two, would you say, is the more mature? Settled? Sensible?

I think I'm more at peace with who I am. And I think my brother is more at peace with where he wants to be and how he wants to position himself. He wants to get this apprenticeship so he can be lined up for that internship, so he can be in line for that junior associateship or whatever. So he can be on the "in track" to get into the best law firm so that, you know, he can get into a big law firm's properties and patent law department. He really knows where he wants to go. I'm not sure where I'm going to end up, but right now, I think I'm having a lot more fun than he is. And I think I'm a lot more at ease than he is. I think – as far as maturity – it's probably me. Probably me. He gets into a lot of fights. I don't get in fights. I don't really see the logic in it. But he gets into a lot more fights. And for that reason alone, pretty much, I could say that I was more mature than my brother. Because, man, you know ... at the bar, he'll start taking off his rings. And I'm just going, "Man, why are we doing this again?"

Well, is he built like you? Is he a big guy, too?

Interview 3

Yeah, yeah. He's built like me. I'm a little bit bigger in the frame, but he's been lifting a lot longer.

Don't you find that people like to challenge muscular people like you? In the bar situation?

Sometimes. But I'd much rather be challenged to a smart-ass competition. Like a "battle of the wits" rather than, "Let's go out in the street and bloody each other." If I'm going to spend all that money at a bar, I might as well meet the people while my inhibitions are down. [Laughs] And I can get to know somebody rather than looking for fights. But that's just me. So, yeah. I'd say I was more mature than my brother.

Let's go back, now, to elementary school. What's the first memory you have in your life – and how old were you?

[Pause] Man! I think my first memory was "Pirates of the Caribbean" at Disney World. Just because I'd never seen anything like that, with all these people running around. I can't even remember how old I was. That seems to be one of the first things I can remember. It was scary, and these pirates were chasing these girls around the town, and there were flames and cannon fire, and they were all happy and drunk. You know. It was weird. But I don't remember any other part of Disney World.

So it was a mixture of fear and awe.

Yeah. Oh, yeah.

Like, "I never saw anything like this back home!"

I mean, a boat! I don't think I'd ever been in a boat before. It was exciting.

Well, now. You started school. Did you attend a private school?

Yeah. It was a Lutheran school. I went to a Lutheran school for nine or 10 years. Prekindergarten through eighth grade. And then I was an Eagle Scout in the Boy Scouts at another Lutheran church, but it was a different synod. It was, like, the two factions of the Lutheran Church. And then I attended the Methodist church with my family. And in all the studying that I've done – because we had religion class every day in the school for 10 years – I can't see a lick's bit of difference among any of those religions.

Yeah. If you'd be Jewish, maybe you might have seen more of a difference.

Yeah. Probably.

And more now, I think, even the Catholic mass used to be quite different from the Protestants, but you go to one or the other now and it's all kind of melding together. It's probably a good thing.

Did you ever wish you had gone to a public school?

All the time. All the time. All the time. My brother and I would always try to

Growing Up Male In America

figure out how much our parents were paying for private school, and we're, like, "God, if they weren't sending us to that dumb school, we could have so many more toys and so much more vacations, and it'd be so much fun!" Also, there were no sports teams at the private school. Well, there was soccer. Soccer was big, because it only required buying a ball. But there was no football, and there was no hockey. Nothing like that. I wish we could have played sports. I wished ... just being in a bigger swamp of kids.

Do you think you received a good education at the private school?

Better than public, for sure.

Really?

Yeah. For sure.

Well, probably the teachers didn't have to spend as much time on discipline as teachers do in the public schools.

Probably not. But actually, I'm quite sure not. Because we ... I got a two-hour detention for chewing gum one time. Yeah. So even though we thought we were reckless, we were a pretty tight-lipped bunch.

Well, that must have been kind of a shock when you got thrust into public high school, then.

Yeah. And we lived in a nicer, big house outside of town in a neighborhood where there weren't that many other kids. That's why my brother and I got so close. We only had each other. But then when I went to the public high school, I knew only one kid, because the other private-school kids went to the other high school in town. There were about 2,500 kids in that public school.

Now, when was this? Ninth grade?

Yeah. The ninth grade.

Okay. Well, you must have felt pretty isolated.

Yeah. Well, the thing about it was, my brother was a senior when I was a freshman. And because he was young for his grade and I was a little bit old for my grade, we'd always hang out together and talk about football. By then, he'd played football for many years. And I'd ask, "Do you think I could play football one day?" And he'd say, "Yeah, I think you could probably play wide receiver or something." And that excited me, because before my growth spurt I was about as big as that little stereo speaker stand. I was tiny. I was absolutely tiny. I was on the cross-country team. I was a runner. I played soccer. But then as I started getting closer to high school, I started hitting my growth spurt. And this was kind of fun, because I'm coming out of nowhere. And my brother hauls me in. He's a pretty well known football player at that point, and he hauls me in there to the ninth-grade coach. And he says, "Yeah. This is my brother." And the coach looks up from whatever he's doing. And I'll remember this for-

Interview 3

ever. He looks up from whatever he was doing and he says, "Perfect." And I was, like, "Well, I'm in! I'm in!" And they put me in pads. I had never worn full football gear before. And they put me in pads, and I was running out on the field for the first time in front of all these, you know, guys that were sitting there. "Who's the new kid? Who's the new kid?" And I was running out there. And I didn't know how goddamn top-heavy I was. I was trying to run out there really fast so I could kind of impress them. And then I started, you know, hunching over. And I was, like, "God, I'd better slow down here, or I'm going to fall over on my face." Just because I had never worn football pads before. But from that point on, I made friends really easily with all the guys on the football team.

So ninth grade starts. The first day of classes, I'm sitting in the biology honors room. There was a scrimmage that day, so all of us team members were wearing our jerseys. And I was, you know, just the prototypical football player. So I'm sitting in there, and there are no other football players in this class. And then all the other kids start filtering in. And this one kid sits down and says to me, "Man, what are you doing in this honors class? Physical science is down the hall." And I'm, like, "Yeah, I know. But I'm in biology honors." And he's, like, "Okay, man. Are you sure?" [Laughs]

Football? Honors? A contradiction in terms!

Yeah, yeah. Yeah. That whole thing. And then I ended up helping that kid, tutoring him in that class. And I remember I got one question wrong on the final and got the highest grade in the class. And who's laughing now?, I thought. Who's laughing now?

Again, you're breaking stereotypes all through your life, aren't you? The dumb jock. Not. I'm a cheerleader.

Yeah.

All right. Where you lived as a child, you were somewhat isolated from lots of other kids, right? So it turns out that your brother and you were more friends to one another.

Yeah. Well, sort of. Yeah. I mean ... we had some friends. We played T-ball and stuff, but you couldn't come home from school, throw your bag down and then say, "I'm going to go out and play" and go play with the neighborhood gang of hooligans or whatever. I mean, I was always in baseball. We were all in baseball and stuff in the summertime. And I knew a couple of kids through that. But pretty much it was just my brother and me.

Okay. Well, religious school for the elementary years. Did you ever have a favorite teacher? I'm always curious as to why somebody like you wants to be a teacher.

Yes. I did have favorite teachers.

You must have had a few along the way who made you think, "Hey, this is not such

Growing Up Male In America

a bad life." Can you remember one of your favorites, way back in elementary?

Yeah. Fifth grade. And he had a laugh that you could hear anywhere in the building. It was a ridiculous laugh. It was like no other laugh I've ever heard. And that just sticks out in my mind. Plus he had all these model trains. He was a big model-train enthusiast. So he would invite six or seven of the kids from our class over to his house to play with his model trains and help him build new things for his train set. I remember his history class. It was the first time I was ever exposed to historical writing and writing about the history of the picture, like, "What's going on in there?" And I'd write. He'd correct it, and I'd always argue with him. Argue everything with him. And he would always end up saying, "Okay. I can see how your mind's working. I see that your mind's working, and for that we'll count it." I had so much fun in his class, and he challenged. That was my first favorite teacher.

And that was fifth grade?

It was fifth grade.

And you've had a few more along the line?

Oh, yeah. Quite a few wonderful, stimulating teachers.

So you've had a number of good teachers to emulate. And you're going to teach history? I think a lot of students are turned off to history, don't you?

Oh, definitely.

It's the history of wars and politics, but there's more to it.

Oh, a lot.

And I hope when you teach, you'll bring in art and music and culture.

The human experience.

Yeah! It's not just a bunch of wars and political takeovers.

All right. You're getting up to about ninth grade, and now there's that big "P" that jumps in called "puberty." Did you start that earlier than most or later than most or about the same time as other boys? I think it's coming earlier these days.

Yeah. Nutritionally. Nutrition seems to make a difference.

Is that about age 14, ninth or 10th grade?

Yeah. Yeah. I'd say it was about normal. From the locker room, from what I could tell.

You'd look around.

Yeah. Yeah.

Some hadn't started, and others that looked like they'd been "men" for three years already.

Interview 3

Yeah. One had been shaving in sixth grade. But, yeah. I think I was pretty normal – a pretty run-of-the-mill type of a deal.

Okay. You had an advantage of having an older brother, too, didn't you?

Um-hum. Well, I mean, we never talked about anything like that. No.

Really? Now, is that a male thing, again? Or don't little girls talk about their periods with each other, either?

I don't know. But my brother and I – nothing. I mean, we were really the brothers' brothers. I mean, we were out to kill each other, and we knew it. He tried to cut off my thumb with a utility knife. He pushed me off a railing at Valley Fair and split open my chin pretty bad. And I stabbed him with a Swiss Army knife. And, yeah. And we were always fighting and always wrestling. Guys, guys, guys, guys, guys. And – I've thought about this a lot – never once did we talk about, "God, Mom and Dad don't seem really happy" or anything like that. Never. Never.

One thing I'm always interested in is about sexual development, which men just tend not to talk about too much. When did you have your first sexual experience with someone other than yourself?

Someone other than myself.

I mean, we'll talk about masturbation another time. [Laughter]

It was probably in, I'd say, the summer between ninth and 10th grade.

Okay. What happened?

Well, it was the summer between ninth and 10th grade. And we didn't have cars. Well, this one kid had a car. And he brought along this girl, and we were hanging out. I hadn't really met her before. He brought her over to my house, and we sat there and we talked and stuff. You know. And then he was, like, "Oh, man. I've got to go." And so there we were, just her and me. I asked, "Well, do you want to watch a movie or something?" So we ended up watching a movie.

So your buddy had to go, but she stayed.

Yeah. Yeah. Yeah. And I said, "Well, yeah. My mom will be back soon … my mom will be back and she can give you a ride." Aw, god! That phrase! But, yeah. "My mom will be back, and we can give you a ride." And then we went downstairs. That was another part of me and my brother hanging out. We could completely go all the way downstairs in the basement of our house. And there was a whole, like … there was a TV and stereo and a little mini-fridge. And there was a bathroom down there. And we didn't have to come up for anybody or anything. We could just stay down there and hang out if people upstairs were pissing us off. So we went down there, and there's a big waterbed. And she and I ended up on the waterbed. And she basically ended up … we pretty

Growing Up Male In America

much had sex with our clothes on. You know. Dry hump. So, yeah. That was the first time that that had ever happened to me.

Now, was she your age?

Yeah. She was in my same grade.

How about you physically, at that time. Had you begun to lift weights?

Yeah. Yeah.

So you were in pretty good shape.

Yeah. Yeah.

Okay. And how did you feel after? I mean, you achieved orgasm, I assume.

Yeah. Yeah. I made a mess of myself. And boy, did I feel dumb. But I just said to her, "Excuse me while I go to the bathroom." And I went out of the room and closed the door. And of course I wanted to close the door. And the bathroom was right there, but the laundry room was also right over there. And I ran over to the laundry room and I was, like, "Oh, what have I done?" Threw clothes right into the washer and came back with another pair of jeans on. I don't know if she noticed that I was wearing a new pair of jeans or whatever.

How savvy was she? I mean, did she know what had happened to you?

Yeah, she was in the know about sex.

She knew that boys do that? That they come?

Oh, yeah. She wasn't dirty or "loose" or anything, but just the fact that she had been in public school, I think, is a whole different kind of experience. More worldly.

Yeah.

Because when I went to the public school in ninth grade, I saw guys grabbing girls' breasts down the hall. I was, like, "What the … what is that?" Well, I had no idea that something was going on. But she knew. And she was, you know, completely savvy. She didn't make me feel dumb about it, and she didn't laugh or anything.

Do people in the ninth and 10th grade start dating, or is it usually group dating?

Well, people in ninth and 10th grade do start dating.

And you did, too? Or did you put that off? Or was it parental pressure not to date? Or what?

Well, I'll tell you. [Pause] I was never one for conventional dating. I always thought that it was too institutionalized, almost. Are you going out with him? Is he your boyfriend? Are you and he dating exclusively? Are you two going steady? And there are so many different levels in there. I mean, to label them almost seems, you know, useless. But I started seeing people and hanging out

Interview 3

with them on a more-than-friends basis around 10th grade. I got my car. That helped, a lot. But a lot of group dating, too. And especially in the seventh and eighth grade, leading up to ninth grade. In the private school, you know, this was what you did. You called people up. Like there were three boys, and you said, "We're going to go to a movie." And you'd approach the three girls as a unit. You know. It wasn't anybody asking just one other person. And if you liked a girl – if you were trying to kind of match yourself up with one of the few girls over there, you would never call *that* one and say, "We're going to movie. Do you want to come with?" You'd always call one of her friends and say, "Do you and Betsy want to come to a movie with us?" Because you weren't interested in her, but Betsy was the one you were interested in. But you didn't want to call Betsy directly. This was how it was done in my eight-grade years. Eighth, ninth.

As you look back on it, it's kind of cute. But the idea of "So-and-so's going with So-and-so" was almost an entrapment. Or you're just bright enough to see how silly those kind of connections can be. Did you date one girl or maybe more for a longer period of time?

Yeah. There was one girl. It was always just this one girl. But when I had time … when I perceived to have time for relationships, it really was this one girl. And looking back on it, I apologized to her a while back, like, a year and a half ago, for being such a moron.

How so?

Well, you know … she was a really, really great girl. She was nice, and she was sweet. And she was gentle, and she was kind. She was intelligent. And I don't know what I was thinking. I would, you know … just kind of string her along. Not committing to being as emotionally invested as I think I should have been. And I felt guilty about that later on. But, yeah. It was with that girl.

How long did that last?

Probably about the better part of two years.

Oh. So that takes you up to your junior year in high school.

This girl was pretty much the summer between my sophomore and junior year, up until the summer before I went away to college. But it was never …

Not exclusive?

Not exclusive.

Okay. So you had your recreational sex?

Yeah. But I didn't, really. I mean, I didn't mess around … well, maybe I did. But … I don't know. It was always her. She meant a lot more to me than I knew at that time. And looking back on it, I can really see that. How she was steady in my life. She had a room in the back of her house, and I could always

Growing Up Male In America

tell when the lights were on. I could always go knock on her window. You know? I could always sneak in the back porch door or whatever. Anyway. I did that a lot. And I remember feeling really good, knowing that she was there. That she would probably always open the door for me.

An anchor.

Yeah.

What you said just now is interesting to me. "I didn't realize, then, how much she meant to me." But in retrospect you do. One of my favorites quotes – although it's paraphrased – is from the German philosopher Nitsche: "Life is lived forward but understood backward." Isn't that nice?

Yeah.

We can sit and reflect ... on our deathbeds we can reflect, "Well, that was a pretty significant thing. But I didn't know it at the time." Some artist said that, once. He said, "Living through the Depression, I didn't realize I was living through an earth-shattering and great event in history until many years later, when I read about it."

Okay. Moving on. Let's talk about masturbation here, a little bit. I'd like to get into how much you shared those experiences with anybody, if anybody – or if that was totally a private thing. First, do you remember about how old you were the first time you did it?

Well, masturbation isn't just touching myself. To become aroused. I can't even remember. I can't even remember the first time for that – arousal.

And the first time you actually came?

Um ... I remember that, because I thought I broke something. [Laughter] I was not aware that things like that happened, as you said. But ... god. It might have been in [pause] ... I want to say the summer between seventh and eighth grade. Maybe before that, though. I don't even know. I just remember how my room upstairs looked. The way the furniture was arranged and where I was in the room. And "Oh, my god. What is going on? What is that?" Yeah. Yeah.

Did you use anything, like an adult magazine for visual stimulation?

Well, I think I used a lingerie ad or something. Yeah. I don't know. A women's catalog.

And then, all of a sudden, the great gusher. And you said, "I injured myself."

[Laughter] Yeah. Yeah. You know?

And then, the first time – the pleasure is so incredible.

Yeah. Definitely. The eyes cross and then ... when can I do this again? Without anybody ever knowing?

And you probably felt – like most people do – that you were kind of alone in this. And you were convinced that certainly your friends weren't doing this.

Interview 3

Yeah.

Now, did you ever talk with your friends about it?

No.

Did you ever do a group jerkoff?

Never. At the private school ... man, that would have been forbidden. I can't even imagine it.

Talking about it.

No. Not talking about it. Not even the act. Talking about it. Thinking about it. Like even if your best friend said [whispers], "You know, what if we all got together in the locker room? Had a circle jerk?" I mean, you'd probably get suspended for even whispering about such a thing.

And your friends ...

Well, yeah. They would definitely not be your friends anymore. Or they would treat you a lot, lot different.

Well, the first few times you masturbated, you were still in a parochial-school situation. Did you feel shame or guilt?

Oh, yeah.

Yeah?

Yeah. Yeah. Yeah.

And did you try not to do it again?

Well, not that. But just absolute secrecy – hide it. I was completely obsessed with secrecy about it. I mean, if the parents left the house or something, I'd rig up things in front of the door so that if they came home unexpectedly, I'd hear them come in. And I'd usually only do it down in the basement, in the corner. And I was just paranoid as all heck.

And yet it's the fight between pleasure and guilt.

What's the most number of times you masturbated in one day? Not that you keep a journal of this, probably. But did you ever have a contest with yourself to see how many times you could do it in one day?

I never had a contest. I never set about it as a goal. But [pause] ... the most I can ever remember doing it was twice in one day.

On average, how many times a week do you tend to do it now?

It depends on the week. [Laughs] Some of the time, I come home and fall asleep almost before I hit the bed. But on average, probably three.

Three times a week?

Three or four.

Growing Up Male In America

You're 21 years old?

Yeah.

Back when you started to develop – you know, when puberty kicked in – you certainly were sizing up other guys, too, weren't you? And you could see some hadn't developed yet and others had. And there you were. Do you ever remember sneaking a peek at other guys' cocks and doing a little comparison?

Yeah.

Yeah. And again, that's another thing you don't talk about with your friends, do you?

No! No, no, no. But, well … actually, I do remember talking to my brother about … not that … not like the way that we're discussing it … but there were two brothers we knew who were in the same grades as my older brother and me. And these guys hit puberty in, like, the third grade, maybe. [Laughter] You know? That's what it seemed like. And this guy was six-four in eighth grade. It was just crazy. And I don't even remember how it came up. Must have been a really jaded conversation between my brother and me or something, but [pause] I said something about, "Wow! He's just got a *huge* unit." And my brother said, "Yeah. And his older brother does, too!" Man! I mean, they were just hung like donkeys in that family.

Both of them.

Yeah. But I never really remember the whole penis envy/inferiority feeling around that guy, for sure.

Would you say you are average, above average or below average in penis length?

I'd say average. From the females I've talked to, maybe … not a little more than average. Just average.

Just average. Do you know … how do you define average?

I don't know. About …

They say between four and six inches, erect. Six, maybe up to seven. I think we're jaded by porn.

Yeah. For sure.

We see those films, and we think that every guy is super endowed.

Yeah. "How can I satisfy a woman unless I'm packing nine inches?"

Yeah. And that's all kind of ridiculous, isn't it? Is your brother about the same length as you? Or is he a donkey? [Laughs]

No. No. Uh … I mean … after we'd lift or whatever and were showering I'd look at him and say, "Jesus! Look at the size of you!" His cock was pretty big. And he'd say, "Oh, no. Jesus, man – you're going to steal my girlfriend away

Interview 3

from me one of these days."

He said that to you?

Yeah. Yeah. And from what comparisons I've made I can't see that at all, because he's bigger.

Okay. You're circumcised, aren't you?

Yes.

I thought with a doctor for a father, you probably would be.

Could I pick your brain about secret fantasies?

Yup.

How do you define a fetish?

I would define a fetish as ... if you're talking to somebody or you're watching TV and all of a sudden you don't know what the ad's for or you don't know what they're selling and you don't know what the show's about – you can't even hear their voice – and you just ... and all you can think about is one thing. Whether it's boobs or ass. Or with me, it's muscles called sterno-cliedo-mastoids. Or it could be feet. Or anything like that.

Define that term, sterno-cliedo-mastoids.

A sterno-cliedo-mastoid is the muscle on a woman's neck.

Really.

Yeah. Attached to the sternum, the clavicle and ... your neck is referred to as your mastoids. You know. Straight up and down. And that muscle sits right straight up and down. Right by your ear.

Oh.

Yeah.

And there's one on either side?

Yeah. And they both end up behind your ears. They actually facilitate turning your head.

So you find that arousing?

Yeah! Whew!

It's interesting. I bet you don't talk about that with the women you date.

Oh, yeah. I do.

Oh. You do?

In fact, on dates, for sure. Yeah. I like it. I like it. And then they're all really interested in knowing all about the sterno-cliedo-mastoid. Yeah.

That's also kind of an erogenous zone for a lot of people, the neck and especially

Growing Up Male In America

the ear. And you start doing a little nibbling around the ear, and then you could have your way with her.

Yeah. Well, not so much. I mean, it's an erogenous zone, for sure. But almost ... I mean, to nuzzle it, but just to look at it. It's just so graceful and so nice. And the line of it is just ... I like it a lot.

I see. If we're going to rank that muscle – we'll put that at number one – where do breasts come in? How about the butt? Thinness?

Priorities?

Yeah. People say, "Well, that's a tit guy." The first thing he sees is that.

Uh-huh. Man. Well, I mean ... huge tits, I just think of the location. Large breasts will knock you off your feet, whether that's your thing or not. If a girl walks in with a really, really tight shirt that's just Saran Wrapped over her chest, I feel like yelling, "Put those things away before you knock an eye out or something." I take care of my body a lot. I'm in the gym, and I'm very aware of anatomical parts and the names of them and their functions. I'd say I'm more interested in just shapely and firm bodies that are in proportion. Athletic people. People, women in the gym who are in there and taking care of their bodies. Even if they're sweating and their hair's messed up and stuff, that's ... I mean, it's sexy just that they're there. That they care. That they want to be in shape. That's really a turn on.

In terms of your routine for the gym and all that, do you ever find sometimes that you're just too tired to work out some days?

Well, what will drive me is the cheerleading. I can feel the difference in my stunting. And I can feel how much better I've gotten from the girls ... the girls I work with in the summer, they don't see me all during the year. Just this weekend, when I was stunting with a bunch of them I stunted with last year, they said, "Oh, god, you've gotten so much better." And I'd feel so much tighter, and everything feels so much more solid. Well, I can tell that I'm getting strong with that, and less back pain. Because I've been working on getting a strong midsection. So, I mean, there are advantages, sportwise, when I think about it. We compete nationally, at Daytona Beach nationals, every year.

Yeah. And it's competition with yourself.

Yeah. Yeah. Yeah. Plus, it's kind of just a high about having power over what you look like. I mean, you have the power to reshape and redefine your body.

Now, when you're cheerleading, what are you wearing?

It's slacks for a uniform.

And what kind of a shirt?

It's just a baggy shirt. It's not tucked in. It's just out, and it's got a little bit of trim on it.

Interview 3

So I mean, it does show the physique.

Well, I mean, the sleeves ride up a little bit on you. And especially when you, you know, hold your arms above your head and stuff like that.

Do you ever get any – oh, I don't know if the word pleasure is really the word – but gratification of sorts, or it gives you a feeling of well being, when men look at you and you can ... they may not say it. They may even say it. "Hey, you're in great shape." Does that give you a certain degree of self satisfaction?

It gives me a little degree of that. But not only that. When somebody says that to me, I think it says a lot about them, too. Because I know how hard it is for guys, especially, to say that to another guy. It kind of makes me feel like they're respecting the time I've put into it. It's as if they're saying, "I respect what you're doing and I can see the value in that for you. Congratulations on the effort."

Have you ever had a gay sexual experience? A homosexual experience? Even if it was just ... well, mutual masturbation? Have you ever had anybody proposition you?

This last summer, I taught at a cheerleading camp out in Provincetown, Massachusetts.

Oh.

Yeah. I went out there. And one day I was wearing a shirt that said "Cheerleader" on it. That was my staff shirt – what you're supposed to wear while you're teaching. I was out on my lunch break, and I ran into a woman friend I'd traveled with many times before. We were good friends. She and I went to college together up here, and we were both teaching at this cheerleader conference. Anyway, she said, "I'm going to go shopping" or whatever. And I said, "Well, I'm going to stay here and eat because I'm really hungry." So I just stayed in this little bar-type of pizza joint type of a deal. And, yeah, a guy came up to me and said, "What do you do?" And I said, "Well, I'm just in town teaching this cheerleading camp." And he said, "Oh. You're a cheerleader. That's cool." And it didn't even really occur to me that he might be gay, because I was just eating my food. And then he asked, "So, what are you doing tonight?" And I said, "I'm probably going to hang out with my partner."

Partner?

Yeah. And he suddenly wasn't so friendly, and he sort of backed away and said, "Oh!" And then I said, "Yeah." Then my friend walked into the bar, and I called out her name. And then this guy just walked away. And I thought, "Hey! What just went on here?" Life is lived forward and understood backwards. Yeah.

There were a couple of loaded words there. "Partner". By that he might have thought you had a gay male partner, and then he knew it was "hands-off" because

Growing Up Male In America

you're with a guy. And all of a sudden she walks in, and "partner" takes on the more usual meaning of someone you work with.

Uh-huh. And she and I weren't sexually involved at all. We were just that – partners. In the teaching.

Right. But the guy was probably confused. You have to give him credit for respecting whatever relationship you had there. Was he older? Younger?

I would say he was older. He was older than I was. Probably in his upper 20s.

Okay. Well, Provincetown, as you probably learned, is kind of a gay mecca. [Laughs]

Yeah. Definitely. I definitely learned that. When my woman friend and I first rolled into town, there were all these guys riding bikes. And she said to me, "Look at all these guys riding bikes in their cute little outfits!"

Uh-huh. Well. But that was about the extent of any gay experience you ever had?

Yeah. That, for sure, was the extent of any experience. I went to a gay bar once, and I walked through the men's toilet into another bar in the back. One of the bathrooms has two exits, or two entrances and exits. And I got disoriented or something. I wasn't drinking or anything, but I walked into another room. This was the hard-core homosexual bar. I just opened the door, and I looked up at the video monitors and saw some heavy-duty man-man sex in those videos.

Did you go to the bar alone?

No. I went with three other guys.

And you knew it was primarily a gay club?

Yeah. Yeah. Yeah.

Okay. Moving on. You've never been in the military?

Nope.

Ever thought of that? Help pay the bills for college?

Yeah. Exactly. Senior year in high school, I thought about that for a while. And walked into the Reserves office downtown. And there was this guy with a southern accent. He stood up from his desk and he said, "Well, hell! You look like a poster boy for the U.S. military. Sit on down there, boy!" And I was, like, "Well …," you know. "Lay back and we'll talk about the poster deal later." But he was pretty pumped about me joining. Then I talked to my dad and he said, "If you make a decision based on money, it's probably going to be the wrong decision." And I will remember that for a while. And then I thought, maybe not. But then they called me.

Oh, of course.

Seventeen hundred times.

Interview 3

I'll bet they did! Well, being in the Reserves is a way to pay the college bills, I suppose. But I've talked with others who were in the Guards, and their big fear is, what if there's a big war?

Today there are so many little rogue nations that the Guards could be called in for anything.

You've said that your brother is probably your best friend. But do you have a close relationship or a friendship with another man?

Yeah.

Non-brother.

Probably two or three. Because the guys on the cheer team, you know ... while the girls are out talking about everything, you don't want to be in the tampon discussion group. So, you know, you bond with these guys. And it really takes a different kind of ... it takes a kind of special breed to pick up the cross of being a male cheerleader, so to speak. And so the guys in there with you are kind of the same stock. So I get along with those guys really, really well. And there are two guys. And one of them is my lifting partner, too, and has been for the past year and a half.

Oh, he's your partner? Just a little joke there!

Yeah. [Laughs] My lifting partner! He's my lifting partner!

There's an adjective in there.

And he chose to go to Puerto Rico for this last semester or two to study abroad. And, yeah, I've really come to understand how much he and I were friends. And what a tremendous advantage it is to go lift with him and have the motivation and have somebody yelling at me during workouts and stuff like that.

And you missed his companionship, too.

Oh, yeah. It was kind of a triangle involving my lifting partner, B—, and another guy. And, you know, me and the other guy lift this season. We were just, kind of, lost. "Man, I wish B— were here." It would be, like, "Yeah. Yeah." You know? "If B— were here, he would probably say something and we'd imagine what B— might say, and then we'd all laugh about it. We realized how much this hurts and how much we missed him.

Now, do you share that with R—? Do you tell him how much he means to you?

Yeah. Well, we e-mail. And at the beginning of the year – you know, when he first left – it was mainly small talk. But then towards the middle of the year, it was, like – in the most non-prison movie kind of a way, you know – "Man, I wish you would have been at practice last night, because it was pretty tough." And, "Man, you know, I miss you." And he writes back, "Yeah. I really miss you, too." And the day he got back up here – his parents picked him up at the airport, and then the next day, he drove up to see us, and we all came over to

Growing Up Male In America

the house and sat around and had a few High Lifes and kicked back.

Do you hug?

Oh, all the time. All the time.

Great. So you're not afraid of the physical touching.

No. No.

You know what I mean. A lot of guys are a little distant when it comes to touching other guys.

Yeah. Well, there's like … there's probably three guys that I call when I go back to my home town. And I got to meet up with one of them for no reason. I mean, "Just come over and we'll shoot the shit." And he came over, and we both gave each other a big hug when he walked in the door. Yeah. I'm not afraid of hugging.

Good. Do you ever talk with your close friend B— about feelings?

Yeah. [Pause] Not so much with B—, actually, but with the other guy that kind of completes the triangle. About feelings, quite a bit. And I talk about feelings a lot. Quite a bit.

Okay. Then you're not afraid of that.

No. No. We have good discussions.

From associations with other men, you realize how relatively rare that is, don't you?

Oh, yeah.

Because in a roomful of people you don't know terribly well – they're just acquaintances – there are certain topics you just don't talk about, because that's not what men do. And that's the whole point of this book I'm doing.

Well, yeah, but to be a male cheerleader, you've got to be a special type of the same stock. We would just go out and have a good time. And then we'd, like, come back to one of our places, and the three of us would sit around. And we'd just … we'd take turns. We'd be, like, "All right. We're going to do 15 minutes. Everybody's going to have 15 minutes, and then the other two just ask you whatever they want to ask you." You know? And so we'd ask, like, you know, "Who's your biggest role model? Do you want to grow up to be like your dad?" And stuff like that. And, "What's the best part about your life right now?" Things like that. And we'd have long discussions about lots of things … yeah. "What's your biggest regret?" "If your dad was your biggest role model, when did you feel like you had let him down the most?" And stuff like that. Really, you know, we had good conversations.

Oh, that's great. That's great. And, I think, rather unusual among men.

But jumping to another question: Do you have any regrets? You were talking a

Interview 3

while ago about going back to this girlfriend you had in high school, and talking with her about how sorry you are that you had screwed up your relationship with her a little bit.

> Yeah. I went back and talked to her and just said I was sorry for the way I handled what should have been a better relationship. Which should have been more of an emotional investment on my part, in that I just almost used her to have something steady, to have something constant or something that I could count on. But then I didn't give back something that she could feel was tangible, emotional support for her.

Ah. How'd she respond to that?

> Well, she cried. And then she said, "Well, at least you know. At least you can see, now." What I had done to hurt her. And she told me that there were nights when she'd cry herself to sleep. And that made me feel bad. But at least I figured it out, kind of. And maybe I'll be better because of it. In the future. But, I don't know ...

But it wasn't as if you were, like, using her for sex or anything.

> No. No, I never. Sexual actions never took place. But [pause] it did almost seem like I was using her. I didn't really have much of a model for it. I didn't really have much of a model for how to handle a relationship, even though I had an older brother. I'll tell you right now that my older brother and me – as far as women are concerned – are really different. I mean, in high school, he had a girlfriend that he was going out with, but he cheated on her, messed around with other girls. Like, a lot. Like, as much as he could without getting caught. And I would have to be cover for him so he wouldn't get caught. And so I never really knew what it meant to be really involved with somebody exclusively and in a faithful and honest way.

And that's where you went off the track a little bit with this one girl you saw for two years.

> Yeah. I think so. Plus, I think it was just really selfish. Yeah. Very selfish.

But maybe that's a condition of your age at the time?

> Maybe.

It needn't be. But that's a pretty self-involved age – 16, 17.

> Well, I guess so. Plus, since I wasn't having sex with her or anything, I didn't see my behavior as using her – at that time, at least.

No sex with her at all?

> No. I never had sex with that girl.

You mentioned role models before. Do you find, at this point in history, role models to be rather scarce? Who do you look up to? Don't you wonder how you are supposed to behave as a man in the beginning of the 21st Century?

[73]

Growing Up Male In America

Yeah. Reading historical things, I have a lot of quotes that I like to keep in the back of my head that I kind of think of as almost role-model things. For example, Martin Luther King, Jr. said, "Injustice anywhere is a threat to justice everywhere." That's really come to play a lot in my mind since I took this human-relations class and was thinking about all the different "ism's" and how our society is completely set up to help one group and shit on the rest of them. Just things like that. I mean, how to act, how to behave in society. I think I'm just affirming your hypothesis, here. That there's no one out there to show us the way. How can I look at, you know, dead people – the great thinkers – and think of them as role models?

I think they may have left us some germs of wisdom. But your generation tends to feed on immediate gratification at all costs.

Yeah, I know.

That's what I mean: your dad and his dad had John Wayne. And they had "The War." And they had all those kinds of things that were sort of in balance. The man would come home from the job. The wife would be baking cookies for the kids. Not – god forbid – that we want to go back to that, but now men don't know if they're supposed to cry or if they're not supposed to cry. Or what they're supposed to be. Do you ever ask yourself – among you guys – "What do women really want in a man these days?"

Yeah. All the time.

Isn't it all very, very ambiguous? What is it to be a man?

Well, with the male cheerleader buddies of mine, for sure. We're confused. All these girls say, "Oh, you're so sweet!" What comes out of this side of their mouths is completely opposite of what comes out of the other side of their mouths. And how the hell do men make sense of what they say?

And they want you to be butch and masculine and also sensitive.

Uh-huh. Well, like ... from quotes from a girl: "You're so sensitive. I love that in a man. Blah-blah-blah." And then when we were kind of messing around she said, "I love how you can be so rough." I'm, like, "Isn't there a contradiction there?" Yup. Yup. Yup. I don't have any idea.

Yeah. It's very difficult. And then, you might look at another side of this issue. What are you looking for in a woman? There are still guys out there who say, "Well, I want my wife to be a virgin. Yet it's okay for me to fuck my brains out with all these chicks – it doesn't make any difference – but I wouldn't want any one of them to be my wife." Now that's a great contradiction.

A complete double standard.

Totally. So the whole sexual freedom issue is getting in there that I don't think was quite the issue three generations ago. But I just wonder if every once in a while you sit up and talk to yourself and say, "I'm kind of lonely here. I'm kind of in a strange

Interview 3

battlefield, and I don't know what the two sides are."

All the time.

You know? I think it can be very confusing. I don't know how you find your way. Some find it in religion, I guess.

Yeah. And some find it the weight room. I mean, that really is true. Really, in all fairness in every other aspect of life, things just don't make much sense. I mean, you learn that, the only unbreakable code we've ever had in U.S. military history is the Navajo language. In World War II, the Battle of the Midway was pretty much won because we had a flawless code that could be translated perfectly on site. So we could coordinate radio communication. Whenever you sent an encrypted message, it's got to come off the radio. Huge advantage. And yet, we stole land from the Native Americans. We treat them like ... so second class. You feel great about being American, and then you realize we've pissed on everybody. And so you feel bad about that. Nothing makes sense. But then you just go the weight room and think, "Hey, I've got a dumbbell over here. I'm just going to grunt and focus everything I've got on pushing that weight around." And I feel focused and peaceful.

Have you ever used or been tempted to use steroids or any enhancing drugs?

Yes.

You have used?

No, no. I've been tempted.

Because it's out there and available, huh?

Well, yeah, and because I've been working at nightclubs and bars since I was 16. And one of the nightclubs' staffs I worked on was heavily involved with that. I mean, yeah. We would sometimes go over to one of those guys' houses and hang out. And a guy would come walking out of his bedroom in his underwear, like, pulled down past his ass, with his needle stuck in his butt cheek. And he'd say "Guys, I can't seem to find my needle." And I'd wonder, "Oh, my god. What is he doing?"

And his testicles had probably shrunk to the size of raisins.

Yes.

Can't get it up anymore.

My dad talked to me about it and all the medicinal reasons why not to do it. But then I just saw where these guys were coming from. And, I mean, how one-dimensional. I mean, it almost seemed like selling your soul, to me. It kind of seemed like if you would do that to yourself, that would make you one-dimensional in that you are sacrificing your body and you're making all these other sacrifices just to get this one benefit: a great physique. So that one benefit is now going to be your only achievement. I just didn't want to be any of those guys. I mean, if I had a really positive role model who had used steroids, maybe I would have been more convinced that steroids would be good. But, you know, these guys were all characters. These guys were all bar lifers. You know? These guys were all guys on steroids. And that's not where I wanted to be.

And despite the dangers that everybody knows about, there's still the ... well, that's a wonderful way to put it. Selling your body and soul to the devil, for that one benefit.

And it seems like it's cheapening all the authentic bodybuilding work I do. Because when I stand around and I say, "This has come from nothing except my six calluses on each hand and my working hard to bend my physique to my will and the systematic deconstruction of my body and letting itself heal and build muscles properly." But those guys taking the steroids, it's like saying, "I couldn't do it the hard way, I didn't have enough dedication, I didn't have enough motivation, I didn't have enough will power to do it the proper way. So I made a little pact with the devil for a strong physique." But now he's jeopardized his chances of sexual reproduction.

Right. Not such a great tradeoff, is it?

No. Not a great tradeoff at all.

There's a friend of mine who ... it's not in the same league, because he's very afraid of drugs. He works in a bar, too. And, you know, I ask about Ecstasy and all this other stuff. He did a little coke once, and that was about it as far as drugs are concerned. But he does have this big bottle ... it's like speed. Because it's energy, and it keeps him "up" for his bartending and his college classes and his long commuting drive – all with very few hours of sleep.

Effergerin?

I don't know what this stuff is. I should have written its name down. Let's see. As far as drugs, when you were a kid, did you try – aside from alcohol – did you try pot, or weed?

I tried pot, actually, in college for the first time. I was always offered it, though, in high school. You know. You get to the kegger and then on the way to the keg, there would be four chances for you to smoke pot. "Hey, man. Wanna come burn this bowl, man?: You want halvsies on this joint?" And I just said, "No." You know. No. No. No. No. And I finally get to college. It was the end of the year and I had my grades pretty much in control and I was just feeling really good about myself. And somebody said, "Hey, come on – smoke a little." And I thought, "Why not?" Because it would be a shame not to have experienced it at least once. And this would help me in my teaching later on, for talking to kids in high school. Just not to know what this big dope phenomenon is all about. When I did it, this guy said, "Hey, you're a pretty big dude, so we don't know how much you need." Blah-blah-blah. And I got stoned out of my

Interview 3

mind! Out of my gourd. Completely.

Really!

Unbelievably stoned. Worst thing ever. I was puking. This is completely confidential?

Totally.

Good. Well, this happened on campus in a dorm.

Somehow it doesn't surprise me!

Well, it wasn't my dorm. But I went over to this buddy's dorm. And that place is a maze, you know? I mean, the wings on that building. The elevator shaft is, like, in the middle, and then it branches out in four ways. And they're all, like, mirror images of each other. And you have no idea where you are. And if you don't live there, you haven't a chance. And so we went to somebody else's room. Did it. Got completely high. I remember trying to split my focus between four different conversations in the room at once, and actually almost being able to keep up with each one of those. And I'd laugh at somebody else's joke, and the person who was talking to me was, like, "What are you laughing at?" And I'm, like, "Oh, they just said something funny." But then the guy who I went there with left. He's, like, "I'm good, so I'm just going to go down to my room and play my bongos. And whenever you're ready, you come down and we'll play bongos" or whatever. So he leaves. I sit there and I'm just, you know, having a good time. Toking it up and toking it up and toking it up. Suddenly everybody's gone, except for that one person whose room it is. And he says, "Time to go, dude." I just felt awkward. I don't really remember. But I left, and I went to go try to find my buddy's room. So I'm knocking on people's doors. Like, trying to put on my sober face. And my eyes, you know, are probably this big and just bloodshot to shit. And I'm going, "Yeah. Do you know where my buddy's room is?" And they're just, like, "Get the hell out of here, pal. You're going to get me in trouble!"

So finally I just stumbled around, and I ended up walking into a cheerleader's room that I knew. And I was, like, "Oh, my god." And she's, like, "What's *happened* to you?" And I'm just, like, "Oh, my god. I smoked pot." And I got hot flashes. I took off all my clothes. I was down in my underwear with this girl that I kind of just met. And I was sweating super bad. And the room was, like … I could look straight ahead. The room was going around and around and around. And I was puking in her trash can. And I was so dry mouthed that I asked, "Can I have a sip of water? Would you give me a sip of water?" And I'd hurl that back up. And then I remembered. My brain came back to me and was thinking logically, but my body just didn't. There was no connection between what my mind was thinking and what my body was doing. So I'm, like, "God, this is just horrible. I must look like an idiot. Just a moron." And I remember, she had a really good-looking lady friend. And the good-looking friend comes

Growing Up Male In America

to the door and I'm in my underwear, on all fours, in front of this trash can. And I'm going, "Oh, my god! This is so embarrassing! This looks so dumb! So dumb!" And I went to sleep on her bed. I woke up about four hours later. And I was still high.

It kind of stays with you!

Oh, yeah! And I've never done pot since. And I'm not going to ever do it again, I don't think.

It affects ... a lot of times, the first time you don't feel anything.

Yeah. And that was my first time. You know, I'm a big guy, and they thought they should get me really high, and, I mean, I had one hit off a bong. I remember doing that probably 15 times.

And you were lost and confused in all the hallways of this dorm?

Yeah. And plus, I was paranoid as all hell, and I thought this was the end of my career. I could hear my teaching career coming to a grinding halt.

Well, let's move on, now. Are you dating anyone right now?

Man. Right before I left ... right before I left to go this last weekend down to Iowa, I kind of met somebody. And we went out for cocktails, and we had a pretty good time. And she was interesting, and she was nice and she was attractive. And she might be someone who I might be into a future with.

Good for you! You deserve that.

Now, I'm going to ask you some quick-response questions.

Do you ever pose to attract women? I mean, like ... what I mean by this is, a lot of us know what our best side is and whether we smile with our teeth showing or not. Do you ever do that, consciously?

Not consciously. The only time I do it is to be funny and be overbearing. Sort of like, you know, "So you ladies come here much? I haven't seen you around. I know I'd recognize a face like that!"

All right!

Just being dumb with it.

You know, there's a future for you in acting. You know that?

True or false? I expect that with careful planning, my dreams or hopes for the future will be realized.

False. It isn't going to take careful planning. It's going to take luck. It's going to take being in the right place at the right time. Listen, man. I've been on national TV. I've been invited on a lot of adventures. None of that was planned. I didn't plan to do any of the best things in my life. They just happened.

Okay. Next question: Where did you learn most about sex? Friends? Parents?

Interview 3

Siblings? Internet? Books? Movies?

Um ... [pause]. I'm going to have to say ... my brother. And health class. And porno movies.

Okay.

In that order. In that order, I think.

Mom and dad never sat you down.

Nope. Never did.

Even dad, being a doctor?

Nope. Never did. Never. Not even once. I can't even remember the topic ever coming up.

What about when you have kids? Will you?

When I have kids? I'm going to put it out there right away, I think. I think I've got to. Because, as you said, girls are having periods earlier. Guys are going into puberty earlier. I mean, I think it's all just ... well, the more you know, the less threatening it becomes. The less likely there are going to be huge misconceptions and weird feelings and ... you know. If I have kids, I think I'm going to go at it pretty head on, pretty early.

Okay. I think it skips a generation. Parents didn't, and then you decide you will. And maybe your kids ...

Won't.

Well, they'll learn it somewhere. Won't they?

Do you like oral sex?

Yeah.

Do you like having oral sex performed on you?

Yeah.

Okay. What is the main topic of conversation that you carry on with most women? What does it consist of?

Them. What's going on in their lives.

So you become a listener.

Yeah. And they chat away. Well ... the boss, the owner of the company that I worked for, sometime, you know, we'd talk about ... all these long car trips we had to take, driving to the camps and stuff, with these women. And sometimes we'd just start doing the multiplication tables in our head while we were driving. You know. "Yup. Seven times seven's 49. Yup. Eight times eight's 64. Yup. Yup." And every time I think of a random thought while I'm listening to a girl talk, I'll confide in him. And the other day, I was listening to a girl talk to me,

Growing Up Male In America

and she was talking and talking and talking. And I looked out the window and I thought to myself, "I wonder how much that building weighs." [Laughs] And he about cried laughing at that one.

Okay, next question: My biggest and greatest fear is ...

[Pause] My biggest fear is that I don't ... I mean, it's going to sound cliché-ish and stuff, but I don't mean it to be. I want to experience all that I can. All that is within me. Like not having the girlfriend and not having a really solid relationship. Like boyfriend/girlfriend. So far in my life ... I wonder if I'm missing something that could be a big part of my life, and if there's just an area inside me that hasn't even been touched, that is just waiting. Or I look at some of my classes at school and I wonder if I'm challenging myself enough, or if the field I've chosen to go into is venue enough for me to expand and think and push myself. I don't know. Just that I'll have had more in me than what I gave to this life.

It sounds a little like, "Have I really explored all the possibilities?"

Yeah.

Do you ever have a fear of not being able to perform in sex? Ever worry you're not going to get it up?

No.

Not at your age.

No. I mean, if the chance is there, yeah, I'm ready.

All right. What kinds of things cause you to go into a depression? Or to feel particularly lonely or sad or blue? What can trigger that?

When there's no end in sight. When there's [pause] ... like in the middle of the cheerleading season. Not towards the end of it. I'm really happy to be in cheerleading, but in the middle of the season I'm just, like, "Oh, god. Four hours a night. I beat the crap out of myself. And I just can't see where it's going. Where it's leading." Also, being in the middle of school, where it's just paper after paper after paper after paper, and you don't even notice how your mode of thinking has even changed. When you're in the middle of something, you can't see the end of it and you can't see the point of it and it just seems, like, "Why am I even here?"

You know what you're going to like about teaching? It has an end and new beginnings all the time. The school year comes to an end, and then you look forward to a new semester or a new year starting again. New kids. New people. Now, imagine the day-to-day sameness if you're in a corporate job. Or what your dad does.

Yeah. Exactly.

Because January is the same as July in most other jobs.

Exactly. And you sit at your desk, and you file the PDF forms. And you put the

Interview 3

cover sheet on the TPS report.

Here's another question. I don't think it applies to you at all, but how do you feel about your body?

Um ... sometimes I'm really happy with it. It will never be what I want it to be, exactly, because I'll always feel like I could be in there, pushing it harder. I really feel like I'm in tune with what a useful tool my body is. I love rock climbing and camping and being able to carry a pack on my front side, a pack on my back side and also a canoe down a portage trail. I think my body's very useful, and in that sense I like it. Lately the opposite sex has been complimenting me a lot, so that's good. That makes me feel good.

Are you at about the bulkiest and biggest you've ever been?

Yeah. As far as muscularity. Yeah, for sure. For sure.

And in the right clothes, in the right situations, you draw attention even more with your physique, I'm sure.

Um-hum.

Okay. I think we've covered this, too, but how would you define the concept of happiness? You might hook that into the future. What would make you a happy man when you're 30, 35 years old?

Feeling that I've made a difference. Feeling that I haven't sold myself short. Feeling that I've grown as a person and as a brain and as a body. And improved upon myself and my situation. And improved the lives of people I've come in contact with. Students and people I've taught at cheerleading camps. I mean, the guy I work for at the camps has really stressed this. He's said to me, "You don't even know the impact you have on some of these girls over the summer. I mean, they'll remember you for the rest of their life." That would make me a happy man.

All right. That's great. Who would you say is your favorite male public figure? Movie star, political person, whatever. Who do you admire? Who do you want to imitate or emulate?

I enjoy Jack Nicholson tremendously. Mark McGwire seems like a pretty cool guy. It seems like he's pretty level-headed. Pretty cool. Not caught up in the whole athlete earning millions of dollars and stuff. Just chalking up home-run records. And then to see he is best friends with the guy he was competing against for pieces of home-run history. Yeah, that's cool.

That is classy, isn't it? I can see where you find that appealing: to be unassuming, to do things with grace.

Uh-huh. Michael Jordan, a lot, too. I think he's one of the classiest guys around.

Who's your favorite female public figure?

Growing Up Male In America

[Pause/whistles] Probably ... oh, man.

I don't know what it is, but they seem to come and go more quickly.

I think so, too.

Could be dead. You're a history major.

I'd say Jackie Onassis was pretty remarkable.

Talk about style!

Yeah. Yeah.

Courage.

Yeah. Grace.

Last week ... grace. Last week I was at the Metropolitan Museum of Art.

MOMA.

And there was this exhibit of some of her clothes.

Oh, really?

Plus, audio and videos of JFK giving speeches. But there were the dresses. We'd see the pictures and the videos, and then all of a sudden there was the dress itself, mounted in the display case. Cool.

Okay. Moving on. Since you're involved in athletics and athletic-related things, are you shy about your body in the locker room? Like, do you walk around naked in the shower room? Does that bother you? Or do you tend to keep a towel around you, or what?

I'd say I tend to keep the towel around me, not because I'm shy about my body. Just because I know that some people think it's showing off. If I was with guys I know really well, I'm okay with being naked a lot. But when I'm in a more public locker room situation, I don't walk around naked. My dad is ... holy cow! He's the champion of walking around naked. We went camping once in the Boundary Waters, and we walked around the campsite naked. You know? I'd say, "You know, I'm going to go down and wash up." [Laughs] And we'd walk out onto the lake shore naked and he was, like, "Well, we're not going to be seen by anybody." And he was just walking around. [Laughs] But in other situations, I would put a towel around my waist just because I wouldn't want to make anybody else uncomfortable.

Okay. I've noticed a trend in the last several years, that men seem more shy in the locker room. They just cover up, wear a towel. In years past, it was the "male thing" to strut around the shower and locker room naked.

Moving on. Do you admire your mother?

Yeah.

Why?

Interview 3

Because everybody who ever talks to my mom, you know ... like if a phone call comes for me and she answers the phone, that person ends up talking to her for, like, 15 minutes. And days or weeks later, the next time they talk to me, they say, "Oh, I talked to your mom for 15 minutes. What a wonderful lady!" And the fact that at home she's not having the best emotional base right now – for her to come off as that nice ... I mean, she is putting a facade of family togetherness on something that's really falling apart right now. I think that's pretty special and courageous of her – like with the divorce on the horizon. It takes something special. I can't think of anybody who hasn't – just from talking to my mom – said, "Oh, what a great lady." You know? It would be one thing to hear that once in a while, but it happens all the time.

How lucky you are!

Yeah. What a great mom she is.

And then, as you say, for her to be suffering with this impending breakup. That gives her more nobility and grace under pressure.

Um-hum. Well, she doesn't put up that front to me. She's completely vulnerable in front of me. And she cries in front of me, you know, all the time.

Does she like you better than your brother? Confide in you more?

Yeah. Yes.

She is more comfortable talking openly with you.

Yes.

You know, that doesn't surprise me.

And a huge factor in it is that my brother and I are only half brothers.

Oh!

And that causes a huge family dynamic, here. My dad married a girl he met in college. Married her, and they had a kid. She died when my brother was two months old or something. So then my dad thought, "I still gotta finish school. Gotta get this done." So my brother was pretty much adopted by my grandma on my dad's side. And for the first couple years of his life, he was raised in the South. Then my dad met my mom. Her friends told her, "You've got to come meet this guy next door. He has the cutest little son." My mom went over and met my dad, who's got my brother there with him. Because it's the holidays or whatever. So that's the whole thing ... their relationship starts, they get married, and then they have me. But they never told my brother that his birth mom is dead, that my mom isn't his mom.

How long before they let him know the truth?

Not until he was seven years old, and that's got to be rough. That's got to put a rift in the family dynamics there. I kind of look at things genetically, too. With my dad's brains and the first woman he married – his first wife was a mathematician ... like a higher-level math grad student – she was like a super brain herself. So they come out with my half-brother, who's nearly a genius. On the other hand, my mom's not very logical. And so that also has forced her and my brother to butt heads quite a bit. And there's always been quite a bit of tension between them. And the bottom line that my brother would use when they were having fights is, "Well, you're not my real mom. What are you going to do about it?"

Oh, that made her feel great!

Yeah. Because, you know ... I mean ... what is a real mom? Doesn't it make her real because of the 14 years or whatever that she's put into you so far, you brat, 15-year-old kid? But then ... there's even more of a dynamic in my family. My grandma on my dad's side, who took care of my brother when his birth mom died – when my mom shows up, my grandma wants to take this son away and raise him. So then there's a huge rift between my mom and my dad's mom. This last summer, I stopped off at my grandparents' house, and this was the first time I've ever met with them without my parents there. Just me and them. And they tell me all about how they thought I didn't want to have anything to do with them. Because they would send letters and stuff, and they would try to reach out to me. Calling and stuff. And my mom wouldn't let the letters get through to me when I was a kid. Letters and calls from the grandparents who had raised my brother when he was a baby. Because mom probably thought they were trying to steal me away from her, too. So all this finally comes out, and I'm thinking, "God. Whew! That's a great year!" How's that for sarcasm?

Well, that's all very, very interesting. Do you and your brother resemble each other?

Well, you know what? Some people look at us and say we look like twins, and others don't see any resemblance. But a lot of the mannerisms – our walk, our talk, our laugh – a lot are the same. And that probably has a lot to do with just growing up together. Yeah. I think that's most of the reason.

Well, listen. This has been a wonderful interview. I mean that most sincerely. Are there any final things you want to say that we haven't covered in the interview? Fears, frustrations? The wonderful things about being a 21-year-old at this time in history?

Well, as far as living in this time in history, I really think in my lifetime I've seen so much. One of my great teachers was my high-school creative writing teacher. I tracked him down, and I e-mailed him and thanked him for being such a wonderful teacher. I told him that I was going to be a teacher, too. I shared with him how much I respected him, and I asked how he could possibly have put up with us. He wrote back to me: "Well, you're considering a teaching gig, huh? To most of my students who say that, I say, 'Go out and do some other work first and gain some perspective.' But with you I'm going to say, go ahead. I think you've lived your life thus far and have achieved an increased adventure quotient." That's what he called it. [Laughs] He said, "Yeah. You've

Interview 3

lived your life in a way that your adventure quotient is far above what the average 21-year-old's is. So I think you'll be fine in the classroom, and I think you'll be able to offer some perspective." That he would say that really impressed me, and I thanked him for the confidence he had in me.

I can't remember who wrote it, but there's some quote to the effect that it should never be man's goal to reach a static state of perfection. Rather, it should be our goal to be adapting and adapting and adapting. And I think that has been kind of forced upon our generation. I think that concept has affected not only technology, but our whole culture and the fact that we can't accept things as absolute, static. Things are changing so much faster and in so many more ways than anybody could ever have thought.

Well, I think you've been a wonderful interview. I really appreciate your time.

It's been great!

Postscript – December 2001

This man's parents did separate and divorce. He expects to finish his university degree in history in May 2002 and begin his career as a high-school teacher. Cheerleading will continue to be an important part of his life.

Interview 4

"It's just ignorance, I guess... I don't really blame them for it... That's how they were raised."

This interview was conducted on June 26, 2001. He is 24 years old, 5' 8" tall, weighs 200 pounds and has black hair. He works in a printing company.

First of all, thanks for doing this interview. I hope you find it refreshing and relaxing and not intimidating at all.
Ordinarily I start asking about early childhood, but maybe we can come back to that. Let's take it from the present and then go back. First of all, how old are you?

    Twenty-four years old.

Twenty-four. And that means you're in your prime. [Laughter] *And what kind of work do you do?*

    I work at a print company. I've been in printing for a little over five years now.

Do you like the smell of ink?

    I don't deal with the ink too much. I just finish the books up, pretty much. I work in the bindery department. I just started at my current position a little over a year ago. I worked at another place for four years before that.

Better pay?

    It's a little better. [Laughs] It pays the bills, at least.

What is your highest level of education?

    High-school diploma.

Okay. So you didn't go to a tech school to learn any of those printing skills?

    No.

I suppose it's on-the-job training.

    Pretty much, yeah. That's where you learn. I figure you get in there and figure it out, hands on.

Growing Up Male In America

And you've lived in Minnesota for about how many years?

I moved to Minnesota in 1985, so I've been here more than half my life. I was nine when we moved.

I'm always interested to know: Do you prefer to call yourself African-American? Black? What?

Just black.

Black works for you?

Yeah. [Laughs]

Okay. You know, it gets to the point that you worry about being politically correct, and you're afraid of ...

Saying the wrong thing. [Laughs]

So we'll go with black, then, okay?

Works for me.

Okay. If it works for you it works for me.

All right. Now, let's go back ... way back ... to your childhood and the beginning. Where were you born?

In Greenville, Mississippi.

And that's near ... any major city?

It's three hours east of Jackson, I think. Jackson is the capital.

Okay. That's the Deep South, I think they call it.

Yeah. That's the Delta.

Isn't Mississippi one of the poorest states?

Yup. Three years ago, I checked. They were 49th out of 50 states. The poorest. And they were number one out of 50 states for high-school dropouts.

I wonder why that is.

I don't know. I moved back down there in 1993 for a year because my grandmother was sick and my mom decided she wanted to move back to take care of my grandma. I was about 16 at the time, so I didn't have much of a choice. So we went back down there and I went to school there after being here in Minnesota for almost 10 years. It was just crazy. The craziest thing about it was we moved right next door to the house that we had moved out of 10 years before that.

Wow! Is that strange, or what?

Yeah. [Laughs] We even got to go back through the house and see our old rooms from when we were kids.

Interview 4

I'll bet they seemed smaller.

Yeah. It's definitely different there. It's definitely different.

What kind of work did your dad do?

My dad went into the Army when I was a kid. We haven't contacted each other. I've probably seen him, maybe, four times, five times in my whole life.

Then you were just a little kid when they divorced, huh?

Yup.

Okay. Apparently you don't wish to find him and spend lots of quality time with him?

Naw. I figure ... I don't know. We haven't done it in all this time. I'm not mad at him or anything, but it's just that I've been doing this good without him. There's no use in having confusion. Last time I saw him, I was 17. He was actually supposed to meet me at the Greyhound station at a layover in Memphis, Tennessee, for four hours. And he never showed up. So, I just said, "Hey, maybe he's got his reasons. Maybe he doesn't."

So you don't know too much about him? Like, if he remarried.

Nope.

Or if he has more kids?

Him and my mom never were married. I know he's got more kids, because I met a couple of the other kids because I talked to his mom when I was down there. But he was always gone. The last I heard, he was driving truck. He retired out of the Army.

Did I hear you say that your mom and he were never married?

No. Never married.

Okay.

There's 10 of us. My mom has 10 kids.

Now, he's the daddy of all of them?

No. He was just my father, actually.

Okay. Well, that makes an interesting family reunion, doesn't it? [Laughter] *You're half and half and half. Okay.*

In what religion were you raised?

Baptist.

Okay. That's fairly common in the South, isn't it? In fact, don't they say Southern Baptist?

Yeah. Southern Baptist. I've never heard anything else, actually, until I moved to Minnesota. [Laughs]

Growing Up Male In America

Did you go to nursery school or kindergarten?

I went to kindergarten.

Do you have any memories of that? Because you would have been about five then.

Yeah. I remember hating it. [Laughs] That was my biggest thing. I hated it. Because it was right down the street from our house, and I remember my mom used to walk me to school. And as soon as she'd take off, I'd always hide under the table. So when they took attendance, the teachers would think I was gone anyways. [Laughs] So as soon as they got done taking attendance and they closed their eyes, I'd be gone. My mom always took me back to school. I think I finally caught on to it when she told me that if I didn't stay in school, she'd end up going to jail. She'd get in trouble for me not going to school. So then I just made the best of it. I grew to love it, though. But I hated it when I first started.

Well, school can be so controlling, can't it?

Yeah. [Laughs]

Nap time. Milk time. Play time. Shut-up time. And for a kid who wants to run around and play and have freedom, well … that's a little confining.

About what time in education, in your grade school, did school start becoming a little more interesting, a little more fun?

First grade, probably.

That soon? Okay. There's something magic about learning to read, isn't there?

Yeah. It's just, like, it's so competitive. You know? Just to go and know you're learning something. Because one day you didn't know it and then a week later you know it all. And you just look at it, like, "I had no idea what this was a week ago." So I think that was the thing that got me. Learning how to tell time. Not having to ask people, "What time is it?" Because you know yourself. Counting your own little stash of money, when you get it. So that was … I think that's the part that got me going.

Do you have any memories of a favorite teacher or teachers?

I had a favorite teacher. She was my first- and second-grade teacher, and she was just … I don't know, she was just nice. I had this one teacher in kindergarten, and she was just mean. She was this big woman. I remember her taking kids, and her hands were so much bigger than ours, that she'd just grab their wrists – both wrists – and put them together with one of her hands. And she'd shake your knuckles on the end of the table, at the edge of a table or the edge or your desk. And it's weird, because I never thought about it as a kid, but when I got older I thought, "She could have broken somebody's hand." That was her punishment to the kids. In Mississippi, they are still allowed to spank you, all the way up to junior high.

Interview 4

Well, that's surprising in this day and age, isn't it? Now, in the Catholic Church, the nuns used to do some pretty bizarre things with their rulers and pulling on ears and rapping things over knuckles. But, anyway.

Now, your last name is the same as your dad's last name?

No. My mom's.

Oh, okay. So all the kids share that last name. Now, where do you fall? Are you the youngest, oldest, middle or what?

There's 10 of us in all, and there are four younger than me and five older than me.

Now, tell me about your mom. She sounds like she's a pretty remarkable person.

She is.

To have raised nearly a dozen kids by herself. [Laughter]

She's ... that's mom. Even to this day, she's my best friend. She lives two blocks from me now, and every time I moved, she ended up two blocks closer to me, somehow. And she is just wonderful. We never had a whole lot. We had what we needed. You know? And she just managed somehow – no matter what the cost was, she took care of us to the best of her ability. And I just love her to death for it.

How old a woman is she now?

She's going to be 52 in February.

Well, that's wonderful to hear, because she must have put up with an awful lot, being a single mom. And for you to appreciate it – of course, that says something about your character, too. It means you're a good person. Now, in a way, it's kind of payback time, I suppose. You can kind of give her some time to relax.

Yeah.

Do you get along well with your other siblings?

Yup.

Are they all sprinkled all over the country?

Nope. Everybody's in Minnesota, except for one.

Really? Now, what happened to them? Did they go on to school some place, or did they ...

One of my sisters is a schoolteacher.

Good. So she had to get a little education. Good for her!

Do you live alone?

Yup.

You have to know how to cook, then, don't you?

[91]

Growing Up Male In America

You get tired of frozen pizza after a while. [Laughter]

You know, it's nice to hear that you get along with your sisters and brothers.

Yeah. It's like my whole thing is, you can't hold a grudge. You can't stay mad at people. For one, life's too short. All you're going to do is make yourself miserable. Especially if it's family. It's just like, suck it up and get over it. You've got to talk to every one of them.

Yeah. Yeah. And if you wait until the funerals of these people, that's a little late.

That's the thing. Because my grandma just died two and a half years ago, and we all drove down to Mississippi. We thought my mom was going to take it so hard because she had moved down there to try to take care of her, and she ended up dying. But mom was just the mellowest one of the whole family. Because my grandma's got 11 kids. So I've got a lot of uncles and everything, and they just ... I mean, before the funeral even started, just to see the hearse pull up, they just broke down. And I thought about it all. It's just like they never got a chance to say they're sorry – or they know if somebody got mad at them in the family, my grandma would make everybody happy with that person again. And it's just like my mom just took it all very calmly, and she just walked up to the casket. She just told God, she said, "God, you told me to come here and take care of my mom. So I did, and now I'm asking you to take care of her." And that was pretty much it. And to me it's just like ... it was weird. Because we were just sitting there. Because my mom is real emotional, and we thought she was just going to lose it – but she did really, really good.

That's because she was there to help your grandmother.

Yeah. We all sat there and figured it out, right during the funeral – that she's got nothing to be sorry for. She did everything she could.

That's quite beautiful, isn't it?

Yeah.

Have you talked with your mom about that? Like, "Why didn't you cry?"

Yeah. We asked her right after the funeral. [Laughs]

"How'd you hold up so long?"

At the burial and everything, she was still smiling, talking to people. And I'm, like, "This is my mom?" [Laughs]

Wonderful!

And that's what she told me. She said, "I did everything I could. I never had a reason to say I was sorry about anything." So that's good.

And that makes all the difference.

Yup. That's what I try to tell people. I mean, make up before it's too late, because you never know. I mean, one day that person's not going to wake up –

Interview 4

or one day you may not wake up.

Sure. Absolutely. Now, on to another subject. Do many of your black friends wish they were white? Or could pass for white?

I've got some who could pass for white. Because there are a couple of them who are biracial – half black and half white. And you can kind of tell the difference with their treatment and our treatment. Just like at the school or out at the bar or anything. You know? And I don't … I've never had any of them actually say that "I wish I was white" or whatever.

As you were growing up in Mississippi – and you were relatively young and that's after the whole Civil Rights Movement. But Mississippi is still kind of holding back, from what I hear. Did you ever – once in a while, at least – notice the inequality and wish that it would be a heck of a lot easier?

You know what? To be honest with you, I didn't. And I get that question a lot. But I never did. Because the blacks had their neighborhoods, and the whites had their neighborhoods. If you were black, you wouldn't dare go into the whites' neighborhood – or vice versa. And I mean, at school, we were just kids. You know? So the kids didn't care about it. Because, you know, we're first, second and third grade. And if a white kid or a black kid didn't like you, then they probably would just say nothing to you. So I never experienced it. I can't remember experiencing it when I was a kid in Mississippi.

Okay.

You kind of stayed in your own area. You know? It's, like, you wouldn't go six blocks past where you lived at. You know? Or that whole side of town was just all blacks. You know? Because it's rundown. And the whites – they had their other side of town. You wouldn't ever go over there just to be going over there. You know?

Did you ever have any bad experiences here based upon being a black person?

You get called "colored" a lot.

Do you, really?

Yeah.

Not the "N" word.

Yeah. But you don't hear about it directly. When I first moved here – 11 or 12 years ago – there were only three black families in this town, and now you can go to some areas of town and you don't know if you're in this town or if you're in Detroit or Chicago or North Minneapolis. You know? Nobody has ever come up to my face and said racist words. People driving down the street in their cars, they'll yell something out of the window sometimes. But it's just ignorance, I guess. And me, personally? I don't really blame them for it, because it's just like a cycle. That's how they were raised, and probably

Growing Up Male In America

they've never really talked to a black person. And so my whole thing is, if people want to call you names, let them say what they've got to say. I understand where they're coming from, to a certain point. I mean, people just react to what they know and what they hear. But if you're going to leave a town just because somebody called you a name, what does that say about you? So I'd rather deal with the name-calling any day than knowing I can walk outside and die, just by taking the garbage out or something. I mean, if you want to call me names – if it makes you feel good – go ahead and say it, I guess.

What's that thing that kids used to say? "Sticks and stones may break my bones, but names will never hurt me." You seem to have a very mature and wise philosophy.

Yeah. Because if you go in the ignorant way, then you're no better than they are, to be honest with you. So it's just like "live and let live." You know? And that's my whole thing, too. I'll talk to anybody – no matter what they look like, no matter how they dress or whatever. Just because that person has got his own style doesn't mean that he isn't a nice person. And so it's just, like, talk to him just to find out. I talk to kids now who seemed like they were prejudiced in junior high school and high school, and when we talk they say, "I'm sorry I never gave you chance in high school" or whatever, but I don't blame them for it. That's when I start looking at the parents, I guess. It's just, like, I'm glad that that person did get over it so he doesn't raise his kids like that.

Good. It's so true. Ignorance is based on stereotyping – but once they get to know someone, they realize that they're not a heck of a lot different than anybody else. And that's where I think you're doing a good service. I've only just met you, but you seem like such a genuine and friendly and good person. So that once people meet you, that can wipe out a whole negative stereotype about black people.

I try my best. All I ask for is a chance. I figure you just look at me and you make your negative decision right away. It doesn't really bother me because you don't really care to know me in the first place. And I tell people, "Well, if I based my experience of white people on how I was treated at first by white people, I probably wouldn't have any white friends." It's just like there's going to be ignorance everywhere you go.

Yup. How true, how true. So you're on a mission.

Yeah. [Laughs] I might even write a book one of these days. [Laughter]

And what was school like up here? I'll bet there were a lot of times when you were the only black person in the class.

Yeah. [Laughs] As a matter of fact, I'll never forget grades seven through 12. I remember getting on the bus – we had a bus that was, like, three kids to every seat. And my sister and I were the only black kids on the bus. I've never seen so many white people just look at you. I almost just walked off. "I'll walk to school." And I thought, "Nope, because you're going to have to deal with this every day. I mean, kids are going to be kids. If you show them a sign of weak-

Interview 4

ness, then they'll just tear you up every day." You know? So I just found my seat and sat down, and we got to school and my counselor showed me around. I met one black kid. There was another black kid – and he's showing me around for, like, 10 more minutes, and I don't see any more black kids. I'm just, like, "Okay, here I moved from North Minneapolis, where it was almost nothing but black kids." And I remember saying to myself, "If I don't see one more black kid, there ain't no way I can go to school here." And he showed me my math class, and there was a black girl sitting right behind where I was supposed to be sitting. And I said, "Well, I'm here, now. I guess I've got to give it a shot." [Laughter] So it was different, but I think it was a good thing. Because I think, you hear people say, "Well, nobody will give me a job" or "Nobody … this." You have to do it all yourself. Nobody ain't got to give you nothing. I mean, life is only what you make it out to be. If you don't want to amount to anything, that's exactly what you're going to get. So if you don't think you can learn because you go to an all-white school, and that's just what you're telling yourself – you don't want to learn in the first place. But to me it was good, because I moved from North Minneapolis with all Ds and Fs and then I came here. I didn't know anybody, so I didn't have anybody to talk to, so my whole mind was just focused on studying. At first they had me in all these low-level classes when I first moved. A month and half later, they moved me up to the Honor Roll. And so it was just, like, you've got to do what you've got to do, I guess.

Sure. Sure. But still there must have been some lonely times.

Oh, yeah. But like I said, there were 10 kids in our family, so … [Laughs] And everybody's got their own thing in our family. I think by the time we moved here there were seven of us. I guess three had moved out of Mom's place. And I went to school with one other sister. She was just a year older than I was, so we kind of watched out for each other. There was one of the black guys who went to school here. He and I got to be friends. But there were only five black kids in this 2,500-kid school. All right, you've got to make friends. And it was kind of a cool thing. I remember going to social studies, and at that time – when I started school – the unit they were studying just happened to be on slavery. And one of the white kids came up to me and asked, "Does that bother you? When we talk about that?" I said, "Well, to be honest with you, no. Because none of us had anything to do with that period personally. That's just the way the world was, and there isn't much I can do about it and there isn't much you can do about it." And he just asked me, "Well, I wanted to know." To this day, he and I are still real good friends. And that's from seventh grade, and that's how he and I actually started talking. Because I think kids are curious about things they've never seen. And it's just like you don't meet that many black kids. I mean, lots of kids in that school probably never saw a black kid before.

Well, that kid who came up to you and asked, "Does this hurt your feelings, talking

Growing Up Male In America

about slavery?" That was pretty good of him, wasn't it?

Yeah, it was. And that's why I think we're such good friends today. It's weird, too, because we don't hang out a whole lot, but every time he sees me, he just hugs me. He can be with 50 people, and he'll introduce me to all 50 of them. He's just a good kid. He actually went overseas to play hockey and blew out a shoulder and ended coming back here. He was kind of a big jock when we were in seventh grade. I started talking to him, and I met more and more people every day. It was just like I said, "I'll talk to anybody." One thing led to another. It's funny, because I was going to the carnival a couple of days ago with my kid, and his mom just said, "You know what? The biggest thing I hate about going with you to places is because you know so many people." She just told me that when we walked there, "I'm counting how many people you know." [Laughter] And I just laughed. I said, "Well, for one thing, look how long I've been here." As long as you give me a chance to talk to you, I'll talk to you. I don't care who you are.

Now, let's see. Did I hear you say you have a kid?

Yeah. He'll be six in August.

You're a daddy!

Yup.

Hey, all right! And are you still married?

No. I was never married. But she and I get along really good.

But you still get enough visitation rights?

Yeah. And all three of us still get together. We both take him to things together. We still all get together for Christmas, and we still all get together for his birthday.

Okay. I suppose he's the most brilliant, adorable child in the universe? [Laughs]

Yes, he is. He is. And that's what it all comes down to, too. It's no longer about me. And our breakup wasn't a bad thing. I started dating her when I was 16. We broke up when I was 21. I think from 16 to 21 – male or female – you go through a lot different changes. And we just felt that it would be best for us to part. Maybe we'll end up together one of these days, maybe we won't. But she's a really good mom, and I try to be the best dad I can be. That's what we're doing right now.

And he would be in first grade, now, or about to go into it.

Yeah. He's going into first.

That's a wonderful period in a kid's life, and just think – he'll come home with that same excitement that you did, not too many years ago. And he'll say, "Look, Daddy, I can read!"

Interview 4

Do you get to see him on a regular basis, like every other weekend?

Yeah. Her parents live here, too, and I still talk to them because her mom's a big sports fanatic. We can never all agree on the same teams, so I'm always calling her back about my team or she'll call. She'll send me a card for Father's Day or something. So if for some reason he doesn't have school and his mom's got to work and I've got to work, then her mom will take care of him. But, yeah, at least every other weekend.

Good. Okay. Now, is she black, too?

No. She's white.

Oh, that's interesting! That opens up a whole new door of questioning for me, so let's go there. I have talked with some of my black acquaintances, guys, and they say that white women tend to seek out black men. Maybe it's the myth that black men are well-endowed and better lovers.

The weird thing about that is, white women might think black men are cuter or whatever, but at one time they wouldn't dare touch you. I'd say by the time I hit high school, ninth grade, it was like the biggest fad in the world. I mean, you wouldn't believe how many girls the average black guy can have, and that girl wouldn't really care as long as they could say they've had sex with a black guy. It doesn't seem like it's changed that much, even today. I don't know what it is with the guys. I mean, me personally, I say whatever makes you feel good, do it. If you love somebody for who they are, not what they are, then that's good. If you're with them because you love them, that's good. But if you're with them because you think it makes you look good, then I think you need to find out where you're going.

Yeah. The wrong reasons there.

But it's weird because there are girls now who have two or three kids by black guys. And the way they act, you'd think they were born liking black guys or something. You know? It's crazy. It's crazy. When you hear how the cops say, "Drugs are bringing black guys here," it's, like, yeah, it probably has a little to do with the drugs, but I've known guys who have been here for two days and they'll take a girl home from the bar, and the next day he can move in, and she has no problem with that. To me, that's crazy. He's not working he doesn't pay rent, all of his friends stay there with her, but she doesn't care because she's got this black guy sitting beside her.

Does that work the other way? I mean, do the black women find that white men are interested in them?

Lately I think they do, but I didn't see a lot of black women acting that way. I think black women feel they have to be strong, and they might say this white guy is cute or whatever, but they wouldn't touch him. Or if they did, they wouldn't let anybody know. I'm just going by what I see and what I hear per-

Growing Up Male In America

sonally. You know? I know a couple of black girls who've had kids with white guys, but the white guys they're with think they're just as black as the women.

So it doesn't quite work equally, then, does it?

No. I don't think so.

Well, that's interesting.

I hear a lot of black women – when they move here – that's all they say. "All these black dudes want is white women." I just tell them, I say, "Honestly, you want this dude to go out and work how many hours a week, when all he's got to do is go over here and be with this girl and tell her he likes her." And he can stay there rent-free and drive her car and everything, and she doesn't really care because her parents probably bought it for her.

You know the myth that black men are well-endowed. Is this true?

To be honest with you, I can't say. I tease my friends about that. I say, "You could be bigger than me. I don't know. I'm not going to sit here and ask you to show me." [Laughter] I say to everybody, "It's just a myth. That's all it is. Just a myth." It's like people say that if you've got a big foot, then you've got to be well-endowed.

No. You know what you always say to that? "You know what big feet mean? You need big shoes."

[Laughs] Right. I always tell them, "If it's all in your feet, it can't be all in your meat." [Laughter]

That's great!

I mean, if big feet is the reason, guys would start going into the store and buying shoes three sizes too big.

Yeah.

Me, personally, I wear a size eight and a half. And I don't mind telling anybody what size shoe I wear.

And then if he isn't hung big, then she thinks, "Gee, maybe my information was wrong."

Yeah. [Laughs] "I've been hearing this my whole life." And she could have had a white boyfriend before that who was twice as big as the black guy.

Speaking of sex, do you remember how old you were when you had your first sexual experience with another person? With a woman?

I was 15. I was going into ninth grade.

And do you remember it pretty clearly?

Yup. Yeah. [Laughs] It was the only time I ever had sex in my mom's house, but I knew she was gone for the day.

Interview 4

And was it successful?

Yeah. Short but successful. [Laughter]

Well, then that's a measure of success, I suppose. And was there any oral sex involved at that point?

No.

Okay. Just the standard missionary position. Okay. Do you remember the first time you masturbated?

Yeah.

Was that before the sexual experience with the woman?

Yeah. It was before sex. I was probably 13 the first time I masturbated.

Were you surprised, or did you have any preparation for it or knowledge about it?

I was surprised, I guess I could say. I overheard my older brother and his friends talking about it, and I just remember hearing, "Find some lubricant and shake it out and see what happens." That to me is a good thing, because for your first time having sex and you have never come before, you don't know what the hell you're in for when you're ready to come and you're having sex. [Laughs] And so it's just a preparation. It's kind of like watching soap operas, learning how to kiss or something.

Does the Baptist Church consider masturbation a sin?

I've never heard.

Typically, guys don't talk about masturbation too much with other guys.

I tease my friends about it all the time. It's a lot safer, it's a lot cleaner, and that way I can go to bed without hearing any complaints. I don't have to hear, "Let's go again" or "You're too short" or anything like that. I can just do it and go to bed.

There's a nice line from a movie: "There's one thing you can say about masturbation – you don't have to look your best." [Laughter]

One of my friends got busted. He's got two roommates, and I guess he thought he was just sitting at home alone. And he thought, "Oh, what the hell." And my other friend, his roommate ended up coming home early. He's sitting in the living room jerking off, and the roommate comes home. What do you say? I think personally, if any guy ever says he's never done it, he's lying.

I agree with you. You know what they used to say, too? Ninety-eight percent of all people masturbate, and two percent are liars." Which means everybody *does it.*

When did you first drink alcohol?

The first time I ever got drunk, I was 15 years old. And it's funny how I ended up getting drunk, because I was at this club with one of my friends, and it was

Growing Up Male In America

kind of cold outside. It was in the winter, and I had a coat on and a sweatshirt, and he just had a coat on with a t-shirt. His coat was smaller than mine. I remember asking him, "Why in the hell aren't you cold? I mean, I'm standing here, freezing." He just said, "Well, it's the alcohol that makes your body feel a lot warmer than it actually is." And I said, "Well, let me try some." And that was the first time I ever took a drink. I was 15 years old, and it was grape-flavored Cisco. It tasted pretty good, but before I knew it, I was *drunk* – and there was nothing I could do about it.

Did you throw up?

No. I've never thrown up. But I just remember going to play basketball ... I had a basketball game the next day. And I didn't even know what a hangover was. He didn't tell me about the side effects of it. He was just happy I was drunk. [Laughs] Because I was his little buddy, and here we are, both drunk. I had a basketball game. As a matter of fact, I was playing basketball with one of the Jehovah Witnesses guys, and he was an older guy. He was out there putting moves on me left and right, and I'm, like, "What's wrong with me today? I've beat this dude every time." So he was just, like, "What's going on?" I'm, like, "Nothing. I'll be all right. I just need some water." So I ended up taking a break and I sat out, and I was just thinking, "What the hell did I do last night?" And I thought about it. "Ah! I got drunk last night." And I didn't drink again for two years – not a beer, not one thing. I didn't even talk to girls who had alcohol on their breath.

But you do have an occasional drink now?

Yup.

You wouldn't call yourself a heavy drinker, though?

No.

How about drugs? Ever tried any?

I tried marijuana. That's the only drug I ever tried.

I hear that a lot.

I was too scared. I mean, you grow up hearing about all the heavy drugs. I've seen people do crack or snort coke, and it's scary, what it could do to you. I smoked marijuana for probably about three or four years, and then I got tired of that after a while. There were some times when I smoked weed when I didn't like how I felt. I felt too high, like I wasn't in control of the situation. And this is supposed to be the weak drug, you know?

These days you hear the stories of Ecstasy, which is the hot drug for young kids. Going to the rave parties and all that.

I know a lot of people who are doing Ecstasy right now. And it's sad, because it seems like some of the music they play at the bars now caters to you on

Interview 4

Ecstasy. All my friends – even the guys I hang out with now – they've all tried it, but I told them, "There is no way I will do it."

Aren't you proud of yourself?

I am. I am. [Laughs]

I mean, think about this. You're raising a son, for one thing. But even if you weren't, you have built a standard that you're going to live by. And you apparently don't give a damn about peer pressure. And if somebody says, "Aw, come on, try it! Try it!"

They say, "Hey, smoke a joint." And I say, "You smoke a joint, I'll smoke a cigarette." They'll tease me every once in a while. I have one friend who wants to save the world when he's on Ecstasy, and another friend will play with himself in front of everybody when he's on Ecstasy. The first time I actually ever heard about it, I was 17 years old. This dude at the club was telling me about it. And even then I was just, like, "There ain't no way I'm trying it." You know?

Because the reactions are so different from different people, and you wonder, "What would I do?"

I have a lot of people say it feels so good, and the big thing with guys is you can have sex all night. Like one of my friends, he always talks about ... he will have sex with this girl three or four times and he'll never come. And I say, "Ain't that the best part?" You know, the moment that you come. And I'm, like, "You're on this Ecstasy, and you just can't come?" And he's, like, "No matter what, I can't come."

Well, let's shift gears a bit now. Are you still a practicing Baptist? Do you go to church?

Yup. My mom has bible study at her house.

Okay. So you don't have to go to one of the churches in town.

No. She asks me to sometimes but ... I don't know. I think a lot of people go to church out of guilt. Me, personally, I don't feel guilty about anything. And I think ... I mean, God knows every person because he made every person. You're going to go to heaven or hell depending on your heart, not how you lived your life. So I mean, everybody's born in sin. It's just like, you know what's right and what's wrong. You don't go out there and just live your life on the edge just because you think God's going to save you or whatever. I've always believed in God with all my heart. I got baptized when I was seven years old, which is the youngest of my last three generations. Like I told my mom, even then the church didn't want to baptize me because they felt I was too young – but I knew in my heart I felt God. So that's what I went with. You know? And my whole thing with church is that I don't want to go because somebody wants me to go. I want to go because *I* want to go. And that was my biggest thing, when I moved out here, with the Catholics. I never knew that

Growing Up Male In America

every Wednesday all my high-school friends had to go to this religion thing. You know? And I swear, that's why I think so many kids would rebel. Because it's not like you're going because you want to – you're going because your mom makes you, or you're going to get in trouble if you don't go.

In the Baptist Church, you don't get baptized until you reach what point?

Until you see God in your heart.

I see. You know what Catholics do? They baptize babies within two weeks of birth.

And you see, that was a big thing, because my kid's mom and her whole family are Catholic. But I wouldn't let my son be baptized when he was a baby. I told them, "Honestly, he's my son. If she and I can come to an agreement on it and until he says, 'Daddy, I'm ready to take God into my heart and I want to get baptized,' he won't be baptized." You know? If he wants to do it, he will do it on his own. Not just because I felt it was the right thing or the expected thing.

She's Catholic. Does she take him to mass?

He'll go with her every once in a while when she goes with her mom. And we're going to the church in the Cities on Sunday, me and my mom. And he lives in the city, so I'll probably pick him up and bring him to a Baptist church. More the black culture.

So, it's not like he's a member of one church or the other.

No.

And you're waiting for him to make the decision.

Right. Whatever he decides.

I can't tell you – but I will – how happy I am that you agreed to do this interview, because I'm learning a great deal. And you know what else I'm learning? I'm learning to know one other human being, and that's what I do. I love to talk to people.

Me, too. [Laughs]

Your father was in the military. Had you ever thought that that might be a way for you to go?

Never once.

Didn't appeal to you at all? Okay. I wondered if it was because your dad was in the service, and you said, "I hate Army people?" [Laughter]

That's how I used to think, but to me it's just not for me. I guess I never even thought about it before I had a kid, but once I got him I knew there was no way I could be away from him for so long. And I just never thought about it anymore.

Okay. Now to some quick-recall questions.

Interview 4

What is the most hurtful thing a friend or a relative has ever done to you?

Probably just lying. Because I think lying is probably the easiest thing to do, and it hurts to know that you trusted this person, and that person just looked you right in the face and lied to you.

I think lying is kind of close to stealing.

Yup.

Do you ever pose to attract women? Like, do you know which side of you looks better?

[Laughs] Nope.

What do you see yourself doing in about 15 years? For a career and for maybe a location?

To be honest with you, in 15 years, all I can say about it is if I'm alive, I know I'll be doing something. No matter what it takes to make it, I've always considered myself somebody who does what it takes to make it. I don't know if I'll be here in this town, but if I'm alive and breathing, I know I'll be doing something important.

And your son, you know, will be 21.

Yeah. [Laughs] We'll be hanging out. [Laughter]

Okay.

Maybe I'll be watching him in the NBA or something.

Yeah. Is he tall?

Yup. His mom's tall. All my brothers are, too. Everybody's at least six feet except me.

How tall are you?

Five–eight.

Are you happy with your body? Are you overweight?

I'm 200 pounds.

Two hundred? Is that a little overweight?

Yeah, yeah. For my height, I guess.

Do you ever try to trim down?

No. I figure you live once.

Do you work out?

No. I play basketball here and there, that's about it.

Okay. Where did you learn about sex? Did your mother ever sit you down and talk to you about "the birds and the bees"? About the facts of life?

Growing Up Male In America

Nah.

Where did you learn about sex, then?

Friends. Because everybody had an older brother or something, and they were probably doing it already and were talking about it. You just kind of sit in and learn a little bit, I guess.

Do you see porn films now and then?

Yup.

Are they good or bad? I don't mean quality. [Laughter] *Is it a good idea?*

I think it's a good idea. I mean, whatever makes you at ease doing it. I think people today worry too much about what the next person thinks.

When you talk with just men – you're sitting around and there are no women around – what's the main topic of conversation?

Probably women. [Laughs]

And what else, maybe?

Women. Sex. Drinking.

Sports?

Yeah. Here and there. But I think if the women aren't around, probably the talk is mostly about women.

Now, what about when you're in a group and it's mainly women. What sort of things do you talk about then?

If it's somebody you've had sex with, you'd probably talk about sex. Or if it's somebody you want to have sex with, you'll probably hint about sex. And if they like sports, depending on the sport, you can talk about the sport. Or kids. Because I know I talk to a lot of girls about my son if they've got a kid or whatever. But there's a lot of single parents in this day and age, so a lot of talk is about kids.

Okay. How often do you think about sex?

[Laughs] In an eight-hour day at work, I'd say probably 25 or 30 times.

Yeah. You're not unusual. [Laughter]

Finish this sentence: My biggest or greatest fear is ...

Not being a good father. That's the only thing I'm really worried about. That's why I give that my best shot. I don't really care what anybody else thinks, but I do care what my kid thinks about me. And so to me, everybody else may come and go, but he'll always be my kid. So therefore I'll always try to make him happy.

Are you circumcised?

Interview 4

Yup.

Is your son?

Yup.

When he was born, did they ask you at the hospital if you wanted it done or not?

Yeah, they did. Because I remember the day he was getting circumcised.

I see. When you get depressed or lonely, what sort of thing is it that puts you into that depressed mood?

Sometimes just walking outside, I guess. Just seeing how much the world has changed from 10 years ago. To be honest with you, in my opinion, the world isn't really getting any better. You know? And you've just got to look at it as one day – sooner or later – this society is just going to self destruct. I mean, think about it. Ten years ago, you never heard about guns and a shoot-up at a school, but now you hear about it twice a month. You know?

And you know who they usually are? Boys.

Yup.

That's another thought that occurred to me when I thought about doing this book. What is it about little boys that makes them do such violent things? Girls tend not to.

Yeah. I mean, just like the little boys who are going to prison for the rest of their life because they shot another kid. You don't hear about little girls doing that, though. You know? Or little boys want to try something they saw on TV, and then they end up hurting somebody seriously. So that's the thing. I mean, just how fast the world can change. And then for me, I've got a son who has to grow up in this world, in this day and age. Hopefully he looks at life like I do a lot. It doesn't matter what this person does or what that person says, you know what kind of person you are. Live off that.

And kids who are 14, 15 and 16 are out all night at parties, and their folks have no clue where they are. Mom and dad are too busy with their jobs and their socializing to notice and really know their kids.

That's another thing I don't believe in – being that wrapped up in your work that you can't talk to your kid. I've seen a lot of good kids go bad because of that.

All right. Moving on. Are you happy with the size of your penis?

Yup.

I think you said that earlier – or words to that effect. And that's why you wear the shoes three sizes too big. [Laughter]

"If it's all in your feet, it can't be in your meat!" [Laughter]

Growing Up Male In America

How do you define the concept of masculinity, or being a man?

It's being exactly your own man, I guess. Not what the next man should see you as or what he thinks you should be. It's all what you want to be. I mean, a lot of guys go to the weight room and they get big because they think it's the guy thing to do. You know? But that big guy could be probably the most sensitive guy in the world. He's probably getting that big just so he does intimidate you and you don't bother him. So I think it's just being your own man. Whatever makes *you* and what motivates *you*. That's what makes you a man, I think.

Now, you were raised without a father present, and your mom was the strong influence. Are there any men who are – and they can be in movies, they can be in politics, they can be anywhere – who have been role models for you?

My stepdad. My mom met him when I was 11, I think. And not once do I ever remember him saying, "Don't do this" or "Don't do that." If I had a question about anything, he would answer to the best of his ability. I mean, this guy came in and took care of seven other kids who weren't his. You know? To me, that's a big thing. Because guys nowadays, if you've got one kid – if the girl's had one kid – the guy doesn't want to be bothered with it. Or he'll be there but he won't take care of the kid. This guy busted his butt for 15 years taking care of us, making sure we looked nice when we went to school – no matter what he looked like or what he went through. And I don't remember him ever just saying, "This is wrong" or "That's wrong." He'd say, "You know right from wrong. You get into trouble, if I can get you out of it I will. If I can't, then you've got to deal with the consequences of it."

Where is he now?

Well, he and my mom split up, but he and I still talk, though. He and my mom actually still talk, too. Yup. He's a good guy. I mean, he'd never do much with us, but him just being there was enough. To know that if you had a question that you didn't want to ask your mom, you could go ask him. You know?

And also by having your mother such a strong influence, I think she helped you to understand and develop your feminine side, your sensitive side, your feelings.

Well, I think I've asked all the questions that I have. So thank you very much. I appreciate your willingness to do this.

No problem.

I enjoyed talking with you very much, and someday I hope to have the honor of meeting your son. If he's at all like his daddy, he must be a delightful kid.

Yeah. He's a real good kid.

Thank you.

Interview 4

Postscript – December 2001

This man is still enjoying his work at the printing company, and he is still devoted to being the best possible father for his son.

Interview 5

"He had a very bad temper when he drank."

This interview was conducted on December 2, 2000. He was 30 years old, 6 feet tall, 185 pounds with light brown hair.

Thanks very much for being willing to sit for this interview.

You're welcome.

I think we'll just start with your early life and go from there chronologically. What is the first thing you can remember?

The funny thing is, I don't have a lot of recollection of really early years. My mom remembers things in great detail. But probably the main memories that I have revolve around holidays. Like it's always the happy times that you remember the most.

Yes. That's often true.

Probably one of the first memories is Christmas at my grandmother's. The whole family would get together on Christmas Eve, and they'd always do dinner in the remodeled basement. Every year they had someone come in and play Santa Claus with jingling bells. And you could hear him stomping around and putting gifts upstairs while we were in the basement. They wouldn't let us go up there until he was gone. So that's probably one of the first memories.

How old were you when you learned about Santa Claus? That there wasn't one?

Oh, gosh.

Twenty-seven, you say?

[Laughter] I'm 30, and I'm still kind of not sure. I was probably six or seven.

But you always want it to continue, don't you?

Yeah. I mean, still to this day, Christmas is, like, the biggest thing for me. And it's just ... the whole, you know, the music, the decorations, the whole thing.

Growing Up Male In America

Are your folks both alive?

They are. I'm not very close with my father at all. My parents divorced when I was, like, four or five.

Oh, that early.

And I always pretty much lived with my mother. Except for a few years when I lived with my dad. Being so young when they divorced may be one of the reasons I have very few memories at all of them being married or of seeing them together. It's kind of strange. I asked my mom about this last weekend: "How old was I when you got divorced?" And she said she thought I was five. I thought it was even earlier than that.

Well, then, it makes sense that you wouldn't remember. And then they probably were not getting along too well, either.

Probably not.

So that takes you back to about three or four.

Yeah.

Did she remarry?

A couple of times. [Laughs]

Okay. So far, huh?

My mom's great. I have one sister, and that's it. Just the two of us kids. My mother and my sister and I are all really close. Growing up, it was always just the three of us. I mean, there was a man here or there in her life. [Laughs] But she got married twice after that. But then she had some long-term partners between those marriages.

Did you get along well with her other two husbands? Or were you out of the house by that time?

With the first one ... well, it's kind of funny. Because my sister ... my sister and I actually have different fathers. Although my father adopted her when they got married. But my mother married my sister's father – my sister's six years older – married him, had my sister, ended up getting divorced. Married my dad. Had me. Got divorced. Then married my sister's father again.

Wow! [Laughter]

And that marriage lasted a couple more years. And she realized it wasn't the smart idea to do it again, and so they got divorced. And I was pretty young at that point. The other person she was married to for 13 years. They just got divorced – oh, about six years, five years ago. And him I really didn't like. They got married in 1983. I was 13 at the time. And at the time they got married, I was living with my biological dad. My stepfather had a daughter, but he was never really around her much. Wasn't around children much. He was

Interview 5

retired from the Navy, had been in the Navy for 23 years. Didn't want children around. He made it really obvious. When my mom and her next husband first got married, as I said, I was living with my dad. And then she and her new husband moved to Virginia.

You mean the state?

The state of Virginia. Right. And at that time, I stayed with my father. A hard decision to make, because mom asked me if I wanted to go with them. It was probably April of 1983 when they moved to Virginia. I just wasn't happy to live with my dad. So the following Christmas of 1983 – I was going out to Virginia to visit for Christmas, and then I called my mom and said, "I want to stay in Virginia. I don't want to come back." So I ended moving to Virginia with them then. It was very obvious that the stepfather did not want me around at all. And it made life real difficult.

And you were about 13?

Thirteen. Yeah.

That's a difficult time in a young man's life, even in good circumstances.

Yeah. And I think because of it, it forced me to grow up a lot faster than I should have. Because I was always worried about not causing any trouble and not giving any reason for any kind of argument. Because I didn't want to be, you know, in the middle of him and my mother, arguing. So that kind of continued all along. I mean, there were some good times, but ... I can remember, he used to ... he was never physically abusive, but very verbally and mentally abusive. Eating dinner was always just a really tense time. And the things he'd say. And I can remember almost for – right after I moved in – for close to a month, I hardly ate anything at all. I dropped a ton of weight and just ... just ... the smell of food would make me sick. Just because it would bring back all these, you know, arguments and everything around the dinner table.

Were you a chubby kid?

Not really. I mean, to a degree, I've always kind of battled weight. But I wasn't really overweight. I mean, I probably carried ... I always probably carried, like, 10 pounds more than ... 10 to 15 pounds more than I should.

But not one of these seriously fat kids.

No.

Because that opens up another whole area for some kids. Going through puberty and before and they're really overweight.

Yeah. I mean, like I've said, I've always kind of battled weight. And I've always felt like I was a little overweight. And I've always been kind of insecure about that.

You're the right weight for your height about now, I suppose. What are you? About

Growing Up Male In America

175 or so?

About 185 now.

One-eight-five. Okay. Well, you're 10 pounds overweight!

Again! [Laughs] Again, I need to lose about 10 pounds! [Laughs] As I noticed this morning when I stepped on the scale at the gym.

Anyway, back to what we were talking about. This alienated feeling that you have with your biological dad, or let's say you just didn't get along. Have you ever confronted what it was about him and you that made the chemistry not work?

Yeah, pretty much. I didn't notice it so much when – well, of course I have very few memories of my mother and father being together, but like I said, I always lived with my mother, but would spend weekends with my dad. And he was always very good to me and my sister. I don't have any bad feelings toward him at all for any reason like that. But he is, or he was – and I guess you always are – an alcoholic. I never really saw it that bad. He had a couple of long-term girlfriends. He finally did remarry. But he had a very bad temper when he drank. And I can remember a couple of times – when I was at his house on the weekends and he was fighting with his girlfriend. I can remember a couple of times actually hiding his liquor. And that caused even more of an issue. And I think that's one of the biggest reasons that I rarely drink at all now. Hardly ever. You know. I'll have a glass of wine every now and then if I go out somewhere for dinner or whatever, but for the most part I really don't drink. He always drove truck for a living, and shortly after I moved to Virginia – probably 1984 or 1985 – that's when he was drinking heaviest, I think. And he got two DUIs within a very short time period. Lost his license. Spent three days in jail.

DUI while driving the truck?

No. He wasn't drinking at work. But because he lost his license and spent some time in jail, obviously he lost his job as a truck driver because he was without a license. So ever since then he's been working in a lumber yard, and he just seems to have no ambition. But I've pretty much done things consciously in my life not to end up like that.

Well, there is some evidence, isn't there, that there is a genetic weakness that causes it to run in generations?

I've heard that. Yeah. Early on, I would see him on a regular basis, every other weekend or whatever. But after I did move away, I'd go years without hearing anything from him. Like nothing at Christmas or birthdays. You know. Three or four years would go by, and then I'd finally hear something. And that happened all through high school. And it got to the point where I would have to be the one to initiate the contact. Which I was kind of getting tired of, after a while. It's, like, "You're the adult. You're the father."

Interview 5

Right.

I mean, he didn't even know where I lived for a while. I was in the Air Force for six years, and right when I got out I moved to New Jersey. And out of the blue, I got a call from him. I was living with a guy, in a relationship. And I got a call. And this [person I was living with] was a very jealous person. And I hear him on the phone. And he's angry and says, "Who's this? Who is it?" Then he gives the phone to me. "It's your dad." I hadn't heard from him at the point for probably three or four years. And what's really sad is he … well, the reason he called was because my grandmother had died. But what's really sad is, he had to call my grandfather here to find out where I was or how to get ahold of me. You know? And since I've been back in the Midwest, I've seen my dad a couple of times. I moved back about five years ago. But it's very uncomfortable being around him, just because we are so different and have so little to talk about.

Now, you identify yourself as a gay man?

Right.

About what time, in all of this – if ever – did you "come out" to him?

Actually, my dad is the only one that I'm not "out" to. He's remarried now. His wife knows. She basically came out and asked me if I was gay. "Well, yeah," I said. And his stepdaughter [laughs], she knows – she figured it out!

But since you see him so rarely, what's the point?

Exactly. That's it. I mean, he's kind of one of these macho hunter types. Into football. And I was never really into sports. When I was younger, he'd try to take me hunting a couple of times. Which, you know, I'd go. I liked traipsing through the woods, but I hated the "killing Bambi" part. But he's just like a "man's man" type guy.

Well, even if you did tell him and he didn't take it too well, what's the loss?

Exactly. So, I mean … I kind of want to tell him just to know that I've told that to everyone. Because I'm so open about it to everyone else.

Let's go with the gay thing a little bit.

I love being gay! [Laughs]

But you said you knew it all along.

I always kind of felt different, knew I was different from other boys. I was kind of attracted to the boys in class. And then growing up, it was watching TV. Watching the men. And then all through high school and going to the mall and sneaking a peek at the *Playgirl* magazine. [Laughs]

My first actual sexual experience was when I was 17. I was living in Virginia at the time. I met someone at the beach. He was down from New Jersey, and he was on his honeymoon. Being married to a lesbian. [Laughs] And her

Growing Up Male In America

female partner was along with them. She was one of his best friends, the lesbian. And she was having problems at work, I guess. People saying that she was gay and wasn't out or something. So marrying this guy was basically a marriage of convenience. They were on this supposed honeymoon with her partner. Anyway, I met him on the beach one day, and after watching him for hours, we finally started talking.

So he was a little older.

Yeah. I was 17. I think he was 21 or 22 at the time. So we talked for a while. The way it started was, he was asking me if there was a theatre nearby or something. And I said, "Sure. If you want, I'll come back later and I'll show you guys around a little bit." Because by this time I had met, you know, this lesbian friend of his. I didn't know they were married. I thought she was just some woman he was there with. And so I ended up going back to his room, and his wife and her lady friend left, and it was just him and me in the room. We ended up going to dinner and coming back, and things happened. My first sexual experience!

Was it good? Sometimes first times can be clumsy.

Yeah. Yeah. I mean, it was kind of clumsy just because it was the first time I had ever done this. I didn't know anyone else who was gay. I had no gay friends at all. I never really talked about that subject to anyone at all. Well, one person.

But he was experienced and knew what he was doing.

Yeah. And I wasn't uncomfortable, even though I didn't really know what I was doing so much. We didn't have intercourse. Actually that didn't happen until a couple of years later. But this first time was a good experience.

I think one of the advantages is you were attracted to him. It wasn't just somebody who kind of came on to you.

Yeah.

Which sometimes can happen with a kid your age.

Shifting gears a bit, now. What religion were you raised?

Lutheran, technically. But we didn't go to church much.

Okay. What nationalities are you composed of?

On my mother's side, it's Swedish and Norwegian. And then on my father's side, it's Irish and German.

When you think back to going to school as a little kid, in grade school, and feeling different, were you ever so different that kids treated you differently? Or did you fit in pretty well?

I think probably when I was younger, I think I fit in more. I played hockey

Interview 5

when I was really young. Played baseball for a little bit. And I think that's probably when my sports experience ended. [Laughs] Probably about age six or seven. So I don't remember, as far as my grade-school years, really feeling any different. But through junior and senior high school, that's when I definitely felt more of a kind of wall. And also, I never really had any really close friends when I was young. I mean, we moved around a lot. That made it hard to make those friendships. Because I know my mom has all these memories of being young, and she still has best friends from when she was in grade school. Which is amazing to me, because I never had that. But I didn't really feel that different. But through junior and senior high school, that's when I got teased. You know, being called gay.

I see. Did that hurt?

I did get some taunting. So obviously I must have been a little more obvious. [Laughs] But then again ... and I think part of it was being with the stepfather at that time, from 13 on. And that's part of the reason I didn't really make great attachment friendships. Things were so uncomfortable at home, I didn't really want to bring friends home. I had a next-door neighbor who I was really close with, a female friend, and her family became kind of a second family to me, because they kind of knew what was going on. Like, her mother and I were very close. And every time things got rough at my house, you know, I would go over there and hang out.

That was very generous and kind and perceptive of them.

Yes. So that made it easier. But, yeah. Like even through high school, I never really had close friendships.

Those you did have, were they more with girls than with guys?

Yeah. Most all of my long-term friends, or longer-term, have been with women. Girls.

I suppose getting to be too close a friend with a guy would challenge your secret, too. And all of a sudden, double dating would happen.

Probably. That's probably part of it. And also I think growing up with my mother and my sister – you know, being around women. By no means do I think that's why I'm gay.

I totally feel that I was born gay. I always felt that. But my friends, basically, when I was younger were my mom and my sister. And my mother's extended friends. With the women.

What kind of activities in high school, junior high? Sports ended about five years earlier.

Yeah. Sports ... I didn't do any sports at all in high school. I think athletic things were always kind of uncomfortable for me, and I was always tall for my age. And people always thought I was older. It's funny. When I was younger,

Growing Up Male In America

people always thought I was older. Now that I'm older, people always think that I'm younger. But, like, going through high school, because I was tall and a guy, I had all this pressure to be on the basketball team.

Oh, of course.

And as I said, I was terrible at sports. I knew I was. I wasn't interested in sports, I didn't want to do it. But, you know, I had teachers, I had coaches at school say, "Oh, you've got to play basketball." And I'm, like, "No." During gym, I was, like, the kid that's last picked. Because I just wasn't good at sports at that point. Wasn't interested in it at all.

So was the school big enough that you could have a choice of activities?

Yeah. Pretty much.

Like choir and theatre.

I was in choir, I think, for one year in junior high. In junior high, I never really got too involved in too many outside activities. Probably the main thing was, in junior and senior year, I got involved in the student council. And that I enjoyed. It was finally a way for me to kind of fit in. Like we did a couple of different events which I really enjoyed. We did a lip-sync contest in my junior year. And making the class sign as seniors. And the class float. Doing all that. So that was really the main extracurricular activity I had.

And you see, that was using your intellect and your social skills. And dribbling a basketball, you don't need intellect and you don't need social skills.

Yeah. Exactly.

So at this time, I'm sure you talked to other guys with similar interests, and they'd come through with the same kinds of stories. They also channeled their energies and talents through maybe not the most popular activities.

Yeah, that's true. And my mother's always been very, very creative. She's an interior decorator. So I definitely got more of a creative thing from her.

Did that bother you? That there seemed to be a missing link? You know, "This is a guy thing." And guys go out for the sports.

Kind of. I definitely remember feeling lonely a lot, both through junior and senior high school. Definitely I was feeling very lonely, very different.

How did you handle that? Did you spend a lot of time alone? Go for long walks? Did you have a confidante?

I was definitely more of a loner at that time. I mean, even still, to this day, I wouldn't consider myself a loner, but I still like being alone a lot. I'm single and live alone. I have a close friend who suggested we should move in together about a year and a half ago. And I'm, like, "I really like living alone." You know. If I was in a relationship with someone, that's totally different.

Interview 5

But this wasn't a relationship thing?

No. Just a friendship.

There are some people who are really freaked by living alone, or doing anything alone.

Yeah. Like even when I lived in New Jersey, I was in a relationship for about a year. And that's really ... well ... that's the first time I ever really technically, physically lived with someone who I was dating. And it was those issues of, having to compromise on how to decorate and what to do here and there. And I didn't like having to make that compromise. [Laughs] I mean at this point, now that I'm older, it's not that big of a thing. But still ... in a relationship, I don't mind doing that. But with a friendship thing it would be, like, "No. This is what I want. This is what I'm doing. This is how it should look."

Okay. After high school, you didn't go on to college but you went in the Air Force right away?

Yup. Kind of shocked everyone, including myself. [Laughter]

Something just drew you to the military life, huh?

Yup. So I went home and said, "Mom, guess what! I think I'm going to join the Air Force." She thought it was a great idea. I think more than anything, it was a way to get away from the bad situation with my stepfather. At the time I was in school, but I was working part time in a department store. And they had offered that when I graduated, I could work full time. I started out working in the stockroom. I split my time between there and the men's clothing department. They had offered that when I graduated, I'd be promoted to assistant manager in the stockroom. But I thought about this: Well, either I can work at the store or join the Air Force, and that will get me away from home. Away from this chaos that I've been dealing with.

Well, let's see. You were in the Air force for six years?

Six years.

You have to talk about that. I mean, a gay man in the Air Force. "Don't ask, don't tell" and all that. Now, first of all, you went in when you were how old?

Eighteen.

You were right out of high school? Okay.

Actually, I enlisted when I was still a senior in high school. So I was 18. I'd just turned 18, and I went on the delayed-enlistment plan. They call it delayed enlistment, where you're signed up but you don't leave, you don't go to schooling. Because basically you can pick what job you want, and it depends on what time they send you in. How I got doing what I did, I don't know. [Laughs]

Where'd they send you first? Lackland? Do they still do that?

[117]

Growing Up Male In America

Yeah. My training was in Texas, and my job title was radar operator. The job was really boring. But I did more later on. Even though I enlisted when I was still in high school, I didn't actually leave until November of 1988. So I was home the whole summer. So I went in in November of 1988. Went to Lackland for basic training, which lasted six weeks. And then technical school training, which I think was another six weeks, at an Air Force base in Mississippi. And then I got orders to Germany. Spent three years in Germany – which I loved.

Near any large cities?

That was the bad thing! [Laughs] Well, it wasn't near a city. It was way up north, right on the North Sea. The actual town we were in was close to Bremen, a big city. Kind of the flat farm land, not the pretty mountains and black forests that you think of when you think of Germany. But I loved Germany. A beautiful place. The country is the cleanest place I've ever been.

I was assigned to a mobile radar site. So we actually lived on an Army base and then had to take a bus about 45 minutes to get to our radar site. The radar operator, basically, would sit and track aircraft. So we had to play a lot of the war games. Go deploy to the field and tear down the radar from our site and set it up in the field.

Was this kind of fun, though? I mean, here you are, 18.

Well, kind of. Well, I did things I'd never dreamed I'd ever be doing. One of the things was they had this huge city-size bus that would come in. They made a couple of us in the dorm get trained on driving this bus, and I was one of the lucky few chosen to learn to drive this bus. [Laughter] So here I am, a 20-year-old gay boy driving this huge city-size bus through the cobblestone streets of Germany. Funny as can be. We went to Denmark a couple of times. Right outside of Amsterdam. I don't regret ever being in the Air Force, but I was very glad when I got out. The experience I got was very valuable. We'd have to carry M16s and crawl around in the dirt and play the war games. I was actually on what they called the Nuclear Biological Chemical Defense Team – where if it was a chemical-warfare thing, there was this team of people who would have to go out with gas masks and detect what it was or what type of agent it was and do the tests.

That sounds very sophisticated, and very demanding.

One thing about that that was really scary was the fact that when I was in Germany, the Gulf War was just starting up. And they had mobile radars down there that they were using. We didn't end up going, but we were on a "stand by".

That must have been a tense time for you.

Yeah.

I mean, war games are one thing.

Interview 5

It was scary enough just knowing that you're that close to possibly going.

Then you came back here? And where were you stationed?

I did a flip from being in Germany – where the gay life, even being in the Air Force, is totally open and very accepting – to Salt Lake City. So I thought I would just hate it, but then I got to enjoying it. Salt Lake's really not a bad place.

There's a Mormon or two in Salt Lake City, isn't there?

Just a couple. [Laughter] They definitely run the state. And at this time I was still a radar operator. So what we would do was, we'd go and evaluate radars all around the country and all around the world. I spent almost a month in Japan, evaluating the radar there.

Did any of this carry over into work in the non-military world? What kind of work are you doing now?

Actually, the work is totally different. When I first came out of the Air Force, the closest job would have been an air-traffic controller. But I really wasn't interested in that. So I ended up going into the hotel business, working in hotels. I started out working the front desk of a hotel and then doing some night-audit accounting work. And when I moved back here to Minneapolis, I went directly into the accounting office at a couple of the major hotels.

What preparation did you have for that? Or was that the learn-on-the job type?

Basically on the job.

Did you like what you were doing in the hotel business?

For the most part. But I'm not in hotels anymore. Now I'm working for a company doing merchandising.

Okay. Well, now. I want to jump back to the Air Force.

Sure.

I'd heard that basic training in the Air Force wasn't as rigorous as in some other branches of the military. Is that true?

It's not. I had no problem with it. It's more head games than anything. But I got through it as an honor graduate. On our base, an honor graduate.

Okay. Now here you are, a man who had a little difficulty with close friendships with men before your Air Force days. And now you're thrust into a nearly exclusively man's world. Did making friends and significant ones and deep friendships happen?

It did, but my closest friends were other gays in the military.

Okay. Which is what I was going to ask.

Yeah. It was actually kind of strange, because like I said, going into it ... obvi-

Growing Up Male In America

ously, when you enlist, they – at least at that point – they still had the question, "Are you gay?" I forget what the actual question was. Of course, I said "no." Checked "no" – knowing full well "yeah." Well actually, I later came to find out that my recruiter even knew I was gay. [Laughs] Which is kind of a really weird story which I still don't fully understand to this day. But going in, I kind of knew – not so much knew what to expect, but knew it could be an issue to a degree. I never really had any issues at all, though. As I said before, through high school, junior high, I was kind of teased now and then for being called gay or queer, and I don't really think I really acted effeminate. I don't think I do now. Looking back, actually, I think I did seem more effeminate in high school, but not consciously. Now, having just seen a video of my high-school graduation and a party afterwards, I'm just, like, "Oh, my god. How could they *not* know I was gay?" I'm flitting around here and there and oh, yeah. I was gay. But I don't know if I consciously did it or just subconsciously was just acting differently.

I had a friend when I was in Salt Lake City – a female friend – who knew I was gay. I met her at a gay bar. And we were good friends. Still are. She used to laugh because we'd go out to the clubs in Salt Lake City and dance, and I'd be my gay self. But then I'd go back to the base. And she'd say, "I could see a physical change in you the closer we got to the base. It's like you sit up straighter and you just kind of get this 'straight' look to you." [Laughs] So I don't know if I always did that from the time I went into the Air Force or not. I probably must have. I mean, even in the Air Force I heard an occasional comment from time to time. You know, a gay comment. But very rarely. My friendships were mainly with other gays in the military. It's kind of a like a little subcommunity within the Air Force. Like I said, all through high school and through my first experience, I never really had any gay friends. I had a cousin who was gay, and we talked about it. Like write letters back and forth and communicate that way, but he was the only person that I'd ever even communicated to in any way about the gay issue.

How old were you then?

When we met and had the first discussion about it, I was 14. He was 17 at the time, so he was a few years older. That's another whole long story, but I'm sure we can touch on that later.

We'll make a note of that.

But being in Germany was really the first time ... well, the first time I was out on my own, obviously, and then the first time I ever dealt with any kind of a gay community or had any gay friends. And being overseas, going into any bar or anywhere, really, it's so easy to spot an American. Or at least in Germany it is, or was at that time. Shortly after I got there, I made friends with someone who was German. His mother was full-blooded German, and he was born in Germany. And his father was American. So he was able to, you know, join the

Interview 5

U.S. Air Force. But his mother still lived in Germany. And I got to be friends with him and through time found out that he was gay. Well, he was fluent in German, obviously, with his mother being German. So the first gay bar I ever went to, he and I took a train into Bremen. And he had never been out there, either, but he had heard about this one bar. So we took the train and a taxi to this bar and, you know, we both walk in. And we're both, you know, probably about 19.

Now, you didn't wear your uniforms, did you?

No. Definitely not. You definitely don't wear the uniform. Well, we walk into this bar, and it ended up being some kind of leather bar. And, you know, first we were the youngest things in there and just didn't fit in. We had on our little disco clothes, ready to go dancing, but everyone's in leather, and they just kind of look at us like, "What the hell!" So we're, like, "Okay. We're going to have one drink and we're out of here." So we had, like, a glass of wine and asked the bartender, you know, if there are any other bars nearby. He told us about this other bar, so we went there, and it kind of became our hangout. But then, you know, being in a foreign country, it's very easy to spot Americans. And if you're in a gay bar and you see an American, chances are he's military. So I had, you know, quite a few friends over there, both Air Force and Army, who were gay, and those guys became my closest friendships. I mean, I was friends with some of the straight men I worked with, too, but the closest friends were gay. Actually, my best friend when I was there was a woman who was in the Army. She lived in the dorm next to me. We became best friends and were always together.

Good. And that probably became the deepest kind of friendships that you had had ever in your life.

Yeah. Definitely.

Lasting? Do you keep in touch?

Unfortunately, no.

Speaking of friendships, I think even in high school, I was closer with some of the teachers than I was with some of the students. Growing up, people always thought I was older, so my friends were always older. I don't think I was smarter than anyone else, but I kind of had a higher intellectual connection with older people. And I just always migrated that way.

I've heard that from more gay guys, that they found themselves bored by a lot of their fellow students.

That's part of it. In high school and even moreso, I think, in the military, one thing I found and noticed with other gay people I have known is that you almost become an overachiever in order to prove to yourself that, yeah, if someone does find out I'm gay, you know, they may be against that, but you'll

Growing Up Male In America

have all this that you've accomplished to balance that out. I know I did that all through the Air Force. Several different times I was "Airman of the Quarter." Made "Airman of the Year" when I was in Utah. Probably 1992 or 1993. "Airman of the Year" both for our unit and then our higher headquarters in Florida. And I noticed that overachievement with a lot of other of my gay friends. We were getting the awards and were the overachievers, striving to prove ourselves.

I see. I don't know what it is about teachers, but gay students tend to seek out gay or more "understanding" ones. And they strike up a kinship. That's very nice.

Yeah. Like I can think of three teachers who were special. I can hardly remember the names of any friends or acquaintances in high school, but I remember the teachers' names. You know, I would go to their classrooms after school, and we'd sit and talk for quite a while. And I was closer friends with them than I was with most of my fellow students.

And you maybe never thought of it, but if you could turn that around, you were probably a great, significant part of those teachers' lives, too. They respected you and probably enjoyed those times very, very much. So here's your assignment, now. You must make contact with those teachers and tell them how important they were to you in those high-school years.

I remember one in particular. She was so much fun.

She's probably still teaching.

Probably. Another thing: I think she kind of reminded me of my mom. My mom's very outgoing and kind of crazy and can talk to anyone. I still have a hard time striking up a conversation with someone [new]. I've always had a problem with approaching people. Especially people I'm interested in, more than anything – but with anyone, really. Whereas my mother can strike up a conversation with anyone. It's just amazing to me. And she's kind of wacky and does kind of funny, wacky things, and I think I saw some of that in this favorite teacher, as well.

When did you first fall in love? Let's go beyond "having a crush" or being interested in somebody and flirting and all that. When did something really develop into love?

Well, let me see. Love. When I was in Germany, I had this very strange relationship with a German man. A very unhealthy relationship. When I met him, he was supposedly breaking up or had broken up with his partner. So we got a little involved – and then I found out that, no, they hadn't really broken up or they'd gotten back together. But yet he was still seeing me on the side. It was a really strange thing. But anyway, I think that man was definitely the first one I more than had a crush on. I'd call it love. And we weren't really ever even together sexually. But this went on for probably about a year and a half, and these feelings for him were very deep and intense.

Interview 5

Did he ever break up completely with his former partner?

No.

So you were always the "other man"?

Yeah. So, very unhealthy. As I said, I was probably 20 at that time. Nineteen or 20.

Any men you've been in love with since then?

[Pause] Yes. When I was in Utah, I was in a relationship for about nine months with someone who I could definitely say I was in love with. Again, it was another unhealthy relationship. I was probably 22 when we met. He was 29. Had a seven-year-old son, and he had been in a seven- or eight-year relationship with another man. And that relationship had ended a couple of months before we met. Well, these two guys also had a baby daughter together. They arranged for a lesbian couple – friends of theirs – to have this child, but he and his partner had full custody of her. So this other guy was always kind of involved, you know, as far as seeing this baby. And he supported her. He was very jealous of me and wanted to get back together with his former partner, so it was always a very tense situation. But we were together for nine months.

And then when I was in New Jersey, I was in a relationship for about a year. I thought I was in love. But … [pause] … I think I loved him, but it got to the point where I didn't like him anymore. I didn't like, you know, the type of person he was and so it just didn't work out.

You get a little gun-shy after a while, don't you? I don't know if it's easier, when you're younger, to jump in and jump out of relationships. But you get a little older and ask yourself, "Do I really want to go through all this again and risk that this, too, will not work out?"

Yeah.

But look at it the other side. The glass is half full or half empty. You had a wonderful year, a wonderful nine months.

Yeah.

So. Did you ever have sex with a woman?

Nope. Never.

Okay.

In high school, I had two girlfriends. [Laughter] And even then I knew I was gay. So, no. It was kind of just the pressure of, you know, "You have to have a girlfriend." When I first moved there, moved in with my mother, my first real friend was the daughter of a coworker of my mom's who she kind of tried to fix me up with when I moved out there. "Oh, you have to meet this girl. Take her out." So we dated for a couple of months. The only thing that ever happened was a kiss, and I can remember being uncomfortable then.

Growing Up Male In America

Did the young lady ever push it? Did she want more than a kiss?

Not really.

It must be difficult to be bisexual. Because whenever it gets a little too tense and uncomfortable in one corner, you can always jump into the other corner, and it can be a little cooler for a while. And yet, maybe that's more difficult. I don't know. But as you said early on, you knew from the beginning that you were exclusively gay.

Yeah.

Let's see, now. Let me go to some random questions. Just give your immediate response.

Where did you learn the most about sex? By the way, if some of these questions seem like they're kind of heavy on sex, it's because I think that that is a defining thing about our humanity.

Oh, yeah. I agree. It is.

A lot of people don't think so, but maybe they're in denial. [Laughter] *Anyway, where did you learn most about sex? Friends? Parents? Siblings? Internet? Books? Movies?*

Probably movies, I guess. I never really talked about sex with my parents.

They never sat you down and had "the talk"?

I don't think so. I think I was always just kind of more mature and more aware of things. I would watch art movies. I also learned some things about sex from friends.

Did you go to the library and get books? Because if you didn't have close friendships in high school, you probably were somewhat uncomfortable talking about such private things.

I can remember going to the mall bookstore and seeing books like The Joy of Sex.

But it's a very open time at this point in history, isn't it? You ought to try … no, I don't recommend it! [Laughter] *Try growing up when I did. I was a teenager in the 1950s. People then just didn't talk about sex. It was all very hidden.*

Next questions: What's your greatest or biggest fear?

Probably not having a relationship with someone. Not having anyone to share my life with. My 30th birthday was kind of hard for me. Not that I really minded the age 30, but just that I kind of had these goals, per se, set for myself. You know, by the time I'm 30, I wanted to, have a nice car, have a nice enough home, have a relationship. And you know. Thirty rolls around, and I had a really crap car that was falling apart. I was living in a studio apartment that was really small. I wasn't dating anyone. So I'm, like, "Uh! I'm 30 years old. I've been out as a gay man since I was 17, and the longest relationship I've had has

Interview 5

been a year. What's wrong with this?" So, yeah. I think the biggest thing that scares me is that I'm never going to find someone.

Okay. Despite the fact that you don't mind living alone, right?

Well, I don't mind living alone, but I really like being in a relationship.

Okay. Next question: When you get lonely or depressed or down-in-the-dumps or "blue," what, typically, causes that? And the second part of the question is, what do you do to make it better? What's your best escape from being "down"?

[Pause] I've been depressed with work a lot. [Laughs] It's been very stressing lately. I've been really down about that. Um … I think it is being alone. As I said, I enjoy living alone, but I guess not having someone in my life, that's a downer. I go out, every weekend, out dancing. And people see me out having fun and having a good time, and I think they get this misconception that I'm this crazy "party-er" and that's all I ever do. And that's fine. I'm doing that now, because I am single. But I'd much rather be, watching a movie with a partner. So I go out and see all these people, these couples together. And then I go home to an empty house. Go home alone. And sometimes that just gets me down. I just think, you know, "Hello! What's wrong with me? Why am I alone still?" And so, most of the times I get depressed it's over that.

But what you don't do *is stay home and continue to say, "I'm alone. Nobody likes me. I have no one" and feel self pity. You go out and get involved*

Yeah. I go through phases where I'll think, "Oh, poor, poor me. I don't want to see anyone. I don't want to talk to anyone. I don't even want to think about it." But that only lasts a little bit before I have to get out and dance. You know? Music's a big thing for me.

Do you play a musical instrument?

I don't play anything.

You're a good singer, though?

Aw. God. Only if it's a really loud bar and you really can't hear me at all. [Laughter] I'm singing everything, but not well. Actually, when I was young, I did play clarinet for about a year. But never really pursued it past that. But, yeah. I have a huge CD collection, and I'll just start out with, you know, the "sad" songs. Love songs. And finally say, "Enough of this," and I put on something faster.

What kind of music?

It's pretty eclectic. Growing up – and people think this is crazy, especially because I'm gay [laughs] – but growing up, all I ever really listened to was country until I was probably about 12. Like, all my dad ever listened to was country. So growing up, that was the biggest thing. And then when I was 12 or 13, I got more into pop. That's when Madonna came along. I love Madonna. I

Growing Up Male In America

love most of the "top 40" pop as such. You know, danceable music.

Do you ever go back into the 1940s and the big-band era of the 1930s and 1940s? Swing? Glenn Miller?

I liked hearing it. And my mom really likes that type of music. My mom really likes big bands, swing-type stuff.

Sinatra?

Yeah.

Some of the old standards.

Yeah. I enjoyed that. I don't think I own any of it. I've got a couple of classical CDs. Pachelbel's *Canon* I'll put on to just to relax. I've kind of gotten into Latin music lately. It's one of the things I want to do, is I want to learn Spanish. I have a lot of Latin friends, and I've dated a couple of Latin people here and there, and I'm, like, "I want to know what you people are saying about me. Really." So I've always wanted to learn Spanish, so that's one of my goals. And I love Latin music. They have the whole rhythm and everything.

And you say you have dated Ricky Martin? But he can't talk about it? [Laughter]

Yeah. You know, we keep it quiet and ...

Yeah, well, that's okay. I won't tell.

He knows I'm here doing this interview, though. [Laughs]

Okay. If you don't mind saying, what's the most embarrassing thing you have ever done? The thing that keeps coming back to haunt you, saying, "Oh, my god! Why did I say that? Do that?" You know?

Well, the one my mother or anyone else never let's me forget is I got a ticket for urinating in public. But there's a whole story behind it! [Laughs]

Well, go ahead!

Oh, my mother loves this now. She didn't at the time, but she loves reveling in the story, now. It was probably – I think I must have been in 10th grade, because the friend I was with was in 12th. We had been at a high-school football game. And I had gone to a football game with this one guy who I had this huge crush on, and somehow we'd gotten some alcohol. I don't even know what it was. You know, something you mix with Kool Aid. So, there was a little pond behind the football stadium, and we were sitting out at this pond with a couple of people, drinking this stuff. And I just got blotto. Well, I was young, so I didn't drink much anyhow. It just totally blew me out. So. Then we were driving around in this guy's car. And there I was, about 16, totally wasted. And my friend saw this girl that he wanted to hook up with. Because he was just as straight as they came – damn it!

Sorry!

Interview 5

And so he says, "I gotta go talk to this girl. I've got to go talk to this girl. I'm going to let you out here. I'm just going to drive around with her a little bit, and I'll be back in five minutes." So he dropped me off at this 7–11 convenience store. Drunk as I was. Well, I had to go to the bathroom really bad. I have a very small bladder, which curses me all the time. And I'm in the 7–11, and either they didn't have one or it was busy or something, I don't know. It was about midnight, I guess, and it was really dark out. So I went out around the building. So here I'm behind the building, and I peed on a dumpster, facing the wall. I finished, and all of a sudden there's a spotlight on me and there's a cop down the street. He hauls me over asks, "What are you doing?" He asked if I'd been drinking. "No, no. I haven't been drinking." I could barely stand. So being a cop, he had to take my information down. The cop let me go, but he writes me this ticket. And I'm supposed to appear in court for this. I'm terrified to tell my mom about this, so I wait until the very last minute … until the day before the court date. So the night before, I come out with my tail between my legs and hand her this ticket, and she's, like, "What's this?" She was supposed to be at a work meeting the next day three hours away, and she had to cancel it in order to go to court with me. So we had to go to court and sit there all day long. We were the last case they called. The judge looked at it and noted that the ticket was for "peeing in public" as a moving violation. So it ended up I had to pay a fine and I had to write an essay about responsibility or something like that. So my mom didn't like that at the time, but now she just loves telling that story about my big criminal activity.

Moving on: Is there one person, at this point in your life, who is your closest confidante – friend, lover or former lover, could-be lover, whatever – with whom you share everything?

Yeah. My best friend, who lives in Florida. I met him when I lived in New Jersey seven years ago. I met him at a bar. We became really good friends. And, you know, he was still there when I moved back here. He and his partner moved to Florida and bought a house down there. But ever since I moved back here, we've kept in touch. We talk at least once a month. Usually every two or three weeks, I'll call or he'll call. He was kind of like the mother hen, you know. He was always mothering me or, you know, scolding me for doing something or, you know, wants to hear about things like who I've been out with.

Is he a little bit older?

Maybe about a year or so, but basically the same age. But we're very close. He's, one of those people who has always been there, and always if something goes wrong, I'll call him. Or when I'm upset about a breakup, I'll call him.

How wonderful.

Yeah. I mean, he's a person who always remembers birthdays. Always will send a card. He sent me a card for buying a new car. Wherever he even found a

Growing Up Male In America

new-car card, I don't know, but he did. He called me a couple of weeks ago and said that, his partner had just redone their wills and that he listed me in his will.

I think a lot of us have these really older friends who have helped us through the things they've been through.

We've already talked about some fears. Do you ever have any fear – when you get involved with someone, of being – oh, any number of these things: inadequate, not good looking, inexperienced, clumsy. What if I can't perform? What if, what if, what if?

Yeah.

What's the nature of that?

I've always been very insecure, anyhow. From looks to just anything, really. And I think even more than that, I've had a lot of bad experiences where I've been with someone who has cheated or been running around. And I've denied it for months. But then you always think, "Well, if they're with me, why are they going to someone else?" You know? "Why? Am I not good enough for you?" Or, "What am I lacking that you're going looking elsewhere?"

Do you ever wonder, in the middle of sex, if your partner is enjoying it? Especially if it's somebody you just met and this is the first time or the second time.

Yeah.

And it's hard to talk to that person at that point.

Yeah. Yeah. I've had that situation. And, you know, I've had the situation where before anything starts and we're taking clothes off, I think, "Okay. I've got this extra five or 10 pounds I've tried to hide while I'm wearing clothes, but now he's going to see it all. He's going to look at my body and say, 'Oh, gotta go. Bye-bye!'" So that's a big concern of mine.

But they don't leave, do they?

No.

No, of course not.

But I always still have that insecurity. Even if I didn't have an ounce extra, I'm sure I'd still feel that way.

That is my next question. How do you feel about your body? And you just pretty much answered it. You know, most gay guys look much better than straight guys, in general. They have to.

[Laughs] It's a dog-eat-dog world out there!

It's not easy. And nobody loves you when you're old and gay. That's a play on words from an old song. Regarding your body, what needs improvement?

I think I've always been pretty insecure about my body. The only part of my

Interview 5

body I've always really been happy with have been my legs. My legs have always been in pretty good shape. Moreso now than at any time, I think, because of all the dancing that I do. I did some biking a couple of years ago. Actually, I did the AIDS bike ride to Chicago three years ago. And I got three awards in swimming classes. I never minded wearing shorts, but I'd be terrified to take my shirt off. "No, I'm not taking that shirt off." Basically I need toning everywhere. I'm intimidated by weights. I don't know what I'm doing enough, and I get intimated by all those buff guys lifting those huge weights, and I've got this little 50-pound thing. My workouts are mainly aerobic.

Don't you use the machines?

Yes, I do the machines. But I don't do as much weight work as I should. I go through phases where I'll go to the gym, and then I won't go for months on end. And then I'll notice I've put 10 pounds back on, and I go to the gym again.

Are you pleased with the size of your penis? Would you call yourself average, under, over?

I'd say I'm average.

So that's not ever been a problem. Like, "Gee, I'm kind of little."

I mean, I'm insecure about it. I don't think I'm small, but I definitely have those insecurities sometimes.

You're circumcised, aren't you?

Yeah.

I'll bet in Germany you found quite the opposite.

Yeah.

Okay. I was wondering: what do you see yourself being or doing in 20 years, when you're nearing 50 years of age? Where do you want to be? At what place?

Well, you know, I like my job enough. I'm good in finance. And I've done it, you know, for so long, I'll probably keep doing it. But I've always wanted a more creative job. Like when I was working with the AIDS ride. I chaired a committee that did different events and planned different parties. I really enjoyed event planning, and I always thought about pursuing something along that line. But I just never have yet. And now I've got the job and the security here.

Especially you have your mother in the background, and she's creative.

Exactly. She's so creative.

And she's happy doing what she's doing, I assume?

Right. A decorator until death, she will be. I've thought about going back to school, too. From being in the Air Force, I have money from the GI Bill to use

Growing Up Male In America

for schooling, but I just don't know if I want to make a huge direction change. And if I do, it's like starting all over again, at the low-pay range. I'd be stepping down from where I'm at now.

That's the trouble with creative, artistic jobs. They don't pay.

Exactly. Not that money's all that important to me. If I have it, I spend it. [Laughs] I would never hook up with a guy just because he had money. I have a lot of friends, who are looking for a Sugar Daddy. It makes no difference to me how much money someone makes. In fact, when I was in a relationship for a year, in New Jersey, I basically supported him. He was going back to school to be a hair stylist and was working a small part-time job that paid very little. I had no problem with that.

But at the same time – thanks to my mother – I have pretty expensive tastes. Just growing up, we always had nice things around. We were definitely not wealthy, but she always worked the extra hours she had to to have nice things. And I've got the same kind of taste as she does. So because of that, I need to be making somewhat decent money. Another thing about my future is that I also hope to be in a relationship. You know, 10 or 20 years down the line, I want to be with someone. I'm an affectionate person by nature, so I need to be able to express that.

I suppose you want to get to the point in a relationship where you finish each other's sentences? You see that with people who know each other very well.

Yeah.

It's so sweet, when you see people who have been together for a long, long time. The only sad thing about that is that one of them's going to die before the other, and then the surviving person is lonely again. But think of all the good times they've had in the interim!

Definitely.

Okay. Shifting gears, here. Were you ever shy about being naked in the locker room, either in school or at the present time?

Oh, yes. I think for one reason: the fact that I always felt a little bit overweight. And then, again, having the gay feelings, and it's, like, "Whoa! What if something happens? What if something pops up that shouldn't?" And also, "What if they see me looking too much?" You know? What's going to happen? So, yeah. Definitely.

It's amazing how we make it through adolescence at all, isn't it? Gay guys in particular – always being truly an outsider. It's difficult enough just being an adolescent.

Yup. Definitely.

Okay. How frequently do you masturbate?

Interview 5

Oh ... three or four times a week.

Okay. Some of these questions are for straight guys. Do you ever notice the size of other guys' penises in the showers? And at the urinal?

Oh, yeah! [Laughs]

I thought that would be a wasted question, here. [Laughs]

Is there anything about your biological dad that you admire? I mean, he has his problems, and you're conflicted quite a little bit, but ...

You know, I think ... deep down, he has a really good heart. You know. Like even when I see him now – the few times that I do – it always really hurts me that he seems so alone. Even though he's remarried, and that's kind of a weird relationship. A very strange marriage. But he just seems like a very lonely person, and I know things really hurt him a lot.

Was he ever very disclosing to you?

Not really. I think he holds his feelings in more than he ever opens up. He was an only child, and I think he was really close to his dad, my grandfather, who died when I was six or seven. The two of them were very close. I don't think he was ever close to his mother. And he closed in even more when my grandfather died. So I don't think he ever really got his emotions out. And his mother was very religious, so that prevented any freedom to let his emotions show even more. I mean, with me, he'd always give me hugs and kisses when I was a kid, but I think he held a lot in.

Do you think this is a condition of straight men?

I do.

I think gay guys with their feminine side let their emotions out more.

And I think straight men are so worried about either being conceived as gay or weak. Just sitting at work every day, it just makes me chuckle. I say so often that if there were no sports, straight men would have nothing to talk to each other about. That's all I ever hear them talking about. It's just amazing. [Laughs] It's kind of funny.

How true that is. And I've always thought how very homoerotic it all is. That a big thrill for a lot of straight guys is going in the locker room to see the players in various stages of undress. And when some player has an injury, the straight guys will talk for hours about his groin muscle or his ankle or his shoulder – all this interest and attention in these players' bodies.

Yeah.

In a way, that's one focus of this book. Why do straight men "worship" their jock gods?

Yeah.

[131]

Growing Up Male In America

And I think it should be good reading, perhaps holding a mirror up to oneself. Just think how, if your interview makes it into the book and some kid who's 11 or 12 and he thinks he might be gay and he feels so alone, and then he will read about your experiences and he won't feel so odd, so different.

Yeah. I mean, growing up, I never had the one person I could talk to except my cousin. And even then, that was only in a superficial sort of way. When I was a little older, I did some briefings and stuff with a gay youth group. It just was amazing to me, even then, how much more open they were and how much better things were for them than they were for me. They had this outlet that I never had, and they had somebody they could go to, even if they couldn't go to their parents. Or if they did come out to their parents and there were bad things, they had this one outlet or this one support system.

Right. It's wonderfully different today.

Right. The books that are out now and the Internet and all that.

And the talk shows. It's all out there, discussed openly. We have TV shows with gay characters of substance and not ridicule.

I love *Will and Grace*.

I think it's so well written. And one of the writers is gay, so that's a nice perspective. But just think back when Lucy and Ricky Ricardo were sleeping in separate twin beds and you couldn't use the word pregnant, and any gay character was for comic relief, not taken seriously.

It still cracks me up when I see that, with two different beds.

I think how sad and lonely the current older generation of gay people must have been in the 1940s and 1950s. Not to have anybody to talk to, and sneaking into dark and dank little gay bars, fears of being seen in or near bars, afraid of losing their job and all the rest of it.

When were you born?

February 11, 1970.

And your mother is how old?

Fifth-three or 54.

Dad's about the same?

A couple of years old than her. Like two or three years, I think.

And I'll bet your mother doesn't act like what some people expect a 53-year-old to act like.

Oh, god, no. And my grandmother – my mother's mother – is 20 years older, so she's 73 or 74.

And just full of life.

Interview 5

She's a riot. When I did this AIDS ride, when I was doing this public-relations committee work, one of the events that we did was a ballroom dancing event. Just to kind of get riders together before the ride, to meet each other. So I invited my mom and my grandmother to come to this ballroom dancing thing. I thought they'd enjoy it. My grandmother danced all night long, with guys younger than I am. Here I am, walking around with my mom and watching my grandmother. And I said, "Mom ... look. Grandma's got a boyfriend, and I don't!" [Laughs]

It's not fair!

And, you know, it's like with half of my friends who have met my mom, if I haven't seen them for a while, before they even ask how I am, they'll ask how my mom is. Like, I can remember when I was in Salt Lake City, when I was in this relationship for nine months and I was in the Air Force. Technically I was living on base, but half the time I was living with this person I was involved with. My mom knew I spent time there at his place, but I still wasn't out to her yet, officially. But I remember, I was in the kitchen, cooking, when the phone rang and my partner picked it up and talked for a while. I didn't think anything of it. I'm still cooking, you know. Five, 10, 15 minutes later, he's still talking. And I finally asked him, "Who is it?" "Oh, it's your mom." I'm, like, "Was she ever going to ask to talk to me?" [Laughs] And she didn't even know. I mean, I think she probably figured out that we were together. But as far as she technically knew, he and I were just friends. And here she's spending 10, 15 minutes talking to him. Doesn't ask where I am. She's just a ... she's a riot.

Yeah. She sounds like a lot of fun. Just think, what if you had had a situation where you didn't get along with your mother – if she was some stony, cold fish. And there you'd be, stuck in the middle of your loneliness and your feeling-different-ness. And with no one to share things with.

I know. My mom's the type of person who always has to have a man in her life. I noticed that while she was going through the divorce. It was very obvious. And I know she doesn't do it intentionally, but when she starts a new relationship, she lets everything else go by the wayside, including family. I remember once when she was dating someone, the same thing was happening. Two friends of hers who were always there for her when she was dealing with the divorce and having a hard time, when she started a new relationship – she never saw them. And she wasn't even talking to me because she had to spend all this time with this person. And I'm thinking, "This isn't right." And at that time my sister was in Japan, because my brother-in-law was in the Air Force. So I'd call my sister and we'd talk, and one of the conversations was like, "When did we become the parents?" You know? It's like I feel like I'm watching over my mom now. [Laughs]

Interesting.

Yeah. But I mean, it's obvious that she just can't be alone.

Growing Up Male In America

Now, where does a woman of 53 meet guys? In her work? Because many of them would be gay, you would think.

I don't know. But she can go anywhere and just meet people.

Whenever you feel you're going to get old and have no one, just look to mom!

Look to her. Exactly.

Well, we're coming to the end of this interview. Is there anything else you want to talk about which we haven't covered? We've talked about growing up where you are now. We've talked about being a gay man in the new millennium, and before. [Laughs] And the military experience and family and friends – and hopes and fears and frustrations.

There is one thing. I met R—, a nephew of my stepfather's, when I was about 14. We lived out East then, and he lived in Kansas. My mom, stepfather and I were on a road trip to Denver, and we stopped over in Kansas. So that's when I met R—. He was about three years older than me. As I said, even then I knew that I was gay. I can remember being attracted to him but never for an instant thought he was gay.

Oh. That was a question I had.

We were there for one night, and R— took me to a roller rink or somewhere. And he introduced me to some girls, so I never for a second thought he'd be gay. But you know, we just kind of hit if off and had a good time. So after that trip to Denver, R— and I kept in touch. We'd write and we'd call every now and then. R— was going to come up the following summer to visit us. But through his letters, more and more, there'd be, like, hints here and there – kind of trying to test me to see if I was different. Things about being gay. But I know his comments started out real slow as far as testing me to see how I'd react to it. To the point where once he talked about having a friend who was gay. R— said that he wasn't, but he had this friend who was gay. R— said he spent a weekend with this gay friend, but nothing happened. And then, well … something happened between R— and this other guy – and now he thinks he's gay, too. And I said, "Well, I think I am, too." So now it was out in the open between R— and me.

We kept writing and calling back and forth, and then we started having feelings for each other. And we said that when he came to visit, we'd be together. This went on for several months. And then I got a call from him one night, and he told me that his mother had found out he's gay and that she had told his uncle, my stepfather. They forbade him to talk to me anymore, and they made him go to counseling. The way they found out was that my stepfather had found a letter in my room from R—. I didn't realize this until then, but my stepfather used to go through the things in my room. So that's how he found these letters from R—. Basically, the letters clearly showed that both R— and I were gay. My stepfather really never dealt with the issue with me at all. I found out later –

Interview 5

after I came out to my mother – that he had lied to her about a lot of it. But after he found out that his favorite nephew was gay, he immediately called his sister and told her all about it. My stepfather basically disowned R— at this point. Supposedly his favorite nephew. Totally disowned him because he was gay. He told R—, "Don't ever talk to me again."

So from that point on, I knew very well how my stepfather felt about the gay issue. And yet he never really had any conversation with me about it. Nor did my mother. And I don't know exactly what he ever told her. I mean, he told her something about R—. But he hid the whole issue about and me and R—, for whatever reason. I decided not to push it or bring it up because I was in high school, then, and living at home. And even after I had moved out and was in the Air Force, I still never broached the subject because I didn't want it to be an issue between him and my mother. I didn't want to put her in the middle again, because a lot of times she was in the middle. So I think she knew about me all through high school, how bad things were and the way he treated me. I could see her conflicted feelings and her feeling bad and feeling guilty. But at the same time, he was her security. She had to have a man in her life and didn't want to lose the marriage. So that's why I never really said anything.

I always knew my mother and my sister would have no issue with it. I knew they would be fine. I knew they pretty much knew. Like with the talk shows? If there'd be a TV talk show about a gay issue and I'd be watching with my mom, she'd make comments like, "What's the big deal? People are just so intolerant." She was hinting. You know. Trying to push me to say something.

And to let you know that you had nothing to worry about.

Right. So I never thought there would be any bad feelings there. But I didn't want it to be officially out in the open, where she'd have to confront it with my stepfather. So I didn't officially come out to her until I was out of the Air Force and I moved to New Jersey. I had moved back in with them for a couple of months until I moved into my own place. I had been out one night – I don't even know what happened – but I came back and was really unhappy. It was around midnight, and I was sitting downstairs watching TV. My mom had been in bed, but she came down and sat next to me, and she could see I was unhappy. She asked, "What's going on? You look unhappy. What's happening?" And then I have the big, gay drama scene! I break down in tears and tell her "I'm not happy, Mom! I'm not! I'm gay!" And she said, "Yeah? So what's the problem?" [Laughs] And I'm, like, "What do you mean, what's the problem?" [Laughs] She's really the only one I've ever come out to, because she basically handled it with the rest of the family.

Is she content and happy to talk about gay matters with you? About dating, relationships, if you're in love?

She's tried to fix me up with guys now and then. [Laughs] She's trying to fix me up now, actually.

Growing Up Male In America

What a mother!

Yeah. She's totally open and always asks if I'm dating someone.

That's very nice.

Last Thanksgiving, she said, "I thought maybe you'd like to bring someone with you." And I said, "No. I haven't been seeing anyone – and my other friends have things to do."

Well, moms always want their boys – their gay boys, especially – to be happy. And how wonderful that you have her. By the way, did you stay in contact with R—, your cousin – the one your stepfather disowned?

Well, I did. I was probably 15 when all this happened, when everything blew up. As I said, they'd forbidden him to talk to me again. I didn't hear anything from him for a long time. Then shortly after I turned 18, I got a phone call. My mother answered the phone, and she was carrying on a long conversation. And I asked "Well, who is it?" And she said, "It's R—." My cousin. I could see my stepfather kind of bristle. And I said, "Okay." And I talked to R— and he said, "Well, I figured you're 18 now, and they can't tell you what to say or do anymore. So I want to see how you're doing." We kept in touch after that for quite a while.

Good for R—!

Yeah.

Do you still keep in touch now?

I haven't talked to him for a while. It's been quite a while.

But you were on the edge of a crush on him at that point. So what happened?

Nothing happened there. And actually, I've only seen him once, other than the first time we met. I mean, we had talked so much by phone and by letter, but when I got in contact with him again when I was 18, he was living in Ohio and was in a relationship. The only other thing my stepfather ever said about him was that they had found out that he was HIV positive. I could almost see it in my stepfather's eyes: "I told you so." Or "That's what you get" or something like that. Of course, I felt just horrible. Because even though there was no relationship between us, this was someone I really cared about. This was the only person I was ever really able to talk to about these feelings. A few years later he came and visited for a while.

How's he doing?

Good. He's been really healthy. At one point, he had bouts of sickness and the doctors were doing some experimental drug testing. But, yeah – he's really been doing well.

You're healthy, aren't you? HIV negative?

Interview 5

Yeah.

You heeded all the right advice, apparently.

I guess so. Yeah.

You've had, I suppose, your share of friends or acquaintances who have died?

Some of the people I know are infected. I had one friend in Salt Lake City who's passed away. But the other people I know ... like one of my best friends here, now, has been positive for several years and has never really been sick.

I hear that's happening more and more. Improved medications.

Which is really lucky. Yeah. That's really good to see.

But back a decade or two ago, a friend of mine in San Francisco said that he was sometimes going to two and three funerals a week!

Yeah.

Well. We're at the end of this interview. I can't tell you how grateful I am that you were willing to sit and share so many of your experiences with me.

I've really enjoyed it.

Thanks again.

Postscript – December 2001

Nearing age 32, this man has changed jobs due to downsizing in his former one. He still works out at the gym, loves to dance and party, and is still searching for a significant relationship.

Interview 6

"I can't change the way people are, so what am I going to do about it?"

This interview was conducted on January 24, 2001. This man is 29 years old, 5' 8" tall, weighs 170 pounds and has brown hair. He is pursuing a university degree in mechanical engineering.

Thank you for doing this interview. Let's begin with your earliest memories about your childhood. Was it kindergarten or nursery school, or was it even before that?

I'd have to say ... thinking back, I think kindergarten is my first clear memory.

And that's when you're about five, I suppose.

Yeah. Five, I think.

And any particular thoughts?

I got in trouble for running my trucks across the kindergarten area inside and smashing them. That was one memory. And a classmate snapped all my big Crayons.

The first thing most people remember is school, I guess. Now, how many are there in your family? How many siblings?

I've got an older sister, then me, then a younger brother and then a younger sister.

And you're 29. That makes you an "older gentleman."

[Laughs] I think you got me by quite a few years!

With a couple of years thrown in for good measure! All right. Are your parents together?

No.

How old were you when they divorced?

When I was two, I guess. Before I recalled.

Did you have visitation?

Growing Up Male In America

No. I ended up moving in with my dad when I was 16. But up until then, I had probably seen him only about 30 times. Couple times a year. Christmas and some other holiday.

And you lived with your mom until you were 16?

Yes, with my mother. And then I was a hoodlum.

You were?

I was a little shithead with my mom, yeah. Then I quit school, and then instead of staying out of school, I had planned on moving and going to work somewhere. I decided to go live with my dad. He asked me, actually.

At the age of 16 or so.

Fifteen or 16.

And by this time he had remarried?

No. He's married now, but at the time they weren't married. She was just living with us then, so it was like they were married but they weren't.

Okay. Do you keep in touch with your parents now?

Yup.

And you aren't still living with your dad?

No.

But your mother – you'd see her occasionally after the age of 15, 16?

I see her about once a week now.

Okay.

She's in town here.

And your dad is in town here, too?

No. He's in a town about 85 miles away.

Do you get along with your siblings?

Yup.

Always have?

Yup.

Do you remember, back in grade school, what kinds of people you gravitated toward as friends? And what qualities they had?

My whole life – even back then, when I was a kid – it was always the nice people that I get along with. You know, like the cocky people and the people who put themselves above everybody else, I never had time for.

No time for that.

Interview 6

And we were poor growing up, too. So then I'd get a lot of hell from people, you know. So then the people that didn't give me hell were the ones that I'd hang out with, you know?

Poor. How poor were you? I mean, you had clothes to wear and food to eat, didn't you?

Barely.

Really.

Yeah. It was four of us with my mother working, and back in the days when we were really poor, I think mom was fighting with dad to get support. He was being a jerk and wouldn't pay, so we were pretty dang poor. We were food-stamp poor, you know? And government-cheese poor.

Well, being poor and then the divorce can make for some great tensions, certainly. Did school chums give you a rough time because maybe you didn't have fashionable clothes?

Yeah. But that didn't last very long, though, because I started beating the shit out of those who gave me a rough time. Really. Pretty soon people learned not to give me a hard time. Now I look back and say that's stupid. But back in those days, that's how I dealt with things. Because you don't think too carefully about stuff when you're a kid.

That's true. And maybe you came in a little defensive, too, because of the money and family tensions – just waiting for somebody to make some smart-ass remark. When you think back to elementary school, what, if anything, were you most afraid of? Or what scared you as a little kid? We're talking six, seven, eight years old.

[Pause] Well, not much scared me, as far as being afraid to do things. But, like, being accepted and stuff like that was always a concern.

Sure.

Back at that age, you really care what other people think about you. And I guess that's about it. I mean, I didn't … I wasn't one of those kids that walked around with fears, you know?

I'm curious. Since your folks were fighting a lot then and eventually separated and all that, did that cause you to be kind of fragmented or torn?

I wasn't around for any of that. They were separated by the time I was old enough to know any better.

Okay. But you knew, from your mom, that there was some tension there.

Oh, yeah. I mean, I guess I heard that, you know.

Like when she was trying to get the money.

Right. Yeah.

And your dad was – what's that word? Recalcitrant?

Growing Up Male In America

Yeah.

Do you like that word? [Laughs]

Never even heard of that one, actually. It's pretty impressive.

Thank you very much! [Laughs]

Yeah. You're welcome. [Laughs]

Did you have any favorite teachers in those early years?

Um … yeah. I had a couple of favorite teachers. I'm not sure why. They were both women. One was the third-grade teacher, and the other was the fifth-grade teacher. They kind of stick out. Oh, and my first-grade teacher, too.

What was it about them that impressed you?

They were really friendly.

And yet you knew the discipline.

Yeah. You could tell they cared, I suppose. Looking back now, hindsight's 20/20. You can tell that they really wanted you to learn a little bit. In elementary school, I mean, it's a little about learning and mostly about growing up, in my opinion.

Ah. That's a good point. Yeah. I think you're right.

I remember one episode in third grade. For class, the teacher acted like she was mad at us and threw peanuts at us. I thought that was kind of cool. And that sticks out in my head, you know? Like acting like she was mad and pelting us with peanuts.

And she was just faking it?

Yeah. She was faking it. Oh, ah … when you were in trouble, too, she used to put on lipstick and give you a huge kiss on the cheek so you'd have to walk around with lipstick on your cheek. And that was a bad deal when you were in fourth grade. So … that kind of stuck out, too.

Did you ever go back and see those teachers, many years later?

Oh … many, many years later, I walked through school, but I didn't get to talk to any of them. But I went there and kind of looked at the place. It was kind of cool.

It seemed smaller.

Way smaller. Yeah. The chairs are so small, too.

What religion were you raised?

I'm not really any religion. We didn't attend church or anything like that. Actually, for a while, when we were younger, we did go to this one church for, like, a month. I don't know what church it was, but my mother was baptized

Interview 6

one way, and the minister said that she had to be baptized by submersion, and if she didn't, she was going to go to hell. I remember her telling us that. She didn't like the fact that just because she wasn't baptized by submersion he thought she was going to go to hell. Then we quit going to that church. Yeah. He told her straight-up she was going to hell.

Did you have any favorite other adults, like some neighbors or somebody you looked up to? Since your dad wasn't there, maybe a father figure or somebody who guided you in some way?

Not really.

Do you remember your time in junior high?

My middle school?

Yes.

Seventh, eighth grade. That's when we left elementary.

Okay.

Up until ninth grade.

Oh. That's when you quit school, wasn't it?

Yeah. I got kicked out of high school,. They had me sign papers emancipating me, so I didn't have to go to school. That's because I was under 16. I was such a little shithead.

When did you start dating? What kind of experiences did you have with dating girls?

Dating? Or the first time I had sex? Or the first time I had an interest in women?

Yeah. All of those. Let's talk about the first time you noticed that you were interested in women.

I was young, young. Probably 10, 11.

Really? Now, had puberty kicked in for you then?

Yeah.

At the age of 10?

I was the first one with hair anywhere. You know what I mean? I was the first guy who could grow a beard.

Okay. So phy ed ... those years in phy ed are such strange years, because some kids haven't started to develop and others already have.

Yeah. Yeah. And others don't have hair anywhere yet. [Laughs]

So, do you remember the first girl you dated and maybe just got to know? And is that also the same first person you had sex with?

Growing Up Male In America

No. I can't really recall. I grew up in a trailer park. So there were a lot of girls around. You go through that flirty stage. It was not necessarily sleeping together, but just messing around a little bit. Nothing stands out.

Heavy petting?

Um-hum. Exploring.

Exploring. And certain women were more willing to get in on the exploration than others?

Those were the ones I always seemed to get along with real good, too.

I see. If you developed kind of early, you possibly were masturbating earlier than most of your friends. Do you remember the frequency?

How often? Quite often.

What do you call often?

Every day. Every other day. Back in those days, when you're going through all your chemical changes, yeah.

You're all glands.

Yeah. That's all you are. And, you know, looking back, it's kind of funny.

Do you remember the first time you masturbated?

Came?

The first time you came. Did you know what to expect?

No.

Did your dad ever sit you down and have a talk with you about sex?

No.

Did your mother?

No. I figured it all out by myself.

Where did you learn it?

Just ... I listened to other people.

And how old were you when you had sexual intercourse for the first time?

Intercourse? I was 12.

Ah, that young?

I know. It's pretty sad, when I look back on it. I wouldn't change a thing, though.

And was this somebody you kept a relationship going with?

No.

Just a kind of a one-time deal?

Interview 6

Yeah. I remember her name. I remember her vividly. Beautiful, beautiful girl, too. Long, red hair.

And was she older than you?

Yeah. She was 15.

She was 15, and you were 12.

Right. I always went around with people that were older than me. I don't know why that is. Even to this day. When I was in high school, all my buddies were out of high school. So I mean, I just hung out with an older crowd, I guess. Even back when I was 12. I fit in really good, too.

Well, it's probably because you are a little more mature, after having hit puberty earlier.

I'm sure there's a lot of reasons, you know. I mean ... different maturity levels.

Well now, here you are, sitting in a wheelchair. I'm really curious to know what happened, and when. Can we talk about that?

Yeah. It was July 3, 1999, and I had just started my own roofing company. It was the last day of the second job that my company ever did. So I showed up for work before the sun came up and worked until after it went down. Done. Completed. So I stopped over for a few beers and had probably five pitchers between five of us in a few hours and fell asleep as I was driving home. At 11:00 at night.

So it's not like you closed the bar and kept drinking or anything.

No, no. I didn't drink any more and go home that night any different than any other night. It's just that I was just so tired, and it was a long, hot day on that roof. I don't know if you've ever worked on a roof or not.

I know people who do.

If it's 100 degrees outside, it's 150 degrees on the roof because of the black tar. Like I said, I was just shot. And I fell asleep. And hit the ditch.

Were you alone in the car?

Yeah. Thank god. It's the first thing I asked when I was able to talk. "Did I hurt anybody?" But I can't remember the accident or afterwards or anything like that.

So what happened? From what they told you and from the little you can remember, did you roll the car? Or hit a tree?

There was actually a girl driving toward me in her car.

Okay.

So I went into her lane and then veered back over, like I was going back into my lane. And then I just kept going into the ditch.

Growing Up Male In America

I see.

So I swerved over to the left and then hit the ditch.

Did you roll?

Yeah. But I guess it was just flipped. I got ejected and landed 30 yards from the vehicle.

Ah. You didn't have your seat belt on?

I think I did.

And still?

Yeah. I never, ever went anywhere without my seat belt on. I mean it was, like, before I put the key in, I'd click my belt every time. So I think I did.

And yet, still, you got ejected from your car!

Yeah. Thirty yards.

Thirty yards! And where did you land?

I don't know.

So, what's the injury?

It's called T4 Complete, which means I'm completely paralyzed from the T4 vertebra down. The girl who was in the on-coming vehicle saw me. She's the one who found me. I guess, when she found me, I was trying to get up but I couldn't. I heard later from a friend of mine that she had told somebody that. I guess I was trying to get up, and she said, "Just hold still." And I guess I said, "Well, I'm not going anywhere." You know? And I guess I just laid back down and passed out.

Do you remember, when you were trying to get up, was there pain?

I can't remember that.

And then you passed out. Were you in a coma for a period of time?

Yes, I guess so.

You woke up in the hospital.

I woke up in one hospital. That's the first hospital I can remember. But I was in another hospital first. They transferred me by ambulance, but I can't remember any of that. I'm sure I was out like a light.

And they probably drugged you to relieve any pain you might have when you woke up.

Oh, they drugged me, I'm sure. I'm sure I was always on drugs – major drugs – for the first month. It doesn't hurt anymore, though, thank god.

Good. So what happened then. I mean, was there therapy?

Interview 6

Cheesy therapy. Looking back, it's fairly – I don't want to say it was ridiculous, but it wasn't very helpful. You know, if I had money I'd start my own therapy clinic because I know what is good and what is bad. Therapists who are walking can only do so much. You know what I mean? They don't really understand.

Yeah.

There was therapy. I held the record for the shortest stay ever in my doctor's career. With my kind of injury. Which is interesting, I think.

So, how many vertebrae are there in a spine, anyway?

I have no idea. A bunch.

I see that you have use of your arms.

I have use of my arms, and I have feeling down to one of my nipples. Like, I can feel this nipple but I can't feel that nipple.

Really. Do they ever predict that the nerves will regenerate or improve a little bit? I mean, what's the prognosis?

If it is going to improve, it would happen within the first year. After that, you're not looking very good as far as recovering. You know what I mean?

So this accident happened in mid-summer of 1999, and it's now ... how's my math? Two years this summer?

It'll be two years in July.

Okay. So ... I'm really curious, now, what kind of emotional frame of mind you're in. It must be a tremendous shock to hear that prognosis. Did you go through any emotional depression? Care to talk about that?

No, I didn't. I've had a lot of people ask me that. They'd say I wouldn't be able to take it and I'd go in a corner and die and all this stuff. But in my case, I've had a lot of fun. I dated a lot of women. I'd done my fighting, my drinking. You know? So with me, it's just, like, well, it's time to slow down, anyway. You know what I mean? So it's not as bad as people think. It could be a lot worse than the way I am.

Right. You could be as serious as the Superman *actor, Christopher Reeve.*

Or I could be dead.

Or you could have collided with a bus or car and killed many people. You can always look to the good in a bad situation.

I always look at the good. My whole life, I've always been that way. And especially now. One thing that I'd say that this injury has done is made me look at everything different. I mean, things that I thought were important back when I was younger are ridiculous to me now. It's like how could you ever put any value on something so silly? You know what I mean? Whereas now, I know

Growing Up Male In America

what's really important. So, I mean, it's changed me – and I think for the better, as far as my attitude goes.

The first time I met you, you seemed to me to have a tranquil, almost oriental philosophy of acceptance, and I think you just put that into words.

Oh, yeah.

Regarding your condition, I suppose there are some people who would fight it and be very bitter and angry.

Yeah. I have friends also in wheelchairs who are like that. I'm, like, "You're just going to have to accept that your life is changed." You know, I can talk to people in wheelchairs like this, you know, but many people can't accept their condition. I have a friend who's also in a wheelchair, and he just lives to whine. Lives to be disabled. You know what I mean? Hard to explain.

I think I understand.

I can barely talk to him because he's always a gloom-and-doomer, and everything's bad and the world's bad and everything like that. I told him, "You know, your life isn't as good as it was in the first place, but you're taking what life you have left and wasting it, sitting there whining about it." You know what I mean? He's afraid of everything. "Don't do this. You're going to get hurt by this." You know? And it's, like, who cares? You know what I mean?

Does he ever wonder, "Why don't people like to hang around with me?"

I told him it's because he's so gloomy. That's what I say. I don't want to say that, but it's what I say. I say, "You're a pretty good guy, but you whine so much."

You're a friend. You can do that.

Friends can do that. And I'm in a wheelchair, too, so I can do that even more than somebody else.

Yeah. But he doesn't take it to heart, apparently? He doesn't figure it out?

No. But I feel very sorry for him. I really do.

How old a guy is he?

He's younger than me. His accident was when he was 18. Diving into the water and broke his neck.

You made the point before that you've lived a good deal and had many experiences before the accident. You got a lot of stuff out of your system. But what about kids who, at the age of 10 or 12, have dived into a rock or had an accident or something, and they haven't had those kinds of experiences which you had?

I do think about such people, not being able to know or experience lots of things, and I'm sad for them.

Could I ask you some personal questions, now?

Interview 6

Anything you want.

Can you function, sexually?

Yup.

You can achieve an erection?

I can achieve an erection and have an orgasm. And I'm not supposed to be able to.

Now that's a mystery to me. I mean, if you're paralyzed from your chest on down, do you have any feeling lower down?

It's way hard to explain.

Help me out! Try to explain. [Laughs]

Yeah. [Laughs] Way hard. No pun intended.

Yeah – I get it!

Um ... as far as erections go ... when I crashed, right away my penis wouldn't work at all. Like at the hospital. Not at all. And I'm a totally sexual person. I mean, whether I'm in a relationship or not in a relationship, I like to have a lot of sex. And so it was ... it sounds weird, but to me that's like almost taking away most of your manhood. You know what I mean? But if my penis wouldn't work, I wouldn't feel complete. So I do take Viagra. And there are some shots that I have, too, in case I need that for an erection. Then with the erection, I can have an orgasm and all that. It's really weird, though. Even I don't understand it.

You'd think everything from your chest down would be out of commission. But the biggest ... what did somebody once say? The biggest sex organ is really up here, in between your ears.

Um-hum. That's where it is.

And that's the thing that's controlling your penis, I guess. It doesn't necessarily have anything to do with nerves.

Well, I've been asked that question. Like, "How does it feel? What does it feel like?" By so many people, and the only thing I can say to them is, like – let's say you're having sex. And you take all your physical feelings and shut them off, and you just feel what's in your brain. You know, it's still really, really, really good. You know what I mean? And it's not all ... just all the feeling down there in your crotch. Let's say that some girl was giving me head. Now let's say she ... if she was all soft and gentle, I wouldn't be able to feel it. But if she's more aggressive, using more pressure or whatever she's got to do, then that's what makes it really good. I mean, I can feel that. So there is something physical.

You know that you're feeling sexually stimulated.

Growing Up Male In America

A lot of it has to do with the visual side of it – you know, watching her give head. I find that visuals help a lot more now than they used to for me before. During sex, I mean. I like to watch what's going on. You know what I mean?

Well, there you go again. It's in your brain.

It's in my brain. A lot of it is in my brain. But not all of it is in my brain. Let's say if I wouldn't be able to have an orgasm? Sex would not be satisfying for me. You know what I mean? But, no. You need to finish.

Have a little completion.

Yes. Exactly.

You must need to find a special kind of woman. Do you find that women have a different attitude when they see you wheel into the room or when you come up to an attractive woman and strike up a conversation? Have you found some resistance?

Some. When I first got out of the hospital, when I first got in the chair, I didn't realize I was disabled yet. You know what I mean? I tried interacting with people and asked girls, and some of them went out with me, but I also got a lot of, "Yeah, it sounds good." But when it came right down to dating, they were not interested, really. You know? But they'd act like they were interested. I don't know why anybody would do that. Some people are funny that way. There's a certain type of woman that I do date now. They've got to have an open mind. There's actually a lot more women than I thought there would be who do have an open mind.

Good for you!

Actually, I think I'm dating more now than before my accident.

You devil! Do you like women who are a little older?

I like women.

Just women. Okay.

As long as their brain is mature, and as long as they're of legal age. [Laughs]

Do you want to marry some day?

Yes.

Okay. You want to have kids?

A bunch of them.

And make your mom a grandma. Has she been made a grandma yet?

Yes, she has. I have a daughter.

You do?

Yeah. A little girl.

How old?

Interview 6

Three on March 19.

And she was conceived before the accident?

Before my accident, yeah. Not long before, but before.

Did you ever marry the mother?

No. It was just a dating thing, actually, and no fault of either one of ours – but she had said she was on the pill, so we didn't take any precautions. I found out later that she wasn't and she had lied to me because she was trying to get pregnant. Which really doesn't matter now, because I have a beautiful daughter. She really is beautiful, too.

Okay. Very good. In your younger days, did you experiment with drugs at all?

Yeah.

Extensively?

Extensively.

Lots. A whole range of things?

The whole gamut.

The whole works. And do you still?

I smoke marijuana. I might do cocaine for a New Year's thing or something. It's so expensive, though. But that's fun every now and again. But that's it right now. I don't drink liquor anymore, and I don't drink caffeine. I don't smoke cigarettes.

Did you smoke cigarettes before the accident?

Yeah.

And you drank. Would you say you were a heavy drinker?

Yeah. A heavy drinker.

Was that maybe due to the laborer types of guys you worked with as a roofer?

Um … that's part of it. People I hung around with. But there were still times when I didn't hang out with a lot of people. Even when I lived in the middle of nowhere. I still drank some. I've always been one to like a good buzz. It's nice to catch a buzz and relax and forget about stuff every now and again.

Now that you're in a wheelchair, do you find an attitude – a "stare attitude" – when you come into a room or when you're downtown? Do people treat you differently because of your disability?

Yeah. To a point. I mean, they do definitely treat me differently. Some people do stare at me. Yeah. But does that bother me? No.

Is that part of your total acceptance? Your accepting nature?

I can't change the way other people are, so what am I going to do about it?

Growing Up Male In America

Stay home? Avoid people? No.

Good for you.

It's just ... if you really think about it – and if everybody would just think clearly when they're younger, too, and just think – what somebody thinks about you has nothing to do with your life. Nothing at all. They could think you're the best or the worst, and it's not going to have any ramifications.

But you know as well as I do that what other people think about you is what guides most junior-high, senior-high and college kids' behavior.

And that guided me, too, to a point.

But you reach a recognition after a while?

Whether be it from age and experience or, in my case, a traumatic experience. There are some pretty stupid people out there.

Well, you're right. And you realize that what others think really doesn't matter very much.

Not a hell of a lot. No.

Did you at any time, after the accident and the hospitalization, take on a stronger religious attitude?

No. Just the opposite.

How so?

I've never been really religious, and I've always had my doubts. But now, since this accident, I see people who – and I know this may sound bad – but I see people who dedicate their lives to God and stuff like that. And I just think, what a shame. But maybe they're right and I'm wrong. Nobody will ever know, I guess. And my policy is I'm a nice person. My attitude is I'll be nice to everybody, as nice as I can be. And if that's not good for "a god" – if there is one – well, then, pardon my French, but fuck him! You know what I mean? I'm here to live my life now. Not to be afraid that something bad might happen. Well, something bad already did happen.

Did you go through a "Why me?" phase after the accident? "Why did this happen to me?"

No. I did it to myself. And if I ask myself, "Why me?," I know the answer. Because I got drunk and fell asleep behind the wheel while driving – that's why. I don't know if I buy into that whole "everything happens for a reason" thing. I mean, maybe I was meant to go into this chair and be an advocate for something. You know? Maybe I was put in here to settle me down. If there is a god, everything will be clear, I guess, some day – but I'm not going to sit and dwell on it now.

Do people ask you to make speeches for kids or other people who have just had a

Interview 6

traumatic accident and are in a wheelchair for the first time?

I've talked to some college groups and at a hospital. I'm more open and honest than most people are, so I don't hesitate to talk about anything with anybody. Whether it be bowel movements or how sex works. You know what I mean? I don't have any problem being open and honest. I'm not afraid to talk. There are a lot disabled people who aren't comfortable talking in front of a group of people.

I would imagine.

Whereas, me – get as many people as you want. What are they going to do? What's to be afraid of? I wouldn't mind talking about anything. Like, right now – for medication, I went from seven medications down to two. One is prescription medication for my bladder, and the other is marijuana. Marijuana replaced six medications that gave me huge side effects, so I'm in the midst of writing letters and getting involved with the legalization of marijuana for medical use. I mean, it's ridiculous that you can't use pot if it helps you. I'm not a criminal.

So this isn't something the doctor is recommending? It's something you do on your own?

Something I tried on my own that worked out. My own research. I had smoked before. I looked at my symptoms that were being treated, and I told my doctor in the office, "I'm not taking any more of these medications." And he said, "Well, you have to." And I said, "No I don't." "Well, then, what are you going to do?" I said, "Well, you'll see." And when I got out of the hospital after three months, I told him about smoking pot for relief. He said, "I don't know how you got out of the hospital so early. It's amazing." And I said, "I know why I did." And he said, "Why is that?" And I said, "Well, it's because I got off of all of your bad drugs and started smoking pot." I'd go to the parking ramp three times a day in my wheelchair and smoke pot out in the parking lot. And I really, truly believe that's why I got out of that hospital sooner than the doctors expected. It worked with me! I'd never hurt anybody. I'd never steal anything. I'd never even kick a dog, if I could. But yet I'm labeled as a criminal because I smoke pot, and I could go to prison. And I can get denied financial aid. I'm involved with this activist woman, and she wants me to go talk in front of the state legislature. So I might. Never know when one day I might be out somewhere, talking.

And you'll be famous and I'll say, "I know him!"

"I know him!"

Now, what's happening? Your leg is shaking.

I need to smoke pot now.

Oh. Otherwise that kind of a tremor will continue and get worse?

Yeah. That's what I have to smoke pot for.

Growing Up Male In America

Okay.

It's for treating that, and there are three other drugs that I could be on to treat that – but the side effects include dreariness and being lethargic and being constipated.

So, you just smoke a little.

Smoke a little weed, and it goes away.

Okay.

Except I have to pay for it myself.

Well, that's a downer – pardon the pun! [Laughter]

I'm very grateful to you for sharing so much about yourself in this interview. Thank you very much.

All right.

Postscript – December 2001

This man is continuing his university studies. As an indication of his sense of humor and his acceptance of his situation, on the information sheet I asked interviewees to submit, he indicated his height was three feet, six inches!

Interview 7

"As a kid, I really didn't get involved in school activities because people tagged me as an underachiever."

This interview was conducted on August 29, 2001. This man is 25 years old, 5' 11" tall, weighs 140 pounds and has light brown hair.

I want to thank you very much for your willingness to do this interview So let's think back to your childhood. You were born in a little town in Minnesota?

Yes, a very little town!

And how many in the family?

I'm the oldest, and I have two half sisters. I'm 25, one sister is 17 and the other is 13.

Half. Well, that suggests that your mom and dad didn't stay married. Now, when did the divorce happen? How old were you?

I was probably four or five months old, so it happened before I even knew. The name that I have isn't even my biological name because shortly after I was born, they divorced. And it came out later that he wasn't my biological father.

Have you found out who your biological father is?

I have not. I have searched and tried to find out and I can't. My mom is holding a piece of knowledge that she won't let go, so it's always left a big question. My mom knows who this person is, but she won't tell me.

She was never married to him?

She was never married to him. Relatives keep it very quiet, too. I've heard numerous things. I've heard rumors that I was the product of a relationship between my mother and her cousin. It's also come up that it was one of her high-school classmates. My mom tells me over and over it could have been a number of guys. She had me when she was 17, so she had not even graduated from high school yet.

Growing Up Male In America

Which makes her still very young, now, because you're 25?

Yes, 25. She's 43, so she's still pretty young.

Well, that's interesting. But before you were born, she married the man whose name you have?

Yup.

But then they were divorced?

They were divorced. She was married before age 18 and divorced before age 19.

Do you ever keep in touch with him?

I do not. He surfaced, though, once, some time ago. He asked some questions about me, and that was really it.

A little mystery in all of this, isn't there?

Yeah. [Laughs]

So you're growing up in that little town. Was it on a farm?

I grew up in the city, but my grandparents and all my cousins lived on farms, so I actually got the small-town life and living on farms kind of aspect of life. Over the summer, I'd spend the whole time out at a cousin's farm, kind of getting that experience. Doing chores and building forts and things like that. That whole kid thing on the farm.

Did you go to a public school?

Yes, it was a public school, very small.

Did you graduate from high school in that district?

Yup.

And the graduating class had all of how many?

Sixty-one. It had a huge farming area around it.

Were you close to your mother's parents?

Very close to them. I actually called my grandpa Papa for most of my younger years. So he was the male, fatherly figure in my life. And he did so many things. He was the guy I always took my car to as I got older, and he fixed it and helped me and gave me advice. I'd come out and mow the lawn, and he'd give me allowance money. He took me to dentist appointments and all that kind of stuff. So I looked up to him a lot as I was growing up. He was kind of a shy, quiet guy, but he cared deeply about me, my mom and all of us. There are 30-some grandchildren, and he was spending this amount of time with me. Amazing!

Is he still alive?

Interview 7

Yup. Both Grandpa and Grandma are still alive.

Okay. And every opportunity you get, you let him know how much he means to you, I hope.

I do. It's kind of a weird relationship now, as we've gotten older. Those compliments and things almost make him too uncomfortable, so I have to be careful and gauge when you can release some of that stuff, because whenever you do, you can tell it makes him uncomfortable and squeamish.

And I bet a big hug is not comfortable for him?

I used to hug him every time, and now when I hug him every so often, those hugs are kind of stiff.

I'm finding in many of these interviews that very same thing. There's just a distance. And sometimes – especially those men of Scandinavian heritage – they don't even have to think of the answer. It's just, "No, we just don't hug. We maybe shake hands."

Who were your favorite teachers in elementary school?

The one from elementary school who stuck out in my mind was a first-grade teacher. She was just so kind to everybody. I mean, every day you'd come to school and she would give each individual a piece of candy. That's the one thing that stuck out in my mind. She went to each student all the time, and you had your few minutes or seconds of attention from her. She always had really creative art-project things going. Elementary is hard to remember, what the specifics were or who impressed me. I think it was teachers later on in life who made more of a difference than those in my younger years.

Actually I had a really strange experience when I was in first or second grade. The special-ed coordinators told my mom that I had some learning disabilities and some functioning problems, and they didn't think that I would amount to much as a student or a person. They told my mom that I was slightly retarded. This was back when you could actually say those kind of words. For some reason, I wasn't developing educationally, like other students were, and I think that affected the way my mom treated me when I was growing up. I did finally, as time went on, catch up, after I spent some time in special ed. So as a kid, I really didn't get involved in school activities because people had me tagged as an under-achiever and slightly retarded.

That must have raised hell with your self esteem! Like, you didn't feel that you were as good as the other kids?

I was very lonely. I just kept to myself. I was a young, quiet, little kid. I was not going anywhere fast at that point in time. I just never went out of my way to get involved in anything. Just real quiet.

In high school, then, you got into music?

Growing Up Male In America

Yup. Instrumental. Everything really changed as I got older. I think the one big thing was my mom got divorced from her second husband. He came into my life right around that kindergarten and first-grade time in my life, and he was the type of person who told me, over and over "I hate you." He would physically sit me down and tell me how much he hated me on a regular basis. It was that kind of mental abuse. And then there was physical abuse, too. That just continued on and on, and I was so put down. I just never really had a chance to be who I wanted to be or to do anything, because I was always told "no." I was always grounded, I was always in trouble in his eyes, and since I wasn't his biological kid, he hated me. But as soon as my mom divorced him when I was 14 years old, it was like his hand came off the top of my head, as if he had been holding me under water and I was drowning.

Well, that was a terrible time for you. To be told by this guy that you're no good and that he hated you.

I felt worthless, abused.

And in such obvious and overt ways. What a terrible thing for him to do! But anyway, with him out of the picture, you started developing a little more self esteem and you saw that you were pretty good after all, right?

As a teenager, I became the man of the house, in a sense. I was the one babysitting after school with my sisters, and once I got my car I transported them. I dropped my younger sister off in elementary school and then I'd take the other sister to babysitting, and then I went to high school. Then after school, I would take them all home and then I'd rush back to high school to participate in whatever activities I was in. I started out in track and then band and theatre, acting.

Oh, you did some theatre?

Oh, yeah. Tenth through 12th grades. I loved it. I was always one of the lead characters in the one-act plays that our school produced, and I always went to the competitions. At that time, too, theatre was looked down upon as not the most popular activity in school, but still people really didn't care. The teachers would have us perform in front of the whole school a number of times to get the other students exposed to theatre and also to get us exposed to audiences.

Sure. And it's amazing, isn't it? Some of your fellow students became your fans, didn't they?

Yeah! After you're done, people say, "You do that? I could never get up there, but you did it."

So at this point in your life, you're kind of flowering in high school. Which one or two teachers in that time made the biggest impression or impact on you?

My band teacher, I think, made a pretty big impression on me. He pushed me a lot to try harder, to do better. I was always trying harder, and I really found an

Interview 7

interest in music and the many different things that I could do. He just kept opening up doors for me. "You can go to state. You can go as far as you want if you practice." I just continued to excel, and whenever there were fun opportunities, he would first come to me and invite me to be a part of things.

And after your upbringing with that stepdad who kept saying that you're no good, all of a sudden somebody comes along who says, "You're damned good." That must have been wonderful for you.

Yes. This band teacher saw something in me, and I'm grateful to him for providing me with an outlet for me to shine.

Tell me more about your high-school years.

Well, I did get a job when I was 17. My sophomore, junior and senior years, I had a job. I started out working at a fast-food restaurant. [Laughs] I actually liked it. I could always go after school and sneak the cheeseburgers and eat. Most of the people who worked there were older and some of them – I hate to say it – were not going too far in life, and they just drank and did all sorts of party things in life. So they were always kind of intriguing and exciting to me because they were rebels. So that's where that part came into my life. But then I was in track in seventh through 12th grade, and I did get up to be track captain, so that was a nice kind of achievement.

Well, you were mixing the arts and athletics.

I didn't even think about that.

Was your mother working at that time? Was she making good enough money, or were you still kind of struggling financially?

We still kind of struggled. We never had much money. But she always somehow or another had money for us all the time to do the basic things in life. I never really wanted for anything, except maybe I didn't want the Levi's, I wanted a pair of designer jeans instead and never got them. She has worked as a clerk at a major medical clinic for almost 25 years now, so she's really got a niche in there. She still doesn't make a huge or hefty salary.

But it's comfortable. It's a living wage.

Yeah. She can retire comfortably from there, too.

What kind of a social life did you have in high school? I mean, you had your social life at the fast-food place, and after work you went with those people, the rebels, and you had track, but what kind of people did you hang with at school?

My social life started out when my stepfather left. Once he and my mom divorced, things kind of settled down for me, but before that I was getting in more and more trouble. I started hanging out with the people who egged the cars, the people who rolled the tires down the street and left them there so a car would run them over. Just kind of the kids in school who were disruptive. I somehow managed to fit in with that group. I didn't really do a lot or say a lot, but I hung around them. I tagged along with that group. And it was about that same time, when I was about 15, that the whole feeling of, "Gosh, something's weird here" set in. That's when I started discovering I had this attraction towards men more than females, and trying to deal with those feelings was very difficult. Where do you go with these feelings? How do you find someone like you? Am I strange? It came early to me because one of my cousins all of a sudden one day came on to me and we had this brief sexual encounter, and I thought, "Wow! I like that." But afterwards he pretended that nothing had happened. At that point, it just triggered this in my mind, "Wow! That was something I liked." But I didn't understand why other people didn't talk about those things or why it wasn't accepted.

And then to have your cousin not acknowledge it made it more strange, I suppose. Obviously, at that time, you were something of a romantic, and you were kind of hoping you could maybe discuss it at least – if not with your cousin, with someone!

[Laughs] Yeah! Like, where did this come from? Where did you get this idea?

How young were you when you started having certain leanings or feelings of a gay sort?

Gosh, probably back to age five or six. I noticed basic thoughts. Actually, this happened when I was probably 10, with the cousin. I was really young. I didn't even realize people did those things. He was four years older than me, so he had progressed more and was more developed.

If you're about 10 when this happened, certainly puberty hadn't started happening to you yet.

Nope.

And yet you still had sexual feelings or yearnings?

The feelings were there, but the sexual stuff wasn't. To me it was no big deal. But I liked what I saw and what I did. It was like whatever I was waiting for finally happened. I thought, "Well, that all makes sense now." Those younger feelings of hanging out with your buddies and liking them was never a sexual thing. It was more the friendship, the group, the company. But then along comes this sexual experience, and then it just all made sense.

Did you ever go through a period of saying, "There's something wrong with feeling this way"? And because of that societal repugnance, you dated women?

The whole thing, yeah. I was terribly afraid of hearing my mom or someone say, "What are you, queer or a faggot?" or those kinds of comments. By the way, those sexual encounters continued on with my cousin. Every so often it would happen again. All of a sudden I began to wonder if mom noticed something different in me and would ask, "What are you, a queer or a faggot? You're only 11." Right away I began to know I did something wrong. You

Interview 7

don't ever let it out, and then you quickly realize from other people, as you get older, that those gay people are not who you want to be. They're something that's not accepted. You can't talk about it. You begin to think there's nobody around you who even thinks like that. It's like you have nowhere to go with this information.

Did you feel that way? "I'm the only one"? Except your cousin was.

Yeah. I knew he was, and I kept thinking, "Gosh, why can't he and I talk?" We never talked about anything. It was just always a sexual thing, and it was over.

I find that interesting because you're young and living in a fairly open society compared to decades past. What religion were you raised, if any?

Methodist was the upbringing. So it was kind of a liberal church, but almost all the members of the church were in their 50s, 60s, 70s, heterosexual, married. There were never any disruptions. Everything was perfect.

That made it all the worse. So you didn't feel like the Methodist church would be a haven.

No! [Laughs] I never liked church, either, so I was in there for the time I had to be there, and I got out of there as quickly as I could. There was never any opportunity to talk to any of those people.

Well, now, puberty. Let's talk about that.

Explosion time. [Laughs]

Yeah. Like a friend of mine said, "It's when you're all glands." Did you develop early or later than most?

I would say earlier. I remember in seventh-grade track, I was one of the first few people who had a growth spurt. I had pimples all over my face and body hair. I had it quicker than the other guys.

Seventh grade ... that makes you about 13.

Yeah. I remember comparing myself sort of with other guys. You'd see different bodies in different stages of development and think, "Oh, I look different from him or him or him."

And the ones who developed later were walking around saying, "When?" Everyone else had hair, and some were even shaving and their penises were full size.

Yeah. [Laughs] I remember those late developers not fitting in in the locker-room scene. They didn't shower, and they hid in the bathroom stalls and things like that. So, yeah. It was strange.

But that wasn't your situation because you were leading the pack. It was already happening.

Yeah. I already had those sexual thoughts. It was especially interesting at that age because the locker room was the only place that I could really see other

Growing Up Male In America

men – not that I thought I wanted anything from them or would say anything to them or go after them – it was not like that. It was just the thought of, "Wow, here's other men." And I actually could look at a man's body. There was my outlet. I saw a guy naked. And it didn't matter who it was. I didn't have to have an attraction for a specific guy.

Do you remember when you masturbated for the first time?

It was really strange. It actually happened when I was having sex with my cousin one of those times. It was totally unexpected because when we'd been together previously, I was feeling good only because, "Wow, he likes me." There's this male thing. But all of a sudden I came at one point, and it was like I thought I was going to explode. I felt like my whole body was changed. I don't know how to describe that feeling.

And you masturbated about how many times a day or a week?

Geez, I suppose twice a day. I mean, it was probably an average at that time. It was always, like, everything you bumped into or touched, it felt like it was just time to relieve yourself. [Laughs]

Did you ever have sex with a woman?

I did. A few times. Maybe three or four times. And that was not until I was almost a senior in high school.

Was it satisfactory? Were you able to function or perform?

Yeah. I functioned, performed, no problem. We were very close friends as we got to ninth grade, and we were in lots of school activities together. It was just a close-knit relationship, and we just kind of became boyfriend and girlfriend. We got along so well. I always enjoyed her company, but then it got to the sexual stuff. The making out and the caressing and all that stuff. That stuff, to me, almost felt like a way to keep her happy, and so I would do those things. But for me, I didn't have the interest. It was, like, "Gosh, I've got to do this now for an hour, and then I'm going to get home and masturbate."

Did she start falling for you, emotionally?

She did, yeah.

There must have come a time when you had to break it off, because you were getting to be a senior, and some women start thinking about marriage already.

We had talked about having children, what we would name them and all those kinds of conversations. Later, we even went to the same college together. I looked back in the high-school yearbook, and there's a picture of us hugging on graduation day. [Laughs] So that was the life I was projecting to everybody, because we were both very outgoing people.

Did you ultimately come out to her? Tell her you were gay?

No, I didn't. I almost did when I came to the point of ending the relationship.

Interview 7

We went away to college, and we were together for the first quarter of college. But then she went out and had fun with some other guy.

Now, during this time, had you – besides those earlier sessions with your cousin – had you started acting on your gay impulses with men? In high school? Or certainly in college?

In high school I ran into another student who probably was gay. We were staying overnight at another friend's house, and we were wrestling around and all of a sudden it just turned from wrestling into a sexual experience. After it happened, I think that was the worst I had ever felt in my life. It was like somebody outside of my family knows that I feel this way. So I felt horrible. I went home and took a really long shower. I called that guy the next day and asked, "Did you remember what happened?" I was feeling weird, I didn't quite understand what happened. I tried to call him and I tried to play it off like it didn't happen, and he agreed with me that it didn't happen. But then, those feelings – puberty – we started hanging out more and more, and he started coming over. Basically, he was coming over and just giving me head on a regular basis throughout the week, and that would be it. He'd come over, do that and leave.

That first time with him, had you been drinking or smoking or anything?

No. I was probably, like, 15. It was wrestling, and it just got out of hand. [Laughs]

Actually, that's very sweet, in a way, that you felt guilt about that. Almost like you were concerned for his feelings.

I was ashamed. "I can't believe I would do that." It was dirty, it was bad.

And this thing of taking the long shower – isn't that something? It's like going to confession or washing with holy water. [Laughter] Well, anyway. Now, let's get to your college years. You've broken up with your lady friend. Did she take it badly?

Well, the night I broke up with her, I tried to come out to her. I had never said to anyone that I was gay, and I tried to tell her. I had it in my mind. I pulled my car off the side of the road and I told her, "I can't go out with you anymore. It's over. You can go your own way, I'll go my own way." She was screaming and crying and upset, and she said, "Why are you doing this to me? Why?" And I tried to say, "Because …" and I tried to say it but I couldn't. Finally I said, "Some day you'll know." And she's, like, "Why can't you just tell me now?" And I said, "I can't." So I totally backed away from it, so the relationship just ended.

And you said, "I can't" – and it meant, "I just can't say it yet."

Yeah. Right. Those words could not be spoken at that time.

Have you seen her since?

Yeah.

Growing Up Male In America

And you've opened up to her now?

Kind of.

Or she has a pretty good clue?

She knows now that I am gay, but I think the whole relationship wrecked the friendship that we once had. But it was not long after that ended in November that I had found my first boyfriend.

And you're in college at this point?

By this time, when you're in college and you're about 19, you were sure of your sexual orientation? Had you used the word "gay" yet?

I did. Not long after I broke up with the girlfriend, it was Christmas break, and I went home and spent time with my family. And that's when I felt, "Things are different." I knew I had to come to terms with this issue. I felt like something was going to explode out of me. I felt like I was trapped, and I didn't know where to go with this information and I was being held down and I couldn't release it and I didn't know *how*. It was a horrible feeling. So I started talking with this other friend, who was a friend of my ex-girlfriend at the time. We all kind of hung out together, and she used to live across the street from me when I lived in the small town where I grew up. She and I talked more and more as the breakup happened, and then one night I just broke down and was crying on the phone, and I said, "You know, I ... I ... I ..." It went on for about 10 minutes, and then I finally said it. "I am gay."

All right, Did you ever come out to your mother? Have you?

Yes.

Recently? Or was it about that time?

It was about that time.

Okay. That awful Christmas vacation at home where you were about to erupt. When you got back to school, did you tell certain close friends?

Nope. I kept it a secret. But in a few months, it all gets really crazy. Events started happening in my life that really made everything make more sense. I had come out in a very painful way, in a sense. The way things happened, they really peaked at a bad point in my life.

Let's talk about that. You said something about you developed a friendship with a boy.

Yup. And that's kind of where it all started. So after I told that girl I knew, finally, that I was gay ... then I knew I could go somewhere with this information. I had seen this little ad in the paper that said, "Gay friend ... do you know someone who's gay? Or are you gay and have questions? Call this number." I went in the bathroom, called the number. The person who answered said, "We'll meet you somewhere. You can come to our group." I said, "I don't need

Interview 7

to meet you somewhere. I'll come to your group." They told me when and where the group met. I hemmed and hawed about it for a while, and I didn't finally go to a meeting for several weeks.

Now, this is some kind of support group in your home town?

Yes.

But not where you were going to college?

Nope. This was in my home town during a quarter break from college. I had to do something, so I called the number again, and they told me they had a group meeting that next Tuesday, and I went to it. It was, like, as soon as I walked in the door there were a few people, and immediately I felt uncomfortable because they were staring at me and I felt like I was being watched and out of place, and I didn't know what to do with all these people talking to me. I was so nervous I couldn't even take it all in. I didn't know any gay lingo, I didn't know any gay body movements or anything. The eyes or anything. But I noticed there was this black man off to the left of me. A very attractive guy. He kept staring at me and staring at me, and he'd walk past me and look at me. I went into the bathroom, and he followed me into the bathroom. I was very nervous. I came out of the bathroom, and I had never been … it's kind of like I was in a whole new world. I was surrounded by all these gay people and I didn't … I actually knew they were all gay and they knew I was gay, so it was like totally new, different and exciting.

And you never saw that many all in one place before?

No. So people were talking to me and were curious, and I just kind of sat there. That's what you usually do, you sit there and discuss. There were maybe 30 people in this place, and this black guy kept staring at me. I was thinking, "Wow! He's very attractive." So then naturally I'd look over and then look away. "Oh, god, he's looking at me." Finally somebody says, "Well, we're all going out for drinks. Would you like to go with us?" And I was, like, "Wow! Here I am. You want me to come with you? Sure!" So I went to this place with them.

Now, how old were you?

I was still 18.

It couldn't be a bar, could it?

It was like a pub. They had food in there, pool tables and stuff.

Okay. So you were legal.

Yeah, I was. There is no gay bar in that town, either, so it was like a straight hangout place. Kind of like a TGI Friday type place, but with pool tables and stuff like that. So we went in and sat down, and right away this black guy sits down right across from me. Here he is, now, within two feet of me, and he

Growing Up Male In America

starts asking me questions. We started talking, and right away I was like ... basically, I fell in love with this guy right away. He was very attractive. He said all the right things, did all the right things.

Was he about your age? A little older?

He was 10 years older than me, and I had no idea of that at first. I didn't even think to ask that question. That was, like, my first date in my whole life, in a sense, because it was somebody I was really attracted to in *all* aspects, instead of just friendship or just sex or something.

This would be about 1994?

It was 1994. Almost 1995.

Did you arrange, then, to get together and go out to a movie or something?

Yup. It was, like, "Do you want to come over to my house?" Or he said, "Let's go somewhere else and have some drinks." And he bought a pitcher of beer, and I drank the beer. Before I knew it, I was like ... I had drunk beer before, but I hadn't drunk a lot in high school or college. The beer quickly hit me. We talked and he was, like, "Why don't you come back to my place?" And I said, "Sure." I was all for that. It was a *good* experience, my first time, because he didn't pressure, he didn't go fast. He was nervous. He was making it kind of fun in the sense that, "I can't lay next to you or I can't do this." So it was pretty relaxed. We didn't do anything more than just touch and feel and hug, the first time. But after that point, it was, like, I was with him almost every day for three years. So it started the relationship right there, and every day we would just hang out, talk.

You did have sex eventually?

We did. Not long after. He opened my eyes up to anal sex. I had never had anal sex before. He showed me, taught me, we discussed.

And it was safe?

It was safe.

He helped you?

For a little bit. And he helped with that. He was very adamant in the beginning about being safe. We talked about HIV. He said, "This is what you should do. Be careful of older men. I'm an older man, but I'll do this with you." So we were together with each other pretty much every night. I don't even think he had a job. He didn't really have much going for him. He didn't have very many clothes. He said he had just moved to this town and lived with a relative.

As time went on, maybe a few weeks, this question came up. He said, "Would you ever date somebody who has HIV?" What would you do if you found out you knew somebody with HIV?" And I had heard of HIV a few times, but I had no idea what it was or anything like that. So I said, "Of course. If I knew

Interview 7

somebody with HIV, I would be there for them. It's not a big deal." I didn't even know what I was answering. So he and I ended up getting a place together a month and a half after we had first met. We got a little one-bedroom place, and soon I started seeing all sorts of bad patterns in him. Money missing, pill bottles, different things about him.

Well, it was kind of confusing then, because a lot happened in a short period of time. I basically changed my college career. I changed from the four-year college I was attending and enrolled in a community college the third quarter. Then we moved into the apartment together. That's when there were money issues. I don't think he ever worked. I don't know.

This can kind of erode the love, can't it?

Yeah, it can, but the sex was every day. It was the affection that I was wanting and hoping for. He was a good, smooth talker. He had the looks. He had everything that I could hope for, except he had all these underlying things that kind of eroded any love over time. Which is a good term, because within three months I was in the emergency room, and I found out I had HIV. And that's kind of what happened.

So it can't have been safe sex all the time, then?

No, it wasn't. It was only for the first few weeks.

But he never quite admitted that he was HIV positive? He never came right out and told you?

No. But when I found out, I told him, "I was just at the hospital, and I finally found out what's wrong." Because for like a month before I even found out, I had lost so much weight. I ended up in the emergency room because my body was falling apart for a month. That was all it took. I was just wasting away. Then he said, "How do I know you didn't give it to me?" And so it just started this whole thing about me ... he never fully said he gave me HIV or it came from him. It was always it came from someplace else, and then it became this underlying thing we never talked about in our relationship. This relationship, which lasted three years, was three years too long. Because it had abuse, it had verbal abuse, it had the HIV in there. Lying, cheating, stealing. I found out about a year and a half to almost two years into the relationship that he was addicted to crack. So that came in there. It was, like, everything. He went to jail three times in our relationship, and I just kind of supported him. It tore my family up, as you can imagine.

Yeah. And some of your friends are probably saying, "Why do you stay with that guy?" And you probably didn't know either why you stayed.

It's like they can break your heart, they can do anything to it, and you'll still love them, you'll care for them, you'll give them that 100th chance. But at some point you finally reach a sense of reality.

Growing Up Male In America

What was that point, when it ended?

Well, all of a sudden, he went to jail again. He was away from me. I could get some space, some perspective. He wasn't there to talk to me. He wasn't there to change my mind. He wasn't there to tell me what I had to do. I was, like, out of his control. He couldn't get to me, he couldn't find me, any of that. I could finally just walk away. I made the decision to go do what I wanted to do, and he was away from me long enough that I could be strong enough to be on my own.

Now, about this time, did you seek any professional help to assist you in sorting through this stuff? Did you ever go back to any gay-support group?

Nope. Well, a few times.

You didn't feel too much support. [Laughs]

Well, it was the whole HIV thing. When it came out that I was positive, it was like I was a black mark in the community. So here I was. I had to tell my mom I was gay, and then two months later she found out I had HIV. That was very hard for her to deal with, and for my grandparents to deal with. They were hearing all these things. My friends from high school just couldn't believe I was gay, and then came the rumors about the HIV. And that destroyed all that. The embarrassment that I felt from all of that made me feel pretty much like dirt, is how I felt at that point. It was like there was no reason anybody should look up to me or would want to do anything with me. All those things I had done in high school, it felt like they were worthless.

And in a sense, your feelings toward yourself reverted to what you were going through earlier in your life: worthlessness, no self esteem.

Very true.

And you probably sat a lot of times and thought, "I'm not making a hell of a lot of progress, here. I'm back there."

Yes. It was so painful. I knew I could do so much better in so many different things, and there was no way for me to tell people. I didn't plan for this. This wasn't something I wanted to have happen to me. Nobody understood, really, what was going on because I couldn't tell anybody, really, what was going on inside my mind, in a sense. Few people knew what it was like to be gay. My family didn't completely understand. They were trying, and then the HIV came in and then nobody knew what that meant.

It was almost like they accused you, in a way. It's like you did this on purpose. You're gay, and therefore every gay guy gets this.

Yeah. You're gay, that's why you're HIV positive.

And therefore, for many judgmental people, that's proof enough that being gay is a sin, and HIV is your punishment.

Interview 7

Right. I'm a stereotype. I walked right into so many stereotypes. After I started working with different organizations, I met some people at the Minnesota AIDS Project at the time and talked to them. They were good at redirecting some of those bad thoughts that I was having. "Why did this happen to me? Is it because I was gay?" And they helped answer some of those questions, and they helped me realize that it wasn't just because I was gay, that didn't mean that's why I got HIV. But it was hard to realize that I had stepped into all these stereotypes – and what are other gay men going to think of me? And the other thing that filled my mind was, at the age of 19, where – even if I got out of this relationship – where would I go? I had to find somebody, some people who have HIV. Where is that? At that age, it's a panic situation.

Well, yeah. Just think of all the stuff that's happening. You're coming out, kind of. You fell in love. That was a disappointment, on several levels. I see these 18- and 19-year-olds sitting out in my classes, and they've got a front. They seem so sophisticated and so cool, and they act like they really know it all. But in truth, they don't. They're still 19-year-old kids.

There's so much to learn. And sometimes, as in my case, it can happen so fast, before you even have a glimpse of what's happened. So much happened in that period of time that when I look back, it's like I lived 10 years of my life in that small period of time. I learned so much about myself, about other people, and I think it has guided the rest of my life. I have followed a lot of the things that I've learned as far as trusting people, relationships, how things work out.

Back at that time, did you withdraw and become more cynical? And your word "trust" is a good one. After you trusted this guy and then he turned out to be not at all what he seemed to be, did you ever become more skeptical?

I am a little more skeptical, I think. And that didn't happen until after, so it took years of being whomped on and bad things happening, and the lies and all sorts of different things after that. I have a friend who's going through a similar situation – a good friend of mine who saw what I went through and now is going through the same stuff. And it's like I'm telling him all these different things, and I look back and think, "My god, I don't know how he can think like that." Then I look back and remember, "I thought just like he is thinking." I have to let some of that go and just let him go through it at his own pace. After all, nobody could tell me anything when I was going through it. I did what I wanted to do – and anything that was wrong, anything that happened, it was not wrong. It was okay in my eyes.

Isn't it funny that they don't hear what you have to say? It must be the frustration that parents go through all the time. Parents who've screwed up in one way or another when they were kids, and they say to their kids, "You know, this is going to get you in trouble. Don't do it."

And they do it anyway.

Growing Up Male In America

Somehow you have to ride down your own path and experience all the bumps and turns along the way. When this guy – your first love – got out of jail for the third time and you had finally decided to break the relationship, what was his reaction?

He was very angry. When he got out, he was back to calling me every day, trying to reach me. He would come to my job. He'd write all these love letters and send them to me, give them to me. He'd buy me food, buy me clothes. All the same crap he used to do, trying to show, "I can provide you with all these things. I can do all these things for you. I've never loved anybody as much as I've loved you."

And you thought, "You know, that might be true! Maybe he's changed." And you were almost won over, weren't you?

Yup. It was hard to resist those feelings and to hear him say those things, because what if he's really telling me the truth? And then it was, like, "No."

How long did this relationship last?

Well, I met him when I was 18, and I was 22 when it was definitely over. There was something else happening, too. I finally met a good friend. He wasn't a good friend in the beginning, but he was another gay guy that I could go to the clubs with and just talk to, share things with, drink, dance and party with. There was no sexual tension. It was just a friendship thing. He started showing me things. "There's Minneapolis. You haven't been to Minneapolis?" We'd go to Minneapolis on a regular basis, and he introduced me to his other friends, and he started opening up so many other doors for me. That first guy back home just became a distant memory. Not so much a distant memory, but a whole different life that was ending and a new one was beginning. It was, like, I could look back at that and realize that that's not something I would ever want to be involved in again. I could go forward and meet all these different people, and it was healthy, it was fun, and I didn't have this person nagging and ripping on me and hurting me.

That's the word that's a nice one, isn't it – "healthy"? Some people think it's unhealthy to go to the gay clubs. "Hang around the bars? Is that healthy?" I maintain that it is. You may run into some creeps there, but you also run into other people who are people with some of the same struggles as you have, some very nice people.

Yup. Coworkers you end up seeing. Nowadays, you see all sorts of different people.

Sure. Well, you had a lot of experience in your 22 years, all crammed in there. As you said, about five or 10 years' worth?

Yeah. In those three years with that first relationship especially.

Did you leave the community college then?

I graduated from there, finally, and then went back to the four-year university where I'd started before, but I majored in social work. I met a great teacher. She was new there. She came from California. Not long after I met her, she said to me, "The first time I met you, you had this great smile and you were sitting in the back of the classroom, and I'll never forget your face. But the first thought in my mind was there's a lot going on behind that smile." When she told me that, it was, like, "Wow!" That was a powerful statement, and she has stayed in contact with me ever since I graduated from college.

You have a degree?

Yeah. In social work, a bachelor's. So I did finish it. My final year in college, I was on my own, and I got an internship in Minneapolis. My good friend who introduced me to the healthy gay life in Minneapolis has been my best friend for the last four years now. We talk every day.

He's a non-sexual friend?

Yup. Never been sexual with him.

Because you have a permanent partner now, right?

Now I do, yeah.

For about, what? Two years?

Yup. Two and a half. It will be three in March.

Well, good for you! So, you earned the college degree, and you changed to a major in social work from history and secondary education. Why the change?

It was because of a teacher. When I was at the community college, I had this professor. He taught the history of New England from 1600 to 1792 or whatever. It was the Salem witch hunts and stuff. He returned a term paper that I had written, and it had an F on it. I had never gotten an F in my whole high school career. I was an A honor-roll student in high school, and in all my college classes I was hoping to do the same. But he gave me an F. I asked him, "Why did you give me an F?" His response was, "You didn't work hard enough. You didn't follow directions." He was very negative. He didn't want to hear anything that I had to say. He just dismissed me, basically, when I asked him questions. From that point on I went back to my dorm room and said, "I'm not going to major in history. This is going to be one of the last history classes that I take." That experience just totally redirected my whole thought process.

Wow! That treatment by that teacher must have made you very angry. And well it should have!

When my mom and I went to visit the college, I had gotten my ACT score. It was low, and I knew that, but in high school I was involved in almost every activity I could be, and I was almost getting straight As. The admissions person said, "I can't accept you into college because of your low ACT score." My mom started crying. She got up and ran out of the interview. I remember it so

Growing Up Male In America

clearly. We had been sitting around a table with probably 15 other students and parents, and he pointed at my mom and me and said, "I have to take you two aside and talk to you about your admission." So he took us aside in another room and said, "I can't accept you. You're not college material." He was going on and on about this, and my mom was sitting there crying. I saw all of these tears falling out of her eyes, and she got up and ran out. And I said, "Oh, mom! Mom!" Finally that admissions guy said, "Well, I'll accept you, but not on the basis of campus acceptance criteria." So he was basically saying, "You're in, but not on our recommendation. We're just accepting you because your mom's crying and you're upset."

Essentially he was saying, "Sink or swim – and we think you're going to sink."

Yup.

Well, that bad experience with that history teacher led to a good result, because you got into a different field and you're doing what you like.

Right.

And you're helping people. Do you mind talking about your health situation at present? Since you work through the Minnesota AIDS Project and all.

It's kind of becoming this nemesis now. It's like, here I am working in HIV and with a degree in social work. At some point, I know I'm ready to make the break from it because I've volunteered and been a part of the Minnesota AIDS Project when I was in college. I live with HIV, so then I now work with people with HIV. It's like I work with people and I live with it, so it's always this HIV stance. I need to get on to something else. But healthwise, ever since 1995, when I first tested positive, it has been over six years now that I've had HIV. So when I look back at where I was back in 1995, I was in terrible shape for about six months.

So you were really quite sick when the infection first came. What about medications?

As to medication, I only take two pills a day now. One in the morning and one at night. That's it. And my viral load is at zero. My T cell counts are normal. I'm undetectable. So I'm a fully functioning adult, but I still have HIV. I could transmit it, but my immune system is basically carrying its own weight. It's functioning correctly.

And after six years, right?

Six years.

Okay. What's the prognosis these days?

There's this underlying prognosis, I think. That's my theory. There's this thought out there that HIV is still a very devastating disease, and people still die from it. But if you take care of yourself properly and do everything that's

Interview 7

recommended, I don't see any reason why you couldn't live a normal, healthy life. I could live, you know, until I was retirement age and retire. If the medications work like they do now and continue to work, I probably will never live a different life than anyone else. But if things were to change, if the medications didn't work, I'm not supposed to live past probably 12 years. That's the prognosis. But I haven't reached that yet, and I work with people who have reached almost 17 years.

Does the future worry you?

It's kind of a worry, but HIV is a small part of my life now. It comes up at different times, but I don't think about HIV every day. I don't worry about it. It doesn't cause me pain in my life anymore. Also, everybody doesn't need to know about it. I have a part-time job that I keep just because I've worked for the company for so many years. I fill in when they need me. Nobody there even knows anything about HIV, so it's interesting to hear their comments and questions they ask about my job with the Minnesota AIDS Project. "How can you work with those kind of people?" And I'm, like, "You work with those kind of people every day." *I'm* here – but I don't say, "I'm here" to them!

You're right. They don't need to know.

Well, now, I'm curious to know about this marvelous relationship you have going on currently. Two and a half years. Where did you meet him?

The past comes back to haunt, in a sense! He was a friend of the "bad guy" – the guy I was with for three years, where everything kind of fell apart in my life and was all up in the air. By that time, I had come to Minneapolis quite a few times and went to clubs and house parties at this guy's house. He had a partner at the time. But I never really thought that this would be a guy I would ever be interested in or there would ever be any relationship thing there. He had a relationship, I had a relationship. So I'd been to his house a number of times over a couple of summers. Once my relationship finally broke up, we got to like each other and he started showing some affection towards me. It was kind of very different. It was nice, but it was like something I had never had before.

Was he still in his relationship?

No. That was over. It was over during that first year I met him.

So he's showing a little affection to you?

Yeah, and it was very nice. I didn't know what to do, really, because I didn't really have any feelings towards him. So we agreed to meet that next week. We went out to a restaurant, and he told me he had HIV and *he* had gotten it from his ex, and his ex had been cheating on him and ended up coming back and infecting him. Then they broke up. It was this whole thing I didn't know about him, and it was parallel to my own situation. So we talked about that for a

Growing Up Male In America

while, and then for the next few weeks we hung out. In the beginning I can say, I really wasn't sure where things were going, and I didn't have any feelings for him and I was scared to let things develop because of the negative things my "bad guy" ex had said about him. So we dated for a few months, taking things slowly.

Then my internship in Minneapolis ended. I needed to move. He had a place, a duplex he was renting. I thought our relationship was going fine because by now we'd started having sex. Probably sex didn't come until like a month or so into the relationship. It seemed to be okay. We got along fine. He's a very easy-going guy. I said, "If it doesn't work out, I'll just rent a room from you." Then I moved in, and we've been together ever since. And so it's been two and a half years.

And in this connection with him, there was never any pressure involved. It was all, "If it works out, it works out," and we both agreed to that, so we both understood where we were at. We were kind of pouring our lives together. We were trying to get somewhere in life. I was trying to find steady work and finish school, and he was trying to find his groove in life. We just kind of connected. Ever since, we complement each other in a lot of different areas.

Now, as to the HIV matter, can one be infected with a different strain even if you're HIV positive already?

Yes, you can. You can get reinfected. Different strains from different people.

Have you ever talked with your partner about that? Since he's positive, too?

Yeah. It's been interesting. I think it's kind of been an educational experience for him, because I think he was assuming that since we both have HIV, what's the point of being careful? And I knew that you can get reinfected. I told him you don't know what all you've got or what all I've got from our past partners. I mean, they could have any one of a variety of strains.

Is your chum about your age?

He's nine years older than me.

Okay. Now, for this part of the interview, just give a quick response. Say the first thing that comes into your mind.

How do you define the term "masculine"?

Masculine is a guy who comes across or presents himself in a way that's more manly – like, a moustache, probably. Somebody who has a fit body. Somebody who has a deeper voice or somebody who doesn't have a feminine style of voice. To me, a masculine guy is sort of the ideal man.

Athletic? Physically fit?

Yes. But I wouldn't say they all have to be extremely physically fit or anything like that. I think there's a line between being manly, when I can be out with

Interview 7

friends and someone about whom I can say, "There's a guy who's a nelly queen over there." You know, people who are throwing you attitude and they're lisping or mincing around a lot. That person's effeminate. But when you see a masculine person, their features are more defined. I guess you could say they seem heterosexual. He could more easily hide himself in a heterosexual lifestyle than some guy who is more feminine.

Do sensitivity and gentleness also fit in your definition of a masculine man?

I think they do, but when I think of sensitivity, it's more of a feminine quality than a masculine quality.

Okay. Moving along. We all go through periods of loneliness or depression. What tends to cause this when you go into a slump?

I think it is when I get a lot of negative feedback. You know, you can be having a great time, everything is going well. Your work performance is going fine, your friends are all around you – and then all of a sudden something happens. Like a friend will stop calling for a while, and wonder, "Why isn't he calling me back? Where is he?" Or you're going through a stressful time at work. As soon as something goes wrong, I think it's very easy for your whole psyche to be thrown off or for things to change, and you go downward.

And what do you do when you get down there?

What I tend to do is sleep a lot more. My way of dealing with it is I just need to go home. I need some peace and quiet. I need some time to myself. I spend a lot more time trying to be near home. But I'm pretty good, though, at overcoming depression. I know when I've had a hard day and things are really getting low, and I just go home and close the bedroom door. I need some time to myself. I'll go to sleep. Take an hour or two nap, and I'll come out of it. I might go for a walk to get some exercise and then come back. And by the next day, things are usually back to normal.

Okay. Do you ever have fear of failure in sex? Like a worry that you can't get it up? Do you wonder about that sometimes?

Yes. It does come up.

Or it doesn't come up! [Laughter] *That was a little pun. Forgive me.*

[Laughs] It does come up in my thoughts! It's just that ever since I became diagnosed with HIV, my whole sexual life turned around completely, 360 degrees. As soon as that happened, I was very ill. I stopped really having any sexual urgings for a while. Just trying to get back to normal was difficult for me. Then once I was healthy again, I just didn't have any interest in sex. Of course, I was still in that three-year relationship at the time, so that might have been a part of it. Even now, in my current good relationship, I've told my partner, "Sometimes you're going to have to initiate a lot of these things, because sometimes my desire is not always there."

Growing Up Male In America

What is the most hurtful thing that a friend or a relative has ever done to you – not counting that terrible relationship with your ex or your abusive stepfather?

A female friend once said, "You can live here at my house for a while, but don't give my kid HIV. Don't give my kid AIDS." That's what her comment was, and that stuck with me. That comment was just like a dagger.

Do you run into that a lot?

I don't think so much, but even my mom has told me things. Back in 1995 – when I was sick and I lived at home for a couple of months when I was trying to recover and I was away from my ex for a little bit – she would say that she used to wash and rewash the dishes that I would eat from. She would come in every night and check to see that I was still breathing. She'd wash the sheets over and over to make sure they were completely clean. She was just very scared that there was some way I would transmit it to my sisters or her.

And here's another small-town thing I'll just throw in here. Before I told my mom I had HIV, she worked at the clinic. A big building. The floor that had the HIV clinic on it was the same floor where she worked. It wasn't really an HIV clinic, but the doctors who worked on her floor saw people with HIV. I was going to a doctor at the same desk my mom worked at, so she would continually ask me, "What's wrong? What's wrong?" And one day, after I came out of an appointment and started crying at her desk, she took me into a room – and that's when I told her I had HIV. So it was at her *work* station that I had to *divulge* my condition to her. She was *so* concerned, and she was so scared.

Final question: Did you ever think about going into the Army or the Navy?

I almost got in.

Really? Which branch?

It would have been the Army.

And that would have paid for college.

Yup. That was my plan. But I had a heart murmur, so they turned me down. So that would have been an interesting experience, coming out. Because I hadn't come out yet, and I would have, probably, getting in the Army and around all those men and …whoa! [Laughs]

I think your story is fascinating, and you expressed it very clearly and very openly and very honestly, and I appreciate that.

Is there anything that you would care to add that you think the readers might like to know about a gay man, age 25, HIV positive? Something that you think might be helpful or interesting or fascinating?

I just had a whole bunch of thoughts come flying at me, but I think when you're coming out, as a gay man, when anybody is questioning their sexuality and dealing with those feelings, you're very scared and you're very shy, and

Interview 7

you're concerned. You're fearful about a lot of things. And people tell you so many things. "Be aware of this. Be scared of this. Don't be around someone like this." I think it's important for people to know that if somebody has HIV or AIDS, it shouldn't be a *discredit* to a person. It's an *aspect* of a person's life. It's just because I have come across this in life and others could have come across it this way in their lives, too. The same with being gay. It could happen to anyone. Don't think that you are safe from it or you are immune to it or you can run from it – because it's present out there, and it disguises itself in a number of ways. You know? It's all about education, I think. It's important, even if you're *not* a gay person or a person with HIV, just to know, to be aware. Know that it's out there, and that the person that you're working with or a friend of yours that you're talking to or your clergyman or anybody in the community you're talking to could be *that* person, and you may not even know it. It's out there. It's present. Young people, especially, can come across it at any point in their lives and not even know it.

And some of the readers of this book will be young people. And I think for any kid who reads this, he might be fascinated by the title: Growing Up Male. *Especially if he's wondering about his own sexuality. He'll hear your story, and he'll hear the accounts of the few other gay guys who are in the book – and those stories might make coming out a bit easier. I think we're lucky to be living in an age where there's a little more education and intelligence about this issue than there was in previous eras.*

Well, I really do appreciate your sitting for this interview, and I thank you very much. It was wonderful to get to know you.

Thank you, too.

Postscript – December 2001

This man is still involved in an emotionally healthy relationship. His physical health remains good and constant.

Interview 8

"My memories are of him just not showing up and me being upset."

This interview was conducted on May 29, 2000. He was 22 years old, 5' 11" tall, 180 pounds with blond hair. He was studying graphic design at the university level.

We're going to begin with early childhood. You're a man of 22, almost 23 years old. And so I suppose thinking back to when you were a little kid is a little difficult. Where were you born?

A suburb of Minneapolis. In 1977.

And your parents are still married?

Well, no. My mother and my real father were married for six or seven years and then had me. They got divorced when I was three years old. After that, I lived exclusively with my mother, and then when I was about 10 years of age, she started dating again. I was also raised by my mother's mother, my grandmother.

Your mom didn't really date much immediately after the divorce?

Not from what I can remember. I remember meeting a couple of guys. Like they'd get back from a date, you know, and the guy would hang out for a little bit. But more or less, that's about it. Then they'd leave, go home. At least I think they did. I don't think my mom dated much because I think she knew it would probably confuse me, and my real father was somewhat in the picture between those years. I think he started disappearing after I was 10 years of age. Or not coming around nearly as much as he used to.

Did you have visitation time with your biological dad?

Yeah. Unless he copped out of it.

Did he do that often?

He did it fairly often. I think part of my mother's memories and my memories

Growing Up Male In America

are of him just not showing up and me being upset. There I was, about four or five years old, with my little suitcase, waiting and waiting for him to show up, and he'd never come.

I can just see it. I mean, it's kind of sad, isn't it? You've got your little suitcase packed and you're ready to go on an overnight or whatever.

And he calls in just for whatever reason and says he can't do it. I think he put most of the blame on work, but who knows what his blames were? I've never been able to ask him. Most of the time he wouldn't even call when he wouldn't show up, and Mom would tell me that he must have got busy at work. But I remember I'd cry a lot when he just didn't show.

What's your relationship, if any, with him now, at this point?

Non-existent. I don't know if he's ... I mean, I'm to the point where I wouldn't know if he's dead or alive.

And he lives somewhere around here? In the region?

From the last time I heard, he lives somewhere in Texas. He hasn't talked to me since I was 13 years old, 13 or 14 years old. He just stopped calling me and keeping in touch.

Did you ever try to regain a connection? Or did you think about it?

I've thought about it. I've thought about talking to his stepsister and seeing what's her theory on this whole idea of a father not knowing his only son. Supposedly only son. Who knows? I think I'd like to go find him. Maybe take a summer off and then see what he's doing. Maybe ask him questions or just kind of blow it all off and just play along for a little bit. And then maybe – if for some reason he accepts me – maybe then start reaming into him and asking him what the hell was his problem? You know. I have other goals in life right now that I've got to obtain first before I actually look for him.

That was my next question. It's not a top priority?

No. But it was almost a year ago. I was almost going to look for him. But then I figured other things were more important, so ...

Is it almost like a sore that's healed? And then to go back and scrape the scab off again?

I don't know. Like, I don't know if I'd get dreadfully emotional. If I started saying, "Why'd you do that?" I think now I've been able to numb myself to the point where it's just not going to affect me.

Did you ever think that in a real way, your mother was both your mother and your dad? She was serving as both parents, essentially.

Yes, definitely.

Well, let's move on. Did you go to public school or parochial?

Interview 8

Public. I actually went to three elementary schools.

Well, now, think back to starting kindergarten. By any chance, do you remember the first day of kindergarten?

Yeah. I remember just one blink of it, and that's just all the kids sitting around in this group, and then I just see my buddy next to me, and then there's just me. And that's it. I know I went to preschool, is that what they call it? And that's all I remember. I don't really remember too much of it. But the thing is, I do know a fair amount about kindergarten, because I read teachers' reports on me. My mother had me sent to a therapist or a psychologist of some sort, for some reason, and I had hyper activity. But I don't think … I never saw myself as that hyper. But I guess, according to these reports which my kindergarten teacher wrote about me … you know, like she was also playing the role of psychologist and tried to psychoanalyze me as a child. The report was six to eight pages long. It was filled with comments like, "Oh, he did this today" and "He cut in front of the line." "Ran off." "Didn't listen." Whatever. I wasn't like that with my mother.

Do you remember any peer pressure in kindergarten? What I mean is, were you aware of who the "cool" kids were and who the outsiders were?

Yeah, there's always the so-called "cool" people. Every person wanted to hang out with them. I think I struggled a little bit to try to socialized with them, but I always ended up fighting them. I do remember … that was in probably, like, around second or third grade. I had my first enemy in school. There was always one kid. I remember his name. I even remember his last name. He was just a little bit bigger than I was, taller and slimmer, but he had the build of a fourth or fifth grader. I always ended up fighting him in the school yard because he didn't like me, for some reason, and I didn't like him just because I think everyone liked him. So I wanted to pound him. I ended up losing most of the time.

You were kind of the great equalizer, huh? If he was so popular, we can take care of him and knock him down?

[Laughs] Knock him out and I'd take his spot. But he always won. He was just bigger than me, and I just didn't have the smarts to beat him, somehow.

Was religion very important in your growing up? Did your mother take you to church, and was there Sunday school?

Yeah. I did have Sunday school for the first grade or so, but my Mom never shoved religion on me at all. I hear parents nowadays – parents saying to their children, "Thank God for this." Or they make comments specifically for a religious reason: "Say your prayers before you go to bed." You know, even if they lightly believe in religion, they still make these generalized comments about religion to their children. Never happened to me. I mean, I quit going to Sunday school or bible study.

Growing Up Male In America

What religion? Methodist?

Well, I was baptized Catholic but was raised Lutheran, sort of. The Lutheran church is where my mother took me. But my mother ... I think it was almost something to keep me occupied. I think that's probably why she took me there. I don't think she's a religious person herself, and we'd never get into debates about God. Never.

At this point in your life, do you call yourself religious?

No. Not at all.

If you think back to those first several years of elementary school, are there any teachers who stand out in your mind as being particularly good or particularly influential, or who made an impact on your life in some way?

Well, I can remember all my teachers. Some teachers were people who showed me what I *didn't* want to be. I wanted to make sure I didn't end up like them, because some of them were just real eccentric. Either they were just too wacky or just, you know, they're there to teach and kind of move you through the doorways and get you out of there.

When you consider how many teachers we're exposed to in the course of our education, it's amazing how few have made much of an impact, isn't it?

Yeah. I guess I could say I've only run into two teachers I can actually carry on a conversation with and hang out with: one would be a professor I had at another school, and the other one is you. Because really I've never carried on a conversation with any other teachers much at all.

In elementary school, how did you think of yourself?

The mentality I think I had going through the first through fifth grade is, "No one is higher than thou." I always knew I'm better than these people, you know. I knew that. Everyone gets labeled a nerd or this or that. I think people labeled me as somewhere between an outcast or out-of-the-norm or a nerd.

Why so?

Well, I don't know. I don't see myself as looking like a nerd. But I don't know. I just never was ever allowed into the popular crowd, and I didn't hang out with them. I just hung out with the people I got along with, and those people I guess were considered the unpopular people. So I think there's only two kinds of people, really. There's an in crowd and there's an out, and I was just in the out crowd.

Did you ever wish you could be in the so-called "in" crowd? The cool people?

I think so. Everyone would like to be in it because they assume that life would be more interesting. But I don't know.

Now, as a little kid, were you thin, overweight, short, tall for your age, or about normal?

Interview 8

I was never really overweight. I think I was just average the whole way through.

You never felt like you were too short or too fat or too tall or too skinny or too any of these things?

Well, I feel short now. [Laughs] I'm 5-foot-11. That's not relatively short. But you stand next to someone that's 6-foot-1, 6-foot-2, you know, you sometimes wish, "Don't I really want to be a little bit bigger?"

Okay. Now, let's jump to high school, and that thing called puberty is beginning to happen.

You're supposed to become sexual at 16. I don't know. It happens earlier for others.

Would you say you developed early or late or about the right time?

Well, I don't know. I never knew when I developed, when I was developed just right. This guy that I saw in the locker room once, he was hung like a horse!

Do you remember what year, or how old you were?

I think that was eighth grade. We were at the swimming pool and just going to change, and he's hung like a horse. And I'm looking at myself and, like, "Shit. This ain't right." [Laughter] I just got a little bit of hair growing. He's hung, so I really never knew if I was growing right. It had to be eighth grade, because I started having sex when I was 15. But even when I look at myself at 15 ... god, I must have been not *as* big. I mean, I was still growing through 16, 17, 18 and up. I didn't actually feel comfortable with my penis. I never actually felt comfortable until I was about 19 or 20, when I actually felt like, "Okay, this is just how it's going to be."

Did you think your penis was smaller than average?

Yeah, I think so. Or was average, I don't know.

Now, when you felt this way, you kept that all to yourself, didn't you? I mean, it's not the sort of thing you sit around and talk about, even to your best buddy.

No. Never talked to him about that. I can remember one time, we were looking through a book, and it showed the stages of what a guy's dick growth should be all through these age groups or when pubes should start growing in. And I'm, like, "Yeah, I'm over here!"

Again, men tend not to talk about these things very much, do they?

Well, they do now.

Really?

A really good friend of mine was telling me this the other day. He said he and two of his buddies whipped out their cocks and measured them. Not each other, they didn't measure each other, but they each measured or compared dicks. I

Growing Up Male In America

don't think they were drunk, either. They're about 18, 19 years old, and they all know that none of them have homosexual tendencies, from what I know. But I'm just assuming that none of them do. And so he and I were just having a conversation or whatever about what each of our dicks are like, because we were just talking about sex. About having small dicks, you know.

I wonder about how many kids are intimidated by the thought that they're so small, and the whole locker-room scene with blatant nudity is scary for them. Did that cause you to feel shy in locker-room situations?

Yeah. I was extremely careful. But I guess maybe subconsciously, that's what caused it. I think I was even before that, you know. Making sure my cock was covered the whole time when I was changing, because in junior high level you have to change into this stupid outfit. Granted, you usually have underwear on, but if you have briefs on, you know, those cling to you. So those obviously tell you if you've got a small one or not. So, you know, you just kind of have a towel wrapped around or what not, you know. You dress and undress real quickly. You know, bent over. You also do it so as not to give any ammo to anybody, you know. Because obviously there's going to be someone in those locker rooms that doesn't like you or just wants to make fun of you for some stupid reason, especially if he goes and announces, when all the girls are there, that you have a small dick. You know, you don't want to deal with that. So it's just better not giving them any ammo and to kind of lay low.

Let's break from the chronology of school at this point and get into some free-association thoughts. I'm going to give you a sentence, and then I'm going to ask you to complete it.

[Laughs] You're not going to give me pictures and ask what the first thing that comes to mind is, are you?

I do have some ink blots. [Laughter] *There's a wonderful joke about the ink-blot tests. A psychologist shows an ink blot to a patient, and the doctor asks him to describe it. The guy says, "Well, that's two people having sex." And the doctor says, "Okay." He shows the patient another ink blot and asks, "What is this?" And the patient says, "That's two people having sex." And the same with the third ink blot and so on – and every time the guy answers, "It's two people having sex." Finally the doctor says, "Well, sir, you know – in every one of these ink blots you keep saying it's about people having sex. You have a one-track mind." And the guys says, "Well, don't blame me, Doc. You're the one showing me all the dirty pictures!"* [Laughter]

I'm going to give you this sentence, now, and then you finish it. "The thing that people do not know about me is ... what?"

I'm pretty open about everything. It can be anything, right?

Anything.

Interview 8

Probably the nude pictures I've had taken of me for some modeling sessions I did a year or so ago. I mean, a few people know about it, but not a lot of people do.

It's not the sort of thing you bring up in conversation?

No, it just doesn't come up.

Do you know why? You're not embarrassed about it, are you?

No. I just don't announce it. Like if someone asks me or says, "What have you been … what'd you do?" Like if I just did a shoot like, let's say, yesterday, if someone asked me, "What did you do yesterday?" You know, I'm not going to tell him. Because it would come back around to haunt me. You know, especially if they told it to the wrong people.

Now, you've done quite a bit of this nude modeling. Are you proud of those photos?

Yeah. I'd like to do it on a more professional level. I have submitted my pictures – or pictures of my body – to other photographers around on the Internet to see if they'd actually consider using me, but I've never gotten any replies back. I only did two shoots. I would like to do it on a more professional level but with photographers who know what they are doing. You know, proper lighting and expensive equipment. Then I'd like to do it. I'd be up for that. The guys who photographed the two shoots I did will be the first to admit that they're not yet on the professional level.

These guys who did the photo shoots, did they know what they were looking for in a model?

Yeah. I think they know what they're looking for in a model. Not as a person, but for a "look" – meaning what other people are looking at. But there are so many looks out there that, you know, there's not just one look that is real popular.

The whole idea of male nudes immediately begs the question of who the clients are for that kind of photography. A big part of the audience for that kind of photography is gay males, isn't it? Are you secure enough in that regard?

Oh, yeah. I think if I wasn't secure with my own lifestyle, which is heterosexual, and if I didn't accept the homosexual or gay lifestyle, I wouldn't do the modeling, for sure. But I mean, it's part of life nowadays. Those distinctions between gay and straight don't matter these days. I was just trying to think back, now, when's the first time I actually thought about two men being together sexually. I don't even know if that came into my mind until I was maybe 17 years old. Guys always kid around about gay things, but I didn't really start knowing about the gay community until I was 17 or 18.

Anyway, you're secure enough on your own that posing in nude photos doesn't seem to bother you. So, what's the thrill for you in modeling nude? Is it a little streak of exhibitionism in you?

Growing Up Male In America

No, not really. I guess when I get liquored up, I get like that. Like at the club where I tend bar, there's kind of a big joke between every one of my coworkers at this bar where I work: I'm the one who bares his ass all the time when I've started drinking. Or every time I'm going to attempt to moon them, they go, "Oh, everybody's seen that!" I don't know. I just do it ... and I just did the nude modeling because, first of all, I was getting paid for it, but also because it was another confidence booster.

I never really started getting another guy's opinion of me until I'd really met a gay man who said I was good-looking. That gay guy was actually the first man who gave me an opinion of what I look like. Straight guys never really talk about, "Oh, this guy looks great." Or "You're good looking." You know, like your best friend, when you're around 17 or 18, he's still not going to come up to you and say, "Oh, you look good in that shirt, or "You should do your hair a little bit differently." Girls will say that to each other. Guys won't.

Just recently, at the club where I work, some good guy friends – and these are really good friends – they'll say, "Oh, you're looking good tonight. You're looking cut. You're looking ripped." You know, they're constantly commenting on how good I look. And these are straight guys in a straight club!

There's one friend I really don't talk about looks with because I know I'm better looking than him. I mean, when you get some girls in the room or even guys, I could say, they're going to find me more attractive than they'll find him. And he's been my friend for 10 years now, but I've never said, "That shirt looks good on you" or "You should wear your hair differently." I know for sure he's just got to clean up his act. I mean, he's got to get some better clothes. He still wears clothes that are from high school.

Well, so much for that. Now, another question: What specific events in your personal life over which you have had little or no control have left a lasting impression on you?

Well, I think probably my father leaving me. I mean, I had no control over that. And I had no control over trying to convince him to stay. I didn't want him to leave. So, I think he had the most profound effect on me. Granted, that's what he did. Maybe a lot of other kids who did grow up with fathers in their home will never understand this, but because my father abandoned me, I will never leave. If I get a female pregnant and have a kid, I'm never going to leave that kid. I'm not going to abandon that kid, like my father did to me. I had an incident where that came out, where I did get someone pregnant, and we decided we were going to keep it, and I told her straight up that I'm not leaving the situation. I'm here to support you. I can't be like my father.

Do you know if you were wanted as a baby? Did your parents want to have a kid?

Yeah. I was planned. I came along when I was supposed to, I guess, because they waited after they got married and were a couple of years into their jobs.

Interview 8

They waited two or three years until they decided to have me. So I was planned. I think my mom wanted a second child. I think she wanted to have a girl because that female would typically enjoy the stuff that my mom likes. You know, cute little things and stuff like that. And I enjoy those things, too, to an extent. I mean, that's kind of where I get a lot of my taste for houses and taste for different things. I get it from my mother, because that's what I grew up in.

Did you ever think that maybe your dad left because of something you did?

Well, I don't know if I ever blamed myself. I was just a little kid and too young to understand. But if he could see me today, I'd shock the hell out of him. I think he'd be extremely impressed, or he probably wouldn't believe that I am his son. I just don't comprehend the whole genetics things. I still do things like my father. Like the other day, my mom said that I still remind her a lot of my father. She said that I get out of the car like my father, or even the way I get in the car is like my father. She said that to me when I was just having lunch with the grandmother and my mom, and she was telling me that. So then when I got in my car, I'm like thinking, "How do I get in my car that's different than anyone else?" I guess just the way I get out of my car and maybe look around or whatever.

You can see if dad was around all the time. Little kids imitate. But where did that come from?

Yeah, that's what I was saying. I don't see how I picked up anything that my father could have given me because of the fact that he was never around. As a person, my father apparently thinks things through a lot, but his rationale got screwed up when he decided not to be around me.

Let's talk about your mom. Since she was the prime parental influence in your life and you do get along well with her, what, in your estimation, does she do right? What do you admire in her?

What do I admire? I think I admire the way that she can be pleasant at all times, no matter what the hell's going on. I mean, she'll always have a smile on her face even if she's pissed off as hell at someone. Or even at family functions, you know, she could give a rat's ass about someone because they treated someone like shit or whatever, and she can just still be pleasant and smile and talk to that person as if there's nothing wrong. I admire that. I can't do that. If I don't like you, I'm not going to sit and waste my time talking to you. My mom treats me like a person, not like a son. She's always said she wants to be my friend, not a parent. But you know, she has to keep that parent level. You always have to keep that parent level.

What's the greatest or biggest lie you ever told your mother?

I don't know. I guess it was the whole pregnancy issue I had with someone, but that never came about because she lost the baby.

Growing Up Male In America

Your mom never knew that your lady friend lost the baby?

> She never knew about it at the time it was happening, but I did tell her later. I could have gotten away with not telling her. I debated it. But I told her after the whole situation was over. I just don't lie to my mother. There's just nothing to hide. I'm not a bad person.

So the relationship you have with her is pretty honest.

> Yes. really. The only thing I haven't told her about was that nude modeling thing.

Another topic: Do you ever cry? What is the sort of thing that would make you cry?

> A bad movie! [Laughs] Just kidding. I don't know. I can be emotional to a point. There are sad movies, you know, like *Philadelphia*. I cried during that. And *Schindler's List*, you know, at the end of that.

What about in your life?

> Yeah, that's what I'm trying to ... my life, I mean I don't ...

Do you ever get depressed or feeling melancholy or blue?

> I used to. I went through a phase where I was constantly crying a lot. I remember doing that. My mom would come into my bedroom while I was crying and listening to music and she'd ask, "What's wrong?" I'd say, "I don't know. I'm just crying!" I don't know. I felt like a female, actually. But, you know, still to this day, I don't remember what I was so upset about or if I was upset. I think I just kind of went through a weird stage.

Was it at the time of puberty?

> Yeah, it definitely was puberty.

Oh, well. Your glands were going crazy in there.

> So, I don't know, I was 15 or somewhere around there. I would just sit and listen to music. I used to do that a lot. I'd sit in my rocking chair in my room and listen to music and just think. It was nothing specific, just kind of think and analyze or whatever. I used to cry. But I think really the last time I cried was when I was dealing with my pregnant girlfriend. With, you know, the child. When I was explaining to her that I could never really abandon that child, I was crying. One other time I was leaving from my grandmother's house – I don't know if it was Thanksgiving or when it was – but I was just overcome with such emotion. I said, "I gotta go. I'll see you later." And I just started crying on the drive back. I was just getting tear-eyed and stuff like that. And I do play the music to my mood, you know. So then I'm playing opera and shit like that. But I don't cry that often on a regular basis.

Having your mother as the sole parent, did that develop and nurture your feminine side?

Interview 8

    Yeah. Definitely.

And you felt that was a good thing.

    I don't think I'd have it any other way. I mean, it sucks that my father left. But I don't know how my life would be or how everything would have turned out if he was there. So I think, all in all, whatever happened worked out okay, and someone is watching out for me. That's kind of what my mom says. She always said, "Someone's watching out for you." So, I guess, maybe my father leaving would be bettering my life. Who knows?

You could have the attitude, "I'm all screwed up because my dad left." You could go through life carrying all that "baggage" on your shoulder, but you have taken it the other way and said it pisses you off that he left, but you've got to move on and live your life.

    Yeah, there's nothing you can do about it. I think that's why you get a lot of screwed-up kids. They just hold on to everything and just don't want to get past it. And they use it as an excuse.

Now losing the baby ... that was a miscarriage, wasn't it?

    Yeah. To some extent. The surgery is what caused it. She was in for surgery because of uterine cancer while she was pregnant, and they had to remove a fallopian tube and then they had to scrape the uterine wall. After being subjected to all those drugs and being sedated and the emotional trauma. But you know, this is all circumstantial. I'm not sure ... I know she had surgery when she was about two and a half months into the pregnancy. Her body just rejected it.

Do you have an opinion on abortion?

    I've always been pro-choice. Like I said, do what you want. I've been to three Gay Pride Parades and festivities, and I always go to the abortion part and buy a button. I usually give them ten bucks when you're supposed to just give a dollar. I'm pro-choice, you know. Like the famous saying goes, "If you don't want one, don't have one." Another man for women's rights!

You can see all kinds of examples of kids who were brought into the world who probably shouldn't have been.

    Yeah, I know. If it was a woman I didn't like, I'd be more for abortion. If this was just a fling and she gets pregnant, there's no point in keeping the baby. But I've always said to myself, you've got to deal with the consequences of your actions.

Okay. Back to high school, now. Were you involved in extra-curricular activities? Like track or swimming?

    No. Nothing. Not even in college.

Was there a reason? Did you make a conscious effort?

Growing Up Male In America

Well, I never even made an effort. I guess all the so-called popular people were into that stuff, but I just wasn't. Also, I was in a huge graduating class, so I just didn't want to deal with the competition. I knew there was going to be competition. But you see, I never had a father to throw that football or baseball around with me so that I could better my technique or be good at that. Yeah, I could throw a football and, yeah, I can throw a baseball, but even to this day I can't throw a football and have it spiral every time.

So, what sports are you good at?

I'm not good at anything when it comes to sports. I guess I'm okay at … no, I hate baseball, but I can probably connect the bat with the ball. You see, I've never gotten in front of a ball going 80 miles per hour. That scares me because I don't trust the person throwing it, and so I just don't want to deal with that. And my throwing isn't good and that kind of limits me a lot, so I don't think I'm good at any sport.

But you do work out at a gym?

Yeah. It's just a competition to look good, I guess. And then just learning about health stuff, and that's almost like a brain-power thing. I think of sports competition differently than I consider competition in a job. I think there are going to be jobs out there that I'm going to have to work on a team with four or five people and, you know, we've got to work together to finish a project. And sometimes you're in competition with other employees, you know, trying to get that better mark so you can get that better promotion.

All right. Now, let's jump to your college experience. Have you developed some friends at this university? Close friends?

I've only developed one friend who I keep in touch with, and that's you. I mean really, there's no one else in this school that I intend to keep in touch with. You're the only one, really, that I've decided that I'm going to keep as a friend. [Laughs]

That's very kind of you to say that.

I guess I would have liked to have made some friends here, but it's hard to establish any type of friendship with anybody. Unless for some reason you have a friend who has friends and you hang out with them a few times and then they accept you.

But then you had a bartending job in Minneapolis every weekend, and so that meant you had to pick up and get out of town.

I remember I didn't start working at the Minneapolis bar right away when I started college here. I didn't start bartending there until December, so I had all the way from September through December of not working weekends. But I mostly stayed at home. No one struck me as very interesting. You find somebody interesting and it just takes years, I think, for those friendships to get

Interview 8

established. I went to another college for three years before coming here, and I established relationships with a lot of people. I still keep in touch with six of them. I can't call all of them individually. It just takes too much of my time. But, you know, other than that, I think in due time that will end, too, to the point where I'll be keeping in touch with maybe only one of those six. Or maybe just still the same two people. Just touch base.

That's one of the things I find sad about teaching. It's like a train station or an airport. It's a series of arrivals and departures, and you just get to know some students when suddenly they have to leave. I think life is like that, too. You get a job transfer, you move to another town, and pretty soon you don't see each other again. But the friendships that do continue are really rather rare.

Yeah. I can say that I probably will have a continuing friendship with at least three people from the other college. I will always keep in touch with them.

At this time in your life, would you care to disclose who your closest female friends and your closest male friends are – and what is it about them that makes them friends? In other words, I'm asking you to define what a friend is.

I guess my closest friends are three guys. To be honest, those are three different friendships. I mean, they're all close friendships, but I talk to each one of them about three different kinds of things.

Are these three about the same age as you are?

One is 19, and the other two are 23. I like all those three guys in three different ways.

Now, what about your closest female friends at this point in your life?

I have one close female, who I made friends with when I was a freshman in college, and I've kept in touch with her. I can talk to her about anything from masturbating to … whatever.

Does she talk about masturbating, too?

Yeah. She tells me she does it. A funny thing about her is, she gets off on getting guys to masturbate in front of her. She'll just go with the guys, and she'll start talking to one of them and get him to whack off right in front of her. She just loves that. They don't touch her at all or anything. I slept with her once. I was just horny and I figured, well, she's always wanted to have sex with me.

Could I ask a personal question? Sometimes, when friends go to bed with each other, the friendship is strained after that.

Well, it was fine in bed, but I think it's because she's a very sexual person and I am sexual, too. So I think we connected on that level. It was more or less a quickie. It wasn't like, you know, a romantic thing. It was just like, "Let's do it."

It didn't affect the friendship?

Growing Up Male In America

No. She was worried that it would, and I thought maybe it would, too. But, no. We both knew what the hell was going on, and we both were into it, and it worked out all right.

Do you have any female friends who you would call good, close friends but you've never had sex with and you probably never would?

I don't really have that many close female friends. Yeah, I'm dating women now, but I wouldn't consider them really close friends after knowing some of them for a month or so. So I don't classify any of them as friends. Granted, they might know a lot about me, but I don't talk to them on a regular basis.

And you define friendship in a different way?

Yeah. You know, the work people, I can hang out with them and give them hugs and a kiss on the cheek or whatever like that. And they feel real comfortable around me, I feel real comfortable around them. Yeah, yeah. I think any female I choose to associate myself with, if I choose to let them in closer, it usually means I wouldn't mind having sex with them. That's the only reason why I'm going after women, it's because I'm attracted to them. So most of the women I meet now usually end up in sexual relationships.

What are you looking for? Is it "that one" that you can fall in love with?

I'd like to have that, but I'm so skeptical right now. If I'm looking for women, yeah, I'm always looking at them as a possible long-term thing. I'm always looking at them as that.

Do you ever talk to your mother about what sexual behavior was when she was in high school?

You know, I never asked my mom. I don't know why I haven't.

What I was thinking is: in you mother's generation, was sex recreational? I mean, today if things are "right" when the bar closes, people just go home and have sex. Nobody thinks about it too much more than it's just recreation and fun. No commitment.

It's recreation for a lot of people, but I do run into people who are not like that. They're not necessarily saving themselves for that right person – it's just that they don't want diseases.

So, I wonder. You're living in a time that you would call very "permissive" when it comes to all of this. I mean, most people wouldn't condemn you and make you leave town because you had sex before marriage.

Well, if I'm going to have a long-term relationship, she's got to be interested in the same things that I am. There are women I have dated and had sex with, but they're only comfortable in two positions and that's about it. You know, not willing to try other positions. And that turns me off. It also tells me a lot about them, too. They're not experimental or open-minded. I mean, I base a lot of

Interview 8

things on what their sexual wants and needs are. Some women just don't care to have sex.

What qualities do you look for in a mate?

I guess the biggest one is actually they show that they care for me. Not just by saying it, because there are some people out there that don't actually show it. The only time they actually show that they care for you is when you're in bed, or they just make little comments here and there. But they don't actually show it. I want more than just a little gesture. They've got to be able to show that they actually care for me by touching me more or caressing my shoulder. You know, being affectionate. Granted, that doesn't start right off the bat. I guess what I look for first is, I've got to be attracted to them. Brain-wise, they've got to be interesting. You know, observant, intellectual. Common sense is a big plus, because if you don't have common sense, I don't know how you function.

What about a cute, dumb but highly sexual woman?

That type – and if somehow she liked me, more or less I'd just have sex with her. And just say, "Okay. See ya!" Because I don't think she probably would want to be with me. But I don't know if I'd ever let myself get to that point. Most women I've dated, they've had somewhat of a brain.

Okay.

When you see a woman for the first time, what do you look at first? Breasts?

No. I'm not a boob person. I guess I look at her face, and then I look at her ass. [Laughs] I'm more of a butt man, I guess. On the whole, though, it's the face.

I think surveys show that women usually say the first thing they look at in a man is his eyes. But do you know what women really look at more in a man?

I think it's his butt.

Right.

If somebody wants to see you go into a rage, what really makes you mad?

I don't know. To get me to go into a rage? Insult my intelligence. What I tell the women I date is, "Don't fuck with me." And I've told that to several of them. That's the biggest quote I use when I date women.

What would "fucking with you" be? Being unfaithful?

This is what I add to it when they ask me, "What do you mean by that?" I tell them, "If you have any issues or any problems with me, let me know. Tell me. If you feel you have feelings for someone else, let me know. Don't let me find out, because I will. You fuck with me, you're out the window." And I don't get pissed off. I do it in a dead serious way.

Now, if you expect "don't fuck with me" from them, do you use that as your own Golden Rule, too? You're honest and true to the women you date?

Growing Up Male In America

Yeah, I am honest and true. Obviously be faithful to me, but just be honest and respecting and then everything kind of branches off from that easily. I mean, you can't be unfaithful if you're honest. So anyway, if she's not honest or she goes with another guy, I tell her it's her loss. If I like them and I say I want to have a date with them and then they want to end it with me, it's their loss. It's not mine. I'm not losing anything. I can find another woman. It's not that hard.

Have you ever been in love?

You know, I was thinking on the way over here how I define love.

I guess people define love in so many different ways. One strong example of love is if you would sacrifice your life for another person. That's a real strong one. I guess I have a degree of love for everybody, to a point. But I guess I can say I don't know if I'd necessarily sacrifice my life for my three best male friends. I think love is cruel. It makes you do weird things. So I guess, to some extent, I probably have loved one woman. God knows I would never say that to her, though. Nor would she say she loved me. Maybe she knew it. I don't know. She sure as hell never said that, and neither of us was going to talk about it.

Yeah. And some people use the four-letter word "love" all the time, and then it loses its meaning.

Sometimes – the really older you get, and if you're with that same person, I don't know if it's considered love anymore. It's more or less you're stuck with them. If you're married.

So maybe some day love will come your way – but you haven't experienced that yet?

I don't think so.

Maybe glimmers of it?

When I left this one girl, she was really pissed off. So that helps. [Laughs]

That helps. If you do the dumping.

Okay. Let's move on. Question: Where did you learn most about sex? This is kind of multiple choice. Maybe it's a combination. Friends. Your mother. Internet. Books. Movies.

Books and movies.

Where'd you learn the details? Like how to function sexually?

I don't know. I guess books and movies. Because I was pretty much having sex way before all my friends were, so I can't say I learned from friends. Yeah, books and movies, I guess.

Your first sexual experience? First of all, you were about how old?

Fifteen. I had just turned 15.

Interview 8

And what was she like and what was it like and how successful was it?

It was actually at my grandparents' cabin up north. In the basement. Weirdest position, too, in a way. Well, she'd had sex before with another guy. I think she was having sex when she was 14, so she was more experienced than I was. And it was more than once that she had had sex with this other guy. Once we got started, it lasted no more than about … I don't even know. [Laughter] Like, not even a minute, maybe. I didn't stay in her because I didn't know how to pull out or when to pull out. Because, you know, you usually don't have an idea of what this is supposed to feel like. I don't remember even masturbating before that. I was trying to think about the first time I'd masturbated, and it was after that experience with that girl.

Well, that's very interesting. Now, did you have wet dreams?

Yeah. And I knew that I had this stuff in my bed. [Laughs] Oh, I remember the first time I came with another person, and that wasn't by having sex. That was what they call dry fucking. I don't know of a nicer term for it.

Now, about dry fucking – describe that.

Well, we both had our clothes on, and she was on top of me and rubbing back and forth. So it was just like if I had my clothes on right now, and she's just moving her hips up and down on top of me. That's why I call it dry fucking. Anyway, that was the first time I came, and that freaked me out because I had no idea what the hell was going on. And wet dreams? I didn't really put two and two together, really. I didn't know. But then I came and I'm, like, "What the hell is this stuff?" And I'm just wiping it off in the bed. I was embarrassed by it.

These first times are so interesting because they're often so clumsy.

Yes. Oh, definitely. Or very quick. [Laughter]

You mentioned masturbation before. I'm always interested to know about that, because everybody does it, and yet it's one of those things that people tend not to talk about. I think junior high boys talk about it in a kind of a giggly sort of way, but a lot of people don't like to admit that they masturbate, even when they're married.

How frequently did you masturbate when you were 17 and older? How many times a day?

I never did it more than three times a day, and that was a rare occasion. But when I'm dating a woman, of course it's less frequent. The average length of time between my relationships is typically a one-month span. After about a month, I can guarantee that I will find a woman who I will start having sex with and maybe prolong a relationship with, but even when I'm dating, I'm whacking off every once in a while. I guess in the average week, it would be three to four times. Sometimes more, sometimes less. It just depends on if it's a

Growing Up Male In America

slow week on the sex side.

Oral sex. You like that, don't you?

I love giving it and receiving it.

Do you feel that giving pleasure to your partner during sex is important to you?

Well, sometimes I get to the point where I can't even get pleasure, and I don't know why. It's just that I get into a mindset where it's hard for me to even ejaculate or to work myself up to that, because ... I don't know if I'm desensitized a little bit because of masturbating or what. So I don't know if that's why I don't get off as easily when I'm with a woman. Usually any girl I'm with the first time, I never come.

And I suppose some of your partners say, "What's the matter? Am I doing something wrong?"

Yeah. And I just give them a lie. I concentrate too hard on not coming, and then I don't. Which might sort of be true.

It might be true. Anything else you want to say about sex? Do you like it?

Sex is good. The feeling is not all that it is cracked up to be, but for some reason it drives us to want to do it.

You almost wish you could go to kids in junior high and tell them that.

Well, I've told that to my buddy. Even before he had sex, I told him, "Dude, it's not worth it. It isn't really worth it. But you're going to do it anyway." For some reason you see a female and, okay, "I want to have sex with her." It's weird. You just want to bang her, you know?

Well, I guess that's the drive that keeps the race going.

Just a few more questions. These are random, unrelated thought questions. What do you like most and least about yourself?

I guess I like most that I'm easy-going. I consider myself thoughtful and considerate. When it comes to a significant other, I'll bend over backwards for that person.

What is it in your character that you like least? What's something that really pisses you off about yourself?

I don't know if it pisses me off, but I can be very judgmental about people. But usually my judgment of a person is right. I'm usually right in what I think. I'm sometimes wrong, but I'm willing to admit that.

You can usually figure a person out?

Yeah. I can look at them and just depending on how they dress or how they hold themselves, I can determine if I really want to associate with them or not. I'll see someone and if I don't like the way they dress, or I don't like how they're holding themselves. Granted, they might be a good person. But I choose not to associate with them. Especially with some women. I can see women, and if they're slouching or they just don't look confident, I don't even want to bother talking to them, even though they may be confident or they may be really nice people to get to know. And I think I do know a couple of women that just do not hold themselves with much respect, but they are nice people. But normally I would not have talked to them. I think that's somewhat of a weakness in me.

Drug use. We didn't talk about that. I mean, you like your drinks, but have you ever experimented with other drugs besides alcohol?

I tried marijuana … I think, like, on three or four different occasions, *attempting* to get high. I could never achieve it, and I don't know why. I was with different groups of people and obviously different types of weed, and I just couldn't get it. I couldn't get the high or that so-called "being high" mode. I'm not sure why. But usually they say it takes three to four times of doing it to actually achieve it. So, I've never actually been high on weed. And I've never tried anything else other than that.

You really haven't?

No. I have thought of trying Ecstasy. I was real iffy on that, because you never know the purity of what you are going to get. It can be bad shit. I've contemplated "roids," obviously.

Explain what that is.

Steroids.

Steroids. And that's the enhancer for weight-lifting?

Some of it's not even steroids. There's like testosterone injections and whatnot. I have thought of trying that. Just couldn't deal with the long-term effects that possibly could result from it, though.

You know, it surprises me, because you work in a bar, that the frequency and availability of these various substances are right there.

Oh, yeah.

But you apparently have more than enough respect for your body and your mind.

Yeah. I just was always afraid of what it might make me do or that I'll like it. Cocaine has come into my mind, that I might want to try that. But I think what scares me away from it is, am I going to get addicted to it? And that's what scares me. I don't want to get addicted to it. You can't necessarily get addicted to steroids, but you can get addicted to how you look when you're on them. And if you look good when you're on them, then you're not going to get off them. And marijuana … it's not really an addiction; you just get addicted to that high feeling.

I suppose those people who have to face the morning with it every day and can't get

Growing Up Male In America

through the day without it, that might be a form of addiction. But you feel comfortable with alcohol?

Yeah, alcohol's all right.

You can predict what it's going to do?

Yeah, I have a good idea what it's going to do.

Also, as the heavy dope smoker is going to tell you, you can predict the effect.

Yeah. Even smoking cigarettes is an addiction. I tried it. I've only smoked three or four cigarettes in my life. Most of it to prove to someone that I can inhale. [Laughs] It's just not necessary to me to function now. Alcohol, I mean. I drink every once in a while. And yeah, I'll party. But you know, I think it's because it's legal. It's available. And yeah, I have a good time when I'm drinking. But I still limit my intake. I still try to keep it down to every once in a while.

What percentage of your attitudes and behavior comes either from advertising or from peer pressure? And I'm thinking of designer clothes and what's fashionable, what's in.

I don't know. I guess everyone gets influenced by advertisements, everything from magazines ads to commercials. I guess I could say, yeah, I'm influenced. So far, the most I can afford is Ralph Lauren. Which is considerably more expensive stuff than Levi's or Lee, which most people can afford. So I guess I'm grateful that I can afford Ralph Lauren. But I think if I could afford more, I would be dressing like how I see in *GQ Magazine*. Because that seems to be what gets the attention. But I'm not doing it because it's the style but because it's good, you're going to look good. You know? If I was dressed in Armani and then I was dressed in jeans and a t-shirt, I think my being dressed in Armani is going to be more of an attention-grabber than the guy dressed in jeans and a t-shirt.

Do you have a suit?

Yes. It's a Structure. It cost over $500.

Do you have many occasions to wear it?

I wear it at weddings. I wore it just last week. I do own a tuxedo, also, and that is way out of the norm for a person my age to own. But I had a lot of functions that I had to have a tuxedo for, so it was just cheaper to buy one. But you know, whatever you feel comfortable in, you are getting judged by what you wear. I mean I know for sure, if you dress like white trash, you're going to be considered white trash. I don't care if you've got a 152 IQ, you're going to be judged as white trash. I'll judge you as white trash. I guess if you're comfortable, fine. But no one is going to accept you that way.

Well, we have reached the end of the interview. I thank you very much. Thanks for

Interview 8

your time and your honesty.

Postscript – December 2001

This man completed his undergraduate degree in graphic design and is currently employed full time by a computer-related firm. He continues to be a bartender at the trendy club in Minneapolis. He wishes he could find more time to do artwork, particularly charcoal drawings. He has not had any lasting romantic relationships with women but has had several liaisons with many women. Since the interview was conducted two and a half years ago, he has had some "experimental" sexual experiences with a man, and he has used cocaine during those sexual encounters.

Interview 9

"I don't think he wanted me as a son ... he made that very clear to me."

This interview was conducted on July 7, 2000. At the time of the interview, this man was 28 years old. He is 5' 9" tall and weighs 145 pounds. His hair is dark brown.

First of all, thanks for doing this interview.

No problem.

Let's start with now. Tell me a little bit about yourself – like where you were born, what you're doing, where you live.

Okay. I was born in St. Paul, Minnesota. My mom and my biological father were not married at the time, and my dad did not want to get married to my mother, so consequently my mother and I moved in with her parents and her sister. I lived there for two years with my grandma, my grandpa, my aunt and my mom. My mom married when I was two, and then we moved out to a suburb. I lived there until I was four or five – I can't remember exactly. I think I was five, because I remember starting kindergarten in the new house, which was in a really little town. It was like a thousand people, maybe. So I lived there for only about a year, and then we moved to another suburb when I was in first grade, and we lived there until 1987, when I was 12 years old. And during that time period, when I was 12, I had to go into the hospital because I had an eating disorder. I was anorexic.

Was that intentional?

Well, I don't think eating disorders are intentional.

I mean, it wasn't something at that early age that you tried to be thin or anything.

Well, what happened is that I tried to lose weight because I was a little chunky. And my stepdad ... he and I didn't get along at all. He was always trying to get me to lose weight, and he went about it in not a very nice way. I sometimes refer to him as my dad, but he's my stepdad. So anyway, I was in and out of

Growing Up Male In America

the hospital pretty much from the age of 12 until 21. I was in a couple of hospitals for a year and a half at a time. Because I had some serious problems with anorexia and bulimia and just depression and things like that. So it wasn't a very easy adolescence for me. But I think a lot of it had to do with being homosexual and not being comfortable with that, because at the age of 12 I started the eating disorder – and that was also when puberty began. And I think that was one factor, but also just the relationship with my stepdad. And I think the eating disorder started because I wanted my stepdad's approval and I could never get it, no matter what I did. And I think that well, here, I've lost some weight and he was really happy about that. You know? Then I just kept losing more and more weight.

Anyway, right now I'm living in Minneapolis.

How old are you?

I'm 28 right now. I like the location. I'm not employed right now. I'm looking for a job. And I just think my relationship with my current boyfriend is ending because we're fighting all the time and we don't like to do the same things. He's older than I am. And it's been going on for about a year and a half, and pretty much the whole relationship has been fighting. [Laughs] So, what else? That just recently ended. It was kind of the 4th of July weekend.

But you didn't live together?

No, we did not live together ever. We didn't even sleep together in the same bed, just because I can't sleep with someone else in the bed with me.

Oh. So when you would have sex, you'd have it and then you'd have to separate for the rest of the night.

And then I'd go or whatever. I mean, I'd stay a while, though. [Laughs] It wasn't just like I had sex and hopped immediately out of bed.

Your discomfort with sleeping with another person – did you think that was unusual? Or did he think that was unusual?

I think he did, because I know in his past relationships, they lived together and they slept together.

Cuddling and all that.

Yeah. We cuddled but … and even then, I was uncomfortable with it sometimes because I just kind of felt trapped – like I had to get out of it. You know? And I don't know what that is. I'm sure a psychologist could figure that out.

Just think. Maybe after talking about everything here today during this interview, it will all be made a little clearer to you.

Yeah, maybe. It's part of the reason I thought this interview might be good for me.

Well, there might be some truth to that. They say babbling about our inner thoughts

Interview 9

is good.

Just bouncing it off someone.

Right. Now, let's go back to the "not sleeping with someone" issue.

Yeah. I was talking about not being able to sleep with someone else in the same bed with me. So that might have been one of the reasons that my current relationship didn't work out too well. Also, we didn't have a lot of things in common. He's a recovering alcoholic. He's been sober for 11 years, almost 12, and I still like to go out to the bars once in a while. He never liked to go to the bars, which is understandable. But he didn't like to do anything that I liked to do. He didn't like to go to any of the street festivals or the state fair. Things like that.

What – if I could ask – did he like to do?

Well, he liked to bike ride, which I do. Which is fine. He worked on his house a lot. He's really into the interior design thing. I don't know. I guess we were just at different stages of our life. And, I don't know, I love him a lot, but we fight too much and ... I don't know.

Well, that kind of brings us up to the present. You say you're not working now, but what kind of jobs have you had?

Well, I've worked at a grocery store. I haven't had a very good track record keeping jobs. And I don't know why that is. I think a lot of it is because my family pretty much supports me financially, and so I really have no reason to get a job. Although they are getting very frustrated with me mooching off them. And a lot of it has to do with because I think I was just in the hospital so much that sometimes I think that I just don't have the skills or the social skills to make it in today's society. But I've worked at a grocery store. I've worked at a bank. I've worked at a couple of banks. Mostly customer service positions. And I model part time right now. But I am looking for a full-time job, and I'm looking in the customer service field. I finished three years of college, with a major in political science.

Where did you go to school?

I went to the University of Minnesota. Actually, a couple of years ago I was accepted as a transfer student at Georgetown University, into their school of foreign service. But I never accepted ... it just wasn't the right time for me to go. And so ... they gave me a couple of deferrals, which they usually don't do, but now they said if I want to go I have to reapply. Which is kind of a bad thing. [Laughs] So what I think I'll do is I'll just finish here at the University of Minnesota and then maybe go to Georgetown for graduate school, if I ever get my shit together enough to do that. [Laughs]

Well, you're making some determined choices, at least. I don't know which is worse. A lot of kids just rush through college, get their four-year degree and then all of a

Growing Up Male In America

sudden wake up and realize it wasn't what they wanted to do.

> Yeah.

Okay. That takes us up to the present. Now, let's look back.

What is your first memory? Can you think back to how old you might have been and what you might have remembered?

> Well, I remember ... I think I was about five, and I remember my mom and stepdad fighting. And that was pretty traumatic, very traumatic for me. And I remember my mom grabbing us. It was winter, and she was grabbing my brother and me – who was probably one or two at the time – and just grabbing us, putting our coats on and taking off in the car. Because they were fighting, and she just wanted to get out, I guess. And she drove out, maybe went a block and then came back and then went back in and they made up. I remember that was the most uncomfortable for me, is when they fought. And it seemed like they fought a lot.

And this was the stepdad?

> Yup.

Because your dad – your biological dad – never married your mother.

> He was kind of out of the picture.

Did you ever connect with your biological dad at all?

> Yeah, I did. I did when I was 21. He called his sister, who still lived in Minneapolis, who called my grandma, who called me and said he wanted to meet me. And I said okay. You know, I didn't have any expectations.

You had seen pictures of him, I suppose.

> Yeah. I saw one picture with him and my mother at prom.

Oh. Way back.

> Yeah. It wasn't a very comfortable meeting, and I didn't feel any connection there. I didn't feel, like, you know, "my dad" at all. Because, you know, he wasn't my dad. So ... you know, I told him a little bit about what I had been going through as far as the eating disorder, and he didn't seem to really care. He said he did, but it didn't seem like he was genuine.

Okay. Now, what about your stepfather?

> He's dead. He died about three years ago of cancer. Throat cancer.

Was it a pretty turbulent, stormy relationship with your mom and him?

> I don't know if I'd go that far, but ...

I mean, they fought a lot when you were a little kid.

> Yeah. And I think when I had the eating problems, they fought a lot, too.

Interview 9

Because my mom was always trying to defend me, and my stepdad was ... I don't think he wanted ... he adopted me when they were married, and I don't think he wanted me as a son. I think he adopted me just so he could marry my mom. I don't think he wanted me at all. And he made that very clear to me. And as a little kid, I tried to get his approval any way I could, and he knocked me down at every turn. So I think that's very hard for a young kid. I mean, because a kid's innocent. And so, anyway, they did fight a lot, it seems like. I don't think he was the right person for my mother.

How many siblings?

I have a half brother, who's from my stepdad and my mother. And that's it.

That's it. In a way you could speculate, if you had had a little flock of sisters and brothers, maybe you wouldn't have got all the attention or the inattention – is there a word – that he gave you, almost to the point of abusive attention.

Right.

There might have been more protection in numbers, I suppose.

Did you go to nursery school or prekindergarten or anything like that?

I don't think I did. No. Not that I remember.

Did your mother work outside the house?

She did when I was ... let's see, she started working when I was about 11, outside the house.

Okay. So she was in the house taking care of you until you started kindergarten and the first few years of school. Can you remember kindergarten at all?

Yeah. I remember kindergarten. I liked my teacher a lot. She was very nice. And as a matter of fact, one time she was reading us a book. We were all sitting in a group on the floor and she was on a chair, and I just jumped up out of nowhere and gave her a kiss. [Laughs] So I really liked her. I think I was very smart in school. That's what everyone told me. I caught on really fast. I remember coming home after kindergarten, because it was half days, and my mom making macaroni and cheese. You know, boil-in-a-bag macaroni and cheese or chicken pot pies. And then me just planting myself in front of the TV to watch *Sesame Street* or *Mr. Rogers* or whatever was on. [Laughs] But, yeah, I can remember pretty far back.

Okay. Now you're starting in school – first grade, second grade and so on. Were you aware of what your socioeconomic level was? Was it middle class?

Middle class.

I mean, your family income was all right. You weren't poor.

No.

So, do you remember ... I mean it's so important now. Fads and fashions and what

Growing Up Male In America

to wear and the proper jeans and all that stuff. Do you remember any of that going on at that time?

No.

The haves, the have-nots and other kids who ...

I didn't really pay attention. I didn't notice anything then. I think my mom bought her clothes from Sears or Penney's or whatever, and that was fine with me. [Laughs] So ... but I didn't notice, I didn't feel any peer pressure then. Except that I was starting to get a little overweight at that age. And that's about it.

Now when you say overweight, reflect back. Is that like 10 pounds? Or were you a real, real chubby boy?

No, I wasn't real chubby. I'd say 15, 20 pounds overweight. But to me, it probably seemed worse than it really was, because my stepdad was always saying, "You're too fat." So I don't really know. I can't conceptualize if I was that overweight. Some people say I wasn't fat at all.

It's a subjective thing, isn't it? Because people who are skin and bones think that because they can get a little pinch of flesh around their waist, they think they're overweight.

Yeah.

You said earlier today something about how unkind or what unkind measures your stepdad used in the overweight thing. Do you want to go there?

Sure. He would call me fat. He would say I was too fat. He would limit what I could eat at meals. I remember one time I was getting a second serving of something, and he stabbed my hand with a fork and yelled, "That's enough! You don't need that!" And I could never ... my mom always cut the portions up, and I don't know if that was to avoid a conflict with my stepdad or just because we didn't know how to do it ourselves. I don't know. And he would call me fat. Once he was joking with my brother, when I was a little older, that I was the fat one in Laurel and Hardy. Whichever the character was, the fat one.

Hardy.

Yeah. And he was joking with my brother and, you know, I was hurt and I was very angry. You know, I was just like, "How can you do this?" So ... those are just some examples of things he did.

Stabbing a fork? Not hard.

Not really hard. [Demonstrates] Yeah, yeah. But when you're, like, seven or six, it's pretty scary. I was just ... I was very afraid of him all the time. Not just because of that, but just because he had a very mean demeanor. You know? I was very uncomfortable with him. I never wanted to be around him. I remem-

Interview 9

ber I would stay overnight at my grandparents' a lot. My mother's parents. And I remember crying when I had to leave there after the weekend was over because I didn't want to go home.

Now, your grandmother understood this? She was your mom's mom?

Yeah.

I don't suppose you had much contact with your biological dad's mom and dad?

No. Because I didn't meet them until right around the same time I met my dad. I heard that they called a couple times to see how I was, but that's about it.

It's an interesting ... it's almost a play or a novel out there about what they were going through, thinking of this little kid that their son had fathered that they never got the opportunity to be grandparents to. It's kind of a safe thing to speculate upon.

Did your half brother come under the same kind of attack from your stepdad?

No.

He was free and clear of all that?

Well, I think so. My mom has been a staunch defender of my stepdad, up to this day, and she denies a lot of the stuff that I say happened. And she'll say that we two boys were treated just the same. But I disagree. I really do. Because that was his natural son, and I suppose it's a little natural for him to have favored him. Ideally it isn't, but I think that he did. I mean, my brother never had a weight problem, so that took that issue away. But I don't know. He just seemed to connect with his biological son better.

Was your brother more athletic than you?

Yeah. And he liked some of the same stuff that my stepdad did. Like woodworking. My stepdad was a carpenter. They just had more of the same interests. I was more like a sissy, I guess. When I started first grade, most of my close friends were all girls, except for maybe one guy. I just felt more comfortable around girls. And I suppose it makes sense, now, because I felt more comfortable around my mother than my stepdad.

It sounds almost like a textbook, doesn't it? I mean, you were more comfortable with girls. Liking mother, almost resenting dad. I mean, it's all very Oedipal or something. [Laughter]

Was there ever any sexual abuse from the stepfather?

No. Sometimes I wonder, though. Because some of my behavior and some of the problems I've had seem to indicate that. But I can't remember it.

And if it did happen, you might have blanked it out of your memory.

Right.

Growing Up Male In America

You've talked about having girlfriends and one or two boyfriends, too. But back in first grade, second grade, third grade, something like that, do you remember a best friend? One whom you went everywhere with and whom you trusted?

I don't really ... I never really, never had a best friend.

Ever, ever, ever?

Ever. And I still don't to this day.

Oh. Why do you suppose that is?

I don't know. I just don't think I trust people. If I get too close to someone, I start to get uncomfortable. And that includes a male lover relationship. It's just a trust issue, I think. You know, I think it has to do with my stepdad, too. Of course I didn't trust him, and that makes relationships very hard. And right now I'm very lonely, because I don't have many friends. And the friends I do have are kind of fucked up and they like to do drugs all the time. I do drugs once in a while, but not every day. And not 24 hours a day. So, yeah, even up to this day I don't really have a best friend. No one I can talk to.

Is it afraid of opening yourself up and being too vulnerable, so therefore you can be hurt?

Yeah, I think so. And even being aware of that doesn't help. So, I don't know what to do. [Laughs]

You said you liked your kindergarten teacher. She must have done something that was sweet and good and welcoming and loving.

Yeah. I just think she was nice, you know. And I don't know, I think ... I think you really, when you're that young, you just grow an affection for your teacher. I don't know. That's all I can think of. I think she was maybe a little younger than my grandmother, but I think she reminded me of my grandmother. She had kind of the same hair. And when you're little, you know, you associate that with something.

And of course, when you're little, anybody over 25 is old.

[Laughs] Yeah.

Unfortunately.

Yeah.

Did you have any other teachers – first, second, third grade – that you kind of liked or who liked you?

I mean, they were all decent, but I don't remember any of them really making that much of an impact on me. Pretty much first through fifth grade and sixth, you know, they were just teachers, you know.

School was easy for you?

Yeah.

Interview 9

I mean, you learned easily?

Yeah. Actually, in first grade, I think, they put me in a special-ed class because they thought I wasn't learning. I can't remember exactly what was going on, but I remember I was in a special-ed class for a short period of time, and they figured out that I wasn't hearing well or something. So they sat me in the front of the class, and then I did really well. And then I ended up getting into accelerated classes. But, yeah, I did … I got pretty much straight A's all through elementary school, high school and college. I was a perfectionist, and I always … I remember even in third and fourth grade, I was always worrying about my grades. And I would ask my teacher, you know, "How am I doing?" and things like that. And that's kind of unusual, I think, for a kid that age. But it wasn't any pressure from home. I think it was because I just wanted to impress my stepdad, but it didn't work. At least I got good grades.

Certainly your mother watched over you as far as your schoolwork and wanting to make sure you were doing well in school, too, but your excellence in school was really to try to please the stepdad.

Yeah.

But then it got to be pleasurable for yourself, too. I mean, achievement is nice.

Yeah, yeah.

Okay. Were you very religious as a family?

Quite the opposite. I think my mother's parents – my grandparents, who I lived with for awhile – were very religious. I think my mother kind of rebelled against that. She was in a Catholic school and my stepdad was, too, and they were just over it, I think. And they didn't go to church at all. My mom sometimes went on Easter or special holidays. When I went to my grandparents', we did go to church. But other than that, you know, I really had no religion. It wasn't a factor.

What's your ethnic background?

I'm Hispanic. That's what my biological dad was.

What's the appropriate term? Hispanic? Latino?

Hispanic, I think.

It's very confusing as to the labeling, isn't it? Black people, for example – are they "African American" or are they "black" or are they "people of color"?

It changes so much. [Laughs]

It's very confusing. Both your parents were Hispanic?

No, my mother's white.

So, let's see. You went through puberty while you were hospitalized. So that's an interesting and rather sad thing, it seems to me. Did it feel that way to you?

Growing Up Male In America

Yeah. Actually, I think at first it was really scary the first time I went into a hospital for my eating disorder. But after a while I started to like it because I didn't want to go home. So ... and ...

So there was still that strong feeling happening, not wanting to go home?

And in a hospital, the majority of the staff are female. I'd say 90 percent or more. And I was with a bunch of females pretty much throughout my adolescence as well. So I think that is why I am more comfortable with females.

Did you talk to anyone about the physical changes that were happening to you during puberty?

Not really.

I see.

I didn't talk about any of that.

Would you say you developed early or about on time or late?

I think I developed early. And in phy ed, I remember feeling uncomfortable taking showers. Not because of the size, but because I was uncircumcised. And that's the only thing I really remember. And I always was afraid I was going to get an erection, too. [Laughs]

Speaking of erections ... as you think back, was it because of somebody who was attractive or just because it was happening so frequently?

Well, not because the men I saw were attractive, just because they were men, I think. Or boys, or whatever.

You were noticing this already?

When I was 12, yeah. Oh, yeah!

Okay. Being uncircumsised, did you think you were very much in the minority?

I did then.

Most seemed to be cut?

Yeah. My brother was uncut, too.

Well, it seems like everybody is circumcised. And especially when you're not, you feel like an outsider, somebody who's different.

Can you remember back to the first time you noticed, in a sexual way, another man?

You know, this kind of sounds sick. But I remembered as early as five, I think, being attracted to my stepdad. And I think it might have been a confusion thing, where I just wanted to be close to him. I don't know. I've always been kind of attracted to him. I know that sounds sick, but ... whatever! [Laughs] That's the way it was. But I remember then ... and pretty much through grade school I remember always being attracted to men. And this kind of throws my

Interview 9

whole theory of being gay, because sometimes I think I'm gay because I'm looking for this affection and this father figure. And then I hear this stuff: well, it's biological, and you're born that way. And it confuses me. But if it's the case that I'm just looking for affection or a father figure, then that means I can change it, you know? But I remember, all pretty much through grade school and high school, that I've always been attracted to males. So even before puberty.

So when you ... you saw somebody from afar that you were attracted to, did you have enough courage to go up and do something about it and talk to that person?

No. Because I was, like, denying it to myself.

Oh, of course.

So I wouldn't approach them.

Well, you're not unusual in that regard.

Right. Right.

It is amazing to me how many kids are coming out so early now and actually getting in groups and doing something about it.

I think it's easier these days, too.

Was the type of man that you were attracted to somebody who resembled your stepdad?

I think so. And it's interesting that the guy that I'm – well, I don't know what you'd call our relationship at this point – but my recent relationship. [Laughter] That guy is a lot like my stepdad. I think that's why we fight so much. But my other boyfriends – and actually I haven't had that many, maybe two or three – I guess they've all been tall, they've all been blond or brunette – which is my stepdad's color of hair. I mean, these lovers I've had don't resemble him, per se. But they have a lot of the same characteristics.

Do you remember your first sexual experience with another person?

Yeah, I do. Actually, it was a friend, a kid that used to live in my grandmother's neighborhood. When I went over there. I'm sure I was just experimenting. But I was probably seven years old. And we just looked at each other's penises and ... he always ... I remember this, because it was very bizarre. But he always wanted me to pretend that I was a girl. I mean, this was when we were seven years old! Seven! And he wanted me to pretend I was the girl in the relationship, and I just said I wouldn't do that. I don't know if we did anything sexual. I don't think there was any oral sex or anything. But I think we might have rubbed our penises together.

And I remember another time – I stayed overnight at some friend's house when I was about eight or nine. We stayed in a tent in their back yard. And I remember, I was sucking his penis, and this guy was a year or two older than me. I

Growing Up Male In America

remember being fully erect.

You were? At eight years old?

Yes. Well, he was erect, too. I didn't ejaculate, of course, then.

Did this person – in the tent there – did he admit he was gay?

No. I remember him making a comment like, after we were doing this sucking thing for a while, he said something like, "I don't want to do this anymore. I don't want to be fagging out."

I see. But it's one of those confusions, isn't it? It felt good, but you don't want to be labeled.

Yeah, right.

Okay. So you had some experiences early on?

Um-hum.

A lot of those are kind of typical playing-around type things. Do you ever remember getting involved in ... in adolescence ... in circle jerks or mutual masturbation?

No.

Any of that kind of "boys will be boys" type thing?

No. I wish! [Laughs]

Anyway, you were feeling this attraction toward men, and you were acting on it a little bit. And yet you didn't quite know what to call it, right?

Right.

Once you started reaching the point of knowing you liked it and you continued feeling an attraction to men, was this difficult for you?

Well, as I said, when I was 12, I started having the problems with eating. And my gay feelings pretty much stopped then. When I would masturbate, however, I would think about men all the time. Or magazines or pictures. But I denied it to myself, and as I said, I didn't know what to call it. I didn't want to call it anything. And I think that might have contributed to my eating disorder, because I felt very uncomfortable about it. I didn't really have anyone I could talk to. Especially not my stepdad or even my mom. I didn't even want to tell my grandparents, or anyone.

If you were about 12, I'm trying to think what year that would have been.

1983, I guess.

So Phil Donahue and the other talk shows at that time, they were kind of "out" talking about gay life, but as far as local places to go to, it wasn't as available as it is now.

Right.

Interview 9

So it might have been ... so you would call this a rather lonely time.

Yes.

Did you ever try to change?

Well, I kissed some girls in sixth grade and kind of made out with them or necked, or whatever you call it. And I dated a couple of girls in sixth grade, if you can call it that. I never had sex. Actually, when I was seven, I did have ... I remember this one girl that was my friend, and we kind of fooled around. But I was seven, you know? And I remember trying to insert my penis into her vagina. But of course you can't even get hard, I don't think, when you're six.

So you knew about where your penis was supposed to go, huh?

Yeah. Even at the age of six. I was a very early bloomer.

Have you ever had sex with women?

Not really.

Okay. So you don't really consider yourself to be bisexual?

Well, I did describe myself as bisexual on my Internet Web page to attract more men. [Laughs]

Oh. I see. All right. That's what I was getting at. The concept of bisexual is a nice catch-all. It's kind of an escape hatch.

Yeah. That's exactly what I call it, too. When someone says they're genuinely "bi" – I question that.

Uh-huh. Good. Okay. That was my question to you. It's rather convenient to be gay until that gets uncomfortable for some reason, and then you can escape and parachute out and go over to being straight for a while.

Exactly.

And that's what some do.

Now ... I'm still thinking about your adolescence. My god, you poor kid. You're sitting there from the age of 12, off and on in the hospital. How long were some of those times in the hospital?

Well, the first hospitalization was just in a medical hospital, and it was just to get some weight on me. It was a month, maybe a month and a half. Then the second time was more long term. It was three months, and it was in Wisconsin. A special program for eating disorders. And that was hard, because I was away from home, even though I wanted to be away from home. It was still hard not to see my family and my grandparents. They drove down once in a while. I was there three months. Then I got out. And then I lost weight again. Then I went back for six months.

Six months!

Growing Up Male In America

Um-hum. And then I was in a hospital in Topeka, Kansas, for a year and a half. And I was in the psych ward in a Minnesota hospital for a year at least.

Now, was this related to the eating disorders, too?

Yeah.

Was it any part of the coming-out process?

Well, I wasn't coming out then.

Okay. You had pretty well put that on the back burner.

Yes. Well, I didn't even know it. I was so focused on my eating disorder and the behavior with it. Eventually I was bulimic, when I would binge and purge. I think that's why I didn't want to think of my sexuality. Maybe I was trying to avoid it with the eating behavior, you know? If I focused on all this behavior and game playing and fucking everyone over and just making a mess of everything, then I wouldn't have to focus on the homosexuality.

Early on, in these hospital times, did your mom come and visit a lot?

Yes.

And your stepdad?

He didn't.

But wasn't that what he wanted? For you to lose weight?

Yeah. No, he didn't come to visit me in the hospital. He came for one family meeting, I think, and that's about it. And when I was out of the hospital – which wasn't very much – and I remember … this might have been before the second hospitalization, which was the longest … they started getting more long term … we were eating dinner. And I sat across from my stepdad, which was very ironic, at the dinner table, and my mom sat across from my brother. It was a rectangular shaped table. My mom had made meatloaf. And I took a very small portion, it was so ridiculous. It's, like, why bother eating? But that was my anorexic behavior. And all of a sudden my dad got up from the table, took the whole pan of meatloaf in his hand, and shoved it at me and wiped it all over my face. Wherever he could get it. It was dripping off me, and I pissed my pants. And I was so angry, I threw my chair and I just ran out of the house. Meanwhile, while this was happening, my brother didn't say anything, but my mother kept telling him to stop it and stuff like that.

So I ran out of the house and went to one of my friend's. You know, with meatloaf all over me. It pretty much was all gone off of me by then. This was when I was about 13. Ironically, my friend's parents were friends of my stepdad and my mom. So … they didn't know what to do. I told them to call the police, but they said no. But then they called my stepdad. The next day I ended up in the hospital. So … I was good riddance, as far as my stepdad was concerned.

Now, this happens, and your stepdad does that abusive thing to you. Did he ever

Interview 9

apologize? Did he ever take you aside after his rage and say, "I shouldn't have done that. I'm sorry."

No.

None of that?

No.

How does he explain that? How does your mother explain that behavior?

Because of what I was ... not eating, or something, you know. And it was basically my fault. It was meant to be my fault, I guess.

So that's his form of discipline?

Yes. I think he was just frustrated. He was a Vietnam vet. I don't know if that had anything to do with it, but it might have a little. Post-traumatic stress or something. Sometimes I guess I reminded him of some of the people he saw in Vietnam, in the camps or whatever. Because I was very thin. I was probably 69 pounds at that point. I'd lost a lot of weight.

Well, that's pretty traumatic stuff.

Yeah.

Now, the hospitalization in Kansas. A year and a half there? What sort of program or treatment was that? How did you feel about all that?

Well, I didn't like Kansas at all. And I took off from the hospital. It was a locked unit, and I remember following someone out the door when they were leaving to go off duty from their shift. I just took off. It was, like, the second night I was there, and I didn't know Kansas from, you know, whatever. And so I just took off. I remembered going to a drug store, which was quite a ways away, and buying a whole bunch of sleeping pills and taking them. And the next thing you know, I'm in the ER. But anyway. The treatment was basically just to try to get me to eat normally. They watched me in the bathroom to make sure I didn't throw up, and they had us go to group sessions. You know, group therapy, I guess you'd call it. And then individual psychotherapy with a psychologist. And they had a whole bunch of activities that you could do, like woodworking and art and gym. But you had to earn those privileges over time. And it got to the point in Kansas where I was just so depressed, and I tried to kill myself several times there. I was to the point where I had someone with me 24 hours a day, so I wouldn't do any harm to myself. They would sit in the room while I was sleeping, basically watching me sleep. So it was a very hard time for me.

I suppose, after a while, you kind of got used to the fact that there was someone always there?

Yeah. I lost all my privacy. All ... everything. And I guess I did get used to it. Actually, I felt safer because no one was going to let me do anything to myself.

Growing Up Male In America

They were, in a very real sense, protecting you from yourself?

Yes.

I bet any shyness you had about personal toilet habits and showering and all the rest of it pretty much went away?

[Laughs] Yeah.

Do you ever suffer from "shy bladder"? I think that's what Ann Landers called it. When you know you have to pee, and there are others at the urinals, and you can't pee – there's like a psychological blockage.

No, I'm never bothered with that.

No problem in that regard?

No. Even when I'm over at someone's house, I don't shut the bathroom door. Except if I have a bowel movement. But if I just have to pee, I don't shut the door. Just because I'm so used to people watching me in the hospital. And I don't really care, you know? I don't see it as a shy thing.

Okay. Now, your eating disorders – might that be a big part of the coming-out process? And the denial of your gayness, and all of this self-loathing that many guys go through with the coming-out process?

Yes. I think it had a large part to do with it, but I think it had a large part to do with my stepdad, too. I don't think it was just one thing. I'd like to make it one thing, but I don't think it was.

Right. That would be too easy, wouldn't it?

[Laughs] Yeah. But I'm sure the gay issue had a lot to do with it because you start to feel sexual when you're 12, and I remember being very uncomfortable because I felt attracted to men, and I tried to deny that. Then part of it, too, was a physical thing. After I'd lost all the weight, I didn't feel sexual.

Did you have a negative image of your body, partly because of what your stepdad said and did, and also because you were a little overweight? Was that a part of it, too, that "I'm not attractive"?

Yeah.

And so, maybe, by being thin, "I'll be more attractive."

Yup.

And then you get totally out of control and down to 60, 70 pounds.

Yeah.

Okay.

Yeah. That was it. I never felt attractive.

Now, let's go from then to now in terms of attractiveness. I mean, you're an attrac-

Interview 9

tive man. And you work out and have an impressive physique. In a sense, your body now is a reaction to being overweight and to being ultra thin during those awful teenage years. Do you see that?

Yes.

Is that what motivates you at the gym? One more set, a little more weight on the machine?

No. I don't think that's quite the reason. I think it's kind of sad, but I think my physique is the only way I can relate to people, and I think it's the only thing I have to offer to people. If I look good. Then, you know, I get attention that way. Because I don't feel like I have anything else to offer – substantial, as far as personality or friendship or anything like that. So that's how I relate to people, I think. It's through my looks or through my body or whatever. Which is a kind of sad state to be in, but I'm working on that.

Well, if you didn't have your good body, then you'd be even sadder.

Yeah.

See? So you see, you're up several notches. And for what it's worth, you're a very attractive man, even if you didn't have your impressive physique.

Thanks. [Laughs] Thanks.

Now, you said you were in and out of hospitals until you were in your early 20s?

Yes.

Okay. When were you called "cured"?

Well, there's really no cure. Because when I met my most recent boyfriend, I started having the bulimia behavior again. I'm sure there's some connection.

Want to explain what bulimia really is?

Bulimia is where you eat large amounts of food and then purge, throw it up.

Okay. Laxatives, too?

During adolescence, I did use laxatives a lot, and I'm just sick about what I did to my body. It's just not good for your body at all. But when I started dating this guy, S—, is when I started to have the behavior of throwing up. I think it has to do with him reminding me of my stepdad. That whole thing again. And I think part of the reason – this is kind of off the tangent, but I have to say it – that I started dating this guy and wanted to continue in the relationship just to inspire me to work out some of my problems with my stepdad through S—.

Interesting.

I perceive some of the things that S— does as something that my stepdad would do, so I perceive that I've been wronged or I've been unfairly treated when I'm probably not. It's hard to see. But it's a very interesting dynamic.

Growing Up Male In America

Is a part of that dynamic, "I'm bad. It's my fault. I did something wrong"? Or is it, "It's all my boyfriend's fault"?

All his fault. [Laughs]

Okay. Because I would think, the way your stepdad was treating you, there could be a lot of, "I'm not worthy. I'm bad."

Actually, it's quite the opposite. [Laughs]

You've overcome that and gone on to, "The fault is out there."

Yeah. Like I said, some of the things he'll do remind me of something my stepdad might have done, like me feeling left out or something like that. And I'll just react … have a very big reaction. And it's not good. And it's not fair to my friend, and I think that's why we're having so many problems. But, I don't know. [Laughs] He didn't sign on to be my stepdad while I work through my issues, you know?

Or to be your caregiver.

Yeah.

You say it's never really over, these eating disorders. And as a recovering alcoholic, your boyfriend S— would tell you that same thing. What do you do when you see a bout coming?

I don't really see it. Like, I didn't see it early in this current relationship, when I started to have the bulimia again. But in my early 20s, the condition started to get better. And I think it got better because I started to come out of the closet. That's when it started to get better. I mean, it didn't happen overnight, but it kind of happened as the coming-out process progressed. The bulimia sort of … I didn't feel like I had to do it. That was pretty much when I was 21, when I could go to a gay bar. [Laughs]

When did you start working out? When did you go to the gym? When did this become of great interest?

Probably about 22, 23.

Okay. When you started going to the bars and you started noticing that you were attracting attention.

Yeah, exactly.

And you realized that with a buff body, you look the way the ideal gay man is supposed to look, and you get noticed.

Yeah, exactly. I think it was because I didn't get the attention when I was little, maybe. I know it happens to a lot of gay men. But, yeah, that's exactly what happened. I started to get attention at the bars. Partially, probably, because I was newly out and also because I was young. And then I started … well, if I get this attention now, if I work out and get big, I'll get more attention. You

Interview 9

know?

Sure. That's the gay ideal.

And it was very motivating for me. I mean, I was at the gym every day. I still am.

But that can be an obsessive passion, too, sometimes.

When you'd go to the gay bars, did you typically go alone?

Typically alone.

So you dance?

If I'm on Ecstasy I do. Don't use that against me or don't show that to a police officer. [Laughs]

Well, I don't think you're the only one using that drug. [Laughs]

No, I'm sure I'm not. And so, yeah, I went alone. And I would go home with men, you know. Some of the choices I made were not the best as far as the looks department, and basically the sex was just like a mutual masturbation thing, because I've never been anally penetrated.

Why is that?

I don't know. I was just kind of afraid of it, and I know when I've gone to the doctor and they've done rectal exams, it hurt. I mean, I want to have intercourse. I fantasize about it. But the actual process of getting it in there – especially if it's a big penis – forget it. Too much trouble.

Could it be the health issue, too, that you maybe are a little concerned about?

At the beginning, yeah. I always wear a condom. But when I first came out, I was freaked out about HIV and AIDS. I didn't even want to kiss anyone.

So at this point you're a full-grown gay adult in his early 20s. Where does school fit into all of this?

College?

Yes.

Actually, the impetus for me starting school was when I got fired from a job. So then I thought, well, what the hell, I'll go to school. So I started college, even though I was maybe 24. Kind of late, you know.

Political science?

Right.

Were you a good student?

Yeah. I studied all the time, and I did all my work and was very prompt and got all my work in ahead of time.

Do you like to read?

Growing Up Male In America

Yeah. Lately I've been reading a lot of biographies of presidents. I just finished one on Kennedy. Now I'm on to Johnson. I might skip Carter because he was kind of a boring president.

Yup.

You didn't start college until you were about 24 and now you're 28. How near to finishing your degree are you?

I'm about a junior. I stopped about a year ago, when I met my current boyfriend. I don't know why I did. I just did.

I see. Have you and he ever talked about moving into a place together?

We did, but he wanted me to stop a lot of things. He wanted me to stop smoking. And he wanted ... I'm kind of a pack rat. He wanted me to stop being a pack rat. And we have none of the same decorating tastes or none of the same furniture tastes or anything like that, so I think we both knew that it would never happen. [Laughs]

And where did you meet him?

I met him at a gym where I took a spinning class. And he approached me. He started by making small talk, and then we set up a date and went out to dinner. And of course we had sex the first night, even though I didn't want to. It's hard for me to say no in situations like that because I feel like I'm being mean, because I know if I wanted to have sex with someone and they said no to me, I'd feel rejected. So I said yes. I didn't even really want to date anyone at that time. I didn't want to, but we ended up seeing each other more and decided to date.

Okay. Now, he's older than you?

Yup.

Your tastes in men and in the partners you have had, have they tended to be a little bit older?

A little bit older.

What is it about him that attracted you?

Well, at first I didn't give him a second look before he came up to me in that spinning class. So part of me wondered why I started to go out with him. I don't know. But maybe I needed something.

What attracted you to him?

Well, he's very masculine.

Why didn't you just say, "I'm sorry. Yeah. We'll see you around in spinning class next time."

He was very masculine. And that's it. [Laughs]

Interview 9

Well, that'll do it.

And attractive.

In terms of sex with him, are you the top?

I've only been a top, even though people assume I'm a bottom.

All right. Now, for the next part of the interview, I'm going to ask you a series of unrelated questions. Give the first answer that comes to mind, okay?

How would you define happiness?

Free of worries.

Okay. Are you there yet?

No.

Okay.

No. Not near it. [Laughs]

Have you ever been there?

No. I don't think I ever have.

Okay. And so maybe you'll be close to happiness when you are free of money problems, maybe in a nice relationship that's comfortable and a little more at home with yourself.

Yes.

All right. What makes you happy? I mean, like in the course of a day.

I guess, thinking about the past, sometimes. Thinking about the good times I had with my grandparents makes me happy. That's about it.

Are you happier when you're alone?

Yeah. But I get lonely, because I'm alone. [Laughs]

What can make you not just unhappy, but to the point of depressed?

When a lot of things pile up. When I'm having problems with my boyfriend or my family. When I feel like nothing's going right – then I get very depressed. I'm suicidal sometimes. And I am on an antidepressant, by the way. But I often wonder, what am I contributing to this society? Nothing. What am I contributing to the world? What am I contributing to my family? You know? So basically when I feel useless or I'm not feeling good about myself. As I said, all I have to offer is nothing. [Laughs]

But you've come out of that.

Yeah. Usually it takes someone else to do it for me, though. I can't do it internally. I need someone to say, "Oh, you look good" or "That's good that you did that" or something like that. I need validation.

Growing Up Male In America

A lot of what makes me happy is thinking back to the times I spent with my grandparents. Like if I smell cigars – my grandpa smoked cigars – if I smell cigar smoke, that just brings me back there. If I see someone that looks like my grandma, that'll make me happy.

Is she still alive?

Yup. My grandfather isn't, but she is.

How old is she?

Um ... she was born in 1927. Seventy-three.

And full of life, and love?

Um-hum.

When you get into these depressions, what do you do about them? What do you do to relieve them?

Well, when I had my eating disorder, I would probably binge and purge. But since I'm trying not to do that, usually I'll read or I'll try to get someone on the phone who I can talk to. But I don't have any friends, so I don't really feel like there's anyone I can talk to. Sometimes when I get really depressed, it usually takes someone else to get me out of it.

Okay. Another person? So you can watch a video and you can read a book and you can watch TV, and it doesn't quite always do it.

No.

Okay. Do you go to movies alone?

I have.

You don't prefer it.

I don't prefer it, but I have when I can't find anyone to go with.

When you're out of town, do you go to restaurants alone?

Yes. Because I often go out of town alone because, for one thing, I like to get up early, and a lot of people don't like to travel with me because I get up so darn early. And I like to shop and they don't like to shop. So I go out of town a lot alone. And I'll often go to restaurants alone. I'll go to the bars alone. I'll go shopping alone. Do everything alone. Unless I'm with someone. [Laughs]

Moving along. What's the most hurtful thing a friend or a relative has ever done to you?

Well, I remember a couple of things. When I was in sixth grade, I had a male friend over. This wasn't anything sexual, but he was very popular in school, and I thought it was really cool that he was spending the night at my house. Later I found out that his girlfriend at the time lived right by me, so he was using me to go to her house. Another thing I remember is, some of my girl

Interview 9

friends – not girlfriends but friends who were girls – when I was, like, six or seven. We would always ride our bikes to the local bakery and get baked goods. I was a very generous person. I always bought them treats, candy, doughnuts, whatever. I think they started to take advantage of me. One of my friends later told me that one time when we went to the bakery, they were going to tell me – they had this all planned out – that they forgot their money at home or something, just so I would pay. [Laughs] So there's just a couple of things. But not too bad.

Yeah, not traumatic. But very annoying.

Yeah.

What's the most hurtful thing you've ever done to somebody else?

[Laughs] I'm sure other people would tell you millions of stories!

I mean, consciously *hurtful. Is there anything you've ever done consciously to hurt somebody?*

I don't really think I've done anything really that hurtful, on purpose.

Because you're not a hateful person.

No.

Can you remember how you learned about sex?

Um ... I think just from friends. And maybe TV, magazines. Things like that.

Okay. Nobody ever sat you down. Grandpa, grandma. Certainly not your stepdad.

No.

And based on what you said before, there's probably no one person whom you share everything with.

Right.

Do you think there are any heroes in your life? Or in your culture, let's say?

Well, I think one of my heroes was my grandfather.

Why?

Because he was just a very typical gentleman. I always admired him because he was kind of funny. He was a lawyer, and they had some money. And he would always take me aside when I was really little and he would pull out a $100 bill and show it to me. Of course, when you're a kid, you're impressed as hell by that. He would show affection towards me, you know, and that's something my stepdad never did. I guess I saw that contrast between him and my stepdad, and I admired that. I mean, he gave me bear hugs and things like that. And I saw how well he treated my grandmother.

And you weren't seeing that at home with your mom and your stepdad?

Growing Up Male In America

    No, not at all. So he was probably my hero when I was little. Right now, I don't have a hero that I can think of.

I always wonder if there are any heroes for young people right now.

Were you ever in the military?

    No.

Never had any wish?

    Well, when you're supposed to enroll in the Selective Service, I was in the hospital. Not that I really cared. I would have preferred to go into military service, I guess, but I probably wasn't healthy enough to do it anyway.

Do you have a fear of failure?

    No. Actually, quite the opposite. I think I have a fear of success. [Laughs] Because a lot of times I'll be doing something very well, and then I'll quit it for no reason. Like, right before I'm done. With anything. Writing a story, writing a paper for school. Anything. I don't want to finish it for some reason. And I think it's because I'm afraid of success and the responsibility it might carry.

That is interesting.

    I start a lot of stuff and I don't finish it. It's very hard for me to finish things.

Now, you're going to finish that degree, though.

    [Laughs] That's another thing. I quit after three years. It was, like, I have to. Yeah. But I'm enrolled for this fall, so that's a good sign.

Back in the days when you were dating or had one-night encounters with men, did you ever have a fear of failure sexually?

    No.

A fear of getting it up?

    No. Well, sometimes I had a fear of ejaculating and sometimes not being able to. Or it was taking too long. I always felt pressure that way. But otherwise, no.

You know, there's a funny difference between gay men and straight men in that gay men often worry about that very thing: what if I don't come? Will my partner think he's doing something wrong? Or why can't I? And we've all been there. Straight men have to prolong it and they don't want to come too soon, and yet they want to come but they also want to please the woman. Isn't that interesting?

    Right. That is.

Now, let's talk about your body. You're in magnificent shape. What, in your estimation, needs improvement?

    Maybe my calves. They're kind of skinny. That's about the only real problem I have with my body.

Interview 9

In terms of your workout routine, are you at the stage of maintaining now?

Yeah. I'm trying to maintain my body shape. Maybe put on a little more. Because I lost a lot when I went through that recent bout of bulimia. And I've been putting it back on. But I don't know. It's like I said. I've been questioning if it's that important to me to have a good physique. Maybe I should focus on other things. My personality, for instance, or maybe why I don't have friends. So maybe I'm putting too much focus on looks.

Maybe you can do what the old ancient Greeks used to do in trying some moderation.

Yeah. [Laughs]

In terms of penis size, is yours larger than or smaller than average?

It's average.

About average? Okay. Fourteen inches?

[Laughs] Yeah, right!

I think people have a mistaken notion, based on porn probably, about the length of a man's penis.

Yeah. I was reading something on the Internet, and it said the average penis is four to five-and-a-half inches or something. Erect.

A colleague of mine where I teach is doing a casual study on why we don't see male frontal nudity in American films. Of course, the answer that the film executives give is that men would be embarrassed. Yet the camera can zoom right in on the vagina of a woman and almost count her pubic hairs – and that's okay. But all we get is butt shots on men. Right? So he's contacting people on the Internet, asking for responses, and ultimately he urges, "Let's see more penises in our films!" And he's calling his study The Invisible Penis in American Film.

[Laughs] Oh, that's funny.

And he's a straight man!

Okay ... back to you. When you're in a locker room, are you the least bit shy showering in front of other guys?

Not any more.

Okay. Do you consider yourself handsome?

Yeah. I think so. I know it goes day by day, actually.

Are you trying to change the word "handsome" to "attractive"?

Yeah. It's day by day. Some days I feel ugly and I don't even want to leave my house because I feel like I don't want anyone to see me. And other days I feel like I'm the best-looking guy in town, you know? So it varies. I'm sure it has something to do with how I'm feeling about myself that day, overall.

Growing Up Male In America

Does it have anything to do with not having been to the gym in a while?

It really doesn't have much to do with that.

Did you say you go to the gym every day?

Six days. Yeah.

What's the day off? Sunday?

Sunday. Yup.

The day of rest, you know.

[Laughs] Yeah.

And how long a workout do you typically do?

An hour, an hour and 15 minutes. Sometimes I'll go to another gym where I do just strictly aerobics. And so I'll end up going twice some days. Probably twice, four days a week.

Okay. Do you feel that regimen is controlling you, or are you controlling it?

It used to control me. I used to go three, four times a day. And that's when I was losing a lot of weight, about a year and a half ago. And I was very compulsive about the cardiovascular workout.

Okay.

But I feel my routine is very moderate now.

Well, there are people who do three and four hours at a session. And that's a bit enslaving, it would seem to me.

Yeah.

Here's a question I ask the straight men that I don't think we have to ask the gay men – but I'm going to ask you anyway. Do you ever "size up" other guys in the showers or at urinals? I mean, sneak a glance.

Oh, yeah. But probably not for the reasons the straight men do. [Laughs]

What characteristics or qualities should a person possess in order to be your friend? How do you define a friend?

Trustworthy. Honest. Basically that's it. Maybe fun. Because I'm kind of more quiet and reserved, someone who is a little more "out there" than I am.

Do you still see your mother on a regular basis?

Yup. Couple times a week. We've been having a rough time lately because she's just sick of giving me money. So every time I ask for money, we fight.

You're out to her as a gay man?

Yup.

When did that happen?

Interview 9

That happened shortly after I realized that I'm gay. It was really no problem for her. I don't know if she's in denial or if she just doesn't care.

You don't have long, heart-to-heart talks about your current relationship?

No. I don't feel comfortable talking to her about that, either.

Okay. And did you come out to your stepfather?

Yeah. Before he died. I actually told him when he was very sick. He couldn't really talk because of his throat cancer. Somehow mumbled to me that he thought he knew for a while.

Okay. Do you recall how you felt when he died?

I was very sad. I was maybe a little relieved. I hate to admit it, but at that point it didn't really matter, because I wasn't living with them at the time. So he couldn't really do anything to me or make me uncomfortable anymore. But I was sad and I felt sorry for myself, because I really didn't get to tell him all the things I wanted to, even though I know I had the opportunity to. We knew he was going to die for a while, so I felt I kind of missed out on telling him some things that he had done that I didn't like. I guess it was never the right time, especially when he was sick. But I've written a lot of it down and kind of got it out that way.

Good. Do you keep in touch with your half brother?

Oh, yeah. It's just mostly family gatherings. But once in a while I'll call him up and see what's going on.

Now, let's see. He's how much younger than you is he?

He was born in 1975. So that makes him 25? He's getting married next year.

Okay. And he knows you're gay?

Yes.

Masturbation. How frequently?

Once a day.

Okay. Which part of the day?

Usually afternoon.

Really?

Early afternoon.

Of course, being a man of leisure, you know.

[Laughs] Exactly. It's when I'm bored.

Is it after a workout at the gym?

No. Usually I'm too tired after a workout.

Growing Up Male In America

And a favorite place?

    My bed. [Laughs] Kind of boring, isn't it?

I could write a book on masturbation on some of the answers I'm getting in these interviews!

    [Laughs] Oh, really?

Do you ever experiment with toys or cock rings or dildos?

    No, I really never have.

Okay. Would you call yourself a highly sexual person? I mean, do you need to get your sexual release regularly?

    Yeah. Yes.

Now, in terms of drug and alcohol use and so on. Do you remember when you had your first beer or first bit of booze of any sort?

    I wasn't the type that needed to get it, like the second I turned 21. Or even I didn't try to sneak it or get someone to buy for me. But I remember when I was pretty young, at my grandma's, and they let me have a little of their Schnapps. And I remember feeling a little tipsy. But my first real drink, when I was 21, I liked it because it made me less inhibited and I could talk to people more easily. Especially at the gay bars. I don't drink that much at all anymore. Drugs are a different story. I experimented with Ecstasy a few years ago, and it made me feel so damn good. Especially when you're kind of depressed. Then I'm just really uninhibited. I'll say anything to anyone. I'll do anything out in public, pretty much. [Laughs]

Is it true what I've been reading? I mean, that it's a peaceful sort of drug?

    Yeah. It's just like you don't have a care in the world and you feel like everything's great.

How about marijuana?

    I tried that a couple of times, but nothing excessive. And I didn't really like it because it made me so damn tired.

Okay. Marijuana brownies? Cookies?

    No. Never had that.

Would you care to talk about the riskiest sexual behavior or sexual event you've ever been involved with?

    Probably swallowing. I didn't want to do it. It just kind of happened. [Laughs] He didn't tell me that it was about to happen when I was giving him oral sex. But that's probably the riskiest sex I've ever had.

Okay. And what would you say is the most exotic or kinky or unusual sex you've ever had? Have you been in threesomes?

Interview 9

Oh, yeah. I've had a couple of threesomes. I had ... well, one guy wanted to put some electrodes on my nuts, but I didn't let him do it. [Laughs] This was in LA, of course.

Of course.

But other than that, nothing too exotic.

Here we're going to get a little philosophical.

What specific events in your personal life over which you have had little or no control have left a lasting impression on you? How did these events seem to influence your beliefs and your behaviors?

Well, I think I did talk about this, about my stepdad and how I don't trust people and how I look for a male role model in other males and confuse that with sexuality. It's more comfortable for me to talk to women than men and hang out with women moreso than men. And I think a lot of that has to do with my past. And that's about it.

Okay. Since you're a student of history and political science – if there was another period in history in which you could live, what would it be?

Maybe the 1950s. Because the 1950s seemed like it was kind of ideal. Like the *Leave It to Beaver* thing. But I heard the economy was very good and Eisenhower was president. So after the wars, World War II and Korea – that's the period I'd like to live in.

Do you speak any foreign language fluently?

No, I don't. I took two years of French in college – but if you don't use it you lose it. I haven't really used it since I've taken my break from college. But I've traveled to Paris a couple of times, and I made myself speak it there.

It's about the only way to learn it, though, isn't it? To use it.

Yup.

Do you go to the theatre very much?

I don't, just because I really don't have anyone to go with. [Laughs] And I'm not going there alone, that's for sure.

Yeah. Intermissions are kind of odd, aren't they? To have to go out and stand there by yourself. Have you been elsewhere in Europe?

London and Amsterdam.

Oh. Why Amsterdam?

[Laughs] Well, actually, I don't know. I just wanted to try it out. There was a very cheap airfare. I didn't like Amsterdam that much. I thought it was very dirty. I loved London and I loved Paris. I've been to both of those cities twice.

Good for you! Now, is your current boyfriend a traveler? Does he like to travel?

Growing Up Male In America

He does, but he has his priorities fucked up, if you ask me. He just spent a whole bunch of money on his house, so he hasn't traveled recently. We've gone to Boston and New York together, but those times weren't very much fun because we fought a lot. We don't like to do the same things. So ... we haven't traveled since.

On a typical day in New York City, would your friend like to do a lot of walking and sightseeing?

Yeah, he likes to do that. I don't necessarily like to do that so much anymore.

Okay. How about Broadway shows?

Yeah. I think he'd like that. But we just never got around to it.

And the bars?

No. Because he's a recovering alcoholic.

Oh, he wouldn't want to be in a bar. That's understandable.

Shopping? No. Shopping is out. Movies we can do. Basically what we do is movies. We go to eat and bike ride. That's all we do.

Okay. But in New York, you could go to the museums. Would he like that?

Yeah, he likes that a lot. We did that.

Well, we've covered a lot of ground here, and I want to thank you for doing this interview. I think your story is very interesting, indeed.

Well, thank you. And thank you for interviewing me. And thanks for the thought-provoking questions.

Well, thank you very much. It's been a pleasure to get to know you.

Same here.

Postscript – December 2001

The interviewee suffered a relapse with his eating disorder and spent five weeks in therapy during the fall of 2001 on an in-patient basis. His therapy will continue for as long as it takes on an out-patient basis. Because of his relapse, he was forced to leave his studies at the university. He and his domestic partner's relationship has ended. He plans to enroll at the university in the spring of 2002 and continue his studies in political science, with a career goal of public policy.

Interview 10

"I remember the first time we had to work on a cadaver."

This man was 24 years old at the time of the interview, which took place on August 4, 2000. He is 5' 7" tall, weighs 135 pounds and has brown hair.

First of all, in this little conversation, could you tell me a little bit about your background.

> Well, I was born in a larger town, and then my parents decided that that probably wasn't the best place to be raising a family, and they decided to move to a smaller town while my father was getting his degree. We did a lot of moving around, but always to somewhat small towns.

And your folks were convinced that the small town was a better place to raise kids, I suppose.

> Yeah.

Do you agree with that?

> I agree with that. It's also got its pluses and its minuses.

Certainly in a small town, you got to know everybody pretty well.

> Oh, yeah.

Everybody knew everything about you.

> Yeah. Someone got a new pair of sneakers, and it was, like, everyone talked about it. [Laughs]

What is the earliest memory in your life, the first thing you can remember.

> I think the first thing I remember is my second birthday. I remember I was at my grandmother's house, and I had a Bert and Ernie cake with two big candles on it. It was near Christmas, because my birthday's around there, and I could see in the background a big Christmas tree. For some reason I just remember all of that.

Growing Up Male In America

Do you know how Jim Henson's Bert and Ernie characters got their names? They're from the Frank Capra film It's a Wonderful Life. *The two cops are called Bert and Ernie. Somebody said that Jim Henson borrowed from that film, and he named his characters after those cops.*

I never knew that.

Did you go to kindergarten or preschool?

I went to two years before kindergarten, a program called Head Start.

Now, how do you qualify for that?

It's mostly a low-income kind of program. Instead of going to preschool. I think I was three and a half or almost four when I started going to school.

What did they do with you there?

It's one step back from kindergarten. But they'd read you stories and do all sorts of interactive social events. I think they started us reading, possibly.

And your family qualified as low income?

Oh, yeah. [Laughs]

What did your dad do for work?

He had just started teaching, his first year of teaching school.

And of course, that does qualify you as low income!

Yes. [Laughter] And then when you have two other siblings and your mother stays home to take care of you ...

Right. I'll bet your dad certainly can remember what his first annual salary was in those days, and compared to what he must be making now, that's quite a difference.

Oh, yes.

What does he do for work now?

He is a principal at a high school.

Does your mother work?

Yeah. When I was in fourth grade, she started working again half time at a doctor's office as a receptionist.

You have two sisters.

Yes.

Okay. And where do you fall in the family?

I'm the oldest, and we're all 16 months apart.

Since you're studying dentistry now, have you ever thought what influenced you to pursue that?

Well, when we moved to another town, my mom started working for a dentist

Interview 10

as a receptionist. She was there for quite a while. That dentist put my braces on, so I had a lot of interaction with a dental office and saw how all that worked. I remember one day – I was in seventh grade – and my teacher was on this goals kick, and we had this huge goals unit. We had to make short-term and long-term goals. I just remember coming back home that night thinking, "I have to find out ... I have to figure out what I'm going to be tomorrow. That's the assignment. I have to figure it out." So I was stressing over that, and that's when I decided I was going to be a dentist. It's much easier to get through school when you have a focus like that.

How far along in your training for dentistry are you now?

I'm going to start my third year in September.

And you will finish it off ...

May of 2002.

Have you ever had some moments of doubt that you might have picked the wrong profession?

Oh, yes. School is very strenuous, and every day I feel like, did I do the right thing? [Laughs] But I know it'll pay off eventually. I just have to keep sticking with it.

Okay. So what brings you back to "I know it's the right thing"? It isn't just the money you're going to make.

No. Because, I mean, if I was in it just for the money, I would have gone to business school. Because that's a lot easier.

Now, I've always wondered about dentists. What is it about that that you find interesting?

Well, there are a couple of reasons. I guess I like helping people, and you can see results right away. It's not delayed gratification. It's instantaneous. So that kind of influenced me. The other thing is, you get to be your own boss. There are so many avenues you can go into. You're in control. If you want to work for someone, you can. If you want to be your own boss, you can. If you want to take a week or two off, go right ahead.

You realize that you'll be doing the kind of work that most people fear, don't you?

Yes. I've heard that. They're, like, "Oh. You're going to be a dentist. Well you realize now that I'm going to have to hate you. But don't take it personally, though." That's what they always say. [Laughter]

I think the profession has tried a whole lot to change that. Some dentists even advertise painless dentistry?

Yeah.

Well, tell that to somebody who is just about to endure three stages of a root canal.

Growing Up Male In America

 I just finished that class. [Laughs]

Oh. There is a class in root canal?

 Yes.

When do you get to do your first one? Is that still in school?

 Yeah, it's in school. We have to do a bunch of them. But the first two years, we're in, like, pre-clinics. So we don't work on patients. We work on extracted teeth or plastic stuff.

Oh. Do you ever work on cadavers, or will you?

 Yeah. The first semester we had to take gross anatomy with the med students.

That must have been interesting.

 Yes.

Had you ever been that close to a dead body before?

 No. I had only been to one funeral. And it was a cremation. So I had never seen a dead body before. [Laughs]

How did you react? I'm kind of curious.

 I remember the first time we had to work on a cadaver. We were all ushered into the room, and we all had our scrubs on. Everyone was a little nervous, you could tell. We were just walking down the hallway of this old building, and the smell kind of hits you and you don't know what to expect. You walk into this room and there are all these silver stainless steel things – not really coffins, but they're like that.

Was yours a male or a female?

 A male.

And old?

 Yeah. I would say. Older.

It might be a lot harder if you got a 22 year old.

 Oh, yeah.

Did your cadaver have most of his teeth?

 Oh, yes. He had four wonderful gold bridges in there, and as soon as we saw that, then we were just, like, "Oh, my goodness." [Laughs]

You were raised Lutheran?

 Yes.

Are you still a practicing Lutheran?

 Well, I don't go to church regularly.

All right. Now, back to your early years. Do you remember anything particularly

Interview 10

traumatic or awful that happened to you in your childhood?

Nothing overly tragic, I guess.

Like a grandparent dying or anything like that?

No. Both of my grandfathers passed on before I was born, so I didn't have that to deal with. And both of my grandmothers are still alive.

When you were in grade school, did they call you smart?

Yeah.

And what was the word for smart kids in those days?

Gifted.

Oh, gifted! [Laughs]

Gifted. That's what they labeled us. You try to ignore it.

Did you find any resentment on the part of some of your classmates who might not have been so bright?

Not really.

Okay. Because there have been periods when the smart kids were scorned. It wasn't cool to be "a brain".

I think as long as you didn't go around flaunting it and trying to make an issue of it. And I never saw a reason to.

Okay. But teachers must have been pleased to see you pop into their class.

Oh, it was like everyone knew. My father was the principal of the same school that I went to, so they all knew who I was. And, you know, it's a small town, so everyone knows. So maybe that was it. They just knew. That's the other thing, too. You get labeled right away, very easily, in a small town. And you just accept it as that.

Were there any teachers in particular that you liked a lot and some you didn't like a lot? We're talking upper elementary, junior high.

Well, let's see. My fifth-grade teacher I really liked a lot. She let you go at your own pace. She didn't believe in homework, so no one ever had homework to do at night. I guess she wanted you to be a kid as long as possible. But she'd push you always, like, "Do as much as you can." So ... I remember she was always ... I went through two math books in one year, because it was kind of just "Do what you want to do." And she made sure that if you were straggling behind, she'd help you out. But she wouldn't hold anyone back. She would encourage you to do your best.

That must have been challenging on her part.

Oh, yes. She was ... there would be a line from her desk, and everyone would bring up their assignment when they were finished with it or wanted to get

Growing Up Male In America

checked. And she would check it and sit down with you and go through anything. Everyone was progressing at their own pace.

Wow. How she could keep track of all that. It's like juggling.

Yeah.

Were there some teachers who you really just didn't care for too much, and why?

You know, that's ... I never really had any teachers that I didn't care for. I mean, I got along well with most of them. There were some that I wouldn't say I disliked, but when you've got some favorite teachers, you tend to gravitate towards them more.

At about eighth and ninth grades, when you're about 14 years old, how was your relationship with your parents?

I think there were some tensions. I mean, I don't think you can avoid that with anyone growing up. Because you've got that struggle of wanting to be your own person. Independent. And at the same time your parents are there, and they kind of ground you, bring you back down and try to show you the right way. They try to teach you all the stuff that you're supposed to know before they send you off.

Did you ever have a real violent fight with your dad? And I don't mean physical, necessarily. Unless it was.

No. I never had ... well, nothing physical. But I guess we had one or two occasions where ... mostly it occurred later, like when I was 17. I went to college a year early, so I went there as a senior in high school. So then that summer when I came back, it was kind of, like, I had the taste of freedom and all of a sudden it was hard to adjust to home life again. It just didn't work out. So we had a big fight graduation night.

Hum. Great night to have it!

Yeah. It was a good time. [Laughs]

And I suppose you couldn't be on your own as far as living at that point, so you had to come home and abide by the rules of the house.

There weren't ... I mean, my parents never had any strict rules. I think because we kids were pretty good natured to begin with. Like, you know, we never had a curfew. But all my friends had curfews, so I think I was pretty lucky.

How about your mom? Do you get along with her?

Oh, yeah. Never had a major disagreement with her.

Was she a pretty strong force in your growing up?

Not really a strong force. I mean she wasn't, like, overpowering or anything like that. Mostly supportive.

Your folks are still together, aren't they?

Interview 10

Yeah.

Okay. And they've been married for ...

Twenty-seven years.

But they did make the comment once that once my sisters and I were out of the house, this is the crucial time when people either get divorced or they stay married.

All right. Now, let's go back. You're getting to that place in life at age 14 or so – they call it puberty – and for some people this is a very messy time. I mean, the glands. And testosterone is pumping in your body, and adjustments are happening to your body and your mind. Now you were still in this relatively small town when you went to senior high, right?

Well, there was one year that my parents moved. We moved to ... I went to three different schools in one year. It was kind of like a whirlwind. And I was 14 at the time, so it was a pretty traumatic year. I started out in a small town, and then we moved to another town and were there for six months and then moved to another town. We were there for another six months, and then after that we came back to the same small town originally.

Wow! How did you manage friendships?

It was very hard. Once I finally started to make some real friends that I could confide in, I left. Had to start over again.

Do you remember how you felt at that time? Besides lonely.

It was just confusing, and going through puberty as well as trying to deal with all that stuff made it difficult. It was all happening at once, so I just focused on schoolwork more and used that, kind of, as my crutch, I guess. At that age, school is sort of your "universe".

Sure, sure. At least you were intelligent, and you could find comfort and solace in reading and learning.

Yeah.

Do you remember any peer pressure? I mean, here you are in two, three different schools, and the fads and the fashions probably are different in each place.

Oh, yeah.

And was this a little weird for you, too? Or didn't you give a damn about those kinds of things?

Well, you try to fit in wherever you are, I guess. And I guess I just kind of did whatever everyone else was doing.

Now, by this time money was okay at home, right? So could your folks pretty much get you things that you needed?

Yes, but it wasn't like a free-for-all, either. [Laughs] It wasn't like I got every-

Growing Up Male In America

thing I ever wanted.

Now, certainly you remember phy ed, and everybody is developing sexually at a different time.

Yeah.

Was that difficult for you? The nudity thing – was this ever a problem for you?

Yeah. Kind of. Yes. Since I changed schools so much, it was a new school and all new people. The first school that I moved to, the whole middle school was kind of run down, and the gym teacher was kind of a creepy guy. He forced everyone to take a shower, and everyone just assumed that he was into that kind of voyeurism type thing. Kind of creeped everyone out. Whether it was true or not, no one knew. But that's what everyone was thinking.

Now, you have indicated to me that you're gay. Did you have any suspicions about that whole side of your being at the time of puberty?

Not really. If it was there, I just ignored it. Or I didn't know how to identify it yet or to put a label on it.

When did you start putting a label on those feelings? How old were you?

Maybe a year after that, when I was about 15.

I see. If you don't mind, I'd like to explore that side of your life.

That's fine.

Going through puberty and adolescence is tough at best, and if you're straight the world is straight with you because dating and TV and movies, it's all pretty much geared for that. But all of a sudden you have those adolescence difficulties and being on the other side of the fence and being a gay person makes it that much more difficult. As this gay identity was brewing inside of you, did this cause any great difficulties or hardship or trauma or depression for you?

Not really. I guess the only thing that bothered me was that I was really overweight as a kid, so if there was a number one reason for being depressed, that was it. I don't know if being overweight stemmed from being gay, but that really was my main focus.

You are so slim and trim right now.

Yeah. I used to be the fat kid in class, the heaviest kid. I was always the last person to finish the mile, like five minutes behind everyone else, and the last person to get picked for teams in phy ed.

When did you start deciding that you were going to change that?

I don't know if I really consciously decided. It just kind of happened when I started going through puberty.

Oh. You didn't make a definite effort and say, "I'm going to lose this weight."

Interview 10

   Well, sometimes I did. But that was a little later on. It just happened right away, in ninth grade.

Okay. Are you sensitive about ever being overweight again?

   Sure. Yes, you can say that.

Does this make you very much aware of weight these days?

   Oh, yeah.

Like today, if you hop on the scale and you're a few pounds over?

   Oh. I mean, my whole body image thing is just all shot to hell. [Laughs] It doesn't matter. I'm never satisfied.

Did you date much in high school?

   No.

Okay. Do you know why not?

   Well, it was a small town, and I don't know. I just wasn't interested in anything or anybody.

Did any of your friends wonder about that?

   No. Because a lot of people in my class were in the same situation, being it was such a small school in a small town and there wasn't a girl for every guy.

Social activity, then, was pretty much in groups, I suppose.

   Right.

So you hopped in the car and went to a movie or some other activity?

   Well, you quickly tried to become friends with whoever got their driver's license first. If you were lucky enough to become friends.

Okay. Did they have a junior/senior prom?

   Oh, yes. We had a prom.

So you had to go to that, didn't you? Do you remember the lady you took?

   Yup.

Do you ever see her anymore?

   No. It was one of my sister's best friends. [Laughs]

Okay. Was it fun or a good experience?

   It was a fun time.

Did you double date?

   No. It was such a small town, and it was kind of, like, everyone went. It was just like another dance. It wasn't a big deal.

How many were in your graduating class from high school?

Growing Up Male In America

Thirty-two.

Wow! That is small!

Yeah. Our town was a town of a thousand, and the high school, I think, had 250 students total. And that was seven through 12.

Did you ever do any theatre?

Yes. And speech and choir and band. We had a really good theatre teacher, and she was famous in the state. We were always at state for the one-act play competition.

How about sports?

I played golf.

But football?

Yeah. I played football in junior high.

And basketball?

No. I didn't play basketball, but I took statistics during basketball games. I could watch all the cute boys playing basketball. You know? [Laughs] It worked for me.

You were starting to have some sexual feelings at that time?

Oh, yeah.

In high school?

At about 16.

Now, I'm going to ask a very personal question. Here you are, 16, and you know where you're at as far as your sexuality is concerned. Did you have a name for it yet?

No. I guess I was still at that point where I thought maybe it was just a stage I was going through, and I thought I would grow out of it.

Did you find yourself trying to find literature to understand a little bit more about what gay people were like?

No, not really. I still wouldn't even know where to go.

Okay.

Like nowadays they have the Internet. I would have probably gone that avenue. But back then, in a small town, were you supposed to go the library and check out a book? [Laughs] No! If the topic was on TV and no one else was around, I would probably catch myself watching it.

Now, most young men explore sex with other boys. Do you remember any experience like that? Most of the time you never had a name for it, but you just kind of did things. Did you ever?

Interview 10

Not really. I did get kind of close once with a friend, my neighbor. Almost, I guess. Well, we were both young and horny. [Laughs] And the hormones were running all over.

Do you remember the situation, the scene?

His mother worked during the afternoons some days during the summer, so most of this stuff happened during the summer.

But it never reached a point where you actually were sexual with each other?

No. Nothing like that. I would stop short of it because I didn't want it to be true, that I was really gay. I didn't try to pursue it. I tried to pull away from it if the opportunity presented itself.

Do you remember the first time you masturbated? Like how old you were?

Yeah. I was 13.

About how many times a day did you masturbate?

About four or five to begin with. When I was at school there wasn't much time in the day, so only once or twice a day after that.

Okay. What was the most unusual place you ever did it?

Um ... [Laughs] Oh, that could fill up the whole other tape. [Laughs] I guess mostly it was in my room in the basement. It was a finished basement, but then there was a part of the basement that wasn't finished. And so I think most of it happened down there because there was a toilet in there.

And I suppose you always had the fear that somebody would come down and do laundry or something.

Oh, yes. Always. It always had to be very quiet so you could hear anybody coming down the stairs.

And sex ed? Your dad never sat you down and gave you lessons or instruction?

No. It was at school. And I learned a lot from friends.

Okay. That's the other question: where do you think you learned most about sex?

Mostly through friends, school, television.

Movies?

Movies. A lot of movies.

Did you ever have a wet dream?

Yeah.

Nocturnal emission, I believe it is called.

The technical term. [Laughs]

Which I think would be a great name for a nun. Sister Mary Nocturnal Emission.

Growing Up Male In America

When you had messed up the sheet, did you worry that your mother would find this?

No. I never worried about that.

Okay. Did she ever say anything?

No. My parents long ago read some article or saw some show where they thought it was good that children do their own laundry. It showed them a sense of responsibility, so I was doing my own laundry from the age of about 13. [Laughs]

Well, that's convenient, isn't it?

Yes.

Did your folks ever wonder when you would bring home some lady for dinner?

Well, I did bring girls home, so that probably threw them back a little. [Laughs] I had a girlfriend for about a year.

And what period of time was this?

When I was in college. I was 21.

Okay. And you brought her back home?

Yeah. But it wasn't right away. It was, like I suspected that my folks thought I was gay, so by bringing a girl home, I could throw them off, like, "What's really going on here?"

I see. So you dated her for about a year in college?

Yeah.

Were you just chums, or did you actually have intercourse?

We had intercourse.

So, on the continuum of gay to straight, you are not strictly gay. I mean, you are able to perform with women.

Well, when you're that young, it feels good to do it. [Laughs]

Okay. How did the relationship with this young lady end?

Kind of bad. I started having feelings for my roommates, and if you're gay, that's what happens. So I ended the relationship with this girl.

How did she take it?

Not very well at all. It was, like, this long, drawn-out, month-long process. Whole afternoons and evenings, and arguing and yelling and screaming. She couldn't understand that we were through, and she kept thinking that it was just a phase or I'd come back or something like that. She ended up trying to commit suicide and ended up in the hospital over the whole thing. It was the hardest time I ever had to go through.

Interview 10

It sounds terrible.

It was very traumatic.

Especially because you felt some responsibility for her.

Oh, definitely. Even though she didn't know that I ended it because I was gay.

Oh, you didn't tell her that that was the reason?

No, no. I figured if I did that, it would have probably sent her way off the edge.

Now, at this time were there any male friends of yours that you were able to confide in? To say that you were coming out?

Yes.

And were they gay, too?

Yeah. The first person whom I told was also gay, so he obviously understood.

And you had known him for some time?

Right.

Okay. Did the friendship with him continue?

Yes.

When did you start making treks to bigger cities to go to the gay clubs?

Not for a while. I was still pretty closeted because I was living with roommates who were all straight.

Do they know now?

No. They still don't.

They still don't. Do you think you'll tell them?

Yeah. But it's very difficult now because now that we're all out of college, they're all scattered to the wind. So I'm afraid that if I tell one, then they're all going to find out without me doing it properly. Or maybe I never will. Or it's just never a good time.

Did you ever tell a straight friend about your being gay and have it turn out badly?

No, not yet. I think I feel more comfortable telling my family, because it's harder for them to turn their back on you than it is for friends to abandon you.

So, you've told your parents?

Yeah. Two years ago

Did you sit them both down together?

Oh, yes.

You did? How did that go? Whatever caused you to do this?

Well, I was moving down from where I went to college to go to another col-

Growing Up Male In America

lege, and I was staying with them for a week before I moved to my new place. I kept waiting and waiting and waiting. And finally it's Friday and I thought, "I have to tell them now." I knew I'd only see them on holidays, and I felt I was still holding back – like they weren't getting the true me. So I sat them down, and it was, like, oh … we were watching television. My dad was falling asleep in the chair and I'm, like, "Come on. Come on." And I decided, "Okay. The next commercial. The next commercial." And finally I got enough courage and told them. "Mom, Dad. I have something to tell you." And then, of course, my dad flies out of the chair, and they're both concerned. They thought I was dying or something. They probably thought I was terminally ill. And my mom said, "Well, you know, we've got good hospitals around here." [Laughs] And I tell them, "I'm gay." And they're, like, "Oh. Is that it?" It was not really a big deal. I mean, it was a big deal, but they didn't take it like it was a big deal. We went and talked about it, probably for a couple of hours.

So they were good about it.

Yeah. My dad kind of wanted to know more about it, so of course he went and talked to a couple of people. His priest, of all people. [Laughs]

Okay. Did either one of them – as far as you could tell – come up with blame for themselves? Like, "What did I do wrong?"

Not that I can tell. But I'm sure that went through their minds.

Have you told your two sisters?

No. I haven't told them yet, but I intend to someday.

Okay. You're in a relationship now with a man?

Yeah.

How long have you two been together?

A year and two months.

Do you go to family get-togethers? And how do you explain him?

No. We don't do that yet. But his family all know about me, so I feel like I need to start doing my end of the bargain here, soon, with my family.

Now, your folks know that you have a different address and this guy you're living with is more than a roommate?

Yes.

But they haven't met him yet.

No. Not yet.

Oh, that ought to be an interesting meeting. You know, it's kind of funny. When you come out to family these days, they right away think you're dying of AIDS. Somehow, in a way, that's good, because then you say, "Well, no, I'm not HIV positive. I'm perfectly healthy. I'm just gay." And they are sort of relieved.

Interview 10

And they say, "Oh, is that all?!" [Laughter]

You're comfortable being a gay man?

Well, I guess so. It still gets to me once in a while. It would be easier the other way – to be straight – I suppose. But then you think about that and you're, like, "Oh, no!" [Laughs]

And in your case, since you can and did have sex with a woman, you could have opted to do that.

Yes. I don't think it would have been as fulfilling. It would inevitably have been a bad thing, and not at all fair to the woman, either.

Was drinking alcohol a large part of your growing up?

Not really while I was growing up, so much. I was the "goody two shoes" in school, so I rarely drank alcohol. But in college it was easier to get.

Any drug involvement?

No.

Any drugs at all?

None at all. I had never seen any of that. Just beer. [Laughs]

Okay. Now, did you ever try pot when you were in college?

Yeah, but I've not smoked pot on a regular basis. It was maybe once a year or maybe once every two years.

What is the main topic of conversation when you get together with men?

Well, it depends. If I'm hanging out with my straight male friends, it's about women, and when I'm with my gay male friends, it's about men.

Okay. With your straight friends, do you still play the game that you're straight, that you're dating?

Oh, yeah.

I see. Another question: What is the thing that frightens you the most?

I guess it's mostly the thought of dying before I accomplish everything that I want to do in my life. I guess it doesn't necessarily mean dying, but if something debilitating were to happen to me that would keep me from reaching my full potential.

What is it that puts you into a low mood or depression?

Lots of stress. That does it. If I have too many things to do and not enough time, it perpetuates for a long period of time. There are some times when dental school is intense. This past spring semester was just nasty. It was just hell. [Laughs] And then when it's over, after a couple of weeks you feel back to normal again.

Growing Up Male In America

And don't you ask yourself, "Why the hell am I putting myself through all this intense agony?"

Oh, yes. Every day.

Is there something you've done which you wouldn't want anyone to find out about? What's your big secret?

Let's see. Well, I once had a habit – when I first moved to the big city – of going on-line and meeting up with people. You know, chat rooms and stuff like that. There was one time when it had been quite a while since I had had any sexual action, so I didn't care what the guy looked like, and we met up, he came to the door and after having sex, he left.

Didn't you worry? I mean, this could have been dangerous.

Yes. I'm sure it could have been, but it adds to the whole excitement of it. I know I'll probably never do it again, but it was one of those things. For some reason I had a little checklist of experiences I wanted to have in life, and I had to check that one off. [Laughs]

Well, was it satisfactory?

Oh, yeah.

Okay. When you think of your penis – and I'll bet you do ...

I think of it often, yes. [Laughs]

Is your penis smaller than average, larger than average or average?

I would say it's maybe a little bigger than average, if average is five inches erect.

Bigger than average. All right.

[Laughs] Not much, though.

Do you ever sneak a peek at other guy's cocks at urinals and in locker rooms?

Well, not so much at urinals, because that's a little dicey. But when I work out at the rec center, I enjoy the locker room. In fact, I always make a point of wearing my contacts. That way, when I'm in the shower I don't have to have my glasses off, because I'm blind as a bat otherwise. It's a good time.

And your current significant other doesn't mind that you do this?

Oh, no.

I assume he's doing it, too?

Yes. We always compare notes. [Laughter]

Now, tell about your first sexual experience with a man. How old were you?

I was 22.

So that isn't that long ago. Because you're only 24.

Interview 10

Yeah.

So for a long time you had been fantasizing and thinking and wondering about sex with a man.

Oh, yeah.

And masturbating, no doubt. Thinking about men. Did this experience live up to your expectations?

Oh, yeah.

Okay. Good. Because so often the first time is a clumsy experience.

No, no. I was pretty much in control of the situation, so it went the way I wanted it to.

As far as other gay men are concerned, don't you think that age 22 is a little late these days?

I guess I'm just in that old small-town mentality.

How do you define "masculinity"?

I guess being very assertive and assured of yourself. And putting on a good show for everyone and not letting your emotions or your feelings out. It's like putting a wall between you and other people. I don't know if that's what society has told us that it should be, but I guess that's the way I've been shaped to think about masculinity.

Yes. Like not to show your feelings too much?

Right.

Who is your favorite male public figure?

I don't know if it's a certain person, but I guess I'm kind of enamored with the scientists out there who struggle in the lab all the time, searching for ways to help people. Mostly these medical, scientist-type people who work with viruses and bacteria and disease. They're trying to cure these things and their spouse and their kids are back at home, and they kind of put their family life to the side for their interest in their career.

That's a wonderfully cerebral answer.

Do you ever have a fear of failure?

Oh, all the time. I could go on and on about that. [Laughs]

How important is money in your life? You didn't have much when you were a little kid. I mean, you know what it's like not to have lots of money.

I guess it's important to have enough so that there's that safety net, but I don't need a lot of it.

I think you said earlier that one of the great satisfactions you anticipate in life is

Growing Up Male In America

your work, your profession.

That's right. I hope so. If not I'll probably pursue something else that will.

Okay. Let's talk a little bit about your significant other. What's he like?

He's even more Type A than I am. He's hyper Type A. So I'm the more relaxed of the two of us. [Laughs] It can be a little stressful at times.

I was so happy when you mentioned many, many months ago that you had met this person.

He's really a very nice guy. Living with him is definitely a good thing.

Do you consider yourself handsome or attractive?

Well, I never used to because I was really overweight as a kid. So that warped my view of the whole world and myself. Only recently, I guess, I consider myself attractive. But I don't let it go to my head or anything like that. Because lots of times I still see myself as that 13-year-old fat kid.

Do you have pictures of yourself at that age?

Oh, yeah.

What makes you sad? Not depressed, but just sad.

Sometimes, if I'm watching movies, I empathize with the characters.

Do you cry easily at movies?

Not really.

Do you cry at all, much?

Not much.

Have you ever cried with your partner?

No. Not yet.

Has he?

No, I don't think so.

You're both scientist types. I wonder if that training might make you more rational and less emotional?

I asked you about what you were afraid of. What were you afraid of as a little kid?

I was really afraid of the storms. Thunderstorms. Oh, I just couldn't handle it. [Laughs] Because the small town that I grew up in, it seemed like there were always storms there. You know, the sirens, going to the basement.

I see. I was wondering. Thinking back, either to your childhood or even it could be as recent as last week, what would you say is the meanest thing that your dad ever did to you?

I don't think it was anything intentional, but I guess most of it would be that he

Interview 10

wasn't home a lot. He was always at school late or working late. He just didn't seem to be around a lot. Sometimes that would bother me, but other times I thought, "Hey. I get to watch what I want to on television." [Laughs]

On a 10-point scale, where would you put your dad in terms of fatherhood?

Probably an eight, just because if you say something like a 10, someone probably wouldn't believe you. [Laughs]

And as the years go by, your relationship or friendship with him increases?

Oh, yeah. I call him up and we talk. And now it's at that point where he's asking my advice and I'm telling him what I think on certain things. Whether he listens to it or not, I don't know. [Laughs]

Do you ever use the word love with him?

I have on occasion, but it's not a regular thing. My family's not like that. It must be that Norwegian thing, that Swedish thing. No emotion, no hugging, just, "Goodbye." "Hi."

Okay. And if you could put your mom on a 10-point scale, where would you put her in terms of being a mother?

Probably a nine.

Well. Dad's an eight. Mom's a nine. Let's see. Hmm.

Sons are always supposed to like their mothers better.

You come from that Nordic sort of non-touch, non-feel, no open display of emotion background. Now that you are in this major relationship with this man, do you use the word love frequently? Are you finding that you're able to be more demonstrative than you were a few years ago?

Oh, yeah. Definitely.

Well, I want to thank you very much for granting this interview. I wish you the best of luck with your relationship and with your career as a dentist.

Thank you!

Postscript – December 2001

This man continued his studies in dentistry and will complete his degree in May 2002. His relationship with his domestic partner continues and prospers after nearly three years.

Interview 11

"That was hurtful, to be abandoned by people you thought were your friends."

This man is in the Army National Guard and is also a university student studying criminal justice. He is 6' 1" tall, weighs 188 pounds and has light brown hair. He was 22 years old when this interview was conducted on February 24, 2001.

I want to thank you very much for being willing to do this interview.

It's going to be a good experience for me.

What is the first memory you have in your life?

I would say when my brother was born. I remember that very vividly. He was born about three and a half years after I was. But I'm sure there were moments before, but it's just something that's so epic in proportion, it really sort of embedded itself in my mind.

At the age of three and a half, do you remember any feelings about this little "intrusion?" [Laughs] *All of a sudden, he's going to take some attention away from you.*

Exactly. It was jealousy right away. And I think that's common. But it's as if I was getting the attention, and then it was totally put upon him from there on. [Laughs] And even now, to this day, him being the youngest child, he just charges the gas to mom and dad in their name and doesn't have a job. [Laughs] You know.

And you mean, when you pushed the crib over that time, it didn't do him in, huh? [Laughter] *Now your other siblings – you have an older sister and a brother – there's quite a bit of space between them and you two.*

Yes, there is.

How much?

Well, my sister is, I think, 41. And my oldest brother, he's – you know, I honestly don't even remember. I think he's about 35 or 36. And he's married and lives in California. They just moved there into a really nice place and everything.

Growing Up Male In America

You don't see him too much, then, I imagine.

Not too much. Holidays, Christmas and sometimes Thanksgiving.

Now, your parents – I mean, they were married throughout all this. I mean, it's not like a different father or a different mother or anything like that.

My mom was married before.

So these kids – the oldest ones – are hers from the first marriage?

Yeah.

Okay. That's what I wondered. So that makes them your half sister and half brother. How about the youngest brother? You and he share the same mom and dad, right?

Yeah.

About your parents, now – how much hugging and closeness and touching and rocking and sitting on daddy's lap and all that kind of stuff, was there?

Not really too much. It was more the mother/child relationship as far as I was concerned. I think guys are more likely to shake hands, sort of to maintain their poise and never show emotion. [Laughs] But my mom and I are more touchy.

Has your dad improved in that regard, as he gets older?

I think so.

Now, your dad is a farmer.

Yeah.

Could you describe your mom?

Well, she's very talented. She's very involved with the Baptist church. And, you know, she's real into crafts. She likes to have control. More so than my dad. He'd rather just do his own thing and work on a building or something or feed hay and worry about those things. Go hunting.

Now, does she run the checking account and do the books?

[Laughs] Yeah.

Uh-huh.

How did you guess that?

Well, I just had a feeling your dad would maybe be more interested in making sure the Herefords got into the pasture instead of worrying about what the taxes were going to be that year or something. There used to be a term called "smother love" where mothers just control their children – especially their sons. They wouldn't snip the cord. They were watching out for their kids' every move. Is there a streak of that in your mom?

A little bit. Um ... I think that, you know, a lot of moms are like that, though. But it's just part of the mothering instinct, in general. But, yeah. That's still the

Interview 11

way my mom is to this day with me.

And when you were growing up, would you say that she was a strong disciplinarian?

Well, I did have a lot of freedom. When they knew where I was and everything. It was, like, I could call. And they would call, of course, to make sure I was there. [Laughs] But I had a curfew. A lot of kids had to be back by 10:30, 11:00. And I could go out on dates and I could get home pretty late. As long as it was before sunrise, it would be okay.

And your little brother? Does he have a little more freedom?

A lot more. Big time. Yeah. [Laughter] My younger brother has never actually had hard times. Even like in the recession, when the Republicans were in office. It was the early 1990s, and it wasn't until the mid or late 1990s where he actually got to drive. And that was when things were pretty good. And, you know, he's taken advantage of that.

Now, when you were a young boy and getting on up to teenage years, was it expected that you would work on the farm?

Yes. I had chores. And wood was a big deal. We had to split wood. Because I am kind of for the environment myself, I'd feel kind of bad chopping down trees that were just beautiful and in their prime. But we did cut wood a lot. And it was definitely something that we had to do, especially in fall. My dad always said, before deer hunting, "Get out there before the snow hits." And mosquitoes aren't around. And we really had to do that. My brother has never worked very hard. I don't think he's really loaded one or two loads of wood in his life.

What does he do? Run off and party?

That, and … well, he's got a very attractive girlfriend and everything. And he's kind of in with the snooty crowd. Definitely into the sports. That's takes a lot of time, I think.

What sport? All of them? In a small town, I suppose everybody gets involved in everything.

Everything except wrestling, but he was very good at wrestling. He's got trophies and stuff. But basketball interfered with that.

Same season. Did they have much of a theatre program in the high school?

Well, it was interesting you bring that up. Because I was very, you know, looking forward to that. And people kind of stereotype that, you know, being anti-sports and anti-athletic. Which it isn't. It's reality. You know? And I wanted to have a part of that, because that was what I enjoyed. The acting and the being on stage. So right when I was getting involved with theatre, it was a transition period where from ninth to 10th grade I went to a private parochial school. And found that school to be not at all into the arts. It was very, very conservative. And they wanted no part of anything that even had to do with the stage or pres-

Growing Up Male In America

entation, unless it was a biblical sort of play.

What religious affiliation was it? I mean, it wasn't Catholic?

It was Baptist.

Now, was this school – the private school that you went to – all the way up through high school?

The school itself is structured from K through 12. And, of course, they separate the K through the fourth or fifth. And then from there on it's considered high school.

But you didn't graduate from high school from that place, did you?

Yes.

Oh, you did. So you didn't go to the home-town public high school.

No. Well, I did go the public school from K through ninth grade, but from 10th through 12th I went to the private school, hoping to get improvement, get a change, better grades. Just some of the things like that. Basically I wanted a different social experience. But ultimately it would end up to be worse.

Because I think, in your home town, they do have a theatre program in the public school.

They do.

What religious affiliation were your parents? If any religion, how were you raised?

Baptist. Which, you know, if sort of an offshoot of Christianity, in a way. In the Upper Midwest, you know, it's Lutheran, Catholic and Baptist. [Laughs]

Yeah. So, church every Sunday was expected of you?

Yeah.

Yup. And certain restrictions and the good way to live and, I suppose, suspicion on the part – particularly by your mother – that you were partying too much. Did she ever drill you on if you were drinking or using drugs?

There was a New Year's. It was in 1995. And I've been going to this friend's house since then, every year on New Year's Eve. I saw the ball going down in Times Square and the Dick Clark New Year's Rockin' Eve. And I said, "I'm going to beat that thing." So sure enough, I was out, eight minutes before the ball hit. [Laughter] And I came home the next morning. You know. Because it was normal for everyone to just crash there. And so, yeah. It was 5:00 or 6:00 a.m. I wanted to get there as early as I could. And I had a headache and everything. Forcing myself to get there. And my mom questioned that. "Why were you there all night? Normally you're home by 1:00" or whatever. [Laughs]

What was your answer?

Well, I told her that I had some enjoyable beverages, to say the least. It was,

Interview 11

like, there was Windsor or whatever. And I was mixing that with pineapple juice.

Happy New Year.

Yeah.

Now, this is a whole group of people there? At the party?

Yeah. That year, there were three other people. Which were all kids I grew up with. And all these kids are kind of into the arts a little bit. One of them's a DJ now, and he's very talented and good at that. So, uh … we always had a lot of fun getting together. Because when you grow up, you have so many of the same experiences. And it's like you always talk about how things have been.

And traditions in the family, I'm sure, are pretty strong, too?

Yeah.

I always think school is an important thread in our lives.

Definitely.

Did you go to kindergarten?

Yeah. Yes, I did. I was in preschool, also. But it was not until fourth grade when I had a teacher who was really cool.

Was it a man or a woman?

A man.

Okay. That's rare in elementary.

It is. And he's a principal now at one of the Twin Cities suburbs, as a matter of fact. So he worked there for a year, and they laid off a lot of teachers. And all the newer teachers – which he was – got laid off. And it happens. So, yeah. He taught, like, English and social studies. You know, in fourth grade they teach you all sorts of variety.

Do you remember what it was about him that you thought was cool or nice or good?

Well, he always had interest, you know. Positive, good interest in the kids. And especially the ones that were – I don't know if "different" is the word. But, you know, just had different abilities. And I remember he had a broken TV, and I would tell him about how my neighbor would repair TVs, and I was always fascinated by how things worked. So I used to ride my bike down that gravel road and visit the neighbor. And he'd show me, and I'd help him get things and grab stuff. And the teacher had a TV. It was, like, one of those portable ones. And he was telling me that he blew it up when they went up to the lake. Blew a fuse in the thing. Smoke was everywhere. So I took my teacher's TV to the repair person. I did that for him. And he said, "Well, you did the foot work." And he gave me, like, $10. Which in fourth grade is – wow!

Growing Up Male In America

Oh ... that's rich!

Yeah.

Oh, my gosh. I bet – because of your training and just because you're a nice guy – you said, "What?" when he gave you the ten. Did you refuse it?

Well, me in fourth grade – yeah, even then I think I was very modest and humble towards it. So I just said, "Well, that's okay." And he said, "No, no. You did the foot work." So he gave me the ten, and he said, "Well, don't tell the other kids." [Laughter] Because they'd go whining to their parents, you know?

Do you remember the other classmates that you had in those early years? Do you remember the kids who were "in" and the kids who were "out"? You know what I mean? What made the cool kids and what made the not-so-cool kids?

Well, at that time – third and fourth grade, maybe a little bit in fifth grade – there was a time when being the comedian was pretty cool. Just having fun and stuff. And that was me – the comic. And then later – in the fifth and sixth grades and the beginning of junior high – athletics was the thing. I don't know what it is – hormones or whatever – but for the guys it was like a living hell. And I think a lot of people would agree with this. You could be Jim Carrey, but you'd be looked down on unless you were a jock.

And their impression of you as the funny guy changed?

It changed. It was a dramatic change. One year, I was actually pretty cool. And then it was just like I was nobody.

So they knew that you were the life of the party and the jokester, and you could always do little things in class that would lighten things up.

Yeah.

Nothing harmful, but ...

Goofing off in class, too, was more accepted, I think, when you're young. When you get older, it's like, well, we've got to get ready for high school. And when you're in high school, for college. And you don't do it anymore. Unless it's appropriate. Like, I'd say something. I remember the teacher had, in science class, said, "How do rainbows occur?" And this was back, like, in the mid 1990s. And I said, "When Dennis Rodman washed his hair." You know? I would come up with one-liners all the time. And it was just from watching late night. Carson, when I was young, I would stay up. An insomniac, you know. So in the early 1990s, I was more into that stuff.

But it kind of changes when puberty kicks in there, whenever that is. That can spread over a whole lot of time, depending on the kid. And all of a sudden then jock things made them cool, huh?

Big time.

And they could be worshipped.

Interview 11

In ninth grade, I hurt my knee. I got hit from the side. So it was one of those injuries. And it could have been bad, you know. And I went to the doctor. And my coach said, "Don't go to the doctor." He said, "We want you out there. You're our left tackle." And I punted, too. And here I got hit in my leg. Well, how could I punt? And I'm thinking, "Well, I'm going to the doctor. I care about this. I'm in pain." You know? And the doctor wrapped it and said in about a week or so I should come back. And I had a note from the doctor. I went to my coach, and he just looked at the note. He didn't say a word. Didn't say a word. And I thought, "I'm not even going to go to practice." I thought, why the heck go back to that? And deal with all that stuff. And I had my gym shoes in the locker room. And I came back a few days later, when they weren't practicing. I had to go in there when I couldn't be confronted. "What the heck are you doing back here?" You know. And my shoes smelled like urine. One of the players had literally pissed on my shoes through the locker door. And I thought, they must have *really* got mad when I quit the team.

Now, this happened when you were how old?

It would have been ninth grade. So I was 15 years old. That was just before I went to the private school.

Okay. So this was still public school.

That football experience was one of the focal points of my transition and the decision that I would go to the private school. How could I go back the next year after going through about half a year dealing with that hate from the coach and my teammates? And of course, that's kind of an immature way to see it. I should have just drove on and dealt with it.

Now, you said early on that you had kind of an interest in theatre. Did you ever have time in ninth grade, tenth grade, to fit it in? Or was that considered not the thing that guys do?

That was part of it. And it was that pressure that made me avoid getting involved in what I really enjoyed. I was dealing with it in the way I shouldn't have, by ignoring it. And at some point, I did work after school, so it would have conflicted with that. But I didn't have to work. It was all more of a selfish thing. I could have worked on weekends and had enough for gas and go to the shopping mall in a nearby town. You know, the mall. Everyone's place to hang out. [Laughs]

Yeah. The center of teenage activity.

Yeah.

Now, you're coming into puberty by that time, and as you look around the locker room, you notice that some boys have developed early and some boys have developed late and some, you wonder if they ever will. [Laughter] I mean, that is an amazing age, isn't it?

Growing Up Male In America

Definitely.

And there are some boys who don't have hair and nothing's happening yet, and others who look like they've been sexually active for six years already.

Yeah. They've got hair all over, some of them.

Where would you put yourself? Did you develop early, or about normal or later?

I think maybe a little earlier. I don't know. The locker room thing ... I guess, yeah, I was aware of everyone else. I think every guy, honestly, is going to check out other guys and look. Some guys are so shy that they won't even take a shower after practice. Which is pretty bad. But it was around fifth or sixth grade when I was pretty much ... I was growing hair there, and I was asking myself, "Should I shave it?" [Laughs]

So you probably developed a little earlier than most guys since you had pubic hair at age 12.

Yeah. I don't know. I think it's kind of awkward for teenage boys to speak of this, but masturbation might have been something that was going on with some of the guys. I was doing that quite a bit. [Laughs]

Well, let's talk about that. Did other friends of yours talk about masturbation?

It's so weird. Because they wouldn't talk about doing it, but they'd joke about it. They'd take a pop bottle or soda or whatever, and they would shake it up. And we'd be outside at an event or something in the park, and they'd shake it up and then let it fizz out of the bottle. And laugh. [Laughs]

Yeah. And they did this as a joke.

It's a joke. But they'd never admit it. "No. I don't do that. No!" And there was maybe one or two kids who actually admitted it. I mean, come on! Everybody does it.

If you were a typical 14- or 15- or 16-year-old kid, you were horny almost all the time.

Yeah.

How frequently did you masturbate?

Well, it was one of those deals where ... it was more in the shower and the bath. Convenience.

And privacy?

Yeah. And it was safe. I think, as a kid you're wondering, "Oh, what's going to happen?" And you don't know if someone's going to catch you doing it. But at night, also, in my bed.

So, in a typical week, how many times?

Probably 25, 30. But I think, maybe, being on a farm and stuff, I had some time to spare. [Laughter]

And that's a good activity.

Yeah. [Laughs]

But 25, 30 times a week?

Yeah.

What's the most number of times you masturbated in one day?

Well, my record is 17 times. And boy, was I sore by the end of that day! I went on a missions trip in the summer of 1995, and I was in Central Mexico for over two weeks. I was thinking, "Man." You know, all these people around and I had no privacy. [Laughter] I just wanted to take a shower and do it! I don't know what it is with guys, but they would walk in and they'd kick the shower door open. It happened, like, three or four times during a shower. They would kick the door open and laugh. Like, "What are you doing in there?" And I'd be washing my hair. Because, you know, I mean, there's no way I was going to masturbate with people kicking the door open. Because if I got caught, it wouldn't be, like, "Oh. Ha-ha. You're doing it." They'd condemn me for doing that, and they'd run off and tell everyone.

A sin? Was it considered bad?

Yeah!

Well, in the old days of the Catholic Church, it definitely was a sin. You had to confess it to the priest and tell him how many times you did it.

You're kidding.

No. That's true.

Wow. Did you actually do that? Confess it?

Yeah. They say Jews give guilt to their kids. I think the Catholics are way ahead of the Jews in giving you a sense of guilt. And masturbation was called self abuse. In confession you had to tell the priest, "I sinned by self abuse" and how frequently you did it.

Yeah?

It was a sin. But in your case, if anybody caught you masturbating, it would be thought to be not a spiritually healthy thing to do, right?

Yeah. Another thing I was going to bring up – now that we're on that topic – we had a speaker come to our school when I was in 10th grade at the private school, and he talked about abstinence. And I thought, "Okay, here we go. Here's another lecture." You know. [Laughs] And he was a single guy. Early 30s. Youth pastor. And I thought, "Well, okay." So I raised my hand and brought it up, and he said, "Well, you can't have sex before you're married. You can't be intimate, even with yourself." And I said, "What are you going to

Growing Up Male In America

do if there's physiological things that come into play here?" And the guy turned beet red. He was embarrassed. He didn't know what to say. And I thought, "Well, I'm just going to keep going." I was always considered, like, more of the bad altar boy. I would ask questions you weren't supposed to. You know? And bring things up that weren't supposed to be talked about. So I was discussing this. And I said, "Well, isn't there something you can do? Isn't there something you can do to release that and get rid of that?" And, of course, he's turning red. He's ashamed, embarrassed. He probably does it himself. You know?

But he wouldn't talk about it?

He wouldn't talk about it.

Did he ever give an answer?

Yes.

Oh.

He said, "Well, I guess you can do that." And he said, "But …" And I said, "Well?" And he said, "Yeah. If you don't …" And I said, "When you're doing it, if you don't think about another person or whatever, is it okay?" And he had no choice but to say, "Well, maybe." And my teacher was in the back of the class, observing everything. And he was mad and he said to me, "That's it. Get out." And here the speaker's the one that gave the answer. But, yeah, I'm the one who's blamed for it.

Well. Very interesting. Because usually the answer is, from your youth pastor, there are things called wet dreams or nocturnal emissions.

Yeah.

And that's God's way.

But you stop having those – I'm guessing – at 16, 17. You probably won't have any more, after that.

Well, not if you're masturbating 25 or 30 times a week!

[Laughter] Yeah.

Nothing is building up here.

[Laughs] I think I had, like, one wet dream. That's about it. [Laughter]

All right. Very interesting. So you were a pretty randy teenager, and a very sexual one. Did you start dating about now?

Well, being at a private school and there are less people, the girls are almost more like sister figures. You're confined to a smaller space. Socially, you'd have to do things in groups.

Well, when did you start dating?

Interview 11

I was a sophomore,. My first year at the private school.

That makes you about 16 or so. Do you remember your first date?

Yeah.

And she was the first one who didn't seem like a sister?

Yeah. It was a girl from the school there. And it was June, so it was after school got out. And, of course, after that episode where the youth pastor came in, everyone pretty much pointed at me and said, "Yeah, he does it." And I thought, "So what?" I mean, if they want to think that because of the questions I brought up, that's their opinion. Whatever. So the girls, I think, were actually … felt threatened by that. Because here's a guy – if no one else does it [laughs] – here's a guy who's content. [Laughter] You know?

Okay. Now, what was she like?

Real tall and thin. She was in the same grade as me. I was the oldest one in my class. She was the youngest. An only child. So. Of course, her parents – you can imagine the ideals they had. In that way it was a little awkward. I remember her dad saying, "You have to make sure that she's back by 10:00 sharp." And, you know, it was like … he'd point a finger at me and everything. And of course, I was nervous. You know, nerve-wracked. I thought, "Why deal with that all the time?" I thought, "Well, I don't really have a lot of interest anyway."

Where did you go? Was it a movie?

Yeah. Dinner and a movie.

Isn't that great? It's the thing most people do on their first date, go to a film.

Yes. It was 1996, and that was a big year in the box office, I remember. There was a James Bond movie with Pierce Brosnan. It was the first Pierce Brosnan Bond. I mean, he's the handsomest Bond. [Laughs]

So, did you have your date home by 10:00?

Yeah. [Chuckles] When her dad said that, I said, "Nine would be okay. I'll be back by 9:00, how does that sound?" Kind of rub it in a little bit. [Laughter] And of course, at about 8:30 I pulled up in the driveway. I made sure I didn't get a flat tire. I mean, otherwise this guy's going to kill me.

Enjoyable date? Pleasant woman?

Yeah. It was good. Being friends prior to that helped a little bit, too, Which makes a difference. I mean, when I go out with girls now, it's just something to do, more or less. I know it's not going to go anywhere, because I usually don't let it. I'll get their number and maybe I'll see them at a restaurant or bar and talk to them and go out with them maybe once, maybe twice. Then I throw her number away.

Growing Up Male In America

Did you repeat dating this girl?

It went on for about four or five dates, and then I just stopped calling her. Of course, I got a call about a week after, saying, "What's going on? Why aren't you calling me? What's wrong?" I said, "Nothing's wrong. I just stopped calling you."

You must have had some good talks during those dates. And she probably learned that you were a man of substance, right?

I would like to think that.

Of course, I don't know. Maybe people don't talk in any depth when you're 15, 16.

It's funny. She was an only child and was kind of lonely, and I was kind of lonely, too, being in that Christian or private school. It was kind of weird, because there weren't a lot of people.

Now, about this time – I mean, teenage years are weird years. When you're a teenager everything's happening and you're changing attitudes towards social contacts and everything. Did you ever wish just to get the hell out of that small town and go to the big city? Did you feel trapped?

Yeah. And I was, because of the way that private school's credits worked. I was trapped because I couldn't transfer back to public school. They didn't have music. I missed that. Choir. And I was planning to be in swing choir and everything. And all those things I didn't get to have. The credits were screwed up. You know? I didn't take a math class when I was a junior. So from then on, I was trapped there. And I think trapping people is a way to keep them there. Because, I mean, you are paying lots of money to go to a private school.

On the whole, as you look back on that experience with the private, Christian school, did it do a good job for you? Did they have high standards? Did you get a good education, in your estimation?

I learned a lot, quite a bit about religion. And a little bit of psychology stuff. Of course, it was all one-sided. Anything that was controversial, anything that didn't fit their belief was wrong. It was in the materials that we were reading and the notes we got. Things were twisted, too. You know? And I noticed that when I was reading other books. Like Carl Jung. I was reading one of his things. The collective consciousness. All these different things, you know. The environment and stuff. And I mean, of course it just totally contradicts a lot of the beliefs.

And you must have felt you wanted to get out of there – not only out of the school, but did you feel a sense of entrapment at home? I mean, the farm was out in the country.

It was nice, in a way. Because my getting away ... I would always walk in the woods, you know, with a camera. Snowshoe in the winter. And I'd be going down the path. I found that to be a lot of solitude and solace, just in that alone. Being more of an individual and stuff. Of course, the interaction would have

Interview 11

been nice, too, in a city. I didn't want to go back to my junior year after dating that girl because I knew she was going to make it a living hell for me. Or she could easily. She had power. She was attractive.

Because you didn't call back.

Because I didn't call her back. And that was offensive to her, I'm sure. But who knows? I might go making things up or keep saying, "Why, I had no interest." You know? Of course, that would have been sort of a slap in the face to her. She didn't want that. So when I went back, I knew exactly what it was going to be like. And sure enough, it was.

Did you ever read the book by Henry David Thoreau? Walden. When you said you enjoyed going off by yourself and going into the woods and you found great peace and comfort in that sort of thing, that's what Walden is about.

Is it?

And it's one of my favorites, and it's relatively short. He just left the hubbub and humdrum life of society and went off and built a little cabin in the woods.

Let's see. We were talking about high school and first dates. And interpersonal relations, I guess, at this rather confining private school. And the peace that you felt in being by yourself and walking in the woods. You said, taking pictures. Are you a photographer?

Oh, I'm an advocate of photography. I think it's wonderful. Yeah, I'd walk in the woods, you know, and I'd go out there and I'd take shots of that. And we did have an arts festival at school. So I got some of my pictures blown up into 8-by-10s. I did win a ribbon. [Laughs]

Okay! All right! So you like nature? Natural shots?

I guess I'm kind of a naturalist in a way.

You photograph that more than you do people?

A little bit. Yeah. I just like that stuff. I don't know if it's bad or not. And I like being alone out there.

What, in your view, did the strict religious upbringing do to you? For better or for worse? And the second part of the question is, would you call yourself a religious person today? Here you are, 22. And you have certain beliefs and attitudes. Did religion affect that?

Yeah. It did, in a way. I think I kind of put it behind me, though. I have to admit. But I think, even though being church-going or whatever, force-fed a lot of it, I think, to a point. And then when the school combined with that, it was just … it was a lot. It was every day of the week. [Laughs] And then Sunday. Saturday was the only day I had. But now … in ways, I think I'm more spiritual now. Probably not as religious, but more spiritual.

Ah, that's interesting. I'm glad you made that distinction. Okay. So you're not

[263]

Growing Up Male In America

attending church necessarily on a regular basis?

My mom tried to get me to go last Sunday. "You're going. You're going." [Laughs] And, of course, I'm getting ready in the morning and I'm all crabby. [Laughs] It reminded me of when I got back, the first weekend, from the National Guard. The welcome I had was a lot less than I thought it would be. I'm wearing my Class A uniform, and I thought, "Well, I'll look good in church." [Laughs] Yeah. I just didn't get a warm welcome at all. I don't understand that. I guess some people thought I was showing off.

How old were you when you decided to get into the National Guard?

I'd just turned 21.

So that's recent. It was only a little over a year ago.

A little over a year. And I think I waited about five or six months before I could actually start basic training. And of course, the National Guard was real candy. Real easy. You just go there and have a uniform. [Laughs]

Partying! Yeah.

We watched a Vikings game when we were supposed to have a drill. Someone had brought a TV up there to camp.

So that would be a little over a year ago. And where did they send you for basic training?

Fort Knox, Kentucky.

And was that rigorous? Hard?

It was. I tried to stay inconspicuous as much as possible, and I did pretty well at that. I was out of the limelight. I was there, doing what I was asked to do. One kid – they'd say, "Drop. Do pushups," and he said, "Why?" You can only imagine what a drill sergeant would do. [Laughs] And our drill sergeant was a veteran of many years. He was, like, 47, and that's really old for a drill sergeant. And he would run and do all the physical stuff. And it was amazing. This guy's body was like an upside-down triangle. It's like he couldn't stop. He never slept, it seemed like.

So that was not an unpleasant experience for you?

Not that bad.

And how long does that last?

Basic is about nine weeks. And AIT was about nine for me, too. It's called Advanced Initial Training. It's where you study for the job that you're supposed to do in the military. Like, if there was a war, I'd be refueling airplanes and working with airplanes and tankers.

Well, now ... there's that missing period. You graduated high school at 17, 18? Did you go to work then?

Interview 11

I worked for three years doing factory work. I started out at a cabinet-type factory.

Was that up in your home town?

Yeah. The place where all the [laughs] home-town people ... or some of them worked. That's where they ... they just drive to work four miles every day. And that's what I was doing. A six-mile drive. Straight down the road.

Good money?

It wasn't bad.

But the idea of college had not entered your head at that point.

Yeah. But I wanted to work and see what that was like. I thought maybe I could make a success out of it. And I was reading books. No one else I worked with was doing those things. In fact, I bet they don't read! [Laughs]

So the routine of those guys was work all week. Get the paycheck. And go out and get drunk all weekend.

Well, that job lasted a year. I quit the factory job but got another job right away at another factory. The hours were different. So I'm working at this other factory, and I worked there for six months. And then I joined the military.

Getting out of town and away from home and going to basic must have been kind of a wonderful adventure for you.

It was. It was great to be away from home. A lot of kids in basic training were crying. You wouldn't believe it. Homesick. You know, they were just out of high school, most of them.

Sure. I can understand that.

But, I mean, even for me, being away from home was tough. Towards the end, I think I got more homesick. I thought, "Well, I'm really going to appreciate things when I get back home. I'm going to try to be a better person." And the discipline helped a little bit, too.

Maybe now is the time to get into another aspect of questioning. Here you are, about six foot one?

Yeah.

And you're fit, and you're a good-looking young man.

Thanks.

That's all right. It's true. And there is something lurking inside of you.

Yeah.

And you know what I'm talking about.

Yeah. My "orientation".

Yeah. Your gay sexual orientation. Did any of this increase in intensity during the

Growing Up Male In America

Army basic-training experience?

There were a lot of guys around, so … oh, man, it was tough! And then, of course, not being able to masturbate. You'd only get a two-minute shower. Sometimes not even that. "Get out of there! Next guy!" You know? And everything was drilled and very structured. There was a friend of mine who said, "If you haven't masturbated yet at basic training, there's something wrong." And this kid, of course, he was outgoing and stuff. But anyway. He had more gay tendencies.

Were you attracted to him?

Yeah. I e-mail him now. And he was just out of high school, you know, and he was 18 and everything.

Did he ever come out to you?

No.

Okay. But you thought he might be gay.

Yeah. I think so. But we were restricted. You were limited to what you could say and do. You know. If you were under the covers or something. I don't know. It was awkward, to say the least. And I had weeks of it!

Yeah. Especially for you, and there you are in a barracks, and your cot or bed is right next to the other one. The whole privacy thing is pretty much gone. Also being surrounded pretty much by men. You had not had a sexual experience with another man yet?

No.

You must have been almost crazy. I mean, some probably very handsome men were floating through there.

Yeah. There were a few. I mean, it was tough. Because nine weeks of that. Of course, you can't show any emotion. You can't do any of that stuff. And it was … like the last few weeks, I thought, "Man, I don't know what's going to happen here. I'm just going to want to take a walk over the fence."

Did you ever suspect any of the other guys might be gay?

Yeah. There were about three other ones.

But you were never that sure? Or did you ever talk about it with them?

Well, it was weird. Sundays we had cleaning time, so we had time to talk, They call it cleaning time. You clean the barracks and mop the floor and wax it. But there was a lot of down time where we could sit by our lockers and just relax. We'd talk about things, but the gay issue wasn't really brought out. Because if it was, we could risk getting a dishonorable discharge. We had to be very careful. And I think they knew that, too.

So these guys that you thought were gay, did they let you know that they were?

Interview 11

No. Two of them didn't. Just one.

One did though, huh?

Yeah. And it wasn't until AIT.

I see. This "Don't ask, don't tell" thing. It's a mystery to me.

As a matter of fact, there's a story of a guy who was at that same company where we had training. But he was a colonel, retired. And he made a home video thing with him and a male partner. He was homosexual. There was a fire alarm once, and the military people ... because of the way it was set up, they went to his house. But he wasn't home. He was on vacation or something. So the fire alarm went off. And of course they went there. And sure enough, that video was in the VCR. And coincidentally, they played it. I mean, it was personal stuff, and they were messing with it. And of course, they had the right to take away all this man's benefits and everything. And here that's invasion of privacy and everything else. I was pretty mad when I even heard they could do that. But the military has a lot of power. They can just take away everything, if they want.

And a blemish on your record. Is it still a dishonorable discharge?

Yeah. For that it is.

But if they found that in the private home of this person ...

You'd think he'd have some right to privacy.

Yeah. But the military apparently has its own rules.

Definitely.

As you well know. So, there must have been times that you wished you could have talked to someone about your gay feelings. But you never could quite do that in basic training, right?

No. Of course, you were constantly going all the time. So that helped, too. Because when you're busy, you don't think of sex as much. Even though you're surrounded with guys. It's because you're marching and running. But of course, physiologically it's like ... I'm getting all this ... all they'd let us drink is water. And the food is pretty good. You're getting hearty meals. And, I mean, you can imagine the sex drive. [Laughs] All that exercise and good nutrition!

Yeah.

I mean, it was just like ... it was even more than it was at home. So I'm thinking with exercise, I thought, "I've just got to keep busy and keep occupied so I don't have to think about that."

And then in down time, when you're not scheduled, I imagine you kept reading and keeping your mind active.

Yeah, and I'd write. A lot of writing letters home. Reading mail I got. Mail was

Growing Up Male In America

a huge thing in the military.

I would bet. How old were you when you started having some of these feelings, that you were attracted to men?

Pretty young.

By what age?

Maybe eight. I don't know. I would guess that. There were times in the school bus. Like when I was eight or nine. Another kid on the bus who I kind of grew up with – on the way home, we'd take notebook paper and put down our shirts, like we had breasts. You know? [Laughs] And we were just going crazy, you know. Acting goofy and silly. And one of the kids told his parents he was offended. And we were just goofing around. It's not like we're cussing and doing all these other things like a lot of kids do. And he just told my mom, of course, and she took it to the extreme. I was, like, upstairs all night. No food. Nothing. And I look at it now and I think, she wouldn't have done that if I was, like, 13 or 14. But how can you do that to a kid that's just having fun? Things like that were just … even early on, you had to be kind of careful. Society and the system that you were locked into.

Did you – when you were a little kid and you started noticing some kind of an attraction to boys or men – what sort of person were you attracted to? Was it the older fellow farmers or, say, some guy about the age you are now?

It was kind of both, in a way.

So you liked the companionship of men, but you didn't have a feeling, very often, for kids your own age.

It was more … I don't know. I think I could relate to people who were, maybe, older. You know. Not by a lot. But I mean, even when I was in seventh and eighth grade, the high-school students would actually eat lunch at the same time as us. We'd have combined lunches with the older kids. And there would be, like, juniors and seniors.

But some of those senior-high men, they were attractive to you, I suppose?

Yeah. There's one, who's going to law school now. This guy was just gorgeous. I mean, his hair was combed back. In 1993, it was more of the style, too, to have it that way. [Laughs] But anyway, the guy looked like Elvis, in a way. Kind of had that look. I don't know how to explain it. Kind of more of a Ricky Nelson type, but he was almost perfect. You know?

You mean, a handsome person.

Yeah.

Now, when you looked at him – and you were, what? four years younger or something. Had you ever formulated in your mind an idea of what you would like to do? Or was it just, "I like to be with him." Or did you think sexual things?

Interview 11

I did think of sexual things.

Did you think of nakedness and all of that?

Yeah. I don't know. It was, like ... here's a guy that's probably got a girlfriend and everything else. This guy wasn't a jock. He was just a really handsome, cool guy. He was suave and everything. You know what I mean. He was one of those people. And he still fit in, which was kind of nice to see. Maybe towards the end of high school, maybe that's more the way things were – you didn't have to be a jock to fit in. So it was different for me, as a junior higher, to see that. [Laughs]

Did you mentally undress him? Did you wish you could just be with him alone? Did you think about sleeping with him and having sex with him and all of that? Had that formed in your head yet?

Yeah. It was kind of awkward, though, because it's like they don't know what I'm thinking. I mean, you can't say these things.

No. No, you can't. Did you ever get creative and manage to be, maybe, near the locker room when you knew he had phy ed? Or, you know, manage, hopefully get a chance to find him alone, so that you might talk with him, be with him, that sort of thing?

Yup. Actually, it's funny you bring that up. Because we had swimming at those times. And the older guys had phy ed, and we were sharing the same locker room. So that's the way it was. There was another guy, too, who was pretty cool. He wore his hair in a ponytail. His dad was a big shot in the community. He had it pretty nice. But man, I mean, that guy was just hung. You know?

Yeah. And then your interest in the arts – which, apparently, you never got much of an opportunity to explore, at least in school – maybe that kind of cavalier quality of a guy who had the courage to wear his hair in a ponytail made him all the more attractive to you?

Yeah.

And then he was well endowed, as you said. That made it all the more interesting, I suppose, too. And yet you kept dating women. Because the last thing in the world that you wanted was to be classified as a gay man, at that point in your life.

Yeah. Even now, the girls were more aggressive towards me than I was towards them, too. But I was open to dating girls. Just to have something to do on a weekend with them, so I'm not always with guys. And I think my parents kind of wanted me to date. To have that quality or image.

You said once – not in this interview but at another time when we were talking – that you think your mom probably has some suspicions that you might be gay. She maybe knows this but has never uttered it. Is that true?

I'm almost positive. It's almost eerie. Because I'm pretty secretive and stuff. I

Growing Up Male In America

mean, there are guys who enjoy the arts, enjoy those kinds of things, who aren't gay, I'm sure. And so, you know … you can't classify people, I don't think. One hundred percent, anyway. But maybe … I don't know what it is. She just … I think she has intuition that's pretty strong. I don't know. It's a "mom thing."

You're right. It's a "mom thing," I swear it. They just seem to know their sons pretty well. And your mom sees a full spectrum or cross section of people in her work, I suppose.

I think there's a gay guy, too, where she works. Which … I don't know if she finds that threatening or what. [Laughs]

If you did sit your mom down someday and say, "Mom, I've got something to tell you" and you tell her you are gay and you laid it all out on the table, what do you think her reaction would be?

"Get help." She has strong involvement with the church, you know.

And she might think that this could be cured.

Yeah. She'd be looking for a cure, looking for answers. You know. And the road a lot of church people walk on is narrow … the path is a narrow path. And anything off that path, you can't even look. You've got to stay on that path and look straight.

Interesting you should say, "Look straight." [Chuckles] Interesting play on words, there! Now, how about your dad? Say you take him aside, by himself. "Dad, I've got something to tell you." Now, how old is he?

About 65.

Okay. What might his reaction be?

I don't know. He probably wouldn't want to talk too much about it. You know? He'd probably groan. And he would just kind of sigh maybe.

Like, "Are you sure? How do you know?"

Yeah. The typical male …

Yeah. Men are notorious – especially straight men – for not – and especially older ones, sometimes – for not being too terribly verbal about some of these things that "we just don't talk about."

Men hold it in. And I think that's why a lot of guys die when they're 40, 50 of a heart attack. Because they hold emotion in. It's proven. Guys don't live as long. I think a lot of emotion and how you deal with emotions has something to do with it. The stress.

Do you remember how old you were when you first had sex with a woman?

Well … oh, man. I went out with this one girl when I was a senior in high school and she was a freshman in college. I was driving in my truck. I always

Interview 11

had my truck all clean. You know. It was perfect. So I was cruising down. I had just got new tires and rims and whatever, so I was doing all right. And I was with a friend of mine. He was more outgoing, where he would talk to people and get them interested and stuff. And we would go cruising. So he had a girl and I had a girl. And we were in the park, and she just got on top of me. And I thought ... she started, you know, pulling down my pants and everything. This was in a park! [Laughs] And it was getting later, so it was more dark out and everything. So, I mean, I suppose that's ... but I didn't actually go through with it.

Well, she's about to have oral sex with you, you say?

I'm guessing she was going to do that.

Yeah. Okay. At this point, did you – let's get personal, here – at this point, did you respond? Did you get an erection?

Yeah. Because she was on top of me. But not a full erection, not fully hard.

But what went through your mind? I mean, first of all, this is a very aggressive woman we've got here. But what if you're expected to respond and to get equally as passionate? But you didn't.

No. And you know, I wanted to. But ... I don't know. I was scared, too. I wanted to ... I guess before I would do that I would ... I don't know. I just ... it wasn't the time, or something. Or the right person. And, I mean, here's, like, the second time ... it was the second time that we did anything together, you know, as a date. And it was a double date, too. So I mean, here are these other people in the park. It was pretty odd.

Yeah. It's not exactly the idea of a romantic encounter.

No. But usually girls have ... I guess, you know, I've kissed them and stuff, but the oral thing is coming into play. But I've never actually had intercourse with a girl.

Now, when you ... could this be one reason why you would date for a few times and throw their phone number away? Because pretty soon you'd get to a point where something would be expected.

Right. And then they'd wonder. And then they might start talking.

And what if they said, "He kissed me, but that's all he ever did." "Well, I think he's gay."

Yeah.

Because you haven't had sex with a man yet, people could ask – and especially parents and friends – how do you know you're gay, then? [Laughs] And you know what a good answer for that is? When your mother or your dad or a friend asks this? "How did you know you were straight?"

So you just know what you feel – that you're very attracted to men but you haven't

Growing Up Male In America

acted on it, right?

Right.

There's a question that I like to ask: as you would look around at other guys' penises in the locker rooms, would you classify the length of your penis as being a little shorter than average, a little longer than average or about whatever average is?

More. I was pretty good. I don't know what the average is. When it's erect, six or seven inches is average? Is that right?

I guess that's what they say.

I'm much more than that. Like 11 inches when it's erect.

Wow! So you never had to worry that people would think your penis was too short! Another thing: do you ever suffer from what's called "shy bladder"? Do you ever have trouble? And you just can't pee?

Stage fright. [Laughs] Yeah.

Yeah. [Laughs] You're thinking of waterfalls and all that kind of stuff.

I have. You know, maybe because there's guys around me. I don't know if that's part of it. Guys on both sides, and here I am in the middle.

But a lot of straight guys have this problem, too.

Maybe it's just shyness. I don't know. I don't have it as much anymore, though. But especially when I was younger. And maybe it's being nervous.

Well, anyway. When do you think you are going to have that first sexual experience? What kind of a man are you looking for?

Well, I don't know. I've thought about that a little bit. Physically, I guess I can't be too picky. I don't know how to answer that. That's a tough one.

I mean, I suppose you have an idea of what would be a pretty-near ideal man, physically. And some like dark hair and some like blond hair ...

I guess I like the ... when it comes to physical, everyone's got their own thing. But, I mean, someone like William Shatner is ... I mean, he's awesome.

Okay.

Especially when he was younger. You know. *Star Trek.*

What about George Clooney?

Yeah. The Cary Grant-type guy with the Cary Grant jaw and everything.

Had you ever thought what the ideal condition would be once you start becoming sexually active with men? I mean, you're going to be out of the folks' house, now, pretty soon. You're going to go and visit the folks a lot, because you love them. And that's good. But you're going to have your own place, eventually.

And then, when you get through with the Army experience – and you have your own

Interview 11

private place – do you think of yourself as being monogamous? That is, would you want a relationship with one person and "set up house," as they say?

I don't think so. I'm more ... I guess I'd probably be more open-minded, you know. I'd have friends and stuff, and people that could relate to the same things. I guess I could probably get lonely, too, though. I don't know. Maybe that might happen. Maybe not. When you read and have things you enjoy to keep you busy.

It depends on what stage you are in your life, I suppose. Relationships can be very wonderful.

That's true.

But when you're in love, it's really quite a beautiful experience.

Well, listen. We're going to kind of wind up. And what I like to do here is ask some questions and ask you for a quick response. So don't think too long about them.

Okay. [Chuckles]

What's the most hurtful thing a friend or a relative has ever done to you? What hurt you the most?

I guess it happened a couple of time. Twice at the most, really. But it's when you get ditched. Like you'll go somewhere with your friends, and they'll take off and leave. It's, like, well, either they were using you for a ride or you were with them but you're forgotten about. You're left behind, because you had something else you were doing or they had something else. Usually at a carnival or a fair or a sporting event. A lot of people got ditched, I guess a lot more than I did. It only happened twice to me. But that was hurtful, to be abandoned by people you thought were your friends.

It makes you feel like an outsider, doesn't it? And to be left outside of the inner group, that's a lonely, alienated sort of feeling, isn't it?

Yeah.

What would you say is your best ... the best part of your body? And don't be shy about it.

I'm too critical. I honestly can't even answer that.

Well, is it your height?

My height's a little bit above average. It's about where it should be. Six–one is about where the All-American Guy is. That's one good thing.

Anything else?

I don't know. [Laughs]

What? Your chin?

Maybe a little bit.

Growing Up Male In America

You've got a nice, square jaw. And that's kind of the classic ideal. Are you glad about your cock?

Yeah.

It's kept you happy and satisfied?

It's been a good companion. [Laughs]

What do you think about your butt? Good butt?

Yeah. It's not too big and not too little.

Do you wish you pectorals were bigger? More definition?

Yeah. The pushups help a little bit, but I wish they were a little bit more developed.

Okay. Have you ever noticed that big pectorals are the ideal today? A friend and I were talking recently about how the pectorals are so important these days compared to what it was back in the 1930s and 1940s when the so-called well-built man had a fairly flat chest. Just look at the movies of those years for the "well fit" guy. Today, men can even get chest implants.

Isn't that something?

True or false: "I expect that with careful planning, my dreams and hopes for the future will be realized."

I would have to say "true." But I think things are just destined to happen.

Do you write? Creative writing, I mean? Poetry or fiction?

Well, I read. James Whitcomb Riley is good. What was another one, who's just awesome? He wrote one book when he was, like, 34. *Leaves of Grass*. Walt Whitman.

Oh, Walt Whitman. He was gay.

Yeah. He was. And I saw that in his poems. I related to him.

All right!

And I was reading it and I said, "This is awesome." And then after a while, I finally caught on. I read *The Body Electric* and I'm, like, "Yeah."

Um-hum. And he used to hang around on the battle fields and help these poor boys back to health after they were shot. And some of that stuff was never put in his complete collection because they thought it was too personal and homoerotic.

I suppose.

You can get it now, though. It's available.

Really!

And he's talking about the beauty of the young man.

Interview 11

All right. You're in the Army and you're in college and you're in your early 20s and you have friends and neighbors. What is the main subject or topic of conversation – first of all – with men? And, second, with women?

Well, I think now that the football season's over [laughs], a lot of it has to do with the weather. How things are affected. Being in farm country, too. It is a big deal. Because it deals with the whole business of farming, which I understand. But … football. Like when the Vikings lost, our neighbor was so cranky, he could hardly talk to people. I mean, isn't that sad?

That was it?

Yeah. And I thought it was funny. I laughed. [Laughs]

What's the main topic with women?

Well, let's see. I think it varies moreso with them. They're not so narrow-minded where they just see only athletics. With women, it can vary more.

That's quite an interesting comment, there. They're broader and wider in their interests, it seems. I think men really do, too, but they just don't express it as much.

They don't discuss.

And do you notice that men are afraid to talk about their feelings with each other?

Oh, yes.

Whenever you get into a low mood or a little depressed or feeling down, what do you do about it? First of all, what causes it, typically, and what do you do about it?

In the winter it usually seems to be worse. And I think there's a, you know, it's a seasonal effect to a point. But I don't know. It's like … I don't know if it's the artist or what it is, but you say I know I could do this and that, but I don't. And yet I want to ponder it, think about it. Do you know where I'm coming from, kind of? And it's like … I don't know. Eric Clapton has his guitar, and he just plays the blues so much, he has so much heart in it. And that along with the talent. But it's a release of emotion. I think it's like that. Maybe it's photography or writing or reading.

As a kid, were you sensitive?

Yeah.

What makes you cry? It could be more than one thing, I suppose.

Thinking about people that are gone, not with us anymore, that I knew. Like grandparents. [Pause] Mostly people that aren't with us. That's a lot of it.

So when the parents finally go, that's going to be …

That's going to be pretty bad.

It's going to be a rough one. Yeah. It almost always is. Do you cry often?

Well, I've been more accepting of it the last four or five years. You know. To

Growing Up Male In America

hold it ... to drive on, be tough is always hard to do. But what are you going to do? Sit and destroy yourself? I mean, you've got to let it out somehow. Maybe for one person it's crying. I don't know. If it's a means of release, then that's what I do. I cry.

Okay. Let's talk about your future just a little bit. Here you are, on the edge of probably jumping into the gay world. And maybe jumping in to the point of being exclusively gay.

That would be a nice thought. It's a nice thought.

Is that a good thing? Let's forget about having to tell people or if you're going to tell people and all that sort of thing. Do you look forward to that – entering this chapter of your life as a gay man?

If it would be exclusive and ... if I could be open and be okay, yeah.

Because that's what you've been building up for your whole life, since age eight or something.

Pretty much. Yeah.

Yeah. If it were a perfect world, you know, you could have come out at the age of ... when you hit puberty. But you think of that as a more optimistic thing and a good thing and more pleasant thing, that there's a good future for you in the world as a gay man?

I hope so.

And you are convinced that being gay won't be an impediment to being successful at whatever you're going to be?

No. I have no doubts.

Because I can tell you, it won't be an impediment. You'll do just fine.

Well, thanks.

You're welcome. Another question. You don't use alcohol too much, you say. Have you ever experimented with any drugs?

Never have.

You haven't?

No. And a lot of my friends have. As a matter of fact, before I left for the private school, the kids that sat by me at lunch were actually, like, big pot smokers. They were retro-1960s kids. That was kind of the thing in the early, mid 1990s.

But you never tried smoking dope?

No. But I've been in a room where I've been able to smell it. And I thought it reminded me of burnt plastic.

So you don't feel like you've lost out and missed anything for never having experi-

Interview 11

mented with drugs?

I don't think so. I mean, seeing the reactions people had. Some people may be more the John Lennon-type persona when they smoke marijuana. But I rarely see that with these kids.

So. You're, I think, somewhat unusual in that regard. You didn't indulge and experiment when other kids around you were.

Yeah. [Pause] I was away from all the party scene, too, the last three years of high school since I was in the private school. I think I would have tried it if I had stayed in the public school system.

You probably would have had more temptation. Have you ever been in love?

I guess. I mean, I think a lot about it. When I was younger, probably. But then my raging hormones were involved. [Laughs] You know where I'm coming from.

Yes.

But I guess in that respect, yeah, I have been in love. And some of my close friends could say I have been. But it wasn't really … it was not both ways, I guess.

You've been in love from afar. Somebody that you found very attractive and you wondered where the line between love and lust and hormones was. But again, if it's not reciprocated, or in the case of an attraction to another male, if you're not allowed to for one reason or another go up to him and say, "I really find you very attractive, and I wish we could get to know each other better." As a gay person, that's a little hard to do.

I was going to say that I've seen kids – young adults – have girlfriends, you know, and they think it's love. They're in love, they're engaged. But yet they have to share everything they do. They have to know where the other person is going. They have to write notes all the time. There's constant nagging at each other. And I think love should be more non-possessive. Because when you really care, you're going to say, "Have fun." And you have to trust the honesty of your partner.

I understand what you're saying. Well, is there anything else you want to say? I think you have been a wonderful interview.

It's been good.

And I want to thank you very much.

Thank you. You're welcome.

You bared your soul and your mind and your past, and you told me lots of things you've never told to another person. And that's very helpful, and I appreciate it. I'm sure that your interview will make very interesting reading. Just think: kids 10 or 12 or 15 years old might be reading this and reading what you've gone through, and

Growing Up Male In America

they'll say, "I guess I'm not really alone. I'm not the only one." There are kids, gay or straight, who may be wrestling with some of their feelings, their fears, their passions and their private yearnings, and they might feel that they're all alone. And whether they be gay or straight, your comments, your experiences are going to be helpful to them. And parents will read this, too, and they'll have their consciousness raised; they might understand their children's struggles because of your comments here.

Maybe kids will feel it's not that bad.

Maybe it's not that bad. So, thanks again.

Postscript – December 2001

This man is continuing his university studies, is still living at home with his folks, and is contemplating a career in military service.

Interview 12

"I've never been able to quit anything."

This man was 21 years old when this interview was conducted on May 30, 2000. He is 5' 10" tall, weighs 190 pounds and has light brown hair.

Thank you for being willing to grant me this interview. You were born into a Catholic family, am I right?

Yes.

Did you go to a parochial school?

No, I went to public schools.

What kind of neighborhood did you live in?

I lived right off the main street in a medium-sized town in southern Minnesota. There were three houses in a row with kids all our age, and we caused quite a bit of trouble when we were kids.

How many in the family?

Four. My brother and my parents and a little dog.

So it's just you and your brother, for kids. And you're older or younger?

I'm one year younger than my brother.

Did they want just the two of you? Did they ever wish they could have had a daughter?

They never really said anything. They were just happy with what they got.

Do you and your brother get along well?

We were never close. Ever. We always fought about everything. We've never gotten along because there's always been competition. We're both athletes, and we've always competed in everything we do. We still don't talk today.

Really?

Growing Up Male In America

We'll see each other and say "hi" and on birthdays we'll give each other a call and say, "Hey, how you doing? Happy birthday, bud." I wish that was a little better, but that's the way it is.

He wasn't really too helpful to you as you were growing up, I suppose?

No. He used to beat the hell out of me.

Really? Is he bigger than you?

He was bigger until I hit the ninth grade and I started lifting weights with a buddy of mine and I just blew up in size. And then after I got bigger than him, there was just nothing he could do, so he started hating me because he couldn't beat on me any more, so he wouldn't talk to me. He just graduated this year. I went to his graduation. And that's it. It's not that we're enemies, but there's just not a good friendship.

Speaking of friendships, do you remember a best friend when you were a little kid?

I've had a lot of best friends. In elementary, I hung around with athletic kids like me. I've always had a lot of friends. I've always been real good with them. But when it comes to a best friend, that's always switched for me because I've gotten along with so many people. I always just bounced around, but through elementary, it was just me and two buddies who were close.

Okay. Do you remember the kinds of games you played as a kid?

All us kids grew up to be athletes. We had really big back yards, and we played baseball all the time, football. We'd always be playing catch and running around. In first and second grade, we started playing Pump ... which is when somebody stands in the middle and everybody else would have to get to the other side without getting tackled. It starts with one, and if he tackles someone there's two, and so on. The goal is to be the last person to get tackled. That's where I received my first concussion, in fourth grade, playing Pump on concrete. Isn't that a good idea?

Not a good idea. So, as far back as you can remember, there was this interest in competition.

Always. I used to ice skate religiously, and I never played hockey because we couldn't afford it, but I used to skate all the time right after school, until it got too dark to stay out.

Do you remember kindergarten?

Yup. I went to a transition grade between kindergarten and first. I was always a little hell raiser. The transition was ridiculous. All they had were big red building blocks, and all we did was build stuff all day and draw, and I don't know what the hell the point to that was. They gave us fake money to buy stuff when we were good.

And you were kind of a hell raiser.

Interview 12

I was a bad kid. When you grow up in a neighborhood with so many kids around you, you just learned it. It was stupid.

Do you remember, when you started school, who the "cool" kids were? Who the "in" crowd was as well as the "out" crowd?

My brother was always a good athlete, so he was popular. Since I was his younger brother, all the older kids knew me, so I was one of the popular ones. So popular kids always kind of hung around me.

So your brother helped you with that at least, whether he intended to or not.

Do you remember any fears that you had, or things that worried you? In terms of relationships with friends, or not succeeding?

I was so young. I'm assuming I was a really mean person back then, and I didn't like the kids who were less fortunate. But that's the only thing I feel bad about.

So you mean teasing and taunting some of the "geeky" kids?

Yeah. That happens everywhere, but you think about it after it's said and done and how it really does affect people. And you wish it didn't happen. I don't really remember any fears I had, though. I got along with all of them after elementary, once we got into the junior high. I started getting into the peer helpers and was elected secretary, and I started becoming good friends with everybody. I've always been able to get along with everybody. It's just that I remember in elementary that I was a little prick every once in a while. I was kind of frustrated.

Were there any teachers you admired?

There were two teachers I had in fifth and sixth grade. I liked them. They were the only two male teachers I had. I really enjoyed both the male teachers I had. So that was really good. They worked hard with me athletically, and they were always helping me out. They were real strict with me, and that's what I need. I need someone who's real strict, because they knew I could do it. So they just made sure that they pushed me hard enough to the point right before failure, just to get results out of me. Not only in sports, but in the classroom, too.

Was school hard for you in those days? I mean, were you an A student?

No, I've never been an A student. I'd neglect my homework and never really worked very hard. [Laughs] My whole life, I've always been able to do it. I just never put in the time to get it done. I'm the opposite of my brother. He's a space-physics major. He's just brilliant. Just brilliant.

All through grade school, until the time you're about to hop into junior high, what was your relationship with your mom and dad. Did you get along?

Yeah. We had a good relationship up until eighth grade, I believe. So yeah, overall it was really good. But my dad was drinking a lot, and I don't really remember a lot of it. But he tells me that he used to be a bad person a lot of the

Growing Up Male In America

time, but I don't remember now.

What did he do? Reform? Or stop?

He's been sober for 13 years. Had a lot of counseling. He used to swear a lot. Like, he used to get real pissed off all the time, and now he's kind of like a little girl. He's always coming up to you, telling you he loves you. It's a good side to him, though. He's a real happy person now.

How about your mother?

Mom's just always been the standard mom, and dad's real good now. They're both extremely supportive and helpful to me in whatever I do.

How old would your parents be?

Like, around 43. They're young. They're not old. I don't know my parents' ages.

Now, let's try some "fill in the blanks" type questions.

You're obviously in good shape, and you want to stay that way and you want to get in even better shape when you transfer to that other college for football. The form of exercise that you like most is:

Just playing catch and running around, catching the ball. I like to do squats to develop big legs.

Do you shave your legs?

Yeah.

Why is that?

I don't like hair. And with the hair gone, the veins pop out. I'm a real vascular person. I like it when my veins pop out.

Do you shave your chest, too?

Yeah.

Okay. How about your back?

I don't need to yet. My dad's the hairiest individual on earth, though, so I'm assuming it's coming real soon for me.

Some of my favorite music or musicians would be ...

The Boss, Bruce Springsteen, he's my favorite. I like all kinds of music. I like country, I like rap, I like hip hop, I like rock. I just like music.

Do you like to dance?

I like to dance, but I don't know how. So I make a fool out of myself. If I get drunk enough, I'll maybe go up there and just act stupid, but that's about it. I'd like to learn someday.

What is the biggest or greatest lie you ever told your parents?

Interview 12

Back in eighth and ninth grade, when my parents were thinking about getting a divorce and all that bull crap, I started drinking and doing drugs and just being stupid with another buddy of mine. And my buddy and I used to steal a lot. Me and him were stealing constantly because we were, I don't know, just stupid. And we stole a purse one day, and we went over to this guy's house – just crazy guys – and we went to the bank and withdrew $800 out of a woman's account at the bank. That was check forgery, bank fraud, and we got caught. And then my buddy went back a second time and withdrew more money from this lady's account. It took over a year and a half for me to go to court. That was the scariest time of my life, and I had to make up a lie. I got out of both charges. I got a good lawyer, and I lied through my teeth. But that was the biggest lie I've ever told anyone, and I had to tell that lie to everyone because I lied so well I convinced myself. I just had to keep on going with it.

Your parents, too? They were taken in on the lie?

I just told them that I wasn't involved to the extent that I really was. Because I was the culprit. I was the one who did the majority of it.

And you actually forged the check?

I didn't do the forging, but I stole the purse, and I brought it to the guy's house, and I was young and stupid, and I drove the car to the bank. I was just turning 16, just getting my license. And then having to sit there knowing, because the others went back the second time to drain the account because it was so easy the first time. We knew that we were in trouble. After three days, the cops called my parents, and that just ruined everything.

Is that on your record?

No. I got a super-good lawyer, and I was really street-smart back then, so I figured it out and I got off with two misdemeanors and a bunch of community service and restitution.

Yeah, it sounds like it was awful. And it wasn't all that long ago.

It seemed like forever. These days, if someone is cheating on a test, if someone's stealing something, I'll get super-mad. Like super-mad ... I won't even talk to them. It needed to happen, I needed to get caught. Because it changed my life ... and it was probably the most profound thing that's happened to me, and getting caught is what's put me in college and straightened me out. It's good. We need law.

Well, I appreciate your sharing that. That certainly was an experience that shaped your life.

It's the one thing that just ruined my life, but kind of made my life, too.

That's interesting. Okay. This is a true-or-false question: "I believe that with careful planning, my dreams and my hopes for the future can be and will be realized."

Growing Up Male In America

I believe that it could happen. I could accomplish my goals, but I know that I'd have to quit drinking and drugs first. And that's what I've decided. Hopefully, it will happen one day.

Do you believe in fate?

Yeah, I guess so. But also I believe we choose our own path.

Okay. Do you remember your first sexual feelings? You didn't know what to call it at that time, but do you remember going through puberty?

Junior high was just nuts, just nuts. Because everybody's trying to fit in, there's so many different groups. It was really ... junior high is the toughest time for any kid.

Yeah. Can you imagine teaching that grade level?

Oh, God.

Those teachers deserve medals. And how did your confusion work out with you?

It was real difficult for me because I was trying to follow in my brother's footsteps because he's so smart and athletic, and yet my parents were having problems. So I started getting really down and stupid. Junior high is when I started getting real crazy. I started stealing and drinking and smoking weed.

Did you get into any drugs heavier than pot?

No. Not in junior high.

How old were you when you first smoked dope?

I was probably 14 or 15.

When did you first smoke cigarettes?

I remember my first cigarette. It made me dizzy, just dizzy, real dizzy. In the cornfield, by myself. I went probably a mile out in the cornfield. I knocked down a bunch of stalks and made myself a little seat. Lit it up and started smoking. I was inhaling it. I smoked half of it and I'm like, "Man, this is ridiculous. It don't do nothing." All of a sudden I threw the cigarette away and I stood up and fell right back down. [Laughs]

So this was a real cigarette?

Yeah, this was a real cigarette. It was a Marlboro Ultra Red. It was a Red, and whoo-eee. I fell right back down and just looked up. The sky started spinning, and I was really scared then.

Did you get sick?

I didn't get sick, but I felt yucky for probably a good hour. I went home and jumped on the tramp to try to get the smell off of me. And later I got all my friends to do it. [Laughs] "Come on! You gotta do this!"

But at first you did it alone.

Interview 12

I did a lot of things alone first. And then later I got all my friends to do the stupid stuff.

You were the leader and said, "Whoa! Wait till I show you what I did!" [Laughter] And then, what was the situation the first time you smoked marijuana?

The first time I smoked marijuana, it was with two buddies. One of them was the kid who was the pothead in junior high and then later he was the leader of a drug-prevention program in senior high. So he totally flip-flopped. And now he's just average. He'll drink every once in a while now, but he won't smoke, but the first time with pot was at his house and we snuck into his parents' room and stole their pipe and weed.

From his parents?

Yeah. We went out in the garage. He got really stoned, but me and and my buddy didn't feel anything.

You still smoke pot?

Yeah. I probably will till the day I die. I think it just makes me lazy. It makes me just want to sit around. Screw it. But sometimes when I smoke, all I want to do is lift weights. It depends on what kind of mood I'm in. Even during football season, I smoked every day of the week up till Thursday. That's because we had a game on Saturday. I was smoking just at night, just before bed. Put me right to sleep, and then on the weekends after the game, I'd just smoke all day. Drink and smoke all day. Weekends are really bad for me. I would just get hammered.

You know, I'll bet a lot of people would find that a contradiction. Here you are, a jock, and you're in great shape and you want to be better, and yet you're getting stoned all the time.

Yeah. I do it all the time. But I've always been friends with the athletes and the really geeky kids and the potheads. I was friends with scumballs, the guys who wore all black. I was friends with everybody. So I participated in everybody's events. [Laughs] I had the senior party at my house, and the last three people up at four in the morning were the three of us – one of the biggest jocks in the school, one of the biggest geeks in the school, and a kid who never went to school. It was funnier than hell! Just three of the most different people. It was weird, but it was cool. We talked for another hour after everybody else went to bed or left.

How about school? At the present time, are you successful with grades, academically?

I'm doing enough to get by. I'm doing enough to be eligible to play football.

I'm curious about this thing with your parents. They were on the brink of divorce at one point. Describe that.

Growing Up Male In America

It's when my Mom gave my Dad the ultimatum about his heavy drinking, the ultimatum to go to seek a counselor. Otherwise, it's over. And those days, they didn't care what time I came home because they were never home, and so I just went and did my own thing all the time. Never talked to them, never saw them.

Did she drink, too?

No, not at all. She'll have a little wine every once in a while now, like at a special event. She got really weird, though. She started working out at a gym, and she got thin and she got pretty, and I think she thought she was something. And she laid down the law with my dad. And I was upset. I don't really know what happened because I was so screwed up back then, too, but I think she thought she was getting out. She graduated because my Dad busted his butt at his job and put her through school, and finally she got through college and got a decent enough job to live on. And I think she thought she was too good for the family or something. Well, I know she didn't. But I think it was something along the lines of that. Because she started thinking [pause]. I don't know. I haven't really thought about it. [Pause] I'm trying to repress those memories.

That's okay. Take your time. So she raised the family and then went to school. Had she gone to college before?

Yeah. She got her master's. She loves school. She keeps going back. She was in counseling, and now she's a therapist or something.

Okay. Did you get the feeling that at a certain point, she thought she deserved better than your dad and your family?

I think that's the feeling that she got, but I never felt that way.

As far as you know, was she ever unfaithful to your dad?

I don't believe so. But I don't have a clue either, though. I'd never talk to her again if I ever found out that she was unfaithful to him.

Back to school. Were there any teachers or coaches in junior or senior high who were heroes to you? Or influential?

Not really. I got along. I'm not trying to brag, but I was kind of the leader of the school. If there was a problem – like if something real bad was going on, the administrators would talk to me, and I'd go figure it out because I knew every group. And they knew that. But they were all pretty good to me. Until the senior year, when I didn't think I was going to graduate. Then I started being really just a prick, and they started disliking me. But I don't really remember one particular teacher. My coaches were never really great coaches. Like in track season, I'd smoke weed the majority of the week and I'd go around and I'd beat the piss out of everybody. I never really had the influence of a good coach.

Okay. At that time, would you have called yourself "mature"?

Interview 12

I don't think I'm mature yet. I don't know who I am. I think that's my problem. I don't think I ever have. I knew who I was when I was with my girlfriend in high school before we broke up, but I think that's the only time in my life I was really happy. My college experiences have been miserable, because I don't even know who in the hell I am. I just run around popping jokes and doing stupid stuff, making people laugh. Just keeping hammered. That's not what I want to be known for, and that's the sole reason I'm transferring to another college. I'm not transferring because the team here sucks. That's a little bit of it, but I'm transferring because I have to start over. Because my reputation here is over. Because my reputation here is that I'm an obnoxious fool.

Among your friends.

Yeah. And they love it. They think I'm the funniest thing ever landed on earth.

Clowns, who make people laugh, are often sad people.

Could be. The guys who moved out of the house on campus leave me big letters, emotional letters, about how much they like me. And I didn't know they felt so deeply about me. Like these people actually cared about me.

And you had doubts about that?

I just never knew. I never knew my friendship was so deep with these guys.

So you had second thoughts, maybe, about leaving?

Well, ever since I quit the team I knew I was leaving. I'm not going to come back to a team that I quit. But they had stronger feelings for me than I assumed. But they're all great guys. I'm not leaving because of them. I'll always love them. These guys are great. We had a lot of fun, a lot of good memories.

That's good. How long do you think it's going to be before you really feel like you really know who you are?

That's what I've always wondered.

I don't think at the age of 21 very many people really have a clue.

That's what my mother told me. I know what I need to do to be a productive citizen. I just haven't accomplished it yet.

Let's talk about sex. Do you remember the first time you masturbated?

I think I used to masturbate in the bathtub. But I was masturbating before anything even came out. Even to this day, I do it a lot. Usually when I wake up and usually when I go to bed. I just love it! I don't remember the first time, though. I wasn't young.

How old might you have been?

I smoke too much weed so my memory's gone, but I was either 12 or 13.

Okay. Remember, in the locker rooms, being aware of other guys? And some were

Growing Up Male In America

already developed?

> I was always scared because I developed late. I never wanted to change clothes or go in the shower room, and I was always scared when we had swimming. When I was in wrestling in ninth grade, I had a real scary damned time. There was this big, big tailback on the football team. I was in ninth grade, and he was a senior. We were getting changed, and he came along and just flopped and schlonged his big cock right on top of my head. That scared the shit out of me. I'd never experienced anything like that, and I still to this day won't shower with my team. I think just because of that incident right there. I was always real intimidated in the locker room and shower situation.

I see. Can you speculate why pubescent boys are shy about their penis? Because I think they are.

> They just feel inadequate, is the only thing I can think of. It's so intimidating when you see big, super hung Ole Hog standing naked by you.

Well, aside from humongous Ole Hog, when you check yourself against other guys in locker rooms, do you call yourself well endowed, average endowed or under endowed?

> Just another average Joe. I've seen probably more cocks than anybody on earth. I see them all the time. I've been in so many damn locker rooms. But there are so many that are, like, huge and then there are some that you can't even see. So, if you're hanging four inches, you don't have to worry about anything. I'm talking limp, not hard.

Where did you learn about sex?

> I never talked to my parents about sex, but I was always kind of a joker about it with my friends. I don't think I talked about masturbation until probably 11th grade when we started getting comfortable and not caring anymore. It's like everybody's doing it or does it. If you say you don't, you're lying.

But it's not an easy thing to talk about until you get a little freer and older. But at the time, do you remember how you felt? I mean, it was that "secret pleasure," and you didn't share it with other people.

> I've never been caught. I'm probably the one person I know who's never been caught. And that's the traumatic part. Buddies of mine getting caught and telling me their stories – and man, I feel bad for them. See, I never got caught, so I never really cared. Those other guys, their parents caught them. If your mom catches you, that's bad. That's real bad. What do you say at a time like that? [Laughs]

Okay. And as you got older, when you had relationships with girls?

> I started masturbating more. I was still snapping all the time.

Really? You call masturbation "snapping"?

Interview 12

[Laughs] Yeah.

Okay. Did you ever have a group sex masturbation thing?

A lot of the guys I know did. Like in college last year. I mean, we took turns snapping into a cup just so we could put it on some guy's door handle. [Laughter] Just as a joke.

But not in front of each other, though? This cup thing?

No. Well, like me and the kid that I was rooming with at the beginning of this year. He is one of my best, best friends. I'll snap one off right in front of him, it won't bother me none. Like the two of us were driving home from a visit in Wisconsin, and I just tilted the seat back and started snapping. [Laughs] Like it doesn't bother me at all. [Laughs]

Well, that must be a sign of good friends.

Yeah, we're really good friends. Like he's probably coming to this other college down south with me, and we're going to spend the next three years together. So we're trying to stick together. We both made a pact that we're done drinking and smoking and chewing, and we're going to stick to that.

And you'll be motivating each other?

Because that's what you need. You need somebody with you.

Let's talk about your first sexual experience with another person.

I think I was in ninth grade. My first sexual experience – I don't know if it was hers – but we were both virgins, and we were at a buddy of mine's house. And this girl and I tried all night. All night we tried and tried, but we didn't have a clue, you know? And finally I got so sore I couldn't do it anymore, and we stopped.

She was a classmate?

Yeah, she was in the same grade as me. We were going out at the time, for a long time, like 10 months or something like that. But after that first time of trying we got better at it, and we started doing it all the time.

You mentioned you had a relationship with that one girlfriend. What did you say, two years you were together?

Two and a half. Two years and about eight months, in senior high.

Do you think you ever used the word "love"?

Yeah. All the time.

You did love her?

I thought for sure. I was in LOVE, love. But I broke it off with her because I thought when I was going to college I was going to be this big stud, but then I just started being a jerk.

Growing Up Male In America

Did you ever try to get back together?

We did. We tried a little bit, but there was just too much shit going on.

Okay. Now, in the two years you've been here at this university, did you have any long-term relationships?

Nope. Not until I'm 26. That's when I'm going to find somebody.

What is the place of religion in your life right now?

I believe I'm still Catholic. I pray every night, and that's basically the extent of it. Yup. I've got my own relationship with a higher power.

What kind of jobs did you have in high school?

I worked at Godfather's Pizza for three years. I also worked as the projectionist at a movie theater, so that was interesting.

You mentioned your closest male friend. It sounds like it's a lot of "buddy" behavior for your social life now. Clusters of you guys going out together and having a good time. Do you have any close female friends?

Not really. I would like to have some. I never really had a brother, and I always wanted a sister. When my best friend told me we were going to stop smoking so much weed, I quit for 12 days. And that's probably the first 12 days I've quit in a row in four years or something. And I did it because he told me to. But he was smoking the whole time, and I didn't even know it. He just lied to me. [Laughs] But still, he just wanted to do it for me, you know? That's why I'd like to have a girlfriend, because she could help me out with that stuff and make me a better person. That's the plan. No more obnoxious behavior. As soon as I finish this school year, I'm heading home. That's where my best friend is. We're going to start training really hard when I get home this summer. He and I are going to "live" at the gym!

And then you both are transferring to the same college to play football, right?

Right.

He has certain leadership abilities, then, as far as you're concerned.

Yeah. He's funnier than hell, too. I consider him my best friend.

Moving on, now. Do TV and other media advertising have an impact on you a great deal? Like the clothes you buy?

I see something I like but don't have any money to buy it – well, I'll talk to momma. [Laughs]

Do you consider that very important: "designer this" and "designer that"?

I like to look good, or think I look good. I like to try. I like clothes. I like shoes. I like glasses.

Do you judge acquaintances by how they look, how they dress, what clothes they're

Interview 12

wearing?

I gave all that fad stuff up after junior high.

Okay. But it was pretty important then, wasn't it?

Yeah. Obnoxiously.

And expensive. Didn't you feel sorry for the kids in school who couldn't afford that designer stuff?

That must have been horrible for them. There was nothing they could do! Just less fortunate. Ninth grade was when I started getting pissed off when people would start picking on those kids. Because my friends would do it, and I'd get really upset. It seems ignorant to me.

Would you call yourself a pretty even-tempered sort of guy? I mean, calm?

Yeah, I'd say so. When I get mad, though, everybody knows it.

What sets you off?

Stupidity. I don't get mad too often, but when I get mad I do damage. That sets me off.

When people meet you for the first time – let's say at a coffee shop or a bar or in class before the class starts – what impression of you do you hope that they are left with?

I guess, he seems like a nice guy. Because if you don't really spend time getting to know me, there's not much you can really say. But I'm an easy guy to get along with.

Do you think of yourself as handsome? Good looking?

Fair enough. See my nose? My nose has been broken so many times, it's ridiculous. That cut on my forehead here? I got hit by a shed. How do you get hit by a shed?

Well those sheds, they're wild out there!

They go especially crazy when cars hit them. [Laughter]

What do you want to be doing in 20 years, at the age of 41 or something?

I think I would like to be teaching and coaching. I love kids. I always have.

What level?

I think I want to teach secondary in the inner city. Something really challenging. Because I've always gotten along with everybody, and I think I would be able to get along with the kids. They've got so many problems as it is that they need good teachers to help them, and I've had a lot of teaching experience already, and I can relate to some of the stuff those kids have been through because of the stuff I've been through.

Growing Up Male In America

As you reflect on yourself as a personality, what do you like least about yourself?

Procrastination's horrible. I dislike that. I dislike when I don't try as hard as I know I can. I never give full effort to anything except for football. Like the athletes I live with, if we're playing any sport or game, it's just an all-out effort. They won't lose. I don't mind losing. I can handle that because I've never done it. I've never really lost, until I came to this university and they wouldn't put me on the first string of the football team.

Are you going to change your habits at the next school?

I have to. That's the reason I'm leaving. I'm leaving my friends, I'm leaving my family, I'm leaving everything so that I can succeed by myself, because no one thinks I can do it. People back home think I'm a joke as far as school is concerned. I was one of the best athletes ever to come out of there and I come up here, and I needed three Bs in summer school to be eligible to play. I want to go back home knowing I did it by myself.

Well, now you've talked about the things that need improvement. What are the good things about you? What are you proud of?

I've got good people skills. Athletic talents. Easy to get along with. Understanding.

And you're somewhat of a role model for younger kids?

Yup. In high school I was, big time.

Here are just random questions for you to respond to.

How would you define the concept of happiness?

Happiness? That's tough to define. I just want a family, a job I can enjoy, and children that I can raise to be productive citizens. I guess that's happiness to me.

Can you imagine living with the same person for 50 or 55 years?

Well, yeah, I can imagine it. Not right now, but somewhere down the line. I think I can get along with just about anybody. So once I find someone that I can get along with well enough, off we go!

How do you define the word "masculine" or the concept of masculinity?

Hard working. [Laughs]

How do you feel about touching? Do you hug your buddies?

Every time I see them. It's great!

I always thought of that whole generation, when I was growing up, when "men" just didn't touch very much. And I thought of how much they all secretly wanted to but they couldn't.

Just think how much they missed out on.

Interview 12

When you go into a sexual relationship, do you have any fears of failure?

I don't really care. [Laughs] At this point in my life, I just don't even care.

Do you ever worry about whether it is okay for her?

Doesn't bother me none at all. If I have sex nowadays, I have sex and that's it.

Okay. So it's just the act. It's recreational.

Yup. It's pointless. But I want to start that over, too. That's another bad part about my persona here that I want to change. I don't want that reputation anymore.

Do you ever worry about an inability to perform sexually? Impotence, erectile dysfunction?

I'm always hard. If it goes down, it will be hard again in five minutes. I'm hard all the damned day. Sitting in the car, walking to class, that's all I do: hands in my pockets, lift and tuck.

Well, you're 21!

Do you have shy bladder? Some guys can't pee when there's another guy next to them. And in some bars there's a big trough.

I won't use them. I don't like peeing in troughs or urinals because I'm afraid I'll get splashed or something. When I pee, I pee hard. I don't want to splash or get splashed.

But you have no trouble urinating with other people around?

No, I can pee.

I'm always interested in how much of the "gay" thing happens in people's lives. If you look at it, a circle jerk or mutual masturbation is a kind of a gay thing, but it's mainly straight men who do that. In fact, all of sports activity could be called "gay" if you think of it strictly as same-sex ("homo" sexual) activity. But that gets a little clinical and Freudian, perhaps. So I'm going to ask you some more personal questions, now. Not that these others haven't been personal.

Did you ever, at any time, have any sexual fantasies or dreams or thoughts about sex with another man?

I don't believe so. I don't think so.

Because some people say they did, or they do. I guess that would be the bisexual person.

Yeah. But in my case, I don't believe so, though.

Okay. Now, have you ever thought what your attitude would be if one of your teammates finally "came out" to the rest of the team and told you that he was gay?

A guy on my team ... we caught him watching gay porn. We pushed "play" on his VCR, and I don't know what it was called, but it was a full tape of guys

Growing Up Male In America

having sex with each other. And everybody in the house went crazy . "He needs to get the fuck out of the house!" And I'm like, "What the hell's your problem, anyway?" You know? "Let the man watch whatever the hell he wants to watch." The other guys in the house really flipped out about it. There's some people just don't have a clue yet. God knows why.

And it's fear, probably.

Yeah, but it's never bothered me, and I don't think it ever will bother me. Gay guys still bleed red.

I think professional sports is one of the great holdouts of gay coming-out, probably because it's the macho, it's the male thing. Once in a while, you hear of some guy who has the courage to come out and announce that he's gay, but it's usually after his career is over, or they have left it in the prime of their career for one reason or another. So, I don't know.

That would be hard, coming out as gay, if you were a professional football player.

Oh, yeah. Can you imagine? But you'd say you're rather tolerant about gay people?

Yup.

But in many other people, the hate for gay people is incredibly strong.

There shouldn't be the word "hate".

One thing we didn't talk too much about, I guess, is drug use. Now, you smoke weed, dope, pot, whatever, on a fairly regular basis. And you have since you were about how old?

Regularly, about the last four years.

Okay. And you're now 21. So from high school on up.

Yeah.

And you like it?

I enjoy it but wish I could stop it. But for some reason, I never can.

Okay.

But I can't quit anything. I've never been able to quit anything. I can't quit chewing tobacco, I can't quit drinking, I can't quit smoking. If I'm drinking a beer, I've got to smoke a cigarette. And I'm an athlete and know I have to be on the field the next day.

How does pot make you feel?

I just tell people it gets me back to normal. [Laughs]

What does that mean?

Interview 12

Well, it's more just a relaxed state. I can be the person that I want to be. I can giggle and make people laugh and jump around and pop some jokes and just be all jittery, because I have an excuse. Because I'm high, or whatever. And I love doing that. I love making people laugh. And I can do it when I'm smoking. I can do it when I'm not, too, but then I always get so damned depressed. After I'm coming down, I know when I'm super depressed because I start smoking weed a lot. Like during final exam week. Just smoking and smoking and smoking. It's an escape. It's bad. [Laughs]

When you're coming down and you're into a depression, then what's the remedy for that? Smoke more pot?

Well, I don't really even come down fully anymore, I've been smoking for so long, it seems. But when my buzz has worn off, it feels like I missed out on doing something productive. Like I could have been running or working out or studying. I don't remember much of my past because of it, either. Like, I don't remember what I did two days ago. I don't have a clue what I did last week. People have to remind me. I *never* remember names, and that's something that I'd really like to work on.

Do you think smoking pot so regularly is just a phase you're going through?

I don't know. Maybe I just do it to cope with something. Maybe it's just something I need to handle something else right now. I didn't smoke much when I was in that two-and-a-half year relationship with that girl in high school.

Did she ever smoke with you?

Yeah. Like on a rare occasion we would smoke a joint together just to charge things up, just so we could giggle around, you know, and laugh at each other or whatever. But I think I'm just missing something in my life right now. And until I find it, I'm going to be smoking weed.

Do you think you know what that "missing" thing is?

I think it's a relationship. I think it's someone that I can trust. Really trust. Because I don't think I have that right now. Like really, really trust someone. Except my best friend who's transferring to the new college with me to play football. We trust each other.

Well, we're about reaching the end of our conversation now. Do you have any final thoughts you'd like to express?

I think the biggest thing in growing up is trying to focus on controlling what you're doing. If you're doing stuff that you shouldn't be doing, just try to rise above that and make sure that you're controlled and focused on your main goal in life. If I wasn't able to control the bad habits I had, I don't know where I'd be today. I just wouldn't have turned out too well. Just be yourself. You've got to be yourself. And work hard. It's a big deal to work hard growing up, because it's for the rest of your life. That's for sure. Don't judge. Be yourself. Work

Growing Up Male In America

hard. No screwing up.

You're a very interesting man, and I have a feeling you haven't had too many chances to unload and to spill all this personal stuff before this interview.

No, I've never revealed this much about myself to anybody else. Ever.

Has it been uncomfortable?

No, I enjoyed it. I really appreciate the chance to talk about a lot of these personal things. Thanks. But the problem is: What do you honestly close with?

I'll close with this: Thanks to you for doing this interview. [Laughs] *How's that?*

Pretty good! [Laughs]

Postscript – December 2001

This man achieved some of his goals. He and his friend trained very hard at the gym and developed their bodies into terrific shape for football season. He excelled on the football team at the new college, and to date his team has a winning season with no losses.

Interview 13

"Honestly, I come from a family that's too good to be true."

When this interview was conducted on January 21, 2001, he was 23 years old. He is 5' 10" tall, weighs 170 pounds and has light brown hair. A university student, he is majoring in advertising and psychology and plans to graduate in December 2001.

Welcome, and thanks for your willingness to sit for this interview. I really appreciate it.
Let's start with this: What's the first thing that you can remember as a kid? And how old might you have been?

> The first vivid memory is just a memory of a dream. [Laughs] Which is really strange. I just remembered dreams really well when I was a child, and I can still remember them to this day. I don't know what age I was. I also remember events, like playing outside with my brothers and doing weird things, such as working on bikes and playing in the dirt and playing with little army men in the sandbox. Stuff like that. It was primarily with my brothers, though.

You have how many siblings?

> I have three older brothers.

Three older brothers. And how far apart are you all?

> We're all five years apart. They are 28, 33 and 38, and I'm 23.

Now, was that family planning or what!

> I always thought it was. [Laughs] And then about a year ago my parents and I talked, and they mentioned that I was kind of a mistake. But they planned to have kids five years apart – the first three, anyway. I wasn't planned.

And they probably like you best of all, because that's what sometimes happens. So no sisters?

> No sisters. My mother would have liked me to be a girl, actually. [Laughs]

You were raised in a little town in Central Minnesota?

Growing Up Male In America

Yes.

And that's still the family home?

Yup.

Did you say your parents are still married?

Yes. They've been married for almost 40 years.

That's rare these days, isn't it? But your brothers, on the other hand ... some of them have been in and out of marriages, right?

Correct. My brother who is 33 married when he was 22 and divorced at age 28 or 29. They have two children. It's hard on the children. The mother had problems, so that caused a lot of stress in their relationship and a lot of unresolved issues.

Since you didn't have sisters, did you find that you got close to certain little classmates when you started school? I mean, that's where you really got to know what little girls were like.

I've always had good relationships with females. I've always had a good relationship with my mom. Our household wasn't real masculine. It wasn't like my dad saying, "You're going to fight and you're going to be a warrior" or whatever. [Laughs] But I've always had good relationships with girls, and I think I get along better with girls in most instances. But I enjoy hanging out with guys, too. I mean, I have best friends that are both guys and girls.

You're something unusual among the guys I've been interviewing, because you come from a family where the parents are still together. Invariably, so many of these people have come from broken homes. But it seems like you've lucked out.

Yeah. I'm definitely lucky.

All right. Now, up there, in your home town, did you go to nursery school or prekindergarten, or did you just start with kindergarten at the age of five?

Well, this isn't school, but I was in daycare for a couple of years. There was something called Sunshine School. It was preschool or summer school, I guess. I can't remember it too well, but we learned about numbers and stuff. But in daycare, which was before that, which – oh! A childhood memory!

Childhood memory?

Yeah. I remember ... well, I must have been three or four then. But I remember ... we used to sit in a huge circle, like all the kids and the daycare associates or whatever. And we'd play a clapping game. And we'd say the date every day, and we'd say the year, too. And I remember, "Something, something, 1982 or 1981." I remember that. So that's a pretty neat memory. But anyway. So we just played, basically, during daycare. And then I went to that summer Sunshine School.

Interview 13

Was that religious oriented? Like bible school?

No. It was conducted in our public high school. And I think it was just some high-school students posing as a summer-school daycare type thing, where they taught us how to do things and just let us play. It was kind of neat.

Those kids you were with, were they neighborhood kids?

Yeah. They were actually from all areas of the town and some of the rural areas, too. The kids I met there were the kids that I went to school with later in life.

So kindergarten – was that half day?

I believe so. Yup.

You forgot? And you're relatively close to it. [Laughter]

[Laughs] It was, like, every other day or something. For the most part, I think I liked to go. Because I had friends there and I was meeting all these new people. And that was a lot of fun. They made us take naps, which I didn't particularly like. [Laughs] And then they'd make us swish this fluoride mouthwash to protect our teeth, and I didn't necessarily like that. But, yeah, we got to play. We'd just play non-stop. And then we'd go through the alphabet and stuff and learn numbers, again. But it was mainly all play. But we got to cut out pictures and color and all sorts of stuff.

With those big Crayolas.

Yeah, exactly.

And big sheets of paper.

But it was kind of a classroom setting, too, where we all had to sit down and pay attention, with the teacher reading to us. So it wasn't totally disorganized.

Do you remember your feelings toward the teacher? Positive? Good?

Um … yeah, yeah. She was very nice. She seemed a little more strict than I would have liked her to be, but yeah, she was nice.

Okay. Do you remember back – now, you're in first, second grade, something like that – do you remember who were the poor kids, who were the rich kids? Who had the right clothes and whose clothes looked a little shabby?

Yeah. There was a bunch of diversity in the town. The only time I ever noticed that was in sixth and seventh grade. That's when I started noticing the social classes, and the nice clothes and the grungy clothes. But before that I didn't pay any attention. I think some children did realize it before I did, but I was kind of ignorant to that. I didn't really focus on that.

It's interesting that you start noticing that kind of thing about the time puberty's kicking in. And you start noticing how people look. Before that, they were all just little kids.

Growing Up Male In America

[Laughs] Yeah, exactly.

But all of a sudden you start noticing who's cool and who apparently got taken to a bigger city to buy their clothes.

Oh, yeah. Yeah. I got my clothes at a big shopping mall about 50 miles from home.

And you know the tag says a certain designer label and, "Whoa! Cool!"

Yeah. I was a victim of that.

Was school easy for you? I mean, did you get fairly good grades?

I got average or above-average grades. More above-average than average in grade school and in middle school. I got better grades in middle school, I think. Because I wasn't really scholastically focused in my grade-school years. And plus, I was dealing with a bout of depression in my grade-school years.

Really? In grade school?

Yeah. In fourth and fifth grade. I was severely depressed.

Let's talk about that. Because fourth ... let's see, fourth grade you're about 10.

Yeah. Exactly. I know now that depression is not unusual at that age, but I didn't know what was going on with me at the time. My family life was fantastic. My parents would never fight. My brothers were always really nice to me. And I'm really not doctoring this up just for the interview. [Laughs] Honestly, I come from a family that's, like, too good to be true in some respects. But I just came down with this terrible sadness that lasted ... it was probably about a year. And I never would miss class, because I enjoyed school. I got these certificates through first and fourth grade, like, saying I'd never missed a day or whatever. But in the summer after fourth grade and going into fifth grade, I just got massively depressed. And it persisted and even got worse throughout the winter. It kind of started in the fall and progressed into the winter. I would just cry, and I would tell my mom that I was sick and I wouldn't go to school. She just thought it was the most amazing thing. Like, why wouldn't you want to go to school? And she would catch me crying about stupid stuff. She would ask, "What's wrong? Is there anything in school that's happened? What's going on?" And all I could say is, "I'm just sick. I don't feel like going to school." And I don't know, at that time I contemplated killing myself.

At the age of 10!

Yes.

And you didn't seem to know what was going on?

No. I had no clue. I would start crying in class in fifth grade, and it was just stupid, and you feel really dumb.

As a boy, especially.

Interview 13

Yeah, exactly. And so before I'd burst out into tears for no apparent reason I'd run out of the class. My teacher, obviously, noticed me running out all the time, so he talked to me one day, and the teacher asked me what was going wrong or what was going on with me. All I could say is, "I have no idea. I just feel super sad. There's nothing that caused this. It just happened." And he said, "Well, I get depressed, too." And I said, "You don't understand. It's not like just sadness. It's ultra sadness. It's like I don't even want to be here." He said, "Well, I coach basketball, and sometimes I'll get really frustrated in practice and just want to go home and cry." And I thought, "Well, that's too bad for you, but that's not what I'm feeling." He just didn't understand.

So that didn't give you much comfort, huh?

No. So people would try to understand it, and they couldn't. My mom would try to question me, but she wouldn't really question me, because she had no idea. So she just allowed me to do what I felt I had to do to get over this. She asked if I would like to see a counselor or anything. My family's pretty not aware of mental illness things or anything like that. So I determined that I was strong enough to overcome this, which was really dumb. But there would be times where my grandma would pick me up. She lives out on a farm. I would just spend the day with my grandma and go cross-country skiing and stuff to keep my mind off of it. And then, I don't know … then, later at night, it would set in again.

Was that a comfortable place to be? At grandma's house? That was a place to reflect or to forget?

Yeah. It was. Anywhere is a good place to go if you can keep your mind off it. Like, sleeping is awesome, because you're dreaming and your mind is totally in its subconscious, and you're not thinking about what you feel. So, yeah. And she would take me cross-country skiing, for instance. Or in the barn to look at cows and stuff, and that would keep my mind occupied. And my grandpa would talk to me. And it was always interesting, because they would just keep my mind occupied. It was better than sitting at home and dwelling on my sadness. My grandparents were simple people without much formal education, but they understood my problem more acutely than the so-called professionals.

They knew – grandma and grandpa – they knew that you were troubled.

Yeah. But rather than constantly asking me what was wrong, they kept me occupied, they talked to me, they shared their lives with me – a sad little 10-year-old kid.

So maybe there was more therapy happening with grandma and grandpa than maybe even they knew. They had good common sense, just keeping you occupied.

Yeah, absolutely.

So this goes on, and you're going through these ripe years of 10 and 11 being very

Growing Up Male In America

troubled. Did anything bring you out of it? Did they have any medications or anything?

Well, I talked to my grade-school social counselor, and he had no clue. Like … I don't know how those school counselors got these jobs. If they can't identify the simple stages of depression, how could they actually be employed? That was ridiculous. So I was really upset with the faculty, considering what I know now about the illness and what I know about several other illnesses. It's relatively easy to detect and relatively easy to treat. So, now, I'm really upset with the faculty at that school. But that guy didn't have a clue. He just said, "Well, give it a while and see what happens." And I said, "All right." But no one at the school would understand. At least my parents and my grandparents were trying to help me, but at school it's just like … well, "I can't identify with it, so you're pretty much on your own." But recovering from this, I just felt that I had to stick it through. I didn't want to go to a psychologist, because then I would think I'm nuts.

There's a certain stigma attached to seeking professional help for emotional problems, right?

Right. I knew nothing about psychologists or psychiatrists back then. I had no idea. I was just a little kid. So I just dealt with it, and after a while it kind of lifted itself off me, and it went away.

And I'll bet you've spent just a whole hell of a lot of time reflecting back to that, saying, "What precipitated it? Why did it last as long as it did? And how did I come out of it?"

Have you reached any conclusions? Self-psychoanalysis, here, I suppose.

Oh, god, I know. And it's very exhausting. What I determined is that people get brain chemical imbalances just randomly. Most of the time it's caused from something, like family life or your upbringing or just nasty events that happen within your life. But this was just a random chemical change, so there must have been a chemical malfunction in my brain that caused this onset. And then I just went with it, and it cured itself. But that does happen. But that's totally not the way you're supposed to deal with it because it's so easily treated. Like, people will have schizophrenia for years and they won't get treatment, although they know something's not right. They'll just try to deal with it, and they'll go a period of 10 years with this illness. It just causes immense suffering, which is totally unnecessary when you can get treatment for these diseases.

And you felt alone, I imagine, too – that's the biggest part of it – and isolated. You probably found it difficult to have authentic friendships. Well, do kids have authentic friendships at age 10?

I think so.

Did your big brothers come around and hold you and talk to you and try to comfort

Interview 13

you?

Well …

I realize, now, you're talking a 10-year span older than you.

My brothers and I are really close, more now than we ever were. I mean, I've always been really close to them, but it was such an age span that we really couldn't connect like that at that time. But, yeah … my brother … the brother that's closest to me in age would ask me, "What's going on?" Because he was in high school and I was in grade school. Like, I was in fifth grade and he was in 10th grade. So he would ask, "Are you all right? What's going on?" And I didn't want to explain this to him. Because I didn't understand it myself, he surely wouldn't understand it, either. And there's that brotherly thing. You're not going to say, "Oh, I'm sad!" and all this stuff. [Laughs] That would be kind of weird. I felt stupid crying in front of my brothers, anyway. So I would just say, "No. Everything's fine." But, yeah. They would have tried to help if I had allowed them to. But I just didn't.

Sure. There was a mixture of all kinds of things. Pride, and also fear?

I was just scared. I mean, I didn't know what was going on, and I didn't want them to think I was nuts, you know?

And besides that, you probably thought, "Oh, I'm just a kid. They probably think I'm just a kid." Ever remember back, how great four years, five years can be, when you're at that age? I mean, a 10th-grader was a big guy. He was in high school. And here you were, a little fourth- or fifth-grader.

Yeah, right. Right.

And apparently there's that pride thing that you were going through, too. "I'm a little proud to admit that there's a weakness here." So instead you said, "I'm okay." But inside, your voice is saying, "The hell I am!"

Yeah, absolutely.

Have you ever had any other serious dips into depression after that time?

Well, I think I'm predisposed to depression now. I'm in the military. [Laughs]

Are you laughing because you think the military could exacerbate the whole situation? [Laughs]

Well, I don't know. The military is great if you enjoy doing it or you believe in it. I don't necessarily believe in it. I mean, I don't agree with fighting, but I need to get through college, so it's the way in which I had to do it.

What branch of the military?

National Guard.

That's Army, isn't it?

Growing Up Male In America

Yeah. And I have to drill every month.

How frequently? A weekend a month?

Yup. Correct. And two weeks during the year.

You must hold your breath, being in the Guard, when you listen to the news and hear about trouble spots somewhere in the world – and you say, "All I wanted here was an education."

[Laughter] I know. Like, my sister company – they're in the same battalion. Anyway, they got sent to Kosovo for 280 days.

Just now? Recently?

Well, like about eight months ago.

Do you ever wonder sometimes about how different the military is today compared to how it was during World War II? You hear these stories about how after Pearl Harbor, everybody wanted to go and risk their lives for their country. But these peacekeeping things today, where you could have your head blown off because some nut decides he doesn't like you there – it makes you wonder if you really have a commitment to Uncle Sam.

Absolutely. Like, fighting. Like, if a country were to attack our country or it was possible that they're going to come over here and attack us on our home ground, I'll fight for that. Because this is our land. But we're going to fight over some oil reserve in Kuwait or wherever. In Iraq. That's not worth my life, you know? I don't think a material possession is worth any more than life. Or not even close to life.

Especially when the leader of that distant country is still doing fine, and still making his vast fortune.

And still making his nuclear arms. [Laughs] When I was in basic, I would get bouts of depression. But I could deal with that. I don't know if I have the tools now to deal with this stuff. But I dealt with that, and that's probably because of the harsh mental conditions they put upon you in basic. But right after the two months of basic, I had two months of advanced individual training, and I dealt with severe depression for a week and a half. And I didn't think I was going to make it.

Thoughts of suicide?

Um … well … it was different. It was a different type. It wasn't suicide, because I respect my life enough to know that I would never do that. But I just needed to get or do something. It could have been more the situation than my head, but I was just feeling sad and just down. I didn't want to do anything. I just had the classic symptoms of depression. But not necessarily suicidal thoughts.

Had you consulted a doctor? Did you have medicines that you could take?

Interview 13

No.

How'd you do it?

Mostly by thinking, "I can't let this do this to me now." And if you would ever say, "I think I'm depressed" in the Army, they would kick you right out. And they'll keep you in psychological evaluation – or "psycho" evaluation [laughs] – for a series of weeks. Then they'll diagnose you and kick you right out, and you'll have no military career. So I didn't want to do that, because I'd already spent three months in hell in basic and the other training. I would hate to throw that all away. So I kind of had to push myself through my depression.

That's very interesting to me. Probably as a direct result of all this, you're majoring in psychology, of all things. So soon you can go back to visit some of those school counselors who were so inept when you needed them.

I know. I feel like doing it. [Laughs]

Those you encountered back then were definitely not worth a damn.

Yeah. I wonder about their credentials. [Chuckles]

But here you are, majoring in psychology. There's still a stigma. You knew it, even as a 10-year-old, about psychologists or even the word psychiatrist. And mental illness. If only it could be thought of as the same as pneumonia or an appendix attack or something. But it isn't. So having said all that, do you keep your experiences with depression private, or do you talk fairly openly about it with friends?

I talk about it. I feel it's therapeutic to talk about it. Plus, if I can give my story to someone else who could identify the symptoms in someone else or themselves, I think that would save a lot of pain and suffering for them. So that would be rewarding to me. I'm fairly open as far as this is concerned, although it does evoke emotions. Still. Because it was so painful. But, yeah. I speak out about this fairly openly.

Okay. I wonder. You can speculate and never know for sure, but if you were not a psych major and you were in physics or some other discipline, you'd probably be less likely or less willing to be open about it. Is that possible?

Possibly. My roommate's a physics major. [Laughs] And then an astronomy/computer-science major. Triple major. But, yeah. He speaks to me about problems and whatnot, but he's fairly analytical, so I have to pry a little bit to get it out of him.

Yeah. I think that's it. That's what I was getting at. Aren't you glad that you didn't do yourself in at the age of 10?

Yeah.

I realize that's a dumb question. What is it they say in obituaries? "Died suddenly." When somebody kills themselves. But really, the world would be so much diminished by your absence. Because you ... you just give a whole lot. I imagine your

Growing Up Male In America

friends appreciate you so much. And that's not to make you embarrassed. You just seem like such a good person. So. Good for you.

Well, thank you. Thank you.

Okay. Well, you got through probably more trauma and crap in your childhood than most little kids do. Or at least we think so. Maybe there's a lot more like that going on with people than we ever hear about.

Yeah, exactly. I'm thinking ... well, one of my hypotheses is that the majority of people actually go through these bouts. Maybe not as severely as I did as a child, going through all those chemical changes. I'm sure everyone deals with a portion of this depression stuff. So, yeah. It may not be as uncommon as we think.

I think so. And I think it's a very complex world that little kids are being raised in these days.

Yeah. More so now than in the past, even. It's crazy.

Broken homes, child abuse – or the new stepfather who abuses his new wife's kids in any number of ways. Also, the world is fast and complex, and maybe that's why kids tend to gravitate to their computers and their videogames and don't play outside with friends much anymore. That's what worries me, that they're going to be isolated creatures.

You know ... all your talk about chemical changes in your body. That also happens at puberty. I mean, this is a crazy time. Pimples and growth spurts and hair on your body and genital growth. Do you remember, when you were going through puberty, having some bouts with depression?

No.

You got through that pretty much unscathed?

Yes. That wasn't a problem. Um ... another thing. I went through puberty later than everyone else. It was in 11th grade, probably. [Laughs] I was really late. Yeah.

Really? We'll have to talk about that.

I'm still developing, I guess. I just started growing hair on my chest recently.

I don't think that's uncommon.

Okay. [Laughs] Well, I'm growing hair, now.

Usually puberty happens about the age of 12 or 13, or something like that, for boys.

Oh, yeah.

It's about then that things are happening. And so eighth, ninth grade can be a messy time. You've got a classmate who looks like he's been a man forever. [Laughter] Did your late development cause any teasing?

Interview 13

Not that I recall.

Do you remember feeling any personal tension with this? Asking yourself, "When is this puberty thing going to happen to me?"

I was always wondering when it was going to happen. Like, guys were getting hair on their legs and stuff, and I just barely had any. [Laughter] In that respect, I was, like, "What's going on?" But, I mean, I was pretty good friends with everyone, so everyone pretty much respected me and I respected them. So there was never an issue.

When I think about it, wouldn't it be rather unusual for school kids to tease and make fun of something like late pubescence?

Well, it happens all the time. [Laughs]

Really?

Especially girls with boobs and stuff? Thinking they're flat. Or guys? I remember that very vividly.

Okay. What were your favorite activities in high school? What kind of activities did you get involved in?

In my ninth to 11th grade, I was in track, hockey, band.

What did you play in the band?

Trombone. [Laughs] Yeah. And trap set for jazz band. So, I played drums as well. And ... what other activities? I skateboarded all the time. I rode bike. A free-style bike.

Ever do any theatre?

I dabbled in that in my senior year, actually. My senior year, I started choir as well. I was in choir throughout middle school, then dropped it because both band and choir kind of took up a lot of my time. So, yeah, in high school – my senior year – I dabbled in choir again. I just tried out and got on their elite singing crew. Just right in. They kicked a guy out. [Laughs] And so that worked out really well for me. And my girlfriend was in the elite group, too. I realized that I must have some kind of a voice. Although I was a tenor, unlike yourself.

Yeah. School came easy for you? How were your grades?

My freshman year, I just wanted to get straight As throughout high school, just to look good for college. [Laughs] Which doesn't matter, now that I look back on it. But I remember I got good grades. But in my freshman history course, my teacher had it in for me or something. I got a C grade, and I'd never had a C until then. It was a C+, and I was just devastated. So then after that, I just kind of lost interest. "Oh, I'm just going through high school, doing what I've gotta do to get the grade and get out." So I wasn't really scholastically motivated at that point.

Growing Up Male In America

Sure. But you got your B average, I would imagine?

Yeah.

I imagine, since you seem way above-average in intelligence, that you probably didn't have to work too hard.

No. Not through high school.

But also, you had all those activities going on – which makes you a much more interesting, well-rounded person than to be sitting there with a 4.0 average.

Yeah.

On the whole, was high school a good experience? Positive?

Absolutely. I dated a girl that I completely fell in love with. From my 10th-grade year. Actually, my 11th-grade ... the beginning of my 11th-grade year until freshman year in college. Or sophomore year in college. Wow! I'm forgetting all this stuff. [Laughs] It was just ... I haven't bothered thinking about this stuff in such a long time. She's the one that I gave my virginity to. And so that made high school all that much better. Because it was such a treat to see her all the time.

Did she give you her virginity?

Unfortunately, no.

No!

I know!

Ah, well. Doesn't matter. Doesn't matter.

But that's fine.

Good for you. That made you and this girl an item and also good friends. Good. That's very good.

How old were you when you lost your virginity – when you had sex with a woman for the first time?

It was two days before my 18th birthday. October 2, 1996.

And how was it? On a 10-point scale. Successful?

I was a little premature, I think. [Laughs] I mean it wasn't terrible, but it wasn't by any means the best.

The first times with things usually are not the best.

Right. But, I mean, it was so special that that didn't even matter. Because we always talked about it and really set it up to make it this grand thing, and we definitely wanted to share it between the two of us. So that was awesome. It was everything that I wanted or imagined it would be.

Do you find that a little unusual, when you talk to your other friends about their

Interview 13

first time and with whom it was? That there, for you, it was with a significant person whom you knew and respected for quite some time, rather than just any woman.

Yeah. I think in the past it used to be a little more impersonal. Like, people just went out to get laid and they wanted to go lose their virginity, but some of my friends waited until they were in a very serious relationship and that was very valuable to them. So they made sure it was with someone they really cared for. But, yeah, some of my other friends just went out and had a one-night stand. [Laughs] Just, "Hey, there you go." Which I don't agree with.

I wonder if there's something about the male pride, here. You don't want to look like a failure or seem inexperienced, and yet you are *inexperienced. So some guys do it with a complete stranger or somebody who doesn't really matter to get a little practice or something. I think you said a key word just now: For those who waited and had their first experience with somebody they loved or at least respected, the first time was more significant. And you can even remember the day! My god, that's pretty amazing. That you've got that on your mental calendar. That's pretty remarkable.*

Do you remember the first time you masturbated? Did you have wet dreams?

I remember my first orgasm and my first masturbation experience.

Let's talk about that.

Oh, boy.

That's a question that I usually ask in these interviews.

I remember that when I was dating throughout middle school and high school, I was in long, monogamous relationships. And we were really close to each other. I considered it love at the time, until I fell in love with that girlfriend in 10th or 11th grade. But those others were really serious relationships, and so I remember things really vividly. Like the girl that I started dating in seventh grade, we always used to go to a friend's house, and his mom would work evenings or nights. So we'd mess around. My girlfriend and I would go to his room, and he would go with his girlfriend to his mom's room. And we'd mess around. And I had an orgasm just through dry humping or whatever that is. And, yeah, I remember that explicitly. It was something I hadn't experienced before.

That was the first time you came?

Yeah, yeah. I was, like, "Wow! This is pretty neat!"

I mean, you knew the physical result of sexual stimulation?

Well, I didn't … I was pretty innocent. It wasn't anything anybody ever talked about. I knew I enjoyed looking at naked women, naked photos. I knew that was interesting. But I didn't know the physical aspect. And when that happened, when I came – well! I enjoyed kissing my girlfriend and touching her

Growing Up Male In America

and all that, but I just didn't put two and two together. I was pretty naive, I think.

Now, how old were you then?

I was 14, I believe. Then shortly after that, once I had experienced that sensation, I'm thinking, "Well, then, masturbation's really stupid." [Laughs] At that point, I was just experimenting, and that's what happened. Then shortly after that, I was introduced to masturbation.

You were introduced to it?

Well, I wasn't introduced literally. [Laughs]

You learned on your own?

Yeah, exactly.

Now, did you and your buddies talk about this kind of stuff?

No, no. I remember there was a boy in middle school that ... there's a name we used to call him. I called him that name, too, so I was probably a bad guy back then. It was a family event, and he had to sleep with his female cousin, who was in our grade. And she woke up in the middle of the night and he was masturbating in bed. So that was kind of weird. And word about that event got out after that, and since his last name sort of rhymed with "squirting," we called his "Squirtin' —" after that. So that was about as much as my buddies and I ever talked about masturbation – just in a joke sort of way. Other than that, we didn't talk about it because that was bad then. Since he was labeled that.

Were you raised Catholic?

Yes, I was.

And was it still a sin to masturbate?

Um ... well, I heard it was, but that wasn't an issue. My parents are religious, but they didn't say that we shouldn't masturbate. They didn't condone it, but they didn't say not to.

They probably didn't even talk about it.

No. No, they didn't.

And yet we think sometimes our mothers don't notice ...

[Laughs] Oh, god. Don't say that!

... Sheets and towels and things. But they do. And again, they don't like to talk about it. But you think it's your great secret. It's interesting that guys who are coming through the same experience at the same time don't tend to talk about it with each other.

Yeah. I wouldn't even tell my girlfriend, actually. [Laughs]

Did you ever ask her ... no, I suppose, if you're not revealing this, you never could

Interview 13

have asked her if she ever masturbated.

Well, my girlfriend – who I dated in later years in high school – I would ask her if she would because I was interested, and by that time we were having sex. It was really interesting to me. I think sexuality is awesome, and I enjoy every aspect of it. So, yeah, I asked her, "Do you masturbate?" And she was so comfortable with her sexuality, she said, "Absolutely."

Good. She was honest and not embarrassed.

And I asked, "How can you just say that?" And she said, "Well, I do." And I'm thinking, "Oh, boy." And she asked, "Well, do you?" "No." [Laughs] But, yeah, then I had to tell her I do.

Do you remember how frequently you masturbated? On average.

I would say maybe three times a week. Even when I was dating, I was bad. So I mean, I was just a fiend, apparently. [Laughs]

Okay. About three times a week? How about twice in one day?

No. Ah, well, once in a great while, yeah. Just to see if I could do it. It was just a challenge thing.

Once in the morning. Okay. What did you think about when masturbating? Did you think about your girlfriend?

In some instances. Well, I'll start from the beginning. At the beginning, I would think of my current girlfriend. But there really wasn't much to think about, because I didn't really get to see her naked explicitly, in the light. It was always in the dark. And I'm so visual. But I would either watch TV or … this is really weird. I heard about lingerie ads and the Sears catalogs. And once I got the idea from a TV show or something, then I did that. So in the early stages, it was due to a clothing magazine or lingerie ads or something.

You're visually oriented, you said? Or highly so?

Yeah.

Could you envision and create images in your head? Could you without a book or without a magazine?

Yeah. Well, at night, like, if I were to lay in bed, like just before I'd go to sleep or something, then I could stir some thoughts. But I would just recall sexual experiences with old girlfriends.

How old were they? [Laughs] *That was a joke.*

Eighty, 90. [Laughs] Yeah, but I'd just recall sexual events that had happened. The way she was sitting or the way she was on top of me or whatever. But for the most part, it's just basic porn. Like, porn's so visual and it's right there. I don't, like, make little scenarios with the characters in the photo. I just see it for what it is.

Growing Up Male In America

Do you like porn?

Uh, sure.

Videos?

I don't have any videos. I haven't gotten my hands on any, and I haven't mustered the nerve to get one from a video store or anything. But I've watched them.

You just put a paper bag over your head when you go to the rental store. [Laughter] Anyway. Here we're making it silly and funny, but again, you don't share this kind of information with your buddies.

The only time we've ever discussed that was in a game of Truth or Dare. Like when we were drinking or with our girlfriends, and we'd ask weird questions. But even so, there's ... between my roommate and me, I don't want to know that about him. I don't care if he does, but I just don't want to catch him or see him or hear him or whatever. [Laughs] He can do it. That's cool. But I just don't want to know when or where. So that's kind of what's holding us back. I think if we weren't in a living situation, maybe it would be a little easier to talk about, because we'd never have to experience it.

I wonder if women talk about their dates to other women. They do a lot, don't they?

Well, yeah. They're probably worse than the guys.

But do guys do that much? Do they say, after a really great date, great night, they had a wonderful time? Do guys tend to share that?

More sexual.

... More bragging. Like, "Whoa. Here's what happened." Whether it was all true or not.

For myself, it is a little bit of both. If it was just an extraordinary date and this girl I'm with is just fantastic, then I'll be, like, "Yeah, this was great. We did this and everything." And if there was sexual stuff, then I'll say, "Yeah, we even did this." But if it wasn't one that I was very enthused about, I would probably relate just the sexual aspects of it and just say, "Hey, at least I got some head." [Laughs] Something stupid.

Do you find ... you may be a little bit unique in that regard? Or do you find that other friends of yours are equally willing to disclose?

I think I'm just more open than my average friends. Yeah. I choose to disclose pretty much anything. But when I'm sincere about a girl, then I say something, and I like to share it because I think it's a neat event. So it would be neat if someone would listen to it.

I don't want to put ideas into your head, but I'll bet – because I'm getting to know you a little better – I'll bet that you do it in a totally respectful way, for the woman. I mean, it's not like, "Boy, did I take advantage of her."

Interview 13

No.

I mean, if you're talking about the sexual experience with your buddies.

Yeah. Absolutely.

You keep certain things private?

Yeah. And I believe all sexual experiences are unique and special. I value sexuality. I think it's a wonderful thing, and I don't think it should be abused. I think it should be special, regardless of who you share it with. It's just such a neat thing that we're blessed with having.

It is a wonderful thing. I mean, just the thing of an orgasm is just absolutely the most profound physical experience you can have.

Absolutely.

And ironically, our culture has said it's bad. It's to be hidden. It's wrong. And I don't know why that is. And so many of the Ten Commandments have something to do with sex. It's because it is such a strong human force, I suppose, that religion feels it supposedly needs to be curbed or suppressed.

But the more you try to suppress those ideas or sexual thoughts, the more they're going to come out.

When you become a parent, you learn pretty soon that when you say to your kids, "Now, don't go there. Don't do that," it raises the curiosity.

Exactly.

Did you have any favorite teachers in high school? And what was good about them? I hope you had at least one.

Yeah. I've had a couple of favorites. But one in particular was my fourth-grade teacher. He was just a really nice guy. He was an excellent teacher, and he made class fun. We had a biology session or whatever in the course of that year, and we learned about the large and small intestines and the stomach. I got a lot out of his class. We could fool around, but yet we knew when we had to be serious. And he was cool with it all. He didn't say, "You've got to do this" all the time. He was just really good to his students.

Was this teacher ... of course, to a kid, anybody 25 is really old – but did he seem like an older guy, or was he a young guy fresh out of college?

He was an older guy. He was probably 35 or so.

Now, in senior high, did you have a particular one or two that really inspired you and whom you admired?

Yeah. I had probably four really cool teachers. The two that stick out in my mind right now were both female teachers. They were relatively young. They must have been fresh out of college, and they were attractive. [Laughs] They were always really nice, and they had the newer teaching techniques, so they

Growing Up Male In America

made class more fun. But yet they still instilled that respect between the teacher and the student. Yeah. I was kind of a teacher's pet in both of those classes, so I had it relatively easy because they were easy on me. Not as far as grading, but they didn't scold me if I'd screw around or something.

Well, they saw the substance in you, I'm sure.

But there's one that sticks out in my mind. He was a gym teacher. He was also my track coach. I participated in track as well as in hockey ever since I was little. But I was really more talented at track. Like running events and pole vaulting and jumping. He was drafted by the 49ers at one point and was just this excellent guy. He was really nice. He was really strict, but he would also have fun. But he always kept that teacher/student boundary, which I respect. I think that needs to happen all the time. Because as soon as those boundaries start to mix, then there's less respect, in my opinion, and there's not a professional relationship.

And you've certainly had teachers who wanted to be your buddy?

Yeah. And I don't have time for that.

"No. You're my teacher, not my chum."

Exactly. I just think that's the way it should be. But, yeah, that track coach was excellent. When I moved into ninth grade and then throughout high school, he moved up with my class. So he was actually the varsity coach then. And then he kept moving up. And then actually when I graduated from senior high, he was the athletic director.

Okay. So he got out of the classroom and became more administration.

Yup. And I think that's an excellent position for him to be in, because our last athletic director was not doing what he should have been doing, and he wasn't involved as much as this guy is. And he was just excellent for the kids.

And he's still there?

Yeah.

And still kept himself in great shape?

Yeah, yeah. He was still huge. I mean, he didn't lift a lot, but he was just naturally a big guy. He wasn't fat.

Would you say that most of the other teachers you had were duds? Or just not very good?

Well, for the most part, I think we had a pretty good faculty. I think they're all pretty well qualified. Some of the older teachers just weren't as good as the younger ones.

It's like they retired before actual retirement?

Yeah. You're right.

Interview 13

All right. We talked about teachers. Now your parents are interesting to me. I mean, they've been married for nearly 40 years. Still, I suppose, relatively devout Catholics?

Absolutely.

How do you relate to them now? Has there been a rocky up and down in the past? Or has it all been pretty consistent?

It's all been pretty consistent. It's weird. I don't know. I go home every month for National Guard. And my mom just loves it. She would like me home every [laughs] ... I don't know, every weekend, if she could. My dad and I, we have a weird relationship right now. I would like to be closer to him, but he ... I don't know. I think he is trying to understand the way he felt when he was my age and he didn't want to hang out with his parents. So he is trying to give me as much space as possible. And when my mom gets, like, too protective of me or tries to give me too much advice, he's always the one saying, "Hey, he's 23." So he's trying to give me space, whereas now I think I'm beyond that. And I would like to become closer to him because he is getting up there.

How old?

He's 60 or 61. And he's had heart problems. He's had two bypass surgeries. He smoked throughout his childhood, into his 40s.

Your mom isn't too much younger?

Nope. She's two years younger. Fifty-nine or so. Fifty-eight. My god, I can't keep track of ages. But in that respect, yeah, I have a good relationship with my dad. And my mother would do anything for me. And I know I can count on them to do whatever I need them to do.

As the youngest one, did you think you got a little special attention? Special favors?

Well, here's the way my parents explained it to me. From the beginning of my adolescence on, I've had to pay for most of the major items in my life. Like my bikes and my motorcycles. I had to pay for all that. I had to pay for my Nintendos and all my games and just all the miscellaneous stuff that wasn't really practical. So in that respect, my brothers saw me with all these games and stuff, and they thought, "Oh, Mom and Dad are just favoring you. They're buying you all the stuff we never had. We would never get things like this in the past. They just buy you all this junk." But little did they know that I had to pay for everything. [Laughs] I was in debt to my folks since I was 11 until I was 18.

That's enough to bring on an onset of depression!

[Laughs] Yeah. Exactly. But my brothers certainly think I'm spoiled. But then, when my parents are questioned – because my brothers are real upfront with them – they're, like, "Why does he get all this stuff?"

Growing Up Male In America

Are they farmers? Or were they?

No, they weren't. Well, my mother was a country girl. She grew up on a farm. My father grew up in the city.

I'm intrigued by something you said – that you wish your dad and you could be a little closer. Did he ever sit you down and talk with you about the facts or life? Did you ever get anything like that from your folks?

No. Not from either my mother or my father.

And so my next question is – and then we'll get back to the relationship with your dad – where did you learn about sex and intimate relationships? Internet? TV? Porn? What other kids were saying? Where did you start learning about this stuff?

We had sexual orientation classes in grade school.

Really?

Like in fourth and fifth grade. Like, they introduced the female and male anatomy and stuff like that. And it was fairly explicit. And we were really interested. Then we kind of joked about it and we talked about girls' periods. And then we'd get out on the playground and talk a lot about what we'd learned in class. Some people think there is a stigma about talking to children at an early age about these issues, but I think it's an excellent thing, because they didn't make a big deal out of it when they were presenting it in class. But eventually it wasn't that big of a conversation piece. They just informed us in a non-sensational way.

That's amazing, at that age. There must have been people in the community who thought that was not appropriate material.

Oh, I'm sure. I'm sure. And we also got these little handbooks explaining anatomy and the different changes that we're about to experience.

How wonderful for you.

Yeah.

Because the schools know that the parents don't go there, because they're embarrassed. Do you remember the first day you realized that your mother and dad actually performed the sex act?

It was probably when I was, like, 16. I thought I heard them having sex. I hoped to god I didn't. [Laughs] But they may have been. Or else there was just a bunch of snoring going on. [Laughs] But, yeah, at that point I thought, "Oh, my god. Not my Mom and Dad!" At that point, I was having sex with my girlfriend or doing sexual things with her, so then it kind of occurred to me, "Wow. My folks are probably doing this stuff, too."

Now, were you close to your dad when you were a little kid?

Um, yeah.

Interview 13

Whatever close means. Maybe you could define that.

Well, he worked a lot. He worked over 40 hours a week. He was a machinist at a large corporation, and he was on call 24 hours a day. Quite often he was called in the middle of the night. But for the most part, he would work from 6:00 till 3:00 every day, or 6:00 till 4:00 or whatever, and then we would hang out after that and work on my bikes and do other things like that together.

You wouldn't see him at breakfast time, then?

No.

But you had nice long afternoons together.

If I had jazz band at school in the mornings, then I'd be up with him.

And hockey practice.

Yeah. We had an excellent relationship. I don't know, I think I got as much of him in my life as I needed at the time.

But it's a little unusual now to sit down and just have a talk with him? He's closed in?

It's not unusual. It's just that I think he is just trying to do me a favor, because he sees how anxious I get when my mom just bombards me with these questions. "Are you doing well in school? Do you need money? Do you need this and that?" And I'm just, like, "Mom, I'm 23. I can do this stuff. I'm capable." And my dad's, like, "Would you leave him alone? He doesn't need all this stuff." And so I think he was just ... my mom lays it on too strong, and my dad's trying to compensate for that by being a little more detached. Which I respect. But ...

Are you a very huggy family?

No.

I mean, it's not common for you to go up to your dad and give him a big hug when you get home.

No. [Laughs]

Or would he just stiffen up?

Well, my dad would probably appreciate it now. Yeah, he would probably appreciate it now, but I'm just not sure about that. [Laughs]

How about your mom?

My mom was never too huggy until I went off to basic training, and then she started to get more so. And it's hard for me, because I'm, like, "Mom. Shake hands. I'll be just fine."

Are you that way, too? You're not a huggy sort of guy with friends?

No. But with girlfriends, I enjoy hugging them. [Laughs]

Growing Up Male In America

Wonder why!

But my guy friends, we don't hug. But, yeah, our family has never been like that. We've always had this mutual understanding that everyone loves each other and that we don't need to display it like that. Not that it was ever talked about. I'm sure if I wanted to hug them, they would approve of it. It's not like it's not allowed.

Okay. That's interesting. I'll make a prediction that when your dad gets even older, he's going to start wanting more physical contact.

Yeah. My dad's getting that way. I see it with the grandkids.

He'll start loosening up a little bit. Okay.

Oh, another thing I would just like to add to that. With relationships, though, like with a female? I'm extremely touchy. Like, if I really care for the girl, like, I'll always be hugging her. So in that respect ... I've often wondered if my upbringing as being kind of not the touchy type wouldn't reflect upon the way I would treat girls in a relationship. But that's definitely not the case. I'm, like, more touchy, maybe, because I was deprived of that or something back in my childhood. [Laughs]

That may be true. Okay. Did you, as a high-school kid, do much drinking? And do you remember about when that started, if it did?

I started experimenting with beer in my junior year, I think.

Is that late, by your community's standards?

Yeah.

Some of your friends experimented with alcohol at a much younger age, right?

I think so, yeah. I don't know. I just had so much going on that I really didn't have time to go out and get beer and drink. And my parents kind of kept a good eye on me. [Laughs] A very good eye. [Laughs] Just kidding. Yeah. They kept a watch out, and they were pretty ... I don't know, attentive. When I'd come home, they would make sure I was walking straight lines and stuff. [Laughs] And I was in track. I didn't want drinking to jeopardize my track career or my hockey career, because those things were really important to me.

That's also against the high-school league rules. If they catch you.

Exactly. And I was going to college for track.

You were smart enough to know it was probably not good for your body, too. To be excessive. How about drug use?

In 11th grade, a lot of my friends ... I was hanging out with the alternative crowd. The non-conformist crowd. I had long hair.

Really? You look so "mainstream" today.

Yeah. I wore crazy clothes.

Interview 13

Have you destroyed all the pictures from that period? [Laughs]

Well, my family doesn't take many pictures. My friends did, so the only pictures that I have are pictures of friends or that friends have taken. But I do have a couple. I have one, right before I cut my hair for the military. And I have it all down. And it's, like, down to here. [Laughs] That was pretty funny. But, yeah, I do have a couple pictures.

Be sure to show them to your kids. "This is your dad."

[Laughs] Absolutely. But as far as drugs go, these friends were experimenting with pot and mushrooms, and in the senior year they got into acid and stuff like that.

So it was pretty prevalent or commonly found?

Well, amongst my friends it was. But towards the end of the senior year, it was widespread. Like, cocaine use. And crystal meth was widespread between pretty much a lot of the jockey or preppy students, too. Which was really weird, because my friends, there were only a select few that got into crystal meth or coke. But as far as the prep crowd went there was a bunch of people that were on meth.

And this is senior high?

Yes.

And did you get into much?

Well, actually, I dabbled with pot. I knew I wasn't going to take any other drug. Like I would never mess with coke or crank or meth.

Have you ever?

No, I haven't. The only thing I've experimented with is pot and alcohol. So I smoked pot a couple of times. I got really high once. I got really paranoid. [Laughs] So then I did it, like, a couple times after that, when we would go camping and stuff. But that was an interesting experience. But I never got caught up in it. And I still have friends who smoke pot to this day. Just non-stop, like cigarettes.

But you don't?

No, I don't. I haven't smoked pot for, like, five years.

Did you not like it? Aside from the paranoid thing.

I did like it. Well, when we'd go camping, we'd go camping in the summer up at the North Shore. Like a couple of friends and my roommate and I. My current roommate, we've been best friends since seventh grade.

Really?

And we've lived together for four or five years now.

Growing Up Male In America

That's nice.

But he would hardly ever ... I mean, he smoked as much as I did, or less than I did, actually. And so whenever we'd go camping, we always would smoke a little bit. And just laugh. We'd sit at the picnic table and watch the fire and eat and just reminisce. And we'd just laugh nonstop. So we did that a couple of times. But then after the high-school years, we haven't. We didn't go camping with the same people anymore, so pot was never an issue.

Okay. It seems somewhat unusual that you dabbled in some things, but not deeply – which seems to suggest you have a certain appreciation for your body and appreciation for yourself. And also I think it suggests a degree of maturity on your part. You were focused.

Did you have a job when you were in high school?

I didn't have much time, but my parents kind of encourage me to get a job just to get a feel for the work or the job field. So I worked fast food for about a year. That was in 10th grade to 11th grade or a little after 11th grade. Then I worked at Pizza Hut until the end of my senior year. So that's about it. It wasn't a huge income, but at least it got me out there and encouraged me to get a feel for the discipline of work.

At the present time, you've got this job at a computer store in the Twin Cities. That's one day a week, or two?

That's one day a week.

Do you have any other jobs, like at the university?

No, I don't. I'm been offered a couple, but I'd rather not work at the U for some reason. But, yeah. I just do that job at the store one day a week during the school year. When I have some time off from school, then I take a full 40-hour week.

How would you describe the nature of your friendships at the present time?

In sixth grade and part way through seventh grade, I just chose friends who I preferred as people. And then I started getting into the popularity thing. And then it kind of shifted into who the popular kids were. Like, who would I look good hanging out with? But then I would choose the people that I really preferred to hang out with within that group, though. But I would enjoy hanging out with everyone. Or I appeared to enjoy it.

Did you ever have any problem with being excluded from a group that you wanted to be included in? Like you really wanted to be with this crowd?

Not really. I mean, I was in the popular crowd throughout middle school and then high school. And then I kind of broke away from that in, like, ninth grade. I was tired of that scene. I didn't want to be a part of that. So I kind of went with the crazy crowd. You know, the alternative kids, and that was really neat

Interview 13

because everyone was so real. They had nothing to lose. I mean, as far as the high-school society is concerned, these guys were considered outcasts. They didn't have anything to offer and were just a bunch of goofy kids. But they all were real with me, and I was real with them. And that was really interesting, because they were really nice people. And you didn't have to hide anything. You could do whatever you wanted. You could dress the way you liked. You could talk about anything. You could be stupid, and they wouldn't pass judgment. They just saw you as who you are. So that was kind of neat. But as far as my friends today are concerned, I think knowing that type of people back in high school has led me into more stable friendships right now. I look for really sincere people who don't play games.

How about girlfriends, now? Consider back to middle school, when you started dating, compared to now. Are you dating someone now?

Kind of seeing a girl for a week or so. [Laughs] As far as the girls I dated in high school, they weren't the real popular ones. They were kind of in that clique but they were kind on the outskirts of it. Like, they weren't the very popular girls, but they were right in the mix, though. I was dating them, and they were – two of the girls in particular – the one I shared my first orgasm with – they were really cool and they were really honest and sincere, and they still are today. And now the girls I date ... it's really hard dating at this point. Like, the girls are so different now. Like, they play a lot of games. They're just really different now. And I don't get it. Like, there's a lot of materialistic people. I don't know if it's because we're in a large metropolitan area, but a lot of people are pretty materialistic. A lot of girls are. And they're fake in some respects, and some girls think you're just trying to take advantage of them and they don't open up. And they have a plethora of past, hidden turmoil throughout their family lives.

Baggage?

Yeah. And just a ton of stuff. It's really bizarre down here, and I haven't experienced that before.

Do you think it's because they're a different age? I mean, they're in their early 20s or mid-20s, too.

Possibly. Possibly. That's a good way to look at it.

And in high school, they weren't at the bars, probably. Isn't that about the only place to meet people?

Well, yeah. I'm trying to change that. [Laughs] The bar thing's cool, but it seems like the girls you meet there are basically just waiting to be picked up and that's about it. And I don't meet any real interesting people there. I've been asking girls out at school. I'll just be, like, "Hey. You're extremely attractive. I have you in such and such a class, and I was wondering if there's any ... if you would ever like to go out for coffee or talk or something." I prefer to meet a

Growing Up Male In America

girl like that, because I know they're going to school, which I feel is a plus. They have some drive in their life. They're not just out in the work force. And, yeah, that's my plan right now. [Laughs] I've met a couple of girls like that, and it works out really well.

Have you been pretty lucky, then, meeting some substantial women? And they actually can make complete sentences? And they're thinking of more than just looking cute?

Yeah, at school I have. It seems like the girls I meet at school ... regardless if anything ever comes out of it as far as a romantic relationship goes, it works out really well and we become really close. Or else we just become super-good friends, and we just have a friendship that will last for a long time. So, that's really neat.

Which brings me around to this long-term relationship you had with this one woman. And that's over. And when did that end?

That ended about two years ago.

Do you mind saying what precipitated the end? Whose idea was it?

Well, at that time, I was going to another college up north, and I was transferring to a university in Minneapolis. She was going to another private college in the metropolitan area. She was just out of high school. We were dating fine up until then, but I felt my feelings weren't as strong as they once were. I was kind of falling out of love. Which is really weird. I don't understand that. But at that point she said, "Well, I'm going through all these different changes, so I think it would be best if you could just give me some time off. Like a month or so. Just so I can regroup and just get my life in order."

She said this.

And she said, "I just need to meet all these people, and I just need to settle down and get used to the college life. This is such a huge change for me." And I don't think she's good with change. So this was a good excuse, in my opinion. [Laughs] I thought she was being sincere. So I said, "All right. Well, how about in a couple weeks. We don't even have to call. Just give me a call, and we will be monogamous. It's just we're not seeing each other for a while." And she said, "All right. I'll give you a call sometime in the future." And so she called me back three or four weeks later and said, "I think I'm ready now. Everything's going well. I'm ready to get back together." And I said, "Well, I'm not sure I'm ready to do this." Because I felt this was the only point at which I would be able to back out of the relationship without it being a catastrophe. So, yeah. I backed out. I said, "I'm sorry. We should maybe give it a little more time and just see what happens." And then after that point we just never got back together. I told her, "I can't do this. I'm not feeling everything I should be feeling to be in a relationship like this."

Interview 13

Aren't you glad you both were able to talk it out, though?

Yeah.

Instead of having some kind of a stupid fight and just saying, "I never want to see you again!" You both understood each other and where you were coming from.

Absolutely. And now we're excellent friends again.

Great.

All my ex-girlfriends, we're extremely good friends. Still.

Good. That's so important. What a waste of energy to hate anybody. Is there anybody in your life – whom you absolutely hate?

[Pause] There are some people that I dislike, but I don't hate anyone.

Doesn't surprise me. I wouldn't imagine you would tell such people, "You're an annoyance. But I don't hate you. I just don't choose to be around you."

[Laughs] Yeah. Exactly.

Now, into some random-thought questions.

What do you think you want to be doing or at what place do you want to be in about 20 years? When you're in your mid-40s.

I want to be financially well off. I want to be in an excellent relationship with a wife, hopefully. The relationship's more important than the money, as long as I have the mental health or the compassion of my wife or support of my wife. I think that's the most important. And then financial, of course.

Do you want to be retired at the age of 43?

Yeah. I would like to. Sure.

What would you do with your time?

Travel. Spend time with my family. Have children. I would love to be in their lives as much as possible because I know how important that is. I think I have a lot of information to share with them as far as life is concerned. Share just personal qualities with them. Yeah.

I suppose, in your generation, it's not unrealistic that you could be retired in your mid-40s, if you plan it right. It's happening already, you know. You don't have to wait until you're 65 to hang it up.

Another question: Families usually have special names for certain things. When you were a little kid, what did you call it when you had to urinate? Was it pee-pee?

I just have to go pee. Take a pee. Or p-e-e-.

What about when you had to do "number two"?

I have to crap. [Laughs]

Did you notice other guys' bodies in locker-room situations? There you are, gang

Growing Up Male In America

showers and all that kind of thing.

Yeah, yeah.

Did you ever do any comparing of penis size of other guys?

Yeah. I think that's natural.

Yeah. And would you say your cock is bigger, smaller or about average?

I think it would be called average. But in a non-erect format, I don't think that's a very good estimate.

Non-erect, not terribly large?

No. Mine's not surprising. I mean, it's probably average.

So you do sneak a peek at other guys' cocks – in showers, at urinals?

Oh, yeah. [Laughs] If it's around my friends ... well, I'm thinking of my hockey friends, because we used to piss on each other and just do crazy stuff like that. Sometimes we'd catch guys looking at other guys' cocks and we'd say, "What are you doing?" But, I mean, it's going to happen – to glance over once in a while.

Sure. In this culture, we're so private about our bodies. I think athletes have an advantage. They're rather open about nudity because they're hopping in and out of the shower with each other all the time.

You work out with weights, don't you?

Yeah, I do.

How regularly?

Three times a week.

And have you reached your goal?

No.

Are you trying for bulk?

Yeah. I'm trying for bulk and, like, lower body. Over the years, I've gotten a higher percentage of body fat.

You're getting old! [Laughter]

What would you say is the main subject or topic of conversation you have with men now, at this point in your life?

Party situations, like "Do you want to go out?" Like, "Should we go party?" Or girls.

Okay. Computers?

Computers. Yeah. If it's a friend who has some computer knowledge, then I'll bust into the computer thing and maybe spark an argument.

Interview 13

What about conversations with women?

Feelings. Like, relationships. And then partying – partying as being one of the further topics. But mainly relationships and feelings. I enjoy talking about that stuff.

Does that make you, do you think, a little unusual as a man in today's world?

Sure. I believe that does.

So you're not afraid to show or to talk about or to admit that you have feelings and that you aren't suppressing them. Do you feel more open talking about feelings with women than with men?

If it's just a … if it's a woman who's a stranger, I will, I'll feel more open to her than a male who's a stranger. Like, I'll open up to her before I'll open up to a man who's a stranger. But if it's my friends, if we're just close friends, I'll open up to a male or a female. No problem.

And so, I'll bet they appreciate that.

Yeah.

Because a lot of men won't open up.

Yeah. And then they think I'm too good to be true. Then they're like, "Oh, this guy. He's trying to play me" or something. And then … I come across very sincere sometimes and very funny or just abstract. I don't really have a happy medium. I'm two extremes. So I don't blame them for thinking that maybe I'm playing with them, because I am so extreme in those two senses. But, yeah. I guess it's not their fault. I just present myself a little different than the normal person, maybe. [Laughs]

When was the last time you cried?

Probably a month and a half ago.

And I don't mean at a movie or something like that.

No. About a month and a half ago.

Were you alone?

No. I was talking to a female. [Laughs] Yeah.

Okay. Finish this sentence: My biggest fear is …

Social rejection.

Okay.

I'm afraid of what people think of me. Like, if they think I'm just not a likable guy. I'm concerned about that, because I want people to think I'm a fairly likable guy.

But it's not a dominant problem – it doesn't worry you all the time, does it?

Growing Up Male In America

No.

Do you change your basic personality to impress people?

No. But I try to enhance some features that I have to encourage the social acceptability. [Laughs] Social acceptance.

Do you ever feel lonely, isolated?

Loneliness, I could say something about that. My roommate and I, we moved into this new place about a year and a half ago. And formerly we had several roommates in a huge house. There was always activity going on. Then he and I moved into a two-bedroom apartment with each other. And I find myself getting more lonely there, because I don't have the social interaction which I was used to. Plus I'm such a social guy. So I sometimes find myself being a little lonely at home now. And moreso when I don't have a girlfriend

Okay. Now you've known your roommate for a long time.

Yeah.

But he's a scientist type. Does he get himself lost in his own world, or do you share a lot? Do you talk about the day? So, I mean, that alleviates some of the loneliness?

Yeah, yeah. I talk to him.

I mean, he's not too enclosed, is he?

No. But I'm the initiator of the conversation most of the time. If it's something I feel, I'll say, "Hey. You know, this happened at work today." And he's tolerant of the things I have to say. And for the most part, he enjoys what I have to say. But, yeah. He's less outspoken than I am.

So when you're lonely – I think I know the answer to this – what do you do about it? Get on the phone.

Call someone. Yeah. Or hang. I'll say, "Hey, do you want to go grab a drink or hang out, go for coffee?"

Yeah. Yeah. That's the solution.

What have you done in your entire life that most embarrassed you, that you wish you could redo or undo?

[Laughs] Well, the thing that comes to my mind ... well, I'm sure there are others. There's been performances, like in choir and stuff, where I was totally embarrassed because I didn't know the choreography and stuff. But there's one particular instance [laughs]. Just totally bad. But I was masturbating. [Laughs]

Now, this isn't in choir, is it?

No. I was masturbating in my apartment building at the other college. We had three other roommates, so there was a total of five people living in this small apartment with two floors. And there were four rooms upstairs. I was in one of them, and everyone was gone. So I was masturbating, and one of the guys'

Interview 13

friends came over. I wasn't real close to these other roommates, because we'd just moved in. So one of the friends was wandering through our apartment, looking for his friend, my roommate. And I didn't hear him. [Laughs] And I had my door cracked open. I don't know why I had the door open. I just didn't figure anyone was there, I guess. And he walked by, and I saw him and said, "Oh, shit." [Laughter] So I didn't know what to do. I just felt so stupid. This guy said nothing and just continued to walk through the apartment, and then he left. I thought, "Oh, they're going to make fun of me." [Laughs] That's the only time that's ever happened.

So they called you Wacky Guy!

[Laughs] Yeah, yeah. Wacky Guy. That was my name. But no one said anything to me about it after. But I'm sure he knew what was up. Pardon the pun! But he probably masturbates, too.

Gee, what if it had been the girlfriend of one of your roommates?

Oh, wow. Yeah. That wouldn't have been very cool.

As you reflect on your life, what's the most hurtful thing you've ever done to anybody else?

Well, if I feel really threatened or if someone's not being fair with me – like in a rude sense, like if they're putting me down literally and attacking my personality, I get really angry. I can be really vulgar with my language. I can put people in their places really well, and I do it really loudly and make a big scene. I think I've done that to someone in middle school. And then, from that point on, people looked at that person differently. I feel bad about that, because there might be feelings attached to that.

And it probably bothers you because it's so relatively out of character for you.

Yeah. Exactly. You're right.

Have you ever had a gay sexual experience?

No. Never.

No one ever came on to you?

Oh, yes. Men have come on to me.

Yeah. I'm sure that happens.

Oh, yeah. Yeah. Several, several times. I've been approached.

Propositioned.

Yeah.

But you never had a gay experience. Did you ever do a mutual masturbation, a circle jerk with other guys?

No. That's intriguing to me. Like, why straight men do it in a group situation.

Growing Up Male In America

But no, I've never had a male-male sexual experience.

Are you happy with your body?

I'm fairly happy, yeah.

Except the body fat thing.

Yeah. I've had too many dark beers just to put it on. But other than that, I mean, I'm cool with my facial features.

What do you think is your best bodily feature?

My eyes or my muscle features. I have a hard body under all this baggy clothing. [Laughter]

Your eyes are very expressive. I noticed that right away. And you do something that a lot of people don't do, and that is you look right at the person. The eyes are amazing. They tell a whole lot, don't they?

Absolutely.

One guy said his butt was his favorite, his best feature. He said, "Well, the women look at it." And I guess women do notice a guy's butt.

[Laughs] Absolutely.

Let's see. Who would you say is your favorite male public figure? It could be politics, a movie star, athlete. And the same is true with female. In other words, whom might you emulate or admire or has influenced you in some way?

I don't know. A male. Do they have to be alive?

Could be dead.

Newton is incredibly intriguing to me. I don't know much about him, but just the fact that he was so intelligent. I would like to be more intelligent. And just the fact that he created calculus and trigonometry.

That's Sir Isaac, isn't it?

Yeah. Correct. Did I say Newton?

You said Newton. But I thought maybe you meant Wayne Newton, the Las Vegas singer.

No. No, no, no. Excuse me. [Laughter] And the female? [Pause; laughs] It has to be a celebrity?

Could be somebody historical. Dead, living.

[Pause] Wow. This is hard.

Maybe there isn't anyone.

Maybe not. But my mother ... I mean ... yeah, my mother is definitely an admirable figure. She has raised all of us extremely well. She's been very good to my dad, moreso than I think she should have been. [Laughs] He should

Interview 13

share in some of the family activities, such as preparing food and stuff.

But he's the old-style guy.

Yeah.

And eats and then he leaves the table and goes in the other room.

Yeah. He provides for the family. But he's getting better now. But, yeah, when he retired, he just sat around or went fishing. And I don't agree with that. I think that work around the house should be mutual.

Do you consider yourself handsome? You can answer that. Don't be modest.

Sure. I feel I'm good looking.

Anything else you'd like to cover that would give insight for anybody reading this about what a 23-year-old man is going through at this point in history?

I think there are many directions that you can go as far as sexuality and careers and schooling and everything at this age. And it's very confusing for a lot of people. Which makes this age a difficult age. But moreso in the earlier 20s and the later teens. If you just stay focused on what you will enjoy doing in the future and kind of understand your roots and what you're really about and don't lose yourself – focus on yourself and what qualities you possess as a person and what you can share with the world – I think you're going to turn out all right. Just don't lose focus of yourself, because that's the most important thing.

I believe everyone's ultimately a good person. It's just some people happen to do stupid things. As soon as you look at the world in that way, people will respect you. And if you're sincere with people, people will reciprocate. And that's truly fulfilling, in my opinion. And that's what I think life's about: it's just getting along with everyone and being successful at what you do and trying hard at everything that you try to do. [Laughs] I don't know. But I also think sincerity is a huge part of life. So many people don't know how to be sincere. And I don't understand that.

And so many people are filled with such hate. Do you notice that?

Exactly. Exactly.

There's an inner – I don't know – rage, I guess. I mean, isn't it interesting that the kids who shoot up their classmates in schools are all boys?

Yeah.

There's one girl, I think, that I've ever heard about who ever pulled a gun.

I haven't ever thought of that.

One of the reasons for this book is to hear what people in their 20s have been through and what makes them tick. You're so fortunate that you – not only with me, here, but I'm sure you're a very disclosing sort of a personality and you don't hold it in – but there's something that's pretty strange in our culture, it seems to me, that

Growing Up Male In America

causes little kids boys to hold so much in. They can collect an arsenal of guns in the house, and the folks don't even know about it.

> I think *that*'s the sad part – that folks aren't involved in their children's lives, and they don't know where the kids are or what they're doing. I think it has a lot to do with just mutual respect between the parent and the child. And the children are obviously misguided, or they're not guided at all. Parents just don't take the time to show their children what's right and what's wrong and why it's not right and wrong. You just can't say, "No." You have to explain why that probably wouldn't be the best decision. And I think families lack that right now.

Talking with you has been a great pleasure. I have enjoyed it very much, and I hope you can see why I use the word "conversation" instead of "interview".

> Yeah. Absolutely.

Thank you very much for your candid, intelligent and perceptive comments.

> Thank you.

Postscript – December 2001

AUTHOR'S NOTE: A few days after the September 11, 2001 tragedies, I sent an e-mail to this interviewee in which I expressed trepidation and concern that his National Guard unit might be deployed in the war effort. This was his response on September 16:

> "I sincerely appreciate your concern. Yes, there certainly is a possibility that I will be deployed as these events escalate. But there couldn't be a more worthy reason for me to assist in this "war". Incredibly, I am at ease when I ponder thoughts of being activated. I think it's the fact that I absolutely hate terrorism and I'm tired of innocent people being killed for abstract political and/or religious reasons. The fact that we were attacked on our own soil also provides great incentive to assist.

> In the past I was not very patriotic, but these recent events have brought out a patriotic side of me that has never been seen before. I am so very proud to be an American! I would be honored to fight for my country."

Interview 14

"With the guys I work with, I wouldn't even bring up anything about sex and other private matters."

This interview was conducted on August 13, 2001. He is 23 years old, 6 feet tall, weighs 200 pounds and has light brown hair. He works out at the gym several times a week.

First of all, I really appreciate your doing this. This is very good of you. I think the best way to begin is to start with the beginning of your life.
Where were you born?

I was born in California, in a town that's a suburb of Los Angeles.

And you grew up there?

Yes, but I believe I was about two years old when we moved to a small town nearby. I was still too young to remember. Then, a few years later, we moved to another suburb of Los Angeles. I lived out there until I was about 16, and then we moved to Minnesota.

Any siblings?

I have one younger brother.

How much younger?

He is 21 right now. I'm 23.

Are your parents still married?

Yup.

To each other? [Laughter] *If so, that's somewhat rare!*

Right. I think they've been married for about 25 years.

Do you get along with your folks?

Oh, yeah. Very well. I consider my dad almost to be like my best friend. I can tell him anything. Anything sexual, anything personal. The same with my mom. She's pretty good. She's pretty open minded. When I was little, growing

Growing Up Male In America

up, it was different. I felt they were a lot more strict then. But then, as I got older, they kind of let me go on my own and let me fumble around. Basically what happened was, there was an incident. I might as well tell you straight ahead.

Sure. Jump right in.

I was 18 years old. I had graduated from high school, and I used to work at a factory in my home town in Minnesota. I didn't have a steady girlfriend, but I used to work with this girl who was extremely hot. She was pretty good looking. She had the hots for me, and I had the hots for her. She used to come over to my house. We never really went out on dates or anything, but we had intercourse all the time. She would come over to my house – that is, my parents' house. My parents lived upstairs, and I had a room downstairs. One night I was with this girl on the basement floor, and my dad walked in while we were having sex. [Laughter] And from that point on, it kind of changed everything. You know? After that, dad and I had a long talk, and I think he became more open to me and I became more open with him.

I guess a situation like that will do it! [Laughs]

Definitely. All I remember is he walked down to the basement, and the cat followed him down the stairs. He looked at this girl and me on the floor. We were all in shock. I grabbed the blankets. My dad just picked up the cat and walked back up the stairs. [Laughter]

Well, his finding you in such a compromising situation is a "Dad, I'm mature" kind of statement, isn't it?

Right! [Laughter]

Now, your younger brother. Is he here in Minnesota, or did he stay in California?

Actually, he is in Minnesota. As I mentioned to you before, I'm on the good side of things. I'm in law enforcement. I'm a police officer, and my brother is on the other side. Currently he's in prison.

Really!

Yeah. Shocking. He is in the state prison. He is serving 84 months for manufacturing meth amphetamines. His scheduled release date will be 2003. I am asked, several times: "You're in law enforcement. How did your brother end up in prison?" Totally different directions, but the more people I talk with, there's always a person considered to be an oddball or a black sheep in the family. It's kind of difficult for me, at times. It's kind of embarrassing. But what can you do?

Yeah. It's out of your hands. Do you go visit him in prison?

Actually, no. It's kind of hard for me, at this point. I don't visit and don't really have any contact with him. My parents do. They go up and see him, probably

Interview 14

at least once a month. And my brother writes letters to my folks. I'll read them and try to keep up with the updates on him. I don't know. I just feel at this time, it's kind of difficult for me to go into the prison and be in that type of environment. You know? I did work in the county jail here for a year and a half. At least at this time, it's too tough for me to deal with, right now.

At first glance, that sounds like it's a contradiction in terms, doesn't it? Because for people who are not used to a jail, it's a shock, going in to visit somebody who's in there. But you're used to it. Of course, it's your brother on the other side of the bars there, when you go visit, and maybe that's the hard part?

Right. I think it is the hard part. And also ... moreso, I don't want to be hurt or disappointed by him anymore. But let me go back a little bit.

Okay.

When our family was out in California, my attitude was, "Okay. I'm the oldest one in the family. I'm going to run the show." I was the wild one. I was the one always getting in trouble. A lot of fights. Running my mouth off quite a bit. I was a skinny guy, but I was very fast. Yeah.

You've changed.

Yes. I have changed a lot.

You've discovered working out at the gym here, for one thing. So at that time, when you were a teenager, it was you who was the wild one.

Right. Actually, I would say, ever since I could walk. You know? Three years old up to 15, 16 – I was considered the wild one. Most people told me that they thought I would be the one who ended up in prison, and my brother would be the one who would be a cop.

What was he like at that time?

My brother was very quiet. He would always smile, remain calm. Nothing bothered him, and he always wanted to be around me. I was two years older than him. If I wanted to play baseball, he'd say, "Yeah, I want to go play baseball with my older brother." You know? And I would stick up for him. I'd say, "Well, if I'm playing, my brother's playing." That's the way it was. We were tight. If you picked on my brother, I was going to come after you. In fact, we used to go out to the ocean all the time. We used to boogie board and body surf, and we'd help each other. We were the best of friends.

Like I said, I moved out to Minnesota when I was 16 and a half. That was 1994, 1995. My brother was 14. At the time, it was a big change in life. California is a faster pace of life, a different style of living. I really hated Minnesota when I first came here. We moved right in the summer, and I was having a lot of fun in California. I had to give up all my friends. I had to come out here, and I didn't know anybody. In fact, I was so mad about being here that I went back to California for a month, and I lived with my friend. I was,

Growing Up Male In America

like, "No, I'm not staying in Minnesota." After a month out there I ran out of money, and you can't live at your friend's house forever.

So I came back to Minnesota and got a job. I started mingling with a lot of people, making friends, and I realized that I was getting older and needed to start picking a career to get me motivated, so I got myself involved in the Explorers Program – which is a volunteer program for law enforcement. You have to apply for that. They do a background check on you, and it's strictly as a volunteer. You go out and ride with deputies. You find out what police officers do. You work events. You go to university functions for crowd control. You work a BB-gun range for Cub Scouts. You get involved in different police scenarios. Shootings, domestics.

But when we moved to Minnesota, my brother changed a lot. He went from being quiet to meeting and hanging out with the wrong crowd. In fact, my brother and I both got a job at the same restaurant here. A lot of teenage people hung out there. That was the first sign that I noticed something was different about my brother. He started hanging out with some people who were considered "druggies". Then he started experimenting with marijuana, doing the night life, partying and stuff like that. He experienced different things. I don't know if it was because he started to get older or if it was a new stage he was going through.

And how old was he, about this time?

I think he was about 15.

So he's starting to mix around with the wrong crowd.

Right. He's experimenting with marijuana and drinking and stuff like that. Going to parties, juvenile parties, and basically becoming a different person than he used to be. He would come home late, his tone of voice would change, his attitude changed. Instead of being quiet, he got a smile like, "Okay. I'm the adult now. I'm a tougher guy." And he got picked up for a few minor things. For example, some minor consumptions. Drinking under age. Then he would go out to a movie theatre complex with a few friends and break into cars and steal CD players or CDs. Petty theft. I don't know if he did that just to occupy his time or for the excitement in stealing things. Finally I approached him on it because I started to realize, "Hey, you've got to straighten up. Otherwise you're going to end up in jail or somewhere that you don't want to be."

Well, the more I was involved with Explorers, the more I matured. At the same time, I watched my brother decline. He started to become more defensive. "You got away with a lot of stuff when you were my age." You know? It kind of threw me a shock. So I said, "Okay, this is not like you. You're acting totally different." Then he got picked up for a DUI. He went to jail and did his two days, and he was still under 18 at this time, so basically everything from the judicial system was pretty much a slap on the wrist. And I said, "Hey, you

Interview 14

know, things are going to change once you turn 18. You're going to become an adult, and law enforcement is going to treat you like an adult." But he didn't want to hear that. Then he went from drinking to a faster pace of life. He started stealing cars. He got caught stealing a car and did a little time for that, because I think he was still under 18 at the time. So basically another slap on the wrist. He started hanging around with a different set of people. More like the gang-style life.

You were still living at home, I suppose?

Yeah. At that time, I was. My brother started hanging around with what I considered to be gangsters. And he saw the fast cars, lots of money. He was really into that. At that time, I noticed a complete change in him. He just went downhill. Just straight downhill. He's younger, but he was always bigger than me. I think he's 6'4" and 240 pounds. He's a bigger guy.

Does he keep in shape, too, though? Or he is just naturally that tall and that big? I mean, he probably gets a lot of time to work out at the gym in prison.

Oh, yeah. He does now. He's doing a lot of workouts in the prison now. But he did also play hockey in high school. He was pretty good at that. He always had a big chest, but I noticed when he was getting more and more involved with this gang activity, his chest was sinking in, his body shape was dragging and his face was sinking in. I approached him on that and said, "Something's wrong with you," but he still didn't want to hear it. Well that time, I talked with his friends and I found out he was doing different kinds of drugs, like meth and coke. And I was talking with people who knew the effects of drugs, and they said, "Yeah, that will basically eat you alive from the inside out." [Pause] You know. It disintegrates your insides. You lose a lot of weight, drastically. And that's what it was. It was changing the way he looked.

The last time that I remember he was down to about 160 pounds. At that time my mom looked at him and said, "You need to pack up your stuff and get out of the house." She kicked him out. After that, he just ran the streets for a few months, got in trouble. My mom just said, "No, you're on your own. You're not coming back home."

At this time, I was away from home at a technical college, working on my degree in law enforcement. One of his friends brought a newspaper clipping to the house and gave it to my mom and said, "Do you want to know where your son is?" The article said that my brother was found with drug paraphernalia and was manufacturing meth. At that point, my parents pretty much gave up on him. My brother wanted an attorney; he didn't want a public defender. My parents said, "No. You're on your own." So the end result: he got pretty much the full sentence – 84 months. And that was in 1998 or 1999, I can't remember the year. And he's been in prison ever since.

Well, it will be interesting, won't it, once he does get out? Will this have taught him

Growing Up Male In America

a lesson, or will he all of a sudden dip into the same bad behaviors? Well, he's going to be on probation, I suppose, and he'll be watched, won't he?

Yup. He will be on probation once he gets out. That's kind of what I'm waiting for. I would love it if he came out of prison and said, "You know, I screwed up. I did my time. It's done. I'm getting my shit back together. I'm going to get a job. It's over with." You know? If he does that, I'll give him support. I'll give him help, and I'll help guide him. What I'm afraid of – because I don't want to get burned – yeah, he's my brother, he's blood and stuff like that – but I don't want to have him get out of prison and pretend that he's going to change for a month or two and then all of a sudden fall back in the same category. Then I'm burnt. Then I'm hurt. Then I'm disappointed and betrayed all over again. You know? I don't think I could take that again.

I can understand that.

In one sense I want to help him. I want to get him on his feet. But I think at this point, if he wants to do it, he has to do it on his own. If he can do it on his own, then I think he's going to make it.

You say he writes letters to the folks. Does he find it's an unbearable experience that he's going through in prison?

Actually, I have read all his letters, and he doesn't like it at all. But then, who would? At first, it was like he put up a front as the tough guy. "I'm not going to get disrespected in here." Up until that point, he had never been in prison. He'd been in jail, serving a few days here and there, but basically this was his first offense for a major crime. I don't think it was what he was expecting. I know he doesn't like it.

What's his attitude toward you? Here's his older brother, who used to protect him, and you were best buddies when you were growing up – and all of a sudden you become a cop, of all things. I mean, if you could be a CEO of some corporation, that wouldn't be quite so daunting or intimidating to him. But here he is, incarcerated, and you are a cop. It's such a stark contrast. Does he resent you, do you think?

I don't think he resents me. In fact, in his letters, he has mentioned my name a few times. He always says to say "hi" to me. So obviously, he does have respect for me. I think he wants me to *succeed*. He might feel awkward being in that situation, being that I'm a police officer and he's an inmate now. You know? I think if he wants to *change*, he's going to have to accept that.

And you – speaking of accepting – you would accept him back if you have some genuine, authentic proof from his behavior, once he's out, that he's willing to straighten himself out?

Right. Of course. That's kind of what I'm hoping.

Well, that's all very interesting. Do you know the 1938 film Angels With Dirty

Interview 14

Faces? It's about two boys who are very close, but when they grow up, one becomes a cop and the other becomes a gangster. James Cagney played the gangster.

No, I don't know that movie.

Do most people who know you know that you have a brother who's in prison?

Most people don't. What's kind of ironic, too, is that it makes it extremely difficult at times. The person who busted him in that drug bust is my sergeant on the patrol. And, yeah – it's been brought up a few times. But my comeback to that is, "Hey, you know, that's him, not me. It's out of my control. There's nothing I can do." You know?

And they understand that, I'm sure.

They do understand it. But I guess sometimes, I consider myself guilty. I don't know why. I get a weird feeling walking in, thinking, "Okay, these guys know this about my brother. Maybe they have second thoughts about me." But obviously, not too much – because they did hire me. But at times, I always have that thought in the back of my head.

Well, that is fascinating, indeed. I mean, talk about sibling rivalry or something! This is almost Cane and Abel revisited.

Yeah. Exactly.

Well, now let's find out more about you. You were raised in California, up until about the age 16 and a half, right?

Yeah.

Okay. Let's go back to the beginning. Let's start with first grade, kindergarten, whatever you can remember. Did you like school?

I did as far as physical activities. I used to run all the time. Not so much the academic part of school, but I liked being around other students, hanging out, just having fun. Just being a kid. I remember back in elementary, I used to sit back and stare out the window. Watch kids at recess, playing handball and jump rope and stuff like that. I was always energetic. Just the first one out. I got along, actually, pretty good with most of the teachers in elementary. In fact, I used to get awards for outstanding citizenship – basically, my good conduct with other people. I thought I had a real good relationship with my teachers. In fact, a better relationship in the elementary years than, I would say, junior high or high school.

Now, let's get up to junior high.

My junior high was seventh and eighth grade.

Okay. Then high school was nine through 12. You say, it wasn't quite as smooth or fun or something. What was that?

Elementary, I was kind of like the popular kid. I was the fastest runner in

Growing Up Male In America

school. I got a lot of attention. Teachers liked me. I was almost like the teachers' pet. In fact, I really liked my sixth-grade teacher. She was really big into running. The first day of that school year she said, "What I'm going to do is keep a record of the seven fastest people in the class, and I'm going to take those people to UCLA on a field trip." She would have the whole class line up on the track every day, and we'd run from the beginning of the track all the way around. She would mark what place each of us kids was at, and she'd say to me, "You're number one today." And she kept records all year. I was so dedicated and inspired by her that all year I was in first place. Every day. I wasn't going to let any kid beat me, so I got to go to UCLA. In fact, I met Flo Joyner. We had a picnic. It was a lot of excitement and a lot of fun.

But then you got into junior high, and you weren't the top gun anymore?

The beginning of junior high … seventh and eighth grade, I wasn't the fastest kid anymore. It kind of ruined my ego a little bit. I had some competition with four or five, other kids, and I just wasn't the fastest. It was a big school out in California. It was just two grades, but it was 2,500 kids. I just wasn't getting the attention that I had had in elementary. I kind of faded back. The elementary school that I went to was split up. A lot of kids who had gone there didn't go to the junior high that I went to, so I had to make different friends.

And that's a hard time in a kid's life, too, isn't it? I mean, puberty's kicking in, and some are there already and some aren't. And everybody's kind of sizing everybody up, and voices are changing and complexions are going to hell and you're all glands, as a friend of mine said once. So that's a weird time. And then to have to meet a bunch of new people under those circumstances, it's difficult.

Yeah. It was kind of like an urban school. I remember back when I was in elementary, I got into a few fights, but it wasn't like anything major. It was kind of like throw a few punches here, and you break it up. But I remember the first month of school, there were two females that got into it. That happened right in front of me. One of the females had taken a padlock, and the padlock was over her middle finger, and she whacked on a girl's head. I saw that, and it kind of frightened me. You know, it changed things for me: "Okay, you know. I'm in the real world now. I'm big time. I'm in junior high." That's what I thought. It kind of scared me a little bit. There were a lot more fights. It was a lot rougher environment.

Any guns, weapons that you noticed? Among the kids, I mean.

Yeah. It was totally different than what I had expected. My elementary, all six years, I rode my bike to school. Junior high was too far. I had to ride the bus. I had to get used to that. The bus scared me. It was too loud, people were throwing stuff, the bus was just too packed.

You become kind of aware, when you ride a bus even today, that there is a definite class system in this country, isn't there? There are people who act like animals in

Interview 14

our midst.

Yup. And I just wasn't used to that environment. I don't think I really got depressed. I just didn't feel that I was the top gun anymore. Basically, I became more quiet. I got involved in sports, though.

Which ones?

Volleyball. Seventh and eighth grade.

Physically, had you experienced your growth spurt yet? I mean, you're now six feet tall and 200 pounds.

I was always about average for height. Very skinny, though.

So some guys thought they could pick on you then, because you maybe were thought to be scrawny.

Right. I was skinny, but I was strong.

Well, runners tend to be lean. They aren't going to be 250 pounds.

Right. I was pretty strong, even in elementary. When I'd wrestle, I always went for the bigger person, just trying to challenge myself.

Let's see. You got through eighth grade, and then you had to switch schools for senior high?

Then I had to switch schools. That is what I would consider the lowest point of my life, ninth grade.

And that makes you about 15?

I was 14, almost 15. The schools around our city were pretty rough. There were a lot of fights and stuff like that. My parents didn't want me to go to a public school, so they put me in a private Catholic school. A different type of environment, there. In fact, our school had barbed wire on the outside. Not letting you in or not letting you out unless someone was there to open up the gate. Almost everybody I went to school with in seventh and eighth grade did not go to the private school, so I had to start all over again.

So there you were, making new friends again and having to prove yourself in all kinds of ways.

I didn't have anybody to talk to, and it seemed as if people were different. They had the different kind of attitude: rich, classier or religious. I wasn't used to that. We all had to go to religion class, and I kind of felt awkward. I was baptized Catholic, but I don't consider myself to be a good Catholic because I'm not always going to church. And I felt weird and out of place and had a lot of guilt. "Am I going to hell?" I didn't know what was going on in my mind. I didn't know why I should be there. I'm getting pressure to go to church and mass, and I don't know what I'm doing. I remember one time I approached my dad. I was almost in tears because I didn't know what Ash Wednesday was.

Growing Up Male In America

Everybody went up and the priest put the cross on your head with ashes. I didn't know what this was. I didn't go up there. And everybody's, like, "What's wrong with you? You're not getting that?" And I'm, like, "I don't know." So I went home and I said, "Dad, you didn't tell me about Ash Wednesday." My dad was full Catholic – an altar boy, all that stuff – and he said, "Oh, I should have told you." Also, I think I got more puberty in ninth grade than any other grade. I started getting acne, I started getting stressed out, my vision started declining. Like, I had 20/20 vision up until then.

Well, you know, it's because you masturbated too much. [Laughter]

Right. But you know what's funny is, I started losing my vision in ninth grade, but I didn't start masturbating until I was about 16.

Once you got going, learning the enjoyment of masturbation, about how frequently did you tend to do it – per day, per week?

When I first started it, it was once in a while. I felt awkward, like it felt good when I did it, but I wasn't sure if it was right as far as the public or my family were concerned. I didn't know if I was doing something wrong, because at that time my parents were still strict, and I didn't want to approach them on that. I didn't know if, like, I was gay or if I was doing something I'm not supposed to.

Oversexed, maybe.

Yeah.

You never talked with buddies about that, I'll bet.

No. Not at that point. No.

Did you ever have group masturbation experiences with your friends?

Nope. Never did that.

Okay. Anyway, it was a very private thing, but you began to wonder if there was something wrong with you *because you liked* it. *That's understandable. Isn't it too bad that we can't talk as openly about that as indigestion or other bodily functions? What if you had talked with your dad? What do you suppose his response would have been?*

I didn't feel comfortable approaching him at that time, and I didn't really know who else to talk to about that. In fact, it wasn't until a few years later that I talked with a friend, who is now my best friend, about that situation, and he made me feel totally comfortable about it. We talked about it all the time, we joked about it.

Comparing the lifestyles in Minnesota and California, do you think kids started having sexual experiences with other people sooner out there than what you gather happens here? Or is it happening the same all over the place?

I would say a lot sooner in California. I can remember back in junior-high in California, girls in junior high – 13, 14 – having babies. I didn't even think

Interview 14

girls that age could have kids. It threw me for a loop.

Did you ever hear anything about what kind of sexual activity they were having in addition to intercourse? What I'm leading to is oral sex, because I've read some reports that for kids as young as 10 and 11, that's the big sex activity these days.

No, I didn't hear about oral sex until later on.

Well, let's look more at your senior-high years. When did you start dating?

On a serious note, probably my junior year. Actually, it was about three months after I came to Minnesota. I think I was still 16 and a half, maybe 17. I had my girlfriend, my first true girlfriend ... I mean, I had lots of per se girlfriends. I guess this was more serious. Not in love, but steady.

So that didn't happen until you came here, to Minnesota? What kind of activities did you do before that, out in California? Was it pretty much just groups of kids going out places, to movies and to games?

Yeah, exactly. I remember out in California having a couple of girlfriends. She would bring three girls and I would bring three boys, and we would meet at a theatre. We'd sit next to each other, but it was kind of like she was talking with her girlfriends and I was talking with my guy friends. Like we were cool, but nothing happened.

Well, how old were you when you had your first sexual experience with somebody else?

I believe I was about 17 years old.

And you were a senior in high school?

Yeah. I was a senior.

And was sex successful?

Yeah.

Was it the same person that you had been going with for some time, or was it just a ...

Actually, no.

Want to talk about this? I'm very interested about first times.

Let me rewind back a little bit. I went out with my first true girlfriend, and we used to kiss and stuff like that. We'd grope, and that's basically as far as we went. She wasn't a virgin, but I was. At that time, I was curious about sex but I was deathly scared because I didn't want to have kids. My dad always said, "Oh, you'd better not have any juniors." I didn't know what to do. I wanted to, but I just couldn't. Anyway, we ended up breaking up.

Do you think it was because you didn't have sex with her?

I do think that, yeah. So we broke up, and she went out with someone else. We

Growing Up Male In America

were enemies for about a month. Then later we straightened that out and became good friends. I saw her a few months later and basically had kind of a one-night stand, but not really. We had sex. I had sex with her one time, but I don't know how you would classify it.

Now, this is the one you'd been dating and broke up with?

Yup. I had dated her. But when I saw her a few months later, after we broke up, I had sex with her one time.

Okay. And that was your first time?

Yeah.

And she must have appreciated that, that you ... or did you make a big deal about this? "You took my virginity" or "You're my first."

Actually, I made her think I had had sex many times before.

That you were an experienced man.

Yeah.

Of course you would.

And she never knew. I mean, I didn't have any problems. Everything just went with a flow, I guess, because I had known her before. But, yeah, I fibbed and said that I had experience.

Condom?

Yup.

And did you come fast?

No.

Oh! Usually the first time is 10 seconds.

You know what? I heard that, but I think that wasn't an issue for me because I was masturbating a lot. Actually, I still do, to be honest with you. I consider myself way above average compared to most people. Because now I can openly speak with anybody about it. I'm not embarrassed. When I talk with guys, some people say they masturbate a couple of times a week. Me, it's at least once a day, sometimes two or three times a day. And it's almost like a habit. It's got to be at least once a day, regardless.

What time of the day? Depends?

Yeah. It doesn't matter. Sometimes it's at night, before I go to bed. If I had the day off, it could be in the morning. It could be I'll think of something, and do it then and do it at night. It could be three times in one day. A lot of people don't believe me, but it's true.

And I'll bet a lot of people are uncomfortable talking about that. They think it's a private thing.

Interview 14

Right. I used to be that way because I was embarrassed about it. And then I met my best friend during our senior year in high school. He came from Texas, I came from California, and that was our connection. We both came from different states, and we connected because we didn't know anybody else here. He was a really good guy. He was open minded and changed me quite a bit. He'd talk about masturbation and sex, and I thought, "If this guy can say it, so can I." His attitude was, "You know, everybody does it. The ones who say they don't, they lie." We kind of made jokes about it. We'd know personal information about each other. He started when he was 10 years old. And I said, "Are you serious?" And he said, "Yeah." And I said, "Okay. When was the first time you had sex?" He told me, "Eleven."

Intercourse?

That's what he told me, yeah. I didn't know you could even function at 11, because for me, I wasn't even masturbating until I was 16.

Well, I have heard in these interviews that there's a great range. And some are able to be sexually active at 11 or 12, and others take a while. The frequency of masturbation shouldn't make you feel different, even if it's three times a day, or five times on a good day. Did you ever have a contest with yourself to see how many times in one day you could masturbate?

Not really. I think probably the most I've done is five or six times in one day. See, I like the feeling. It's kind of hard to explain, and the only way I can explain it is it's kind of like sneezing. You get to that point, and once you sneeze you feel a lot better. And that's the same thing as masturbating. You want to get to that point, and then there it is.

Do you ever talk to any married guys about their sexual habits?

Yeah. Actually, my best friend is married now.

Okay. And with a guy who's as open about sex as he seems to be, he'll probably tell you that the need to masturbate doesn't stop with marriage. It continues. In fact, the sex with the spouse might kind of cool off, but you still need your release.

Yeah. He's told me that, too.

Do you ever use porn?

Yup. Not so much magazines. They really don't do it for me. But videos do.

And are you dating steady now?

Yeah. I have my girlfriend now. We've been dating for about a year.

Okay. And things are going along toward marriage? Don't you hate that kind of a question?

Yeah, it's a tough question. It could possibly. I mean, I'm in love with the girl. Yeah. I guess that's her intention, too. But I kind of … she has plans to move out of state.

Growing Up Male In America

A job or education or something?

A job.

Is she about your age?

She's two years younger.

So her moving away could muddy some waters or change things.

Yup.

Now, in your job, I suppose you could transfer to other places in the country.

Yeah. But basically the way it works in law enforcement is that if you relocate, you have to pretty much start over. You have your degree and you have your experience, but you have to walk in the door, take the test over. If I wanted to work in Minneapolis, I'd have to start from the bottom. I'd have to go in there, test, interview. I can't just say, "Transfer me down to Minneapolis."

I suppose different counties and cities have different standards.

Yeah. It's not easy to transfer. I wish it was.

Let's talk a little bit about the work you do. Here you are in law enforcement, and you have the two-year degree in ... is that called criminal justice, or is it called law enforcement?

The school I went to, it's considered law enforcement.

Okay. First of all, do you have any plan to get some advanced, formal education? Like, get a four-year degree or get a master's degree and maybe get into administration more?

At this time, no. I don't really like school. [Laughter] No offense to you, but some people like school, and I just ... not that I struggle. I don't find it fun. I like learning from experiences better.

And in your line of work, you certainly get your experiences!

I wonder if you could give me some reaction to this. Have you noticed that some of your colleagues are on a kind of a power trip?

Oh, yes.

That would seem to me to be the wrong kind of personality trait to have in law enforcement.

To me, that absolutely pisses me off when I see attitudes like that. Because I call it "badge heavy" – walking around, basically hiding behind a badge, thinking that you're a god or that your shit doesn't stink. I can't stand that. Obviously, there are times when you have to be assertive and you have to do your job. You have to – by state statute, by law – you have to enforce the rules. If you don't, you'll get in trouble. But I don't believe that you have to go so far fetched as to violate someone's rights or basically ruin someone's life just to

Interview 14

make you look like you're king shit. And, yeah, I do see a lot of that. Absolutely, I can't stand it. That's my pet peeve. I think you should be able to help people. Yeah, people are going to talk back to you and challenge you. It's a tough field. Very tough. You've got to use good judgment, and sometimes you don't want to make it personal but it becomes personal.

I always wonder if there isn't some kind of a personality flaw in some of those people. These people go home, and they're not in charge then. What do they do? Beat their wife? Beat their kids? Drink too much? I don't know. But I would think that in law enforcement, there would be more of an opportunity for that kind of power trip.

Yeah. I would agree with you 100 percent. In fact, we had to learn a lot of statistics in law enforcement, that in our line of work you have the people who are badge heavy. Power tripping. And also there are a lot of statistics that show that cops are pretty much your biggest alcoholics and have the highest divorce rate. The highest suicide rate, too.

Turnover?

Turnover. Depression. A lot of things. Of course, working in law enforcement, you see a lot of things that the public doesn't see, and you have to deal with it, and a lot of times you can't talk about things because it violates policy or confidentiality. Cops see the more sleazy behavior in society. A lot of cops become calloused people. You can't talk with them. They'll just shrug you off, because constantly they're dealing with the problem people of society. And pretty soon they get the attitude, "Well, everybody's a shitbag."

What do you do to get perspective, to get yourself focused, to see the whole picture?

What I do to try to relieve a lot of stress is to work out at the gym quite a bit. Or I try talking with people. I try to realize that there's good in everybody. People make mistakes. I guess I don't doubt everybody and assume that everybody's a shitbag. You know, I try to talk with my coworkers, but I have a harder time just because in the department where I work, I'm so young. I'm 23, and most of the guys I work with are 10 years older than me. It's kind of hard to find common ground. But if I try to approach them and ask them questions, they kind of give me the attitude of, "Don't you know what you're doing?" They don't have time to talk. And I kind of look at them and think, "I hope I'm never like you when I'm your age" – and I wonder how they ever got that way.

Don't ever lose track of that. I have a feeling that you'll never let extreme cynicism get the best of you because you have too much respect for your fellow human beings.

Right. That, and ... you know, I'm in law enforcement because I thought it would be fun, helping people. And if I'm not having fun and I'm not happy ... helping people, I mean, why should I be in it? And if I was to find a job that I like – for example, construction – and if it's fun for me, I can quit now, work 20 years and be done. I find that some people, after talking with these guys, if

Growing Up Male In America

they've been in law enforcement for 15 years, the reason why they're so grumpy or pissed-off at the world is because they're in it so far, and they have no other option of finding a new job. Or they don't want to, or they can't because law enforcement is all they know. And I don't want to get to that point where 10 years from now, I'll be, like, "Oh, man, I should have just quit years ago."

But at this point, you like it, don't you?

Yeah. Right. It's going good so far. At times it's getting kind of stressful, though.

Is the pay good?

Yes. For me, it's decent right now. I'd like to be making more, but it's okay.

You never were in military service, were you?

No.

Okay. Now, I want to ask you some other questions. Did you ever try marijuana?

Yup.

Did you like it, not like it?

That was when I was out in California, basically just to experiment. This was before my law-enforcement career. One night, a couple of friends and I went out and bought some marijuana and some liquor. We thought we were king shit. We rented a tent close by the beach. We did that for a few days. I guess I would say it was fun at the time, but I have no interest in doing it again.

Did you do it for over a period of time, now and then?

No. It was just pretty much that one short period of time.

Alcohol? How old were you when you had your first drink?

I think I was 16.

And what was the alcohol of choice? Beer?

Yeah.

Do you still drink? Casually?

Occasionally. I'm not much of a drinker. I used to drink more than I do now.

When you interview or go through screening for law enforcement, do they ask you if you've ever tried marijuana? And if you have, does that jeopardize the job?

No. Basically, when they do a background screening, they want you to be honest, up front. Because if they find anything you lied about, you're pretty much gone.

Okay. Let's shift gears a bit, now. For the following questions, say the first thing that comes to your mind.

Interview 14

Are you shy about your body in the locker room? Do you walk around naked a lot?

I'm not shy about my body, and I can walk around naked in the locker room.

And would you say your penis length is less than average, average or more than average?

I have been told that I am more than average in length.

Do you consider yourself handsome?

Yeah. I consider myself to be somewhat handsome.

And is your brother as good looking as you?

He has a different look to him. He has darker brown hair, he's bigger, a different build, bigger nose. Not to sound weird about it, I don't think he's as good looking as me. It's hard to say without sounding cocky.

Well, don't worry about being honest. After all, you masturbate frequently, so you must like yourself. [Laughter]

Exactly.

As a teenager or even now, do you tend – I mean, you're a straight man – do you tend to size up other men? Do you notice other guys' cocks at urinals and in locker rooms?

All the time.

Okay. Next question: How would you define masculinity? What does it mean to be masculine?

Masculine, to me, is someone who is strong as far as their body is concerned. A muscular form. It's kind of weird – but to me, I find the male body to be more attractive than the female body. For example, if we were on the beach and there's a guy and a woman, I'd probably look at the guy first. I like guys who have good builds. I don't know if it's something that inspires me to work out more, or just their look. Maybe it's something that I have a fetish for. I just like the guy's look better than the woman's look.

Maybe it has something to do with hardness, firmness. And a woman's body tends to be soft and round.

Right. I know it's hard to explain. I've tried to explain it to myself, but I just don't know why I notice a guy's build first before looking at a woman's.

Here's another question: What is the most hurtful or painful thing that a friend or a relative has ever done to you? And let's leave your brother out of it, because I assume what he has become is hurtful and disappointing to you.

I don't know if this will answer your question or not, but I had a really good friend out in California. When I moved to Minnesota, his plan was to come here a year later, once he got done with school. And we used to talk all the time

[347]

Growing Up Male In America

on the phone. He had made all these plans to move here, but about a month before he was supposed to come out something happened. I don't know if he talked to his parents or what, but the plans changed and then he just no longer called. I was kind of confused about that. I don't have a phone number for him anymore. But, yeah, that time was hurtful to me. I was 17, and he was supposed to come out here, and we were going to go to school together and stuff like that.

And you were best buds in California?

Oh, yeah. But he just cut me off. Since that happened, I haven't talked to him.

And you knew him well!

Oh, yeah. I knew him, I knew his sisters, I knew his mom and dad.

I'll bet you went through a lot of, "What did I do? Did I say something wrong?" And you started blaming yourself.

Yup, right. I wondered if I had done something to make him change his plans so suddenly.

Next question: Where did you learn the most about sex? Now, your dad walked in on you when you were in a compromising position in the basement with this young lady, but did you learn more about sex from friends, parents, your brother, the Internet, books, movies?

I would say mostly from my best friend. He's very open to anybody. I mean, he's not embarrassed because he knows nothing's wrong, and if you don't want to hear it, the hell with it. So I found him really easy to talk to. Before he got married, he was going out with this girl for two or three years, and he used to keep a black book of the days he had sex and stuff like that. And I would always talk to him about it. And he would tell about different sexual positions and stuff like that. I'd get information from him and try different stuff and just went from there. I think I got most of my information from him.

I would imagine that 99 percent of the cops you work with are not capable of talking openly about sex, right? Or there's a defensiveness? Or they use jokes and sniggering laughs and giggles.

With the guys I work with, I wouldn't even bring up anything about sex and other private matters. Yup – they would come back with defensive jokes. "What? You don't do that, do you?" The macho type of response. And basically, when you get that from somebody, you just don't talk to them because you know what they're like.

You've obviously learned that there are people you have to work with, and there are other people that you really get to know. Now, finish this sentence: My biggest or greatest fear is ...

The fear of heights.

Interview 14

Ah! So those guys building the skyscrapers, that wouldn't be you up there? [Laughter]

No. Not at all!

Finish this one: My greatest, biggest fear with women – when I'm with a woman – is ...

Not so much now, I guess, but before I was involved in a relationship, I feared getting a STD.

Do you ever have any fear of not performing in sex? Not getting it up?

Not really. I'm confident in that department.

And you are 23, after all. So you haven't reached the Viagra stage yet.

Yeah. Right. Not yet.

Do you ever go into periods of depression or loneliness?

Oh, yeah. I think what triggers it is ... I don't really like my personality. I don't think I'm a talkative person. I can't just walk up to anybody and communicate effectively. One on one, I can do that, no problem, but it takes me a while to get to know somebody. Like if I go to a party, I can't just walk up to anybody and just start BS-ing. I used to. So sometimes I wish that I had a different personality.

Another thing that triggers that is being at work. If you have a bad day, you screw things up, things aren't going well for you or you've got too much on your mind. My first couple of years in high school, I had acne. I took medication for that, but that depressed me a lot.

Normally I have a clear face, but I've got a few on me. But before, like in high school, it used to be really bad. And I used to scrub and scrub my face. It was very embarrassing for me. I almost wanted to rip my face off. I couldn't take it anymore. I'd go to the doctors, and they'd say, "Oh, you'll grow out of it." That pissed me off, because I didn't want to hear that stuff. I wanted it gone right away. In fact, this went on for a few years. I tried Retin-A and that stuff that would make your face red. Then I got to the hard-core stuff before I finally got rid of the acne. Now, you can't really tell. But a lot of people, when they see me, they kind of perceive me to be cocky or that I'm right or that I have everything. Like a lot of people that I hear, they consider me to be good looking, and they think that I have everything. So they think, "Oh, this guy is gifted" or whatever. For example, I'm young. I'm with the sheriff's department now, and I've got a girlfriend. I've got a nice vehicle. But what people don't see is that I work hard. They just think everything's been given to me. You know? They don't understand that I've been through a lot of tough times. I think people perceive me at first as different than I really am, or they'll make a judgment about me, and that kind of makes me angry. But I don't know. Anyway, I don't take any medication for depression or anything like that.

Growing Up Male In America

What do you do when you get into a dip, and there you are feeling low and in a shitty mood. How do you get out of it?

I try to think a lot of things through. I guess, a lot of times what helps me get out of a depressed mood is I'll set goals, and if I see that I have something to achieve, I'll try to. I'll say, "All right. You're not going to stop me from achieving my goal." And then sometimes when I get my goal, I've got to look for another goal to keep moving on, because otherwise I'm, like, "Okay, where can I go from here?" And a few times it's gotten really bad, just like I can't take it anymore.

Do you ever have suicidal thoughts?

I've thought about it a few times.

Recently? When I say recently, in the last three or four years?

Yeah.

And it might be job related?

It could be. I don't talk about it too much. The only reason that I'm talking to you now is because it's in private. Hopefully the information won't get out.

It won't. I promise you that. Unless this interview is in the book – but even then, your identity won't be revealed.

Okay. But it's tough as far as law enforcement goes because, for example, if you have any sign of depression or you're taking medication for it, it's considered a weakness. It's, like, "Well, if you're not too steady in your mind, we can't hire you." But on the other hand, cops are your biggest alcoholics. That's their way of dealing with depression. They kill themselves. Their divorce rate is high.

Spousal abuse, child abuse.

Yeah. It's kind of a contradiction to say that they want to have people with level heads, but then they put them in the field in stressful situations but they don't want them to go to the doctor or get help for it. They don't want to know about that stuff. And I think that's why a lot of cops will resort to, "I'm depressed. I just saw a guy blow off his head. What can I do? Start drinking." You drink to forget about stuff. "Well, I just saw a 12-year-old get raped. I didn't see it, but I went to a case." Just so many different things. Just weird and depressing things that you would never think really happen.

I think I can understand that. I mean, you watch enough cop shows and you begin to think that the whole world is slimy. Do you ever watch things like LA Law *and* NYPD Blue, *or are they too distant from reality?*

I don't watch *NYPD Blue* or *LA Law*, but I've watched cop shows – you know, actual cops – or police chases. Sometimes *Unsolved Mysteries*. Somewhat more realistic stuff. I'm not so much into Hollywood.

Interview 14

Speaking of Hollywood, have you ever thought of doing any acting, or did you in school ever?

Actually, I did act in a scene when a friend needed actors for a college directing class.

Were you good?

No. I mean, I did all right.

Well, you're the worst judge of whether you were good or not, you know.

I wouldn't mind getting into that kind of activity, but I have to feel more comfortable than I do now because you get me in a big crowd and I get nervous and tend to stutter a little bit. I didn't stutter in that scene at all. Actually, I did a little bit of modeling at one time. I wouldn't mind getting into that. In fact, as soon as I'm done with my training, I'd like to go back and get some modeling going again.

I'll bet you don't go to the cops you work with and talk about your modeling experience, right? You might be laughed at. Or am I wrong?

Actually, you're right. One of my coworkers did find out that I did some modeling, and he spread it around. I've been the laughing stock, and I've gotten a few nicknames. Fabio, Hollywood, whatever. I kind of laugh and let it go. It's nothing major. It's not going to hurt me. But a lot of the guys are into this macho stuff. "Models – a lot of them are gay." I'm, like, "Well, they are – but so what?" I don't have a problem. I'm comfortable with my sexuality. In fact, I can tell you another story.

Go!

About a year ago, I was kind of interested in doing some dancing or some stripping. This is kind of weird, because *this* cannot go back to law enforcement because that stuff nobody knows. But, yeah. You can make a lot of money stripping. So a bunch of friends and I went down to this gay bar. I have no problem with heterosexual, homosexual, anybody. A person's a person. So we went down to this bar in a big city about 100 miles from here, and they had an amateur night – a chance for members of the audience to come up on stage and do a strip dance. So I went up there, did my thing, and I was approached by one of the professional strippers. He gave me a business card and said, "You did pretty good. Are you interested in doing more of this?" I said, "I don't know. We'll see." I gave him a call a couple of weeks later, and he said, "Yeah. We'll set up an interview." I went in and he said, "You could be pretty good." So I did that a couple of times at that bar and made a lot of money. He wanted me back, but I had to stop for a little bit because of my work schedule as a cop. Basically what I did is, I stripped in a g-string at a gay club! I also stripped at a smaller bar in the back.

Was the audience mainly gay men in that back bar?

Growing Up Male In America

>Yup. That's where I stripped, too. I guess you only live once. You might as well try different options, because you never know.

Well, I'd like to come back to your modeling and stripping a bit later, but is there anything further that you want to say that we haven't covered? Here you are, approaching your mid-20s. Are there some things about your feelings or your fears, frustrations or successes that we haven't touched upon?

>I just think that through my experience, I'm finding out – going through the early 20s – that it's kind of a tough period in life. You're basically getting exposed to the real world. I kind of feel like I'm in the middle. I'm treated by adults like I'm still a young punk, but I'm treated by the younger generation kind of like, "You're getting old." So basically you're in the middle, being thrown each way. Nobody will really accept you until you're closer to their age. I feel like I'm an adult. I have a secure job. I'm making payments. I live with my parents, but I'm still making adult decisions. But I think it's kind of a difficult time right now. Another frustrating sort of thing is my career in law enforcement: I'm 23 and the youngest guy in my department. The other guys kind of think, "Hey, he's just a boy."

You know, when I asked where you live, you said, "I live with my dad." And you did say earlier in the interview that your dad is probably your best friend. I'm curious to know something about your mother.

>I have a really good relationship with her, too. Very open. When I'm down, she's always there to help me out. I consider her almost my best friend, too. It's just maybe my dad and I get along just a tad bit better because we're both males. We both go through the same thing physically. We relate to each other. But, yeah, my relationship with my mother is good, too.

Why, at your age, do you live at home? Is that too personal?

>Not really. I'm asked that all the time. I chuckle every time I hear it. I don't know. I get along with my parents so well, and they're gone a lot. They're in their late 40s, but they're just like little kids. They're going out with their friends, having a good time. They have a camper and spend time at a place about two hours away from here. I can come home, and it's almost like I live by myself. I can bring friends, girls, whatever. I've got the freedom. If the freedom wasn't there or if I had to be home at a certain time, I probably would move out.

It's also cheaper, too. Or do they charge rent?

>No, they don't charge rent. [Laughs] Actually, I did move out for two years when I went to college to earn my law-enforcement degree. At that time I was kind of struggling financially, trying to pay for school. My parents did help me out with rent and car insurance. I just bought a brand-new truck. That's kind of my rent payment right there. It's kind of spendy. I would just like to start saving some money now. It's not like I intend to live with my parents until I'm 30,

Interview 14

but my parents don't have a problem with it at all. I help around the house. I'm not a burden on them and they're not on me, so I feel content.

Well, I'm going to write them a letter and say that it's about time they start charging you rent! [Laughter]

I talk a lot about sex in these interviews, and I think that's because sex is such a big part of what makes us who we are. I heard somewhere that men think about sex about every 12 seconds or something. And women less, I guess. Did your dad tell you anything about sex?

I learned a little bit from my dad, probably when I was 13 or 14. Just your general talk. My brother and I and my dad. It wasn't too much in depth.

So it wasn't a formal thing. Just kind of casual.

Right.

Did he seem embarrassed?

A little bit, yeah.

When you have kids, are you going to do it the same way, or are you going to improve on the technique?

I won't know until I get there. [Laughs] I'll just have to wing it.

You said that when you were a teenager you had pretty serious acne. Were you working out with the weights pretty heavily at that time? Did you ever take any steroids or any "enhancers" like that?

I've never taken any steroids.

Let's get back to the stripping and the modeling stuff, now. I'm curious about what motivated you to do it. Let's talk modeling first. Did somebody approach you, or did you just decide you would like to try it some time? And how did you feel when you were having a shoot? How did it make you feel?

The last couple of years, I've had a lot of compliments as far as, "You're pretty decent looking. You're handsome" or whatever. A lot of people asked me if I'd ever thought about modeling. This was about a year, year and a half ago. I was at a concert, and some people from a modeling agency were there. Just out of curiosity, I talked with them for a little bit. I filled out an information form. I didn't think anything more about it. I had nothing to lose. A few days later, they called me back.

Did you have a photo of yourself to attach?

At that time, no. I just filled out the information form.

And they remembered you?

Yeah. I think they wrote some comments on the form After a couple of days, a guy called back and told me to come in, so I went. They looked at me and

Growing Up Male In America

interviewed me, and they said I had potential, really good potential. I didn't really know a whole lot about the business, and I thought, "Well, we can try it and see what happens." I did that, and I liked it. It was a little bit stressful at times, being in front of people and the main center of attention. I got to meet a lot of new people, new friends. I haven't done any more with the modeling in the last five months, but once I get done with my training here in law enforcement, I'd like to go back. What happened is just before I got into this intensive law-enforcement training, there were some modeling auditions in the four major cities – LA, Dallas, Miami and New York – and each city was looking for a different kind of person. I was doing a photo shoot and the head person approached me, and she wanted me to do a runway for her. I did that, and I did a reading for her, and she liked me and my physique. And I got an offer to go to Miami for five days to try to get a contract out in a bigger city.

Did you go?

I did not go. At times I wish I had gone to Miami, but it was a little spendy. You had to fork up some money as far as plane tickets and hotels. But they had everything set up for me to go. It was at the end of July, which was conflicting with my training. Pretty much this whole summer has been shot for me. I'm bouncing around, and I can't really make plans because I don't know my schedule with the law-enforcement training. So as soon as I get this done, I would like to go back and give modeling a shot and see how far I can make it.

Has your face or body appeared in anything, like in a print ad?

I have composite cards on the way. But, no, I'm not in a print ad yet. I've been offered several jobs. I just haven't gone through with them.

Did they ever offer to photograph you nude?

Not nude, but shirt off.

Swimsuit, maybe?

Yeah.

Okay. Now let's get to that stripping episode. Now, that was about a year ago at a gay bar?

Yup. I danced several times, but the first couple of times it was just amateur nights.

That's where they're up on the stage and they pick you out of the audience.

Yeah. They had their drag queens up there. What you do is, you take off your shirt and stand by the rail. And they'll pick five or six guys, and you strip down to your boxers and try to get the attention of the crowd. The first time I did marvelous. I made almost 60 bucks. The crowd went wild, and it was a good night and I liked the attention. It was real fun. I got to go backstage and talk with the drag queens. That was a lot of fun.

Interview 14

Now, you made money. That's tips, I assume.

Yeah.

And people in the audience are shoving money into your shorts?

Yeah.

And that was okay with you?

That was okay by me.

Mainly women?

No. Mainly men. There were only a few women.

You went to the gay bar with five or six friends? Any women, or just men?

I think there was one woman.

Were you dating the woman you're dating now, at that point?

No.

Does she know anything about that chapter in your life?

Yup.

What does she think about that? [Laughter]

She doesn't really like it that much. Like the first time I did it was amateur night. She wasn't there, but I told her about it later. She was kind of shocked. So we had a discussion about that.

Discussion – that sounds heavy.

Yeah. She threw out her views and I told her mine.

What was she afraid of? Too many gay men paying attention to you?

That wasn't an issue. It was just that ... how did she say it? That I was being used as a sex toy or ...

Object.

Right.

The way women usually say they feel.

Right. That my body was being exposed as an object.

Or you were being exploited? Now, you did that amateur night that one time, or did you go back another time?

I went back I think it was two more times for the amateur nights.

With the same friends, or just by yourself?

The second time I think it was half the original group, and the third time I think ... I was going out with my girlfriend. We were dating, and I took her there.

[355]

Growing Up Male In America

The current girlfriend?

Yeah.

And she saw you perform then. Did she have a different attitude?

She kind of laughed it off, but she didn't want me doing it anymore. But that was the amateur time. She didn't really accept it.

How about the man who hired you?

He was impressed with me. He gave me a free g-string or thong. He said he liked what he saw, and he said, "If you want to do it, go ahead." He gave me the okay for it. He hired me right there.

Did you sign any contract?

No.

And is it a salaried thing?

It's a flat fee that you get, and then you get all your tips. They have 30 or 40 guys who work for the organization. They'll just get two or three guys for a particular night.

And where did you dance? On a stage?

Yeah. There's a stage.

Were you up there for the whole night?

They hire you to dance for three hours. The first hour it's on a big stage in a large room, and the last two hours it's in back in a small room that only men can get into – no women. Two dancers work in the back room. There's the one platform on different levels in front of the big-screen TV. Off to the side, there's a pole with a little stand on it.

Where did you dance?

On both the bigger platform and the small one with the pole.

Here's the thing: You said you have no concerns or doubts about your sexuality. You're a straight man. And yet, in that back room, you're dancing primarily to gay men. It's almost exclusively gay men who are worshipping your body and shoving money into your g-string and sneaking a peek at your cock, I'm sure. And you had no reservations or concerns about that?

No.

What were you thinking about? I mean, you're proud of your body and your good looks. Was it the money?

Yeah, the money was a big thing. But it was just, you know, I was getting a lot of attention at the time, and that was a pretty good feeling. I liked it.

Anybody make dates, or try to?

Interview 14

Yeah.

Did they shove some business cards in your g-string or slip them to you?

Yeah. I had a few of those.

Did you ever say that you were straight? Especially when some of the guys were boozed up a little bit and they might get too aggressive?

Actually, what I did was I told them that I was bisexual. That's what the manager told me to say. Or you can tell the customers that you're gay. It makes your audience like you more if they think you're bisexual or gay. But the manager mentioned to say that, so I just went with the flow.

In the interview, did he ask you about your sexual orientation?

Yeah. He didn't say, "What are you?" He kind of knew. He said, "You might be straight." Actually, he didn't use "straight". He just said, "You kind of appear butch." He said that, and he said, "It doesn't matter. But if the customers ask you, tell them you're bisexual or gay. It tends to help the tips."

I can see if you say you're bisexual, there's something kind of alluring about that. It holds out some possibility for the customer to fantasize about your availability. Did you dance in that back room many times? How many different nights?

Only one time at that establishment, and then a couple other times I danced out of state.

Hired by the same agency?

Yeah.

And they provided you with the costume or the g-string?

Actually, those things are pretty expensive.

For so little, you'd think they wouldn't be.

Right. They're, like, 35 bucks for your starting one, and then they've got flashier ones with sequins. Those are, like, $70. Very expensive. But he liked me, so he gave me my first one free.

Okay. Now, about the time you were dancing in the back room, did your lady friend know about that?

Yup.

Did you tell her ahead of time that you'd be dancing before a gay male audience?

Actually, I told her that I would be going down that night, and she did not know what I would be doing, as far as where. And then afterwards I told her that I had danced in the back bar in front of a gay male audience.

And how was she with that?

I think still, at that point, we weren't actually in a steady relationship. This con-

Growing Up Male In America

versation came up a few times – actually to the point where there were a couple of arguments. Then she started questioning my sexuality. But at that point, before I started going to that gay bar, I heard about it but I never went down there. And I had one friend who did, and he said, "Oh, you know, it's a good time. They serve strong drinks." Which is really good. In fact, the last few times that I went down there, I felt more content, or I have a better time in that gay establishment compared to a straight bar. In a lot of straight bars, you have men trying to be macho, where everybody wants to fight. And in a gay bar, you just want to have a good time. I don't feel the least bit threatened.

I've noticed that a lot of straight people like to go to the gay bars. And yet there are some, I suppose, who might be threatened in some way by being around gay people. That certainly is not your case. But gay people know how to party! Anyway, your being in a gay bar and dancing before an audience of gay men made you feel good. It was ego, and it gave you a sense of gratification. Is that right?

Yeah. There have been a few times in my life where I just want to experience things just to say that I did them. If it goes good, I'll continue doing it. If not, then I'll stop. But at least I've experienced it.

You know, you said earlier that if any of the guys you work with found out that you did some modeling, it might make you in your workplace as a policeman a bit uncomfortable. But if it ever leaked out that you were stripping in a gay club, would this be enough for you to lose your job?

Yeah. It could be.

Really?

Oh, yeah. Something like that. Our sheriff would say it's embarrassing to the department. They'd find some policy, or they would look something up in the book to find a reason to get rid of me.

Did it ever occur to you, at any of the three times you danced, that there might be somebody you knew in the audience? Maybe even somebody you work with, who was in that gay-male bar where you danced?

Yeah. There could have been, but at that time I was kind of frustrated with my job in law enforcement, and I wouldn't have been too disappointed if I lost my job as a law officer.

So you thought, what the hell? What's to lose?

Yeah. Right. I figured I could find another job, I guess.

Okay. Final question: Here you are associating, in a way, with gay men in a gay club. Have you ever had a gay sexual experience?

Nope.

Have you ever had curiosity about it? A fantasy? A thought that it might be sexy?

Yeah, that's passed my mind. I think everybody does. Probably just out of

Interview 14

curiosity. You know, I have wondered what it would be like. I don't really know how to explain it.

Well, I think you probably just did. But have you ever thought that maybe that's a side of your life – this is high speculation, here – that maybe *that's a side of your life that hasn't been explored yet? And maybe if you continued to dance in those kinds of places that the right person might come along and you might just try intimacy with that person?*

I think if it was going to happen, it would have happened before now, but it could be a possibility. As of now, the answer would probably be "no" because I'm in a serious relationship with my lady friend, and I wouldn't want to jeopardize that for anything, be it gay or straight. At this point, once you make that commitment to a relationship, it should be 100 percent. I'm committed to her and our relationship, so that's what I'm looking at right now.

Well, is there anything we haven't touched on? Is there anything else that you want to say?

No, I don't think so. We've pretty well covered everything.

Again, thanks very much for doing this interview. You're a very interesting mix of characteristics. You've got a lot of divergent things happening in your life, and that's very interesting. And you've got many years to go. Who knows what experiences you're going to have?

Postscript – December 2001

This man successfully passed his preliminary probationary critiques and now rides without a supervisor in his squad car. He still wants to pursue modeling and other related activities. His serious romantic relationship with his lady friend ended in October – but they remain friends.

Interview 15

"My brother and my dad no longer talk, and it broke my father's heart."

This man is 28 years old, 5' 7" tall, weighs 150 pounds and has black hair. The interview was conducted on October 18, 2001.

Thank you for being willing to do this interview. Let's start at the beginning. You were born where?

I was born in Connecticut. We moved around a little bit, but I lived there up until about midway through March of my freshman year in high school.

Now, tell me about your siblings.

I have two stepsisters and two brothers. One of them's a half brother, one of them's a full brother. I'm the youngest of the three brothers. The middle brother just turned 30, and the oldest is 36; he's the half brother.

Okay. Well, then, tell me about your parents.

My mom had been married ... she's on her third marriage now. Her first marriage, I wasn't born yet. It ended very quickly. In fact, it ended with my oldest brother being the result of that marriage. He wound up being adopted by my father, who is also my 30-year-old brother's father. And then my parents got divorced when I was nine or 10 years old.

Okay. And then she has married again?

Yeah. They both remarried, so now I have two stepparents.

Wow! That makes family reunions kind of interesting! [Laughter]

Not with each other, no. [Laughter]

Does your mom see her first husband, your father?

Never. They don't talk. It's not like they hate each other, but they're out of each other's lives, and they're happier that way. You know, it's funny. When my mom was first getting separated and divorced from my father, she told me

Growing Up Male In America

that as I sat in bed. My dad came in with suitcases and said to me, "You know, I'm sorry, but I have to go." I started crying. My mom came in after he left, and I told her, "Mom, you're ruining my life." She said it just killed her when I said that. I don't remember saying it.

Well, you were caught up in the emotion of the moment.

Sure. I was nine years old.

Later, about high-school age, you moved from there, right?

In March of my first year of high school, I moved to a little town. My mom's new husband, my stepfather, was a minister, and he was hired to take over this small Episcopal church in a town in Massachusetts. Honestly, I was excited about the move because I was moving to a place where there were a couple of ski mountains within 10 minutes of the house.

Now, some would be intimidated by the smallness of the town.

I've always loved smallness – small colleges, small schools. I need attention. I've always been that guy who's the class clown, who needs to have the attention.

Everybody knows everybody.

Oh, they knew me. My first day at the new school, they were, like, "Oh, you're the new kid." I wondered, "What? How do you know my name already?"

Okay. And you were there through graduation from high school, and then when was the next move?

I graduated in 1991. I applied to a bunch of different colleges, and for some reason my mom really loved a small school in Ohio. The soccer coach there really talked me into it. So I gave it a shot. I went there and stayed there for a long time. [Laughs] I didn't graduate on the four-year plan. Oh, god. I changed my major so many times, and then after that I just took my time finishing up. Like, I actually finished in 1997 with a degree in business management, marketing and economics.

You said the soccer coach kind of lured you there. Did you play soccer the whole time?

Yeah. Sure. I started and played on the varsity team for the first two years, and then the last two years I only played a half year.

Any other sports?

In high school I played every sport. I mean, that's pretty much my MO. I've always been really into sports. I guess it's funny, because my brothers and I were so different. My middle brother, B—, is the artist of the family. He's an amazing guitar player, an amazing creative writer and an amazing artist with his hands, doing anything. He's just got a great knack for it. The oldest brother is the finance guy. He's the number cruncher. He lives in New York. He's hit-

Interview 15

ting the books all day, studying, working, making million-dollar deals and loving it. Me, I'm the jock of the family, so in high school I played varsity basketball, baseball, golf. I think the only thing I didn't do was cross-country and wrestling.

You're how tall?

Five–seven.

Was that a problem?

You know, I've always had the little-man mentality. I've always had something to prove, especially in sports.

Now, you're considering graduate study. Are you thinking of teaching?

Yeah. And I'm thinking of maybe doing a Spanish major also because I know that would make me more marketable, and I'd love to learn the language.

You don't know Spanish? But you're of Hispanic heritage.

Yes.

What word do you prefer to describe your heritage? Hispanic? Latino? Something else?

Someone once asked me what the difference was, and I told him that Latinos can dance. [Laughter]

So there really isn't a difference in the ethnic labels, huh?

No. Not that I know of.

Are both of your parents Puerto Rican?

My father was born in San Juan, and my mom was born in the United States but her parents were born in Puerto Rico. I'm not even sure how they met.

Okay. We'll come back later to some of the details of your early days. Did you land a job right away in your field after you earned your degree in 1997?

Yeah, right out of college, I started managing a restaurant in town. Unfortunately, it was kind of a bad situation to get into because I was their bartender and I was their waiter during college, and then I crossed the line to management. I went from being the fun, happy-go-lucky guy to *that* guy. You know, the guy that when I walked in the room, people stopped talking because obviously they were talking about how to screw over the restaurant. All of a sudden, it's my job not to let people screw over the restaurant. But I had a good time there. Made plenty of mistakes. A word of advice: never sleep with your wait staff. That doesn't go over well. [Laughs] Especially when they have boyfriends.

Did you make a fair amount of money there? Pretty good salary?

By the time I left, they were paying me $400 a week. No benefits, which

Growing Up Male In America

turned out to be a bad move on my part. I had got into a fight with a window and lost, so to this day I'm paying $20 a month to a plastic surgeon for 30-some odd years.

Where did it hit you?

Right here, on my wrist. I have a little Zorro scar. I cut an artery and a nerve and four tendons.

I wonder how many people look at it and say, "Um ... attempted suicide."

Exactly. Especially when I went to treatment. Everyone ... that's what they thought.

And plastic surgery is expensive stuff.

It cost about $7,000. [Laughs] Yeah.

Have you had any other major accidents or injuries or wounds?

You know, I don't have many external scars. I've been pretty lucky, especially with all the sports I play. Right now I'm playing in six football leagues during the week, so I'm constantly playing football, but still no major injuries. I've twisted ankles here and there, but that's about it.

How long did you manage that restaurant?

I only managed there for maybe six months or so, and then I traveled to Texas with a friend. His brother was one of the head honchos at a Holiday Inn out there and I had management experience, so I started managing his kitchen, restaurant and bar.

Now, back to high school. Were you a good student?

Yeah. High school was easy. I never really applied myself. Even in college, I never got an A in college. I always looked at college as a balance – you have your social life and you have your academic life, and I tried to keep them about even. So I partied a lot and I went out a lot, and I did enough to get by in school. My mother is very driven. She's going back for a master's now. She just graduated college at the age of 53. She's an amazing woman. So if anybody in my life had an effect on my academic drive, it would be my mother.

She was, by example, showing that education doesn't stop at a certain point.

Exactly. That – and I never really had her say, "Do this, do that." It was more of a supportive role she played.

Have you ever had any trouble with the law?

Yes. I got a DUI in Ohio and another in Texas. I spent one night in jail in Texas. After spending one night in a smelly, noisy jail, my roommate brought my paycheck over. It was just enough to cover the bail. So then I got out. That's actually what led me to Minneapolis, because both of my brothers had gone through an alcohol treatment facility near the city, and my lawyer told

Interview 15

me, "This judge is going to give you a lot of time unless you show him that you want to get better and that you're taking steps."

That was all happening down in Texas?

Yes.

And so if you took steps and went into treatment, that would be okay with that judge?

Yeah. Now, it's a deferred adjudication, so I was given a probation period of four years, and they let me come to Minneapolis. I chose that treatment facility because it's the best, and I got a good deal because they gave me a family discount, I guess. They gave me half off. I wound up going to intensive treatment for 28 days and have now been in the outpatient program for about 18 months or so.

Now, does this mean you don't drink at all anymore?

I do. You know, it's difficult to explain this to people who are in AA, because automatically they say I'm in denial. Now I'm a social drinker.

Did you ever go through any alcohol withdrawal?

No. I was never *bad* – I was just unlucky. I got pulled over and I got in trouble.

What kind of a drunk are you? A gentle one?

I'm an "I love you" drunk. [Laughs]

And now you're planning to move to the East Coast and start a teacher-education program, right?

Yes. It's a really good, three-year program. But, hey ... what's three years?

And you're going to be involved in something you like, and you do like to learn. Do you get along well with your brother in New York?

Now we do. We could never live together, any of us – all of the brothers. We love each other, we see each other and that's great – but we would drive each other nuts. Little things, like the smallest things that seem so irrelevant – like the way he eats. Little things. You know? We would go crazy – but I love him to death, and we're such better brothers now. He didn't tell me he was my half brother until, I think, I was a junior or senior in high school. My folks didn't want me to treat him differently, growing up. I should have known. I mean, look at me! I'm 5-foot-7 with black hair, and he's over six-feet-tall, blond hair. Now that I know, it doesn't bother me at all. I think it did help us. Maybe it's sad to say, but maybe if I had known earlier, I would have treated him different. I wouldn't have respected his authority as my older brother.

Okay. Well, now, your roots are way back in Puerto Rico. Have you ever been back? Have you ever gone there?

Yeah. We did go there once. Actually, my roots go back to Spain, I found out. I

Growing Up Male In America

was doing some tracing back and it heads back all the way to Spain. I've never been there. But we went to Puerto Rico one time. I was nine years old. My parents were separated, and they were trying to rebuild the marriage, so they took the family and we went. My mom said it was probably the worst time she'd ever had. It was horrible. I had a blast. I mean, I'm a nine-year-old kid. I mean, I was scared to death of the sea urchins. But we got there, and there were a few funny things that happened there.

My folks were trying to work on their marriage. We were staying in this beautiful, lavish hotel, and they had a show one night. Our table was touching the stage. It was right up near the stage. Great for a show. The place was packed. The next thing I know, the dancers come out and they're dancing around topless! Oh, my mom was pissed.

And you're nine.

Yeah. At one point my father leaned over and said to my 17-year-old brother, "It's all right if you have a hardon." [Laughs] Dad was just letting my older brothers know it's all right. And my mom, I mean, was just not happy at all. For me, I was just amazed. You know? I didn't care what the show was about – just bring out the topless women again.

And you were nine years old?

Right. We were only there for, I think, five days. It was wonderful – but my mom didn't think so.

Did the trip work to save the marriage?

No. That strip show was the last straw, actually. We did go visit some family, so that was nice.

Did you feel that there was some commonality that you had? Something in common with these people in Puerto Rico?

No. I still felt kind of foreign. I didn't feel like I belonged, necessarily, because I didn't understand the culture and I was too young to really want to understand it. I was just all about having fun.

And maybe there was that American thing – that we're not like these people.

"You're not a state!"

An arrogance. They're just a possession.

But they're not a state yet. No.

When did you first experience puberty? Were you earlier or later than most other boys your age?

Later. I remember the exact moment. [Laughs] I was going to the bathroom. I think I was 13 years old, and I remember peeing, and I had *one* long pubic hair. It was just one, and it was probably an inch long. One day it just kind of appeared there.

Right above your cock?

It was right above, yeah. I couldn't believe it. Just one. I was psyched. I guarded it!

You noticed that there were other kids who were hairy all over.

Yeah.

Did you ever wonder, "Why am I not developing like so many of my classmates?"

You know, I never really did. I guess I didn't have a whole lot of hairy people around me, besides my father. But in gym class, everyone was about my age, and I was older than most in my class, being born in February. So there wasn't a whole lot of hairy people there.

For some kids, it's a real traumatic time, especially if they're late in developing.

For me it wasn't an issue. I was a very confident kid growing up, and I was kind of a fighter, even though I wouldn't start fights, so I had a reputation as a fighter, but I was friends with everybody. I got that from my father. So I was never worried about being laughed at or made fun of.

Did your dad ever sit you down and say, "Here are the biological facts of birds and bees" – whatever you call it.

No, he didn't. Neither of my parents did. I don't remember how old I was. I remember I was really young, and I had asked my father or my mother something about sex, and they had this look on their face like, "Oh, the moment's here!" And then out of nowhere, my brother says, "Don't worry about it. I'll tell you later." So I learned it from my brothers and movies, really. I did have health classes in school, but that was more of a "hee, hee, hee" – everyone's giggling in class when they say the word penis. So I learned the anatomical portion of it in school, but then the sex portion I learned from movies – soft porn on TV.

Do you remember the first time you masturbated, and did you come or was it just that fantastic feeling of pleasure?

You know, I did, and I do remember. I was living out East. It was probably when I was about 13 or so. I wasn't jerking off in the sense of stroking, but I was rubbing the head of my cock. Like a stick, trying to start a fire. And I remember having the feeling like I was going to pee. It just got really good, and it was the best feeling I've ever had in my life. I do remember it, and I've never had one quite like it.

And did you ejaculate?

Yeah.

Had you ever been told, or did you know what to expect?

Growing Up Male In America

No. I didn't know. I thought I'd pissed all over myself. Then I realized it wasn't urine.

Were you doing this through your clothes, or were you naked?

I was naked. When it happened, at first I was embarrassed because I thought I'd just peed myself. I'm 13 years old, I shouldn't be doing that. But then I put two and two together and realized that that was the best feeling ever, and then I realized what I had heard in school.

Did you go to your brother and talk to him about it?

No, no. I would have been laughed at.

And you wouldn't go to your friends and talk about it.

I had a friend there, and we talked about it.

Was he doing it, too? With you there?

Yeah.

So there you were, two guys, naked, masturbating at the same time. Was it a sleepover?

Yeah. It was just a sleepover night.

A tent out in the back yard?

No. We were in my room. Overnight party. I don't even know how it started. I mean, it's not like we looked at each other and said, "Hey, let's do it."

And what was his response? Did he come, too?

No, he didn't. You know, he was my best friend at the time. I can't even remember his exact response. I know it was nothing mean or there was no fun being made at my expense. But I'm not sure of his exact response, though.

Did you ever talk about it later?

Nope.

That's so typical, isn't it?

Oh, yeah. There was this one kid at school who basically got laughed out of school, had to transfer schools, because he got caught masturbating. It's a mean thing that kids do, but in a way, by making fun of him, they were feeling more manly about themselves and their secret activity. "I don't masturbate." When *everybody* in that school did.

Of course.

Yeah. Exactly. But the thing is they felt better about themselves or took some guilt from themselves by ridiculing this poor guy.

All right. That was your first time. Your very first time, with another male. That's interesting for a straight man. Did you ever have any worry about being thought to

Interview 15

be gay?

No. Because I really didn't know what I was doing. I didn't think of it as a sexual thing until quite some time afterwards, when I realized what had just happened. Up until then, it was just like a foot I was playing with or something. It really didn't seem sexual to me.

Okay. Describe your first sexual experience with a girl.

I was young. I was in sixth grade.

That makes you about 12.

No. Maybe I was in seventh then, because it was after that experience with this buddy of mine, but it wasn't long after. I still wasn't in my full-blown puberty. I was still pretty nervous about the fact that I just had peach fuzz going on. We had gone to my friend's place – me, my friend and these two girls. One of them I was dating *because* she told me she would go to third base with me if I dated her. So we're there and we started fooling around, and we decided we were going to try it. I remember her being very nervous because she told me she had had her period, so she could get pregnant. Well, we started fooling around, and we did give each other oral sex. Then we tried to have intercourse, and it was just painful for both of us. I mean, it was her first time. She was very, very tight, and it just wasn't working. I got, maybe, not even halfway in and we stopped, because it was … I mean, I felt like I was getting my banana peeled. It just wasn't fun at all. So I don't really count that as sex.

Okay. But you did have oral sex.

Yeah. It didn't feel like much. I didn't have an orgasm. To this day, I've never had good oral sex.

I mean, giving it or receiving it?

I actually like going down on women, so that's actually something I enjoy. But I've never had a girl who could satisfy me that way. Anyway, we played around a little bit, but I don't know why it didn't feel like I was getting anything out of it. I guess the pleasure was mostly psychological, knowing we were doing something naughty, something that we probably shouldn't be doing.

The first time I *did* have sex and had an orgasm was maybe my freshman or sophomore year in high school, and I had snuck out and gone over to this girl's house. She was younger than me but more experienced sexually, and she had a great body. I wasn't going there to have sex or fool around with her at all. She was going to do a tarot reading for me – and she seduced me! [Laughs] I'd been taken advantage of! I climb in the window to her bedroom, and she did one of *the* best seduction things at this age that you could have done. She said, "Are you comfortable? Do you want some shorts?" And I go, "Sure. And a t-shirt." Because I was in jeans. So she gave me shorts. I put the shorts on, and with her back to me she takes her shirt off and puts another shirt on. It has no

Growing Up Male In America

armholes, and you can see the outside of her breasts on the side of her shirt, on the side of her body. To me that was just ... I was, like, whoa! This is the best ever! Like I said, I hadn't planned to do anything. We just kind of kicked back on the bed and started telling stories. I remember at one point my hand being on her stomach, and then I leaned over and I was really close to her face, and I remember kissing her. Then it just started. We were having sex. And I remember thinking, "This is the greatest ever." Didn't have a condom on and didn't really care. It didn't seem like a problem at the time. It didn't last that long, obviously, being my first time. It was, I think ... it probably lasted, actually, maybe five minutes, but it was just ecstasy. After it was done, I stayed and we hung out for a little bit, and then I climbed out her window. I remember walking home, smiling the whole way home. Truck drivers driving by and I'm waving and smiling. I was *so* happy, and I wasn't happy because this was a girl I wanted to have as a girlfriend. It was that I just had sex.

That rite of passage.

Yeah. The funny thing is, my brother started dating her shortly afterwards.

Well, very interesting. And from there on, you had sex every chance you could?

Yeah. There was another girl. This was the second girl I'd had sex with. We had had sex a few times. Great body, but she had gone out with someone who was just a putz, and I didn't like him and I couldn't understand why she had dated him. I didn't respect her because she dated this guy. Anyway, she and I were having sex at my buddy's cabin, and I remember thinking, "I'd rather be home jerking off right now." I was just not into it. And I remember I faked an orgasm with her that night, just so it would end. I'm sure I probably didn't fool her because I think she would probably know.

Okay. Moving along. I don't know what Hispanic people are supposed to look like, but I'm not sure you fit my expected image.

I don't.

And then if your half brother is blond ...

Nobody ... my father doesn't even look Hispanic, and he was born in San Juan. My mom doesn't. Besides being darker skinned in the summer, being more apt to get tan, he's lighter than you are right now. Nobody really looks it. I've been called Italian and Jewish many times. No one ever guesses I'm Puerto Rican.

So you've never had to suffer any negative remarks?

No. In fact, I've been quite proud of my heritage my whole life, and I've been willing to tell people. I want people to know. That's why I started pronouncing my name in the Hispanic way.

Okay. Next question: Are you circumcised?

Interview 15

Yes.

Is it typically not done among Hispanic people?

All of my relatives are, I think.

Do you ever sneak a glimpse at other guys in the locker room or at the urinals or anything, just to do a little comparison?

Sure.

And you're totally free admitting that. Would you say that the length of your cock is about less than normal or normal or larger than?

You know, I guess I didn't really know, because it's almost like watching hair grow. You see your hair every day. You don't realize it until someone else comes up to you and says, "Well, your hair's getting long." You don't really realize it. And for me, I found out afterwards from women that I was larger. Not women who I was just sleeping with, but women who had heard about me. That was the greatest thing in the world because word of mouth was awesome. You know? I mean, for me. Like, one of the bartenders where I worked came up to me, and I guess my girlfriend had bragged about my penis size, and she said to me, "I heard you're hung." And it was great because I got to sleep with her afterwards, too.

What is it? "Your legend precedes you."

Yes. [Laughs] But then there's the pressure – you've got to live up to it.

Have you ever measured it? Most people do. Erect?

You know, I did in high school. How old was I? I don't even know – it was probably freshman year. It wasn't enormous, it was thick. Like I remember, I was like, maybe, six and a half or seven inches. Seven inches, I think, but I know it was two thumbs wide.

Are your thumbs normal or less than normal? [Laughs]

There you go! I do remember that my size was something that I always had confidence in. I've had friends with small cocks and I've seen how it's affected them.

Have you ever had any fears of sexual dysfunction, or have you ever had a time when you couldn't get it up?

Yeah, it has happened to me. I was with this girl who I had wanted to be with for a long time, and she was just amazing and gorgeous. I had her down in the basement and she was playing with me or whatever, and we're ... I was scared because I wasn't getting it up right away. And I'm thinking, "This is the most beautiful woman I've been with. What are you doing? Wake up! What's your problem?" So I was scared because now, you know, I was scared I wouldn't get another chance. So what I did was I just went down on her and I just started doing oral sex on her for a long time, and while I'm doing that I was playing

Growing Up Male In America

with myself, trying everything possible.

Still nothing?

It was closer to a semi. It was still really not there. So then I just came up and started to rub it on her, and finally got inside of her and then it perked up. But, yeah, after that happened, though, I've had a reoccurring fear. It hasn't happened again, but I'm scared that the fear itself is going to make it happen. It's like a self-fulfilling prophesy, I think. So I think, you know ... I'm sure it's going to happen again. I have no doubt in my mind that it will happen again. I'm just scared that it will happen again at ... I guess there's never really a right time.

No. And it's all in your mind.

The greatest line I heard one time – I don't know if it was a movie line or something – a guy couldn't get it up with this girl, and he says to her, "This never happens when I'm by myself!" [Laughs] But women take it as an insult. Like they take it, like, "Oh, I'm not doing something right. What can I do to do this right?"

Tell me, what is it about straight guys going to gay bars? Why does that happen?

Why do straight guys go to gay bars? I went because I wanted to dance. I've actually been hit on more by men than I have by women. I'm not intimidated by that, but in the same sense I'm afraid I might give off the wrong sign because I don't know what the signs are. I'm friendly with everybody, and I talk with everybody. If I had a serious girlfriend, I would be more apt to go to a gay bar, but I don't know what kind of message that sends.

Incidentally, gay guys coming on to straight guys is a good exercise for the straight guys who get hit on because they can see then what a woman feels like when a guy is just overbearingly pursuing her and she has already said, "I'm not interested, thank you." And you see what women have to go through a lot.

Right. I went to a party, maybe a month ago. A buddy of mine and I were invited to this party, and so we went. We show up there, and my buddy and I were the only straight guys there. All of the women were beautiful, but they were lesbians. We had a blast! We were, like, the token heterosexual guys. We had a group of gay guys around us talking, and we were like guinea pigs. They were asking us, "Well, what do you think about this?" "What's your perspective on this?" And I was joking with this one guy. He kept telling me, "I can't believe you're single." And then he said, "You know, you can be straight and still have a gay experience, and it doesn't make you gay." And I looked at him and said, "That's the worst line I've ever heard in my life." [Laughter] And he just started dying laughing. And I mean, I'm not intimidated in situations. I actually loved it – as long as people know the boundaries. Because you're right, I think – it is a taste of how women feel.

Interview 15

And it's healthy these days. I'm not sure that three, four generations ago, the straight guys would even think about going into a gay bar. But as one person put it, it's the best music and the best lights and the strongest drinks and the best place to dance.

The best dancers.

That first time in the gay bar, were you uncomfortable at all?

I was a little uncomfortable. I was with a good friend's fiancée.

Okay. So she was the only woman in your group?

Yeah. I wound up standing by her most of the night and talking with her. I went out and danced a little bit, but I'm not much of a dancer. And again, I didn't want to give the wrong message out there on the dance floor and then have to some guy think I might be flirting with him. I'm not good at rejecting people. I'm much better at being rejected than actually rejecting someone, because … maybe it's an ego problem that I think, like, I'm going to hurt their feelings.

Had you ever seen that many gay people in the same room before?

No. I was definitely in the minority.

That's an interesting feeling, too. And you probably realized that the whole stereotype thing has gone totally out the window, and the men are not all effeminate little wood sprites.

Oh, god, no.

There are some very handsome, some very manly men there – and some very manly women, too! [Laughter] And some of the lesbians are very beautiful women.

Absolutely.

And some of them can be damned ugly, both gay men and lesbians! But you got over your discomfort at being in a gay atmosphere as the evening wore on?

Uh … no. You know, I really didn't. Actually, I was sitting there, hovering in a corner. I wasn't my normal self, where I'm off talking with everybody and having a good time. Just carefree. I hung out and I laughed with my buddy's girlfriend for a while, and I guess I made it to the dance floor a little bit, but not much.

And if you don't dance, then there you're standing – looking like you're looking for socializing. Was there any fear of, like, "God, I'm going to have to take a pee, now. And who's going to be in the men's toilet and looking? Will I be an object to somebody?"

Oh, yeah. Because that's the stereotype. That's where you get approached. It happened to my friend, when I was living in Ohio. A guy came right up to him at the urinal in a straight bar and reached around and grabbed him. Yeah. It happened to me before. I've been hit on in the men's john. Not at this gay

Growing Up Male In America

place, but in a bathroom in a straight bar. It just seems weird, but like I said, I'm not violent towards anybody. I just tell them, "No thanks. I'm not interested."

You've never had a gay sexual experience?

No.

Have you ever been curious about sex with another man?

No.

What are you – straight?

[Laughter] It's a problem – right?

Now, let's get to just quick-response items.

Fire away!

What are your greatest fears?

Let's see. Fears. I know I had a fear of acceptance. That was a major fear. Fear of acceptance has always been my biggest fear. I don't know if it was a competition with my brothers. I've always had a fear that people won't trust me, and I don't know why. But it's something that I take quite seriously, and if I'm being completely honest – which I normally am – I really get upset when people don't take it as being completely honest or question my motives on it. My biggest fear, though, definitely, is fear of acceptance.

Did you get into fights quite a bit in junior and senior high school?

Yes, but they weren't fights that I started. My father gave me some wonderful advice about fighting. He and I were walking one day after I'd been suspended from school for fighting, and my father ... you know ... I don't want to portray him as not being loving, because he's just full of love. But he took me aside that day and said, "I know that you get into some fights at school. I don't want you to fight. I don't like that. But if anybody ever hits you – and I don't care how big they are – and you don't hit them back, then I'm going to hit you twice as hard when you come home." And he was, you know, trying to teach me a lesson to stand up for myself in the face of something that seems insurmountable – something, someone that's just so big. And I think it was a broader lesson than I took it for at the moment. At the moment, I thought it was all about fighting, but as I got older I realized it was about *life*. About having life stare you in the face and seeming like you have an impossible problem in front of you and being able to look at it in the face and tackle it anyhow and go after it.

You seem to have a great respect and love for your dad.

I do.

Do you think now ... skip a generation, and you're going to have kids of your own

Interview 15

some day. Will you use that same technique on them?

Wow! That's a tough one. You know, one thing I'm sure of is I'm going to spank my child. I don't know if I will or not act the same way or use that same lesson as my dad used. I have a lot of love for my father. It actually got even more intense when I saw the pain caused by my brother. My brother and my dad no longer talk, and it broke my father's heart. But my brother did that because a psychiatrist told him that a lot of the things that happened to him throughout his life were because of my father. "Oh, it must go back to your childhood and your father." And it was just bullshit. So my brother cut off my father completely and even changed his last name back to my mother's maiden name. I don't even talk to my father about my brother because it hurts. I see the pain on my father's face.

In terms of sex education, are you going to sit your kids down and talk about the birds and the bees?

Most definitely. I got this from my mother. My mother was the director of family planning in Massachusetts, and she was so open. Anything I had to talk to her about sex, I had no problems. Anything. STDs. *Anything*, whatsoever. I could call her and ask her. I was never shy, and I never worried about her laughing at me. I'll definitely be open with my kids about it just because I have so much respect for my mother and the way she handles that situation. I never really talked to my dad about it too much.

I wonder if that's a male thing, too – that it's difficult for the guy to talk to his son about these rather personal matters.

You know, I think it might be that way. I think it would be more difficult for me to talk to my father.

When you were a little kid, did you call your dad "Daddy" or "Father" or what?

No, I never called him Father. It changed over the years. I think it started out Daddy and went into Dad – but now it's Pop.

Pop. Okay. Was it difficult for you to change from Daddy? Because Daddy sounds like a little-kid's word.

You know, I don't recall. It just happened on its own. It's not like I ever said, "Hey, wait a minute. I'm 14 years old. It's got to be Dad!"

Well, another question: What causes loneliness or depression? What can trigger that for you, and what do you do about it?

My depression? You know, I've never had too many bouts with depression, and anything I've had has been very small. It never lasted very long.

Okay. Moving along to another question. What have you done that most embarrassed you?

I think my embarrassments stem from how I embarrass my family, the things I

Growing Up Male In America

did. When I was arrested for drug use and for alcohol, like when I was getting my two DUIs. That embarrassed me because I saw that my family was embarrassed about it. Otherwise, I don't get embarrassed too often. I laugh at myself a lot. That's the way I stay low stress.

Relative to this embarrassment thing and my parents: One time my oldest brother was in trouble. I'm not sure if it was a possession charge or what, but it had to do with drugs. He was in jail. I remember being really young, maybe 14, and I remember sitting on my mom's lap and we cried for a good hour. I know she stayed up all night crying. I promised myself that night that I would never do that to her. And then I did, when I got my DUIs and when I got that drug charge in Texas. That was the first thing that I thought of when I got arrested. "Oh, my god, I'm going to make my mom cry over the same thing I swore I would never." It's funny that I remembered that. That was one of the first things I thought of. Even while I was in that jail cell in Texas and still high on the drugs.

How do you define happiness?

Happiness for me is love and fearlessness. Not having to be afraid. My biggest fear is not being accepted. You know what gives me real happiness? I'll do a kind deed and never take credit for it. Like I'll do something for someone that they don't even know I did, because then there's no vanity. It's not about me taking credit. "Hey, I did that for you." You know? It has nothing to do with me then, and it's done for the right reasons.

Organized religion is not such a big deal to you, but some of the basic tenets are?

Yeah. Just, I think, having a higher power. A lot of that comes from AA, too. Just knowing that you're not the center of the universe. To me, that's been a big part of my life as far as growing up, though, in a church with my mother and my stepfather being the minister. I always knew I wasn't the center of the universe, even though I liked to pretend I was. But it also gave me more compassion for people, because I'd see the work that my parents did within the church for strangers and didn't expect anything in return. But the people were always so grateful and so genuine that it taught me compassion.

Okay. The next question is: How you would define masculinity?

My idea of masculinity is confidence, self confidence. Anyone who can be self confident can be masculine. It's not about how big you are, how rough and tumble you are. It's not how high you can jump or how many women you've had sex with. One of the guys who was at that gay bar that night is one of the most masculine guys I know just because he's so confident in who he is. He was at this bar dancing with all these gay guys and his wife's at home. It's not like he has any doubts about his sexuality. He knows he's straight. And his wife knows he's straight.

Do you consider yourself handsome?

Interview 15

You know, I do consider myself handsome, but I've gotten it from how other people treat me and act towards me and the women I've slept with. It's unfortunate, too, because I wish I were more confident in myself to sit here and say I'm a very handsome person. I've met some women who I've not really been attracted to and then I talked to them for a half hour or an hour, and all of a sudden they're beautiful because of who they are and how they act. I think a lot of that has to do with who you are inside and how comfortable you feel with who you are.

Do you ever pose to attract women?

Oh, yeah. I was a poser for sure. I was a big-time poser. I was the guy who had to make sure ... I didn't know where to put my hands, so I put them in my pockets. I'm a big pocket hand putter. I always have my hands in my pockets because it just looks better than me standing around not knowing what to do with my hands. Yeah. So, yeah. I would pose all the time, and I would shoot a lot of pool because that's how I thought I looked the best. That's what my ex-girlfriend told me. She goes, "Man, you look hot when you're bending over, shooting pool." So I'd shoot pool because that was another pose for me. Yeah. Because it means acceptance for me. I love to know that people accept me. And if posing gets me a little closer to that acceptance, well then I'm posing.

Okay.

You know, it's funny. All these questions seem to come back to self confidence, and how to build a healthy self confidence. I thought I knew everything when I was 18, but now I'm not so sure. My stepfather has had a total of nine heart bypasses, and he just had a stroke. We sat down recently and just talked about life and death. I asked him, "What can you tell me now?" He said, "The one thing I'll tell you is you'll regret the things you don't do more than the things you do. So live life. Live life fearlessly, and do it." I loved that quote in *Tuesdays With Morrie*. I can't think of it right away, but I'll bet you know the one I'm thinking of. I know it ends like, "Dance as if no one is watching. Love as if you've never been hurt." That's a great quote. Basically it's just live life and don't live it for someone else.

It's so wonderful. And I could offer you some advice, too: Don't think because you're old you have to stop living. You know? Do you cry often?

Yeah. It's funny. I cry at movies, and the last one I cried at was *The Sixth Sense*. That will make me cry every time. It's the scene where they're in the car, and he tells his mom about her dad, who saw her dance and then he's so proud of her, I lose it. Yeah. But not just at movies. I cry ... yeah, I do cry. It's never in public, though. It's always by myself. I guess it comes back to the confidence thing. You know? I cry over a lot of things. I cry when I'm happy, too. And I cry when I'm thankful. I told you I'm not hugely religious in the sense that I don't go to church, but I do pray almost every night and I don't ask for anything. I'm thankful in my prayers. And I'll cry if I see other people hav-

Growing Up Male In America

ing pain, more than anything. If I see other people getting hurt. I don't cry out of frustration for myself.

Are you going steady with somebody right now?

No, we were, and then she moved away. We tried long distance, and it didn't work. I'm a hands-on boyfriend. I need the attention, you know? It just didn't work. And now I'm trying to avoid any kind of relationship until I move.

When do you move, again?

Next month. To the East Coast.

So between now and then, you'll just find a little sexual recreation here and there, right?

Absolutely.

Thanks very much for sitting for this interview. I really enjoyed meeting you and getting to know you better, and I'm glad you were as forthcoming as you were.

It was a pleasure.

Postscript – December 2001

This man has moved to the East Coast and plans to begin his graduate studies in teacher education in the fall.

Interview 16

"You don't need a permit to be a parent."

This man was 22 years old when the interview was conducted on August 7, 2000. He is 6 feet tall, weighs 175 pounds, and has a trim, athletic build and brunette hair.

Thanks for doing this interview. I appreciate it. Tell me a little bit about yourself, something about your background.

All right. I grew up in Minnesota in a distant suburb of Minneapolis. My dad was the principal of the junior high, and my mom was a secretary at the senior high. So I was trapped no matter where I went. [Laughs] We all had my dad as principal. I'm the youngest of three. My sister and my brother had him, too.

Was it difficult?

No! It was great. And I got along with everybody all the time, so it wasn't really a big problem. I had a lot of friends who were in ninth grade when I was in seventh grade, so it never was a problem, really. And then when I was in ninth grade, I had a geometry class, and dad was the teacher. So I had him for a teacher in my ninth-grade year. And that went great, too, because he was friends with everyone in my grade

Do you get along pretty well with your dad today?

Yup. Get along with him great.

Your folks are still married?

Yeah.

What's the span of years between you and your siblings?

My brother is seven years older. He's 29, and he just got married this summer. And then my sister is 33 right now.

Were you a surprise for your folks, coming along seven years after your brother?

Yeah. Actually, my dad had a vasectomy. They couldn't decide if they wanted

Growing Up Male In America

another kid or not, and they decided that they didn't. My dad had a vasectomy, and two weeks later my mom found out she was pregnant with me. The immaculate conception. [Laughs] Yeah, I think she conceived a week before he had the vasectomy.

Oh, I see what you mean. I thought it was maybe one of those failed vasectomies.

No. He had it, it worked, but he got it about a week too late. [Laughs]

I assume you always felt confident that your parents loved you when you were a little kid?

Yeah.

You never had any fears?

I had a fear of my dad, but it wasn't a fear like a physical fear. It was just, "You don't want dad to get pissed." I remember getting spanked once. I got spanked one time, and he said that's the only time he would spank me. I was little, you know. But I cried really hard. That's the only physical contact I've had with my dad like that. I mean, being a principal as he was, it wasn't something that he did on a regular basis. I still fear him, in a way. [Laughs] You know what I mean?

Well, I read somewhere that fear and respect are very close.

Yeah. Oh, it's a total respect.

Which parent did you prefer or feel closer to – your mother or your dad?

Growing up, it was my mom. Because she was the softie, and I could get a lot of things past mom and she looked the other way. A lot of the time. If I got in trouble when dad wasn't home, she'd say, "You know, you shouldn't do that." But she never told dad pretty much anything I did. But as I've grown older, I respect my dad more than most people that I've ever met. So it's kind of revolved around. Because when I was growing up, sometimes I just hated my dad. We'd get in huge arguments over geometry. It was just ridiculous. But then it kind of rolled over, where the fear turns into respect, just like you were saying. But, yeah, now I go home and can have real conversations with my dad.

You have friends. How does your growing up differ from theirs – if at all?

The guy I roomed with hated growing up. His mom and dad were divorced, and he hated his stepmom. So, I mean, she was just an extreme bitch. And we all thought she was, too. But then he didn't like his dad at all, either, because he was so stern. But now they're getting real close. Just the other day a good friend and I were talking about parents, and he said, "You know, he's my father, but I don't consider him my dad." That's the way he was, growing up.

Must be kind of sad.

I've always kind of thought his dad was an ass, too.

Interview 16

Well, I guess not everybody's meant to be a parent, so there are some failures out there.

You don't need a permit to be a parent.

Do you remember - back in nursery school, kindergarten, first grade, whatever – that there were the kids who were in the in crowd and others in the out crowd? I mean, do you remember if there were cliques?

I think there always were.

Were you aware that some kids didn't have the right kind of clothes to wear, fads and fashions?

I don't remember so much of that in early elementary, like the little kids, but later the kids were already conscious of wearing certain jeans or whatever. I remember in fifth grade, everyone started wearing bandanas on their heads, you know? You couldn't wear hats in school but you could wear these bandanas, so people started wearing them. Then all of a sudden too many kids were wearing them and then no one was wearing them except these other kids, right? And then I remember getting my very first pair of designer jeans. I had the first pair in the whole school, and people were, like, "Oh, what are they?" And then a teacher bought the exact same pair, and then all of a sudden everyone was wearing them.

Yeah. I always felt sorry for the kids who didn't have the money, those who couldn't afford designer jeans or the "in" fashions of the time.

Yeah. I remember poor kids getting picked on, though. I remember one of my friends, actually doing that. Seventh grade. He was just beating on a kid because the kid was dirt poor. And I blew up in the hall one day. Almost had a physical fight with this jerk. I asked, "What right do you have? So who cares if he's poor?" And this was one of my best friends. Still am friends with him. But I'm, like, "You know, you have no right to pick on this kid just because he's poor." And he backed off.

Aren't you proud of yourself for that? I mean, that took some courage.

Yeah. I've done some bad things. But, you know, I try to make up for some things I've done.

Do you do that a lot? Do you find yourself coming to the defense of people if you see injustice out there?

I try, but on certain occasions you can't really say anything.

Do you ever get a ribbing from friends who say, "Ah, don't be so easy. Don't be so willing to go out and help people. It's their business."

Ah, sometimes. Not really, though. I try to hang around with people who are pretty open-minded.

You were raised Lutheran?

Growing Up Male In America

I was confirmed Lutheran. I do not consider myself Lutheran now. I once thought of myself as a Transcendentalist.

Interesting. You've read Henry David Thoreau?

I've read some. And Walt Whitman.

Whitman and Emerson?

And Kant.

Oh. Good old Emanuel.

Yeah. But there's not many today. I mean, it was, like, nature's religion. I always thought of that as being a better path to follow.

Speaking of nature, are you an outdoorsy-type guy?

Yes, I am. I like fishing, camping, traveling.

Do you enjoy being by yourself?

Yes, sometimes. I need some time to just close myself away. Every day. I like to have some personal time.

Ever get into meditation?

When I'm camping I like to sit up at night and stare at nature, and that is the closest I come to touching an inner peace, so I guess that's like meditation. You finally get in touch with yourself again.

Do you ever get lonely?

It's always good to have a conversation with someone, but I mean, I don't really feel lonely ever. Not lonely.

Okay. There are some people who cannot be alone, and they just have to babble all the time.

I know. Those people run their yakkers all the time. That's why I've got to go back to my parents' place every couple of weeks. They have seven acres, and I sit on the porch or sit on the patio and watch the birds. I've done that my whole life. [Laughs]

Did any ministers have much of an impact on you?

Yes. This one was actually a great guy. He was a half-time Lutheran pastor and a half-time psychologist. So I actually went to him and got hypnotized a couple of times for sports. For baseball. Just to get totally focused. I've had some really good conversations with him. I had a really good friend who died when I was 15. She died from leukemia, and that's when my faith just went to hell. Because she was, like, an angel. She was the perfect girl. Everyone liked her. The nicest girl ever. And she died of leukemia.

And you asked, "Why?"

Interview 16

Yeah. "Why?" But then, this minister and I talked about that. He never pushed religion at me. He just always asked me what I thought. He was more of a thinker. The Catholic religion scares me more than the Lutheran religion does.

It sounds like this minister had his head screwed on right. He was doing what you should do – from my point of view – and he wasn't pushing faith down your throat.

Yeah. He officiated at my brother's wedding. My brother was the youth director at our church for two or three years, but since then he's completely fallen out of the church. He thought religion was a sham. It's like a contest in our town, between our church and the Catholic church. Who's going to be bigger? "We need more money to build this, build that." Yet this minister friend is still totally cool with my brother about his choice. He sees it the same way.

Well, you got through elementary school without too many scars. And you got into junior high. It's about then that your body is beginning to change. When did this happen for you? When did you start getting hair on your body and so on?

I remember it was about fifth grade. My buddy was getting dark hairs on his legs. I knew what was happening and saw it happening and stuff. I think I probably was a little ahead of a lot of kids. Like, the end of sixth grade. But seventh grade, I was definitely hit full blown. I mean, I was hairy!

Seventh grade, that makes you about 13?

Yeah. I turned 13 right at the beginning of seventh grade. But, I mean, I'd started puberty before that. But by the time I was in seventh grade, I was already there.

That's always an odd age. Some haven't even begun puberty, and others are there already. Apparently you were ahead of the pack. Did you observe any feelings of insecurity or shyness that some of the kids might have had in the locker room?

Yeah. A little bit. But you see, our school was weird because when I was in sports in junior high, no one ever showered. But I would occasionally, you know, and then in ninth grade I showered all the time.

Why was that, that they didn't shower?

I'm sure kids were embarrassed. Yeah. I'm sure they were.

All right. You're about 13. You say you started getting involved in sports a lot about this time, too?

Well, I was in sports the whole time growing up. I grew up on sports. But that's, like, the age when I really, like, busted out. I was dominating in basketball. Football, especially. You know, when you're a little bit ahead, it doesn't take much. But I had my head on backwards a lot, too.

Did you get any instruction about sex from your dad?

No. It was never talked about. Ever. I mean, I remember my one conversation about sex with my dad, growing up, was, "You know, if you're ever going to

Growing Up Male In America

have sex, you better wrap that thing up." That was it. And the marijuana conversation? It was, "You know, I don't think marijuana is really that bad for you. But I think it leads to other drugs and I know other drugs are bad for you, so you can't do other drugs." And that was once. That's it, growing up. That's the only two things I ever heard about sex and drugs.

Did your mother ever talk to you about sex?

Never once. Still doesn't. Never had a sex conversation with my mom, ever. But I think my dad just assumed that I was supposed to figure this all out, you know? But the reality is that you're totally lost. And when you're pumped with testosterone, you don't even know what you're going through. You have no idea.

Yeah. Like your erections popping up at the worst possible times! Did you have wet dreams?

A couple.

Really. How did you feel? Do you remember how you felt about waking up and noticing the discharge?

I remember the first time. I actually came, and it wasn't a nocturnal emission. It was in sixth grade at a girl's house. I remember biking over there, and we were fooling around. You know, just kissing. You know, like, I remember Bill Cosby talking about how you kiss and kiss and neck and kiss so much your lips are chapped and bloody. [Laughs] Because you know you're supposed to do something, but you're not really sure what that "something" is at all. Yeah. I remember that. And all of a sudden it was, like, "Whoa, whoa. What?" You know, you're all excited and all of a sudden, "Whoa!" And then I had to bike home in sweat pants. [Laughs]

Did you tell her what had happened?

No. It was, like, "Hey, I've gotta go."

And that was your first ejaculation? I mean, you hadn't masturbated before this?

No, no. That's when I started to masturbate.

Usually, for many guys, it's the other way around. How old were you when this first experience happened?

I was 12 years old, at the end of sixth grade.

How many times a day did you masturbate?

When I first started? I remember the first time I did it, I did it right away. And I was done. And I went back to my room and did it again right away. I was, like, "What the fuck?" [Laughs] The first time it was just, like, "Oh, my god!" You're just, like, amazed at the great feeling!

Do you remember any feelings of guilt about masturbating?

Interview 16

Oh, I did, every time. But it would be right when I got done. And they tell you that that's when you're thinking clearest. Right after you release. And I used to say to myself all the time, "The first time I have sex, I'm never going to masturbate again." Yeah. Right. [Laughs]

Yeah. Talk to some married guys about that one!

[Laughs] No kidding. It's like, yeah, "The first time I have sex, I'm never, ever doing this again." But I used to feel really guilty about it. Sometimes growing up, there were streaks when you'd do it two, three times a day. But then you also go on a dry spell, I guess, and don't feel the need to do it at all.

Did you ever, at that time, have a feeling of being alone in this? That maybe nobody else masturbated?

At first. In junior high. Because no one would admit it in junior high. But then by senior high, everyone knew that every other guy was jerking off. Anyway, the guys admitted it.

Women are a little more shy, I think.

Yeah. Until they get to college.

When did you have your first sexual experience with another person?

Um ... sexual experience. I think I had my first "I'll show you mine – you show me yours" kind of thing when I was 12. There were two different guys, and they were both the same age. They were both a year or two older than me. We fooled around and did different stuff.

These were other boys?

Yeah. Two other boys. And then after those times I never ... I mean, that was the last time I had a sexual experience with another guy.

Now, at the age of 12, were you able to come?

Yeah.

Was it mutual masturbation?

No. It was just, like, we did stuff. I think I had oral sex with one of them. We didn't even know what was going on. Never any penetration or anything, because we didn't even know how it really was supposed to work or anything.

Were the three of you together at the same time?

No, no.

You mean you were with each of them at separate times?

Yeah. And it was more than once with each of them. You know.

Was there any feeling of guilt on your part?

Kind of. But then after a while, I wasn't sure. And then for a while, after I was

Growing Up Male In America

13, it was, like, you know, that's the end of that. I'm not going to do that again. And I felt guilty about it for a while. But then by the time I was 16, I was pretty sure of my sexuality.

Did you have doubts when you were having sexual experiences with those two boys? I mean, there you were, sucking on another guy's cock.

Yeah.

And he's sucking on yours. Did you do a little 69 position?

No, I think we kind of rotated. I don't think we had the numbers at that point. [Laughs]

So it was, "It's your turn." "Now it's my turn." Okay. But did you wonder if this was inappropriate behavior?

At the time? No.

Had you heard that there are gay people and there are homosexuals?

Yeah. I knew what it was and everything.

So this activity didn't, in your mind, make you gay?

I didn't feel guilty at the time. Maybe a little bit after.

Did you ever wonder if maybe you might be gay?

Oh, yeah. I had total doubt at some points. I wasn't sure. I mean, I was totally not sure. I was just as excited over one of these boys as the other. Yeah. I remember feeling guilty about it, but then, you know, it would happen again and it was fun and exciting, so …

You stimulated each other orally, to the point of ejaculation?

Yes, a couple of times.

Okay. Did you talk about it? With each other? I mean, did you say afterwards, "That was fun."

At the time, we'd kind of all of a sudden go back to doing whatever we were doing. But it was a big secret. "No one can know about this." And probably at the time, no one should. [Laughs] And we're still friends to this day.

Tell me about your first sexual experience with a woman. Do you still remember it vividly?

Pretty vividly. [Laughs]

All right. Was it successful?

What do you mean?

Did you feel, "Hey, that was all right. That worked." Or was there some clumsiness?

Um … it was a little confusing at first as to how it actually was supposed to go

Interview 16

in. But once I figured it all out, things went okay. I was drinking, that's for sure. I was 16. I waited until I was 16 – and people are still amazed by that because in junior high, I dated girls all the time and got offered all the time. I just didn't do it.

Because, yeah, kids are having these experiences very early.

Yeah. I had a really good friend who I ended up dating later. She had an abortion when she was 15.

I mean, when I first started junior high, that's when you started hearing about people having sex. And it was, like, "Oh. Who's doing what?" But then by sophomore year, that's the start for everyone, basically. But yeah, I remember it. I was at my friend's house, and we were drinking. He had a party, and a lot of those people had left. I remember this girl and I going into a bedroom, and she and I went at it and everything and then slowly made our way to "What do you want?" And she said, "I want you." It was pretty funny.

Was she 16, too?

Yeah. She was a virgin, too. Both 16, both virgins.

And afterwards, you were pleased.

Yeah. Oh, yeah.

She was, too?

Yeah. We were downstairs, friendly all night.

Okay. And that's just the beginning. Did you have a long-term relationship with her?

With her, that was it. [Laughs] But I dated another girl towards the beginning of my junior year. I think we dated for a year and a half. We went to both proms together, and the first nine months were great. And then the second nine months were hell.

How so?

Well, that was the girl who had an abortion when she was 15. She'd always had boyfriends. She was extremely attractive and super cool, but she was super possessive. We went out for about a month and a half, and she thought that pot was more important to me than she was. I said, "No. No it's not. You know, no big deal. I won't smoke pot." So I didn't smoke pot when I was with her. And then we went out for about nine months, and after nine months I thought, "I'm going to smoke pot. I don't care what she says about it." And so I started smoking pot again. I'd go out sometimes and get stoned with my friends. I didn't care. And that was the beginning of the end of the relationship. She flipped, but she wouldn't let me break up with her. She was crazy. She'd spy on my house.

Whoa!

Growing Up Male In America

>Yeah. The nights I wouldn't do stuff with her – when I'd hang out with my buddies – she'd drive by the house. She'd drive by the house to see if other girls were there. Weird, weird stuff.

She must have loved you, or she wanted to control you.

>She would have married me last year. She'd still marry me. I know it, but she's crazy.

Well, you're likable, I assume. You were very sexually active with her?

>Oh, yeah. But we didn't have sex until four months into it.

Really? Was she the one who said no?

>Yeah.

Really. Maybe after having had the abortion and everything. But you wanted to have sex, but she wasn't ready?

>We even went to our first prom together, but we didn't have sex that night. We did stuff – you know, played around – but we didn't have sex. Then two weeks later, we did. After that, she would use sex to keep me from straying. [Laughs] You know how that goes. There were times when I didn't even want to have sex or want her to come over. But then she'd come over and she'd have sex with me. You know, just to keep me interested in her.

Well, after the first nine months and the interest was waning and she was getting more and more controlling, then sex was less frequent?

>More frequent.

More frequent? Oh, that's interesting.

>Yeah, more frequent! [Laughs]

Maybe she was trying to keep you.

>Yeah, yeah. Totally.

And that was all happening until how recently?

>That was the end of my senior year in high school.

Do you keep in touch with her?

>I see her around. But then, she started dating a friend of mine, and they've been dating ever since.

Were you involved in theatre in high school?

>We were fortunate enough to have a drama class, and the teacher at the time told me I should get into theatre when I went to college. So when I got to college, I finally got into an acting class – and it was great.

Good for you. You know, I get the feeling from you that you have a remarkably close relationship with your mom and dad. Am I right on this?

Interview 16

Yeah.

You're very fortunate, do you know that?

I know. My parents were never nosy. My mom found some 1976 *Hustler* magazines in my room. That's how old the porn was that I got my hands on. That was when I was in sixth grade, and my dad and I were fishing together. My mom found them. She totally cleaned my room – and there, under my mattresses, she found them. Then my dad and I had a little talk. He said, "No wonder your door's been closed so much lately" – and that kind of ended it. But my mom never searched my room for anything after that time. It was, like, "This is your space. You know what you shouldn't have in here, but I'm not going to look for it." And that's the same way it is now. There are certain things we just don't talk about, and they know that I don't live like a saint. But they're also really cool about it. You know, I don't remember my parents ever having a fight. Like a real fight. Ever. Never. I never experienced it once. I mean, they've had little disagreements, but they've never had a fight in front of me. Ever. And based on their example, I feel that in a marriage you shouldn't have to work at this. You can talk through everything. If you're fighting all the time, it's obviously not right. It's just not right. You can have arguments, but you don't need to fight.

Okay. Now, you're about to graduate from college, and your major is theatre.

I just declared that. I was supposed to be an English education major.

Do you want to be a teacher?

No. Actually, I wouldn't mind teaching theatre. I wouldn't mind teaching English, either. But after I took a theatre class, you know what? I decided this is what I want to do. And I'm going to try to make this happen. I mean, even if I can't act it out, I think there are a lot of ways I can think it out. There's a lot of ways that you can … I mean, entertainment is what I'm going to be in. Whether it's doing movies or doing little skits or working on some terrible television show that's on at 2:00 in the morning or owning a bar and trying to entertain people that way. That's what I'm going to do. That's the only thing I've been good at in my whole life. Throw the best parties and, you know, make people laugh. That's all I know how to do.

I'll bet when you tell certain people that you want to go into theatre, they are skeptical or cynical or say, "You can't make a living in theatre."

Most of my friends say, "That sounds so much like you." But others just say, "Future waiter of America" and stuff like that. [Laughs]

Let's see. I wanted to ask you some random questions that occurred to me. Again, it's personal – but, then, most of this stuff is.

No!

Yeah! You know, those gay experiences you had when you were a kid – have you

Growing Up Male In America

ever, in the years since then, been approached by a gay man who wanted intimacy?

Um ... it's kind of weird, because when a bunch of us would go out, we'd almost always hit this big bar which has mainly gay customers. It's my favorite bar. You know? I mean, you don't see anything like that anywhere else, you know? But when we'd go in there, my roommate would always get approached by gay guys all the time, and I never would. You know? And I never understood that.

Have you ever thought how you'd handle it if a guy came on to you?

Yeah. I've never been able to lie. But we went out one night to this gay club, and my roommate got approached three times. And two of the times he was, like, grabbed right in the balls. You know? I've never really been approached like that.

And then I visited a friend out West. I found out that the two guys who lived in the apartment below him were a couple. They were gay and they were great guys, and I got along with them really well. One of the guys was totally cool. I mean, he was awesome. He had been married to a woman for eight years before he finally broke it off and said, "I'm gay. I can't do this marriage thing anymore." But his partner was in love with me out there, although I didn't really realize it at the time. I found out afterward, you know. There are lots of pictures of me, and I'd be posing at the pool. I was standing there. And then you'd see one of those gay guys in the background, mouth gaping and looking at me. But, I mean, I sat up late nights with him, smoking cigarettes. Just talking. And these guys were awesome. I still talk to one of them sometimes. But, yeah, I never really got hit on. I guess it just comes off that I'm heterosexual. So ... I mean, I don't know why.

But if you were hit on by a gay guy, you'd be decent and kind about your refusal, right?

Oh, yeah. I think the biggest gay bashers are homophobic. They're people who are hiding gay emotions themselves.

Yeah. I think you're right.

But, yeah. Some of the nicest people I've met are gay. I worked at a big department store, and two of the guys I got along best with were gay. And it was just, like, I don't care. You know? My brother and I talked about it once, and he wondered: is a person gay, or does a person choose to be gay? And my brother's answer is, why would anyone choose to be gay? It would be like choosing to be black in the 1940s, you know? Why would you choose to be persecuted?

Exactly.

It's ridiculous.

When you think back to your gay experiences with your two friends when you were

Interview 16

kids, was that just a phase you were going through? Or was there an affection there for these other kids?

No, no affection, not really. Because it wasn't like anything emotional or love or anything. It was just sex.

You were just getting off, right?

Yeah. One of them and I are still great friends. You know? We're great friends. And that subject is not really brought up, you know? It's just like, you know … that happened, it's in the past. Who cares, you know? What's it matter?

Well, I think probably it happens far more than than most people think.

Okay. When you have conversations with your male friends, what's the main subject or topic?

Sex.

Okay. When you have conversations with women friends, what's the main topic of conversation?

Not sex. Probably just asking what they're up to. Stuff like that. Yeah. But, depending on how well you know them, it revolves to sex eventually. [Laughs] It does, though.

What is your biggest or greatest fear?

Having kids.

Having kids. Why?

Well, it seems like we're just growing into a more dangerous and violent society, and I want to have kids when I'm good and ready. But what kind of world am I going to raise them in? It's scary out there. It's not a nice place.

Whenever you feel loneliness or depression or a combination, what tends to bring that on for you?

A lot of the time I feel like I'm not getting anywhere. You know, like I'm just stalling. Whatever I'm doing, it's nothing. So a lot of times I feel alone at times like that.

What do you do to remedy it?

[Laughs] A lot of times my friends and I go out for a few drinks. But occasionally I have a good cry by myself. But usually I don't feel too down, like majorly down. I don't hit rock bottom very often.

Do you cry often?

Yeah.

Are you embarrassed about it?

Not really.

Growing Up Male In America

But you don't tell everybody.

No.

And I don't mean crying at movies and things like that.

I have a few sad times. Yeah, I cried last night, actually. Which is strange.

Were you alone at the time?

Yeah.

What about?

Thinking about my girlfriend.

Really?

Yeah. I was actually watching *Cheers*, and it was kind of a sad part. And then *Cheers* ended and I didn't shut off the TV and I thought about her for a while. And the tears started coming.

Where is she now?

She's traveling on the East Coast. She'll be home next week.

All right.

Which shall be very, very nice. [Laughs]

What's the most hurtful thing you've ever done to somebody else? That you're kind of ashamed of?

I made my mom cry one time. I came home, and she was asking me lots of questions and I flipped. And I stormed out of the house. My mom was crying, and my brother and my sister just happened to be home. I was in high school, you know. They both came outside and found me and said, "What the hell are you doing?" After that I never even had a confrontation with my mom. To this day, I am totally regretful. I probably made her cry a couple other times at night when I didn't see her crying. Probably when I was up to no good. But, yeah, that really did hurt me.

How would you define what it means to be a man? Or what is your definition of masculinity?

I think being a man is someone who's really powerful, a strong individual. But he also has caring qualities. I want the best of my dad in me, but then the best of my mom, too. Because my mom did things for me that my dad could never do. Like the way she cared about me. The way she'd rub my shoulders. And I could talk to my mom. But then my dad was real stern, the authority figure. I just knew that you don't cross dad. So I think being a man today, you've got to be in between male and female. If you're going to be a good father, a good man, you're going to have to show both qualities no matter what.

Next question: Do you consider yourself handsome?

Interview 16

[Laughs] Yes, I do. Which is kind of embarrassing. I've been told it too many goddamn times. I've heard it all the time, so I kind of realize that I'm not ugly. So I must be all right looking. Hope you don't think I'm completely rude in saying that.

No, not at all. You really are a very handsome man.

Do you ever find yourself posing in the mirror when no one's looking and wondering, "Is this my best side? Is this my best side? Do I look better with an open, toothy smile, or do I look better when I just grin?" Do you do that?

[Laughs] Yeah. I've done it. But I try not to overdo it. But I still look in the mirror and say, "Do I look okay?"

Men today do spend far more time on their hair and clothes than in former generations.

Yeah. And men wear makeup.

Right. What characteristics do you look for in a good male friend?

My best male friend is always willing to hang with me or do what I like to do, and I'm willing to do that same for him. If I was in combat and someone was going to take a bullet for me, who's that going to be? And I look to my best friend and know that he would jump in front of that gun and take that bullet for me. And I would do the exact same thing for him. And that's why he's my best friend. Because he would do anything he could for me and I would do anything I could for him.

Did you know each other before going to college?

Since seventh grade, and we are still best friend. We will be best friends forever.

Okay. Now, about your penis.

[Laughs] Wow! That's sudden! [Laughs] Speaking of penises. Speaking of dicks. That's a better word.

Do you ever find yourself sizing up other guys' cocks?

Oh, yes. That best friend of mine, his is huge.

Really?

Oh, yeah!

Would you say yours is average in length?

I'd say it's average when I compare mine with all my friends.

Do you know what average is?

I thought it was, like, six inches. I heard the joke, "I thought I had a big penis until I heard nine inches was average." [Laughter] It was my baseball coach who told me that one.

Growing Up Male In America

Do you ever take a glance at other guys at urinals and in locker rooms?

Oh, sure. At the baseball games? Are you kidding? Every guy is peeing in a trough.

Do you have a shy bladder, or can you pee easily?

Oh, yeah, I can pee anywhere. No, I don't have a shy bladder. But I have friends who do, yeah.

How frequently do you masturbate now?

Um ... every other day. Yeah. Maybe five out of the seven days of the week. Fairly frequently.

Okay.

Well, you've got to change your oil, or you just don't run right.

Well, use it or lose it, I say.

Yeah. [Laughs]

What is it that can make you really terribly mad, angry?

Bad drivers.

Okay. What makes you sad?

Um ... thinking about my mom.

Do you mean remembering back to when you made her cry?

No, not that. We don't know if she's on the edge of the first stage of Alzheimer's.

Really. How old is she, again?

Sixty.

Ah. Is she aware of this, too?

Yeah, she knows it. She goes to specialists, but they just don't know. They thought at one point that it was one of the veins or arteries to her brain that was constricting. So they told her to take an aspirin a day to thin her blood. That helped a little bit. And you can tell the difference between the morning and night. And she's not bad, but she's just not sharp like she was before. That's why my dad keeps taking her to different doctors. And that's the only thing that ... you know, you'll think of that and you're just, like, "Man, I don't want my mom to be all fucking confused." I mean, you look at Alzheimer's people and stuff, and they don't even know what's going on.

I'm sorry to hear about your mom's condition.

Well, I want to thank you very much for sitting for this interview. I appreciate it very much.

Not a problem at all. I enjoyed it.

Interview 16

Postscript – December 2001

This man left his university studies in his junior year and moved to Las Vegas. He still holds his dream of a career in theatre and film.